TOUR OF DUTY

D1449687

TOUR OF DUTY

Samurai, Military Service in Edo,
and the Culture of Early Modern Japan

Constantine Nomikos Vaporis

UNIVERSITY OF HAWAI'I PRESS | HONOLULU

© 2008 University of Hawai'i Press
All rights reserved
Printed in the United States of America
13 12 11 10 09 08   6 5 4 3 2 1

Library of Congress Cataloging-in-Publication Data
Vaporis, Constantine Nomikos.
  Tour of duty : samurai, military service in Edo,
and the culture of early modern Japan / Constantine
Nomikos Vaporis.
    p. cm.
Includes bibliographical references and index.
ISBN 978-0-8248-3205-6 (hardcover : alk. paper)
  1. Sankin kotai. 2. Daimyo. 3. Japan — History —
Tokugawa period, 1600 – 1868. I. Title.
DS871.5.V37 2008
952'.025 — dc22   2008007212

University of Hawai'i Press books are printed
on acid-free paper and meet the guidelines for
permanence and durability of the Council on
Library Resources.

Designed by April Leidig-Higgins

Printed by Edwards Brothers

For Maria, always

Contents

Acknowledgments ix

Introduction 1

1 Beginnings 11

2 The Road to Edo (and Back) 36

3 The Daimyo Procession 62

4 Assignment: Edo 102

5 Daimyo Compounds: Place and Space 128

6 Life in the Capital 172

7 Carriers of Culture 205

Conclusion 237

Notes 241

Works Cited 291

Index 313

Acknowledgments

THIS STUDY HAS REQUIRED its own form of alternate attendance, with numerous changes in residence between Japan and America. During this time I have incurred a proverbial mountain of debt to many people and institutions.

A Japan Foundation grant allowed me to make an initial research trip to Japan in 1989–1990 to explore various archives to determine whether there were sufficient materials for a monographic study. At that time I made the first of many trips to Kōchi, where I was welcomed warmly by the scholars at the Kōchi Prefectural Library. A Travel Grant from the Northeast Asia Council (NEAC) of the Association for Asian Studies and several grants from the Directed Research Initiative Fund (DRIF) at the University of Maryland, Baltimore County (UMBC) allowed me to maintain some momentum on the project while teaching almost year-round. More sustained work was undertaken in Japan under a Fulbright Scholar's grant in 1993–1994 and from the National Endowment for the Humanities (NEH), with additional support from UMBC, in 1997–1998. Additional funding came from the American Philosophical Society, and an NEH Travel-to-Collections grant paid for a visit to the Mitsui Map Collection in Berkeley.

An invitation to become a Visiting Scholar at the International Research Center for Japanese Studies (Nichibunken) in 2003–2004 gave me a year in comfort to focus completely on research and writing among a fine community of international scholars. More than a few people pointed out to me the incongruity of spending a year in Kyoto to work on a study that has much to do with Edo. Nevertheless, the beautiful foothills of Katsurazaka were a perfect location to contemplate the movements of the daimyo and their entourages on the highways of Tokugawa Japan. The hikes with family and long-distance runs with friends afforded much opportunity to see the bamboo forests and hidden temples for which Kyoto is justly famous. The final writing and revisions were completed during a semester's sabbatical leave from UMBC.

There are numerous people I would like to thank for their encouragement and support. At UMBC, the former and current chairs of the History Department, John Jeffries and Kriste Lindenmeyer, the latter of whom arranged a subvention for some of the images which appear herein. Deans John Jeffries and Scott Bass also jointly provided a generous subvention. While at Nichibunken, the camaraderie and intellectual stimulation provided by many of the other visiting scholars made it a memorable year. In particular I'd like to acknowledge Rien Segers (University of Groningen); Maureen Donovan and Jim Bartholomew (Ohio State University); Eugene Baksheev (Moscow Research Institute); Massimiliano Tomasi (Western Washington University); Hugh Clark (University of Sydney); Victor Rybin (Leningrad University); Bijay Misra (School of Planning & Architecture, New Delhi); Mats Karlsson (University of Sydney); Jutta Hausser (University of Munich); Lee Jender (Academia Sinica); Richard Okada (Princeton University); and Amaury Garcia-Rodriguez (University of Mexico). Of the permanent staff at Nichibunken, Shirahata Yōsaburō, who invited me to join his research team for a year and a follow-up conference, and Kasaya Kazuhiko, who generously gave of his time and expertise, deserve special mention. Of course the invitation to Nichibunken would not have been forthcoming in the first place were it not for the kindness of Jim Baxter. The library staff was extremely helpful and unfailing in obtaining whatever research materials I requested in record time. Okuno Yukio and Sasaki Ayako facilitated all aspects of life at Nichibunken for the entire family with great kindness and cheer.

In Tokyo I would like to thank first and foremost Miyazaki Katsumi of the Tokyo University's Historiographical Institute for his support throughout this project, especially in helping me locate and interpret documentary sources. While a Foreign Visiting Scholar at the Historiographical Institute, I was fortunate to share an office for a time with Ronald Toby. In Japan and in the United States, he gave generously of his time and provided inspirational support. Yamamoto Mitsumasa of the Kokuritsu rekishi minzoku hakubutsukan (Rekihaku) helped me learn to read brush-written travel diaries while more informally instructing me in the ways of the *Edokko*. Personal thanks also go out to Watanabe Kazutoshi (Aichi University), Shindō Kazuyuki and Kayoko, Kurumada Hiroyuki, and Ishida Yuri.

I have many professional and personal debts to various people in Kōchi: first, to the staff at the Yamauchi Shrine Treasury and Archives and its various directors who allowed me access to its rich storehouse of records; and second, to the staff at the Kōchi Prefectural Library, located at the foot of the hill on which Kōchi castle stands, many of whom befriended my family and me, making Kōchi a home away from home for a time. To all of them, as well as to Luke Roberts, who first introduced me to many of the people there, my heartfelt appreciation. On the library staff itself, Hosokawa Shimako made most everything happen from behind the scenes. From Yorimitsu Kanji, whom I had the honor and pleasure of sitting next to in the Tosa *shidankai* (Tosa Historical Society at the Prefectural Library), I learned so much, and not just about Tokugawa history. He also made it possible for Luke Roberts and me to gain access to the Gotō Collection of documents in Aki City, Kōchi, before it was opened to the general public. Luke often braved the scenic but sometimes problematic roads in his car to get us there. Uchikawa Kiyosuke and Takahashi Shiro were kind presences in the *Tosa shidankai* as well. Kiyosuke and his wife Fumi hosted us on numerous occasions with spectacular local cuisine including the justly famous seafood plate, *sawachi ryōri*, and together hiked with us a long portion of the alternate attendance route once traversed by Tosa men. Hirotani Kijūrō and his wife drove me around much of the eastern half of Shikoku, retracing the footsteps of the Yamauchi's processions.

There are two other individuals from Kōchi I must single out because their presence, too, is felt in much of the following text. The first is the late Dr. Okamune Shigehisa, an optometrist from Kōchi who opened up his home to my family in 1989–1990 and 1994–1995 and made us feel a part of his. Dr. Okamune had a model Christian spirit, which he showed by generously hosting more than forty foreign students and professors, some like us, for a year at a time. We shared a candlelight Christmas Eve service, a Greek-style Easter dinner, fishing, visits to his country home, and many other memorable events and ordinary discussions. The second individual is Moriguchi Kōji, of the Kōchi Prefectural Library and subsequently the Yamauchi Treasury and Shrine Archives. From the moment he greeted me on the steps of the Prefectural Library with a big smile and a warm handshake, I knew we would be friends. His enthusiasm for life and his love of history were infectious. He touched many people's lives before his untimely passing in 2000. Part of my scholarly debt to him is evident in the works cited section, but most of it is not. Moriguchi-san sat by my side on a regular basis for the year that I was at the Kōchi Prefectural Library, as well as on subsequent visits there, and he helped me learn to decipher the eccentricities of the brush-written documents that Tosa samurai wrote, pushing me always to do more. This is but a token of my heartfelt appreciation.

There are yet two other people I regret are not with us to see the fruition of this work. One is the late Marius B. Jansen. The seed for this work was planted during his seminar on Tokugawa Japan my first semester as a graduate student at Princeton University. The other is my father, the late Rev. Dr. Nomikos Michael Vaporis, a historian of Byzantine and Balkan Studies, who also devoted his life to service in the Greek Orthodox Church as priest, professor, and dean of Hellenic College/Holy Cross School of Theology in Boston. I can only hope they would have been pleased.

Finally, to my immediate family — Maria, my wife and partner of twenty-five wonderful years, and children Michaela and Aleydis — who alternated residences with me, disrupting their lives to follow me across the seas: I hope there were enough "pleasures" in addition to the "hardships." I certainly could not have done it without you.

The text that follows benefited greatly from the comments of a number of individuals. Luke Roberts, Anne Walthall, and Maria Vaporis generously read through the entire manuscript, making important substantive comments and stylistic recommendations. Jim Bartholomew, Jim Baxter, Michael Cooper, and Susan Hanley all read one or more chapters in some version. Helpful comments were also received from participants in various seminar and lecture settings at Columbia University, Princeton University, Johns Hopkins University, University of Maryland, Baltimore County, Nichibunken, and at the Japan Forum (Kyoto). Anonymous readers for *Journal of Japanese Studies*, *Monumenta Nipponica*, *Japan Review*, and the University of Hawai'i Press prodded me to refine my thinking. To all of them, thank you. All errors of fact and interpretation of course remain mine alone.

I am grateful to the staff of the University of Hawai'i Press, particularly to executive editor Patricia Crosby for her long-standing interest in this project.

Earlier articles from which material has been used are listed below, and I thank the publishers for granting permission to use this material:

"Edo to Tosa — Toshū Edo hantei no ikkōsatsu," *Tosa shidan* 195 (1994).

"Edo e no michi. Tosa hanshi Mori-ke nikki nado ni miru sankin kōtai no sugata," *Kōtsūshi kenkyū* 34 (1994).

"A Tour of Duty. Kurume hanshi Edo kinban nagaya emaki," *Monumenta Nipponica* 51, 3 (1996).

"To Edo and Back: Alternate Attendance and Japanese Culture in the Early Modern Period," *Journal of Japanese Studies* 23, 1 (1997).

"Digging for Edo. Archaeology and Japan's Premodern Urban Past," *Monumenta Nipponica* 53, 1 (1998).

"Samurai and Merchant in Mid-Tokugawa Japan: Tani Tannai's Record of Daily Necessities (1748–54)," *Harvard Journal of Asiatic Studies* 60, 1 (2000).

"Daimyo Processions: Authority and Theater," *Japan Review* 17 (2005).

Note on Usage

JAPANESE WORDS ARE transcribed according to the Hepburn system. Japanese names, including those in the notes and the works cited, follow East Asian usage, with the family name first. I have included macrons for all Japanese place names except for Tokyo, Osaka, and Kyoto, which are commonly printed without them in English-language publications. Macrons have also been omitted on those common nouns, such as daimyo and sumo, found in standard American dictionaries. Domains are usually referred to here by name rather than by the castle town (e.g., Tosa domain rather than Kōchi). Daimyo may be referred to in two ways, either by the family name (e.g., Yamauchi, in the case of Tosa domain) or referred to as the lord from a particular domain (e.g., the Tosa lord or Lord of Tosa). Prior to 1873 Japan used a lunar calendar, and I have followed historiographic convention in expressing dates in the year/month/day format, converting only Japanese years (but not months or days) to the Gregorian calendar. Intercalary or "leap" months are represented by the letter *i*. All translations are mine unless stated otherwise. All works cited are published in Tokyo unless stated otherwise.

Introduction

EVERY YEAR FOR MORE than two and a half centuries, samurai in service to their daimyo marched early modern Japan's highways back and forth from their domain's castle town to Edo, the political capital of the realm and the center from which the Tokugawa family governed its domain. Theirs was no recreational trip. It was a forced movement, known as alternate attendance, or *sankin kōtai*, imposed by legal fiat: The shogun required the daimyo to leave their domains to come wait on him, usually for a year at a time. The daimyo, furthermore, were required to keep their wives and most of their adolescent children in permanent residence in Edo, where they served, in effect, as hostages, acting as guarantees for the daimyo's continued good behavior. The practice was so emblematic of the Tokugawa or early modern period, and Japanese culture in general, that when the Englishman Algernan Mitford visited Japan in 1906 to deliver the Order of the Garter from King Edward VII to the Meiji emperor, a representation of a daimyo's procession was recreated as entertainment for distinguished foreign and Japanese guests.[1] The proceedings, which took place in Hibiya Park, resonated with Lord Mitford, who had experienced Tokugawa Japan in 1866–1867, during its last years. Alternate attendance, more than anything else, evoked the Tokugawa past to him:

> Feudalism is dead, but its ghost haunts me still. I shut my eyes and see picturesque visions of warriors in armour. . . . Processions of powerful nobles with their retinues marching along the cryptomeria avenues of the Tōkaidō, the road by the eastern sea — and I hear the cry "Shita ni iro, Shita ni iro" [Get down, get down], at which all men of low degree go down upon their knees and bow their heads in the dust while the great man [the daimyo] passes, silent and gloomy in the loneliness of the norimono [palanquin]."[2]

These processions remain symbolic of the Tokugawa era even today, as cities and towns through which the daimyo passed regularly stage re-enactments to draw tourists.

While alternate attendance was devised in part as a control measure and this intent is usually emphasized in the secondary literature,[3] it needs to be seen within the context of the development of political institutions in Japanese history. It entailed the elaboration and codification of the centuries-old practice of the lord requiring the periodic attendance of his retainers by his side. It was a form of feudal service, or *hōkō*, one of a set of military-type service owed the Tokugawa by their vassals, the daimyo, in return for the bestowal of land grants and the right to rule those entities. The system as elaborated by the Tokugawa, however, called for the regular attendance of the more than 250 lords for almost the entire duration of shogunal rule, and it effectively consolidated power in a single place, the city of Edo.

Alternate attendance was a bedrock of the Tokugawa polity. Despite the weakening of Tokugawa power that scholars have noted in other areas,[4] it was one of the most durable of the shogun's political controls over the daimyo. In institutional terms it underwent little change. Repeatedly issued in the "Laws for the Military Houses" (*Buke shohatto*), the attendance requirements were altered only once from their formal inception in 1635 until 1862. In this regard alternate attendance stands perhaps as the single exception to the general relaxation of control measures by the shogunate over the course of the Tokugawa period.

While alternate attendance might remind us of other practices observed in European countries, such as Louis XIV's court at Versailles in the late seventeenth and early eighteenth centuries or the medieval German practice of *hoffahrt*, or "going to court," the comparisons are not particularly apt, for in the Japanese case the requirements had far greater historical significance.[5] Alternate attendance not only helped deplete the war-making capabilities of the daimyo, but it also acted as an agent of far-reaching change, generating extensive economic growth, urbanization, and social transformations. With foreign trade largely restricted by political fiat, alternate attendance functioned as a powerful internal economic stimulant. The considerable expenses involved in participation in the system — including transport and travel services, the construction and repair of a network of compounds in Edo, and the maintenance of support staffs there — spread those expenditures along the highways, the development of which the daimyo promoted, as well as in Edo and the domains. Expenses related to alternate attendance could consume as much as 50 to 75 percent of a domain's cash income and greatly restricted the daimyo's rule. It was without question the most important institution affecting economic life in Tokugawa Japan.

The system's impact on the development of the city of Edo was tremendous, as evidenced by rapid population growth, reaching a figure in excess of one million by the early eighteenth century, and the concomitant rise in consumer needs. It also resulted in waves of growth in cities below Edo in the urban hierarchy, as daimyo developed their castle towns and mobilized local resources to meet the costs of alternate attendance. This trickle-down effect impacted urban centers and castle towns as well as local commercial settlements. Osaka in particular was transformed, as daimyo sold tax rice or other goods there to obtain the necessary cash for alternate-attendance-related expenses. This prompted the development of Osaka as a market and finance center and, more generally, stimulated the development of a commercial or money economy and a system of credit. As a result, Osaka's dominant position in the economy was established by the end of the seventeenth century. Its merchants assumed national importance as the mechanism of credit between Osaka and Edo left large sums of interest-free tax money in their hands, funds they used as lending capital.[6]

To cope with the spiraling cost of alternate attendance, domains were forced to adopt a variety of strategies to meet expenses. They rationalized bureaucratic administration and reduced the size of processions. They also increased income through domain monopolies and export-oriented trade policies, which led at least in part to further commercialization of the economy. But, from the early eighteenth century, it was the samurai who bore the brunt of the daimyo's efforts to economize through the repeated implementation of *kariage*, or forced borrowings.

The periodic absence of the lord and a group of his top retainers on alternate attendance also influenced the form and nature of early modern governance. More specifically, it led to a bifurcation of domainal government, with divisions in both Edo and the castle town, each handling a different range of affairs. The Edo branch, for example, largely managed interdomainal relations, while the castle town branch handled the daily affairs of domainal governance. This bifurcation occasionally caused conflict between the two, in some cases leading to the confiscation (attainder) of a domain. The regular absence of the lord created a power vacuum into which his top senior retainers stepped, making many lords largely figurehead rulers. This accelerated the bureaucratization of local power, a predictable outcome of the two hundred years of the *pax* Tokugawa or Great Peace ([*tenka*] *taihei*).

Alternate attendance also functioned, in effect, as a mechanism of intercity mobility for the elite, accounting for as many as one-third of Edo's population. In terms of the volume of circulation and degree of geographic mobility created within a country's borders, alternate attendance is probably without parallel in world history. Despite this historical significance, the system in general and this function of it in particular have been left unexplored. A system of elite mobility existed in contemporaneous China, where officials were recruited largely based on the examination system and were sent across the country to serve in metropolitan and county seats and in the capital. This system caused elite mobility, but of a more specialized type than in Tokugawa Japan, and far fewer people were involved.[7]

In restraining the development of domainal military capabilities by the diversion of wealth, alternate attendance did much to bring peace to the land. After more than a century of almost constant warfare, the daimyo were forced to focus their energies on meeting the requirements of periodic attendance with the shogun and dealing with its consequences. One unintended effect of the congregation of the daimyo and their representatives in Edo was that, on their own initiative, daimyo formed cooperative networks of specially designated diplomatic officials who met to discuss political and economic problems, including how to handle relations with the Tokugawa government. Through the organic development of this new institution, domainal governments were able to resolve disputes independently before they became the concern of the hegemon (the shogun) in Edo, as well as coordinate policy vis-à-vis the shogunate, thus promoting peaceful coexistence and the continued survival of the domains.

This is but a partial and cursory accounting of some of the implications and effects of alternate attendance. In short, it is generally agreed that alternate attendance was the single greatest accomplishment of Japanese leaders, both of the Tokugawa period and of subsequent times. Its significance seems so obvious perhaps that scholars have been content to reiterate generalities without actually examining the system nor exploring in depth its varied implications.[8] There are studies of the physical infrastructure of the network of compounds and the use of space therein, investigations of the life of domainal retainers serving in Edo, and explorations of the material culture excavated from the ruins of Edo's daimyo compounds and other parts of the city.[9] My own research here and elsewhere has engaged with this literature and, as the endnotes will make clear, has greatly benefited from it.

Alternate attendance affected Tokugawa Japan on so many different levels that to write a study of its effects on political, economic, and cultural developments would require, as George Tsukahira noted, "nothing less than a complete social history of Tokugawa Japan."[10] This is perhaps why Nishiyama Matsunosuke, one of Japan's foremost cultural historians, has written that "alternate attendance was of great significance, but there has been no full-scale study of it."[11]

An important reason why there has been so little study of alternate attendance, despite its centrality to Tokugawa Japan, is that the documentary basis for it is so scattered. There is not a full range of sources for any single domain. For example, an extensive collection of official documentation, together with Edo compound maps, procession scrolls, and archaeological evidence, but very few retainer diaries, exist for Kaga domain. Such retainer diaries — a key source for this study — exist in considerable numbers for Tosa domain. Official documentation for Tosa is also voluminous, but maps and procession scrolls are few and archaeological evidence scant. The unevenness in the documentary evidence is manifold. Suffice it to say that given this difficulty, the present study is based on a consolidation of evidence from a number of domains. While Tosa is the main thread that runs through it, supplemental materials are provided from numerous other localities to provide a fuller picture of the system and its impact on early modern Japan.

The principal concern of my research has been, and continues to be, how political institutions impact the human condition. That is to say, while I will not ignore the issue of how alternate attendance influenced Japan on the level of the domain, my main concern is to examine the institution in terms of the individual. Of course, in one sense the domain was nothing more than a collective of individuals. However, my purpose here is to put a human face on the political institution — to render alternate attendance as a lived experience. As much as extant documentation allows, I examine what the trip to and from Edo was like, what the period of enforced residence in the nation's largest city meant to individual retainers, and how that experience affected both their personal lives and careers as well as the cultural life of the city of Edo. For members of the *bushi* status group and their attendants, participation in alternate attendance was akin to pilgrimage for commoners. Both helped break barriers, both political and cultural, and expand the intellectual focus of individuals beyond the domain. The participation of retainers and their subordinates in alternate attendance also had a great impact on their development as consumers. However, samurai were not only consumers but also producers of culture, the latter being a role not normally emphasized. Both of these roles will be explored in several of the chapters. This study also seeks to examine, within defined limits, the social and economic impact of alternate attendance on the city of Edo, as well as its role in shaping a national culture.[12] The history of alternate attendance as a mechanism of political control has been ably sketched by Tsukahira, however, and will not be a focus of inquiry here.

In trying to achieve these various objectives, a principal source for this study will be the diaries brushed by retainers en route to and from Edo as well as those they kept while residing in the city. Together with a variety of other sources — city maps, daimyo compound (*daimyō yashiki*) maps, and official domainal records — the diaries provide the means to begin to write a social history of life within Edo's daimyo compounds. The cultural history of commoner sections of Edo has been explored to some degree in the English-language literature.[13] Much less well known is the fabric of life in the roughly 40 percent of the city contained within the walls of the daimyo compounds. In these urban spaces 25 to 30 percent of Edo's population (250,000 to 300,000 people during the early eighteenth century) lived, one-third to one-half of whom were replenished yearly from the castle towns through the regular migrations of alternate attendance. While the daimyo were forced to have their families in residence in the capital, the political demands of the system largely ignored the personal circumstances of retainers with families. As a result, this is an overwhelmingly male story. Contemporary Japanese, in fact, like to draw a parallel between alternate attendance and the postwar corporate system's demands of loyalty of white-collar workers transferred without family to distant locations.

An important focus of this work is to examine the relationship between the Tokugawa center, meaning the city of Edo and the numerous compounds the daimyo built there to house themselves and their support staffs, and the localities, meaning the castle towns. A goal of the project is to explore the dimensions of the relationship between the two through the flow, back and forth, of people as well as material goods and other forms of culture. In doing this I seek to address a major lacuna in the scholarship. As Yokota Fuyuhiko has recently commented in his intriguing study of the circulation of books in early modern Japan, cultural relations between the castle towns and the three metropolises (Edo, Osaka, and Kyoto) have been greatly understudied.[14] Moreover, I propose to offer a new paradigm for conceptualizing "Edo culture," meaning the culture of Japan during the Tokugawa period, which typically has been viewed as Edo-centric, rather than the culture of the city of Edo itself. In other words, scholars in both Japan and America heretofore have largely misconstrued the process; cultural flow is seen as unidirectional, spreading "Edo culture" from the center to the localities. In fact, we need to recognize that the current use of the term "Edo culture" is often problematic, for the culture exported from the city of Edo was an amalgam of continually changing influences from early modern Japan's many domains. While the flow of culture from the center, Edo, to the localities, the domains, is the most conspicuous, it is equally important to consider the reverse flow as well as the flow of culture from one locality to another due to alternate attendance. This last pattern also sometimes occurred via the center at Edo. In addition, Osaka and Kyoto, where Tosa and many other domains maintained residences as well, must be considered in the cultural and economic networks that linked the domains with the outside world. The dynamics of these various patterns — the degree of interaction between the domains and Edo and to a lesser extent Kyoto and Osaka — are a key measure of the system's role in promoting the diffusion of culture.

Alternate attendance promoted the circulation of culture and demolished social and cultural boundaries, so that by the end of the eighteenth century, or beginning of the nineteenth, there was an integrated or "national culture" in Japan. *Bushi* stationed in or permanently living in Edo formed and participated in cultural networks of many varieties that included members of the other social estates (i.e., commoners). These cultural "salons," as well as the networks established in the three metropolises through the domainal compounds in those cities, created an infrastructure for the dissemination of information and thus made the work of the modernizing elite in the Meiji period (1868–1912) easier.

The economic relationship between the domains and Edo is also an important question that will be taken up here. While it is certain that the Tokugawa's capital became Japan's chief consumption center as it developed rapidly during the first half of the seventeenth century, it is important to examine more carefully the patterns by which the domainal compounds in Edo became integrated into the regional economy of the Edo area, as well as to determine how much they remained tied to their localities. The question is not an insignificant one, for there were somewhere between six hundred and a thousand daimyo compounds in Edo — each lord having at least two or three and some of the larger domains ten or more. Four to five thousand men were housed in the compounds of the larger domains such as Tosa and Kaga during the years when the lord was in residence. These residential and administrative complexes played an integral role in the political, cultural, and economic life of the country as a whole.

The movement of the daimyo's processions back and forth on the thoroughfares to and from Edo demonstrated and was symbolic of the Tokugawa unification of power; it served as confirmation of the centrality of the shogunate's seat of power in the realm. This centrality was further evidenced by the periodic (usually on the first, fifteenth, and twenty-eighth of the month) and irregular audiences given by the shogun at his castle, to which the daimyo made their way from their headquarters in Edo with smaller numbers of attendants in tow. These processions were witnessed by the populace living along the roads, sometimes by other daimyo and their men, as well as by inhabitants of, and provincial travelers to, Edo. In fact the open plaza where the retinue reorganized before the lord entered the castle grounds became a major tourist site. The shogun remained fixed, stationary in his castle palace, while his retainers, the daimyo, were in orbit around him.

The requirement of periodic attendance was fixed in law, but penalties for noncompliance were not. It was clear, nevertheless, as Dr. Franz von Siebold wrote late in the Tokugawa period, that "[t]o offer homage and presents, or tribute, annually to the *ziogoon* (shogun) or military chief of the empire, at Yedo, his place of residence and the seat of government, is the highest duty of every prince [daimyo], dignitary and noble throughout the Japanese realm, the neglect of which would be deemed most unpardonable."[15] In the seventeenth century the shogunate did punish a number of lords with house arrest, reduction in domain, or confiscation for "tardiness" or "negligence" in performing the alternate attendance or returning to the domain without permission, in some cases before the system was even fixed in law.[16] This was necessary during the early decades of institution building in the seventeenth century, but it did not persist. What is remarkable, though, is that until the 1860s no daimyo ever remonstrated against this requirement that so taxed the resources of the domains and consumed so much of the energy of samurai-based government. Furthermore, as will be made clear later, while some daimyo occasionally might have pleaded illness as a pretext to delay or skip a turn of service, none ever denied his duty nor stayed away from Edo for long.

Daimyo compliance with the system is remarkable, too, when one considers the volume of intellectual thought critical of it. Early on, in the seventeenth century, Kumazawa Banzan (1619–1691), though at heart against the very existence of the system, presented a memorial to the shogunate advocating a reduction in the frequency and duration of attendance.[17] Ogyū Sorai (1666–1728), advisor to the eighth shogun, Yoshimune, called for reductions in the length of the daimyo's stay in Edo as well as in the number of men brought to the city. Scholars like Nakai Chikuzan (1730–1829) argued that the system was inherently inequitable; to remedy this he proposed that the frequency of the daimyo's attendance should vary according to the distance of his domain from Edo.[18] Late in the period, when many daimyo became concerned about coastal defense and their inability to finance it, Yokoi Shōnan (1809–1869), advisor to lord Matsudaira Shungaku (Fukui domain), not coincidentally reputed to be one of the poorest daimyo, proposed that the system be abolished. "It is sufficient," he said, "that daimyo send administrative reports from their individual domains. Also, the families of the daimyo, who have been prisoners in Edo, should all be allowed to return home."[19] A wide range of intellectuals, including Hayashi Shihei, Kiyokawa Hachirō, and Nakai Chikuzan, were most critical of alternate attendance because they saw it as a great economic drain on the country. Chikuzan wrote that the economic disarray caused by alternate attendance was "self-defeating as it eroded the nation's strength."[20] Kiyokawa noted that "daimyo have made great efforts to economize these days, but the traveling to and from Edo every time is such a meaningless loss of money. This does substantial harm to the great peace, but the officials in charge allow the requirement of attendance to continue unchanged."[21]

The requirement of attendance on the shogun compelled the daimyo to travel from the seat of their domains to Edo and back. Both *sankin* (attendance) and *kōtai* (alternation) connoted travel or movement to and from Edo. This requirement is underappreciated, it seems, in arguments made about the absoluteness of Tokugawa authority,[22] perhaps because it is sometimes said that many daimyo came to prefer life in Edo to that in the provinces. Regardless of the personal preferences of the daimyo, it was clear to them why they were traveling to Edo: to serve the shogun, the head of the most powerful and highly developed centralized state in Japan's premodern history, by appearing at his castle. Compliance with the requirements of the system signified the daimyo's recognition of the Tokugawa's central authority—this remained true even when the power to enforce its policy was in question.

Similarly, when considering the Tokugawa state, the economic costs of fulfilling the attendance obligations to the shogun are not usually thought of in terms of taxation, at least not in English-language scholarship on the period. James White has asked which is more absolute, "irregular extractions levied by unchallenged bakufu [shogunal] fiat, or regular, formalized taxes levied only with the approval of Parliament"?[23] Yet certainly a strong case can be made here that alternate attendance, while not expressed as a tax, certainly acted as one and merits consideration when contemplating the nature and extent of Tokugawa authority.

The requirement of alternate attendance was a critical part of the relationship between the shogun and the daimyo, appearing second in the Tokugawa's Laws for the Military Houses (*Buke shohatto*) of 1635 and included in subsequent editions, coming right after a reminder that warriors should pay attention to both martial as well as the literary arts (the "twin ways"). In these documents it was most often referred to as *sankin*, which connotes movement from one place to another to serve a superior. The request for *oitoma*, a leave of absence, to quit Edo and return to the domain represented the antithesis of service. It was not a request to be allowed to depart from Edo to perform some duty in the provinces; it was rather a petition for a temporary release from service in Edo. The 1710 version, for example, refers to the lords as being "summoned" (*mesu*) to Edo, which indicates clearly the hierarchical relationship between daimyo and shogun.[24]

While in one sense alternate attendance was simply a complicated ritual that expressed and reinforced the fealty between the daimyo and the Tokugawa shogun, it was nevertheless a ritual that defined early modern society in Japan in numerous ways. The chapters that follow will examine this institution and its effects from a variety of perspectives. The first three chapters are concerned with movement. Specifically, chapter one (Beginnings), explores the origins and legal basis for the system of enforced mobility, the patterns of movement it engendered, and the preparations necessary for the trip. Chapter two (The Road to Edo (and Back)), examines in detail the nature of the trip to and from the shogunal capital for one particular large-scale domain, Tosa, and its men. Chapter three (The Daimyo Procession) analyzes the political and cultural meanings of the processions of the daimyo and their extensive entourages up and down the highways. These parade-like movements were replete with symbolic import for the nature of early modern governance. They were sites of competing — daimyo and shogunal — production, with multiple levels of performance and audience. Shifting gears, chapters four through six are concerned with a type of stasis rather than movement: the physical and social environment that the daimyo's retainers experienced in Edo. Chapter four (Assignment: Edo) addresses the key question of who went to Edo and why. Chapter five (Daimyo Compounds: Place and Space) examines the network of physical spaces in which the domainal samurai lived, the issue of staffing, the relationship between spatial consciousness as it pertains to these compounds, and political power. Chapter six (Life in the Capital) moves from the realm of physical space to the retainers occupying it, examining their lives, at work and at play, as well as their consumption habits. Finally, chapter seven (Carriers of Culture) deals with both movement and stasis in its treatment of retainers as "carriers" of culture, in both a literal and figurative sense. In doing this, the chapter explores the cultural significance of travel for retainers, examines their identity as consumers and producers of culture, and proposes a multivalent model of cultural change.

I

Beginnings

IN ITS TOKUGAWA CONTEXT, alternate attendance represented an important connection with the past, and at the same time it was a significant part of the redefinition of relations between the shogunate and the daimyo that took place during the first half of the seventeenth century. The requirements of participation in the system as it developed in the Edo period consumed much of the daimyo officials' time and energy and severely depleted domain coffers. This chapter will explore two themes related to the notion of beginnings — the origins of alternate attendance and the preparations for the journey — while examining the basic contours of the system.

The practice of retainers traveling to their lord's fortification to serve him has historical precedents going back at least to the late twelfth century. A key component of the Kamakura (1185–1333) shogunate's system of vassal services was the requirement that its housemen perform guard service, depending on their place of residence, in Kyoto or Kamakura, for varying lengths of time, generally between three and six months. Under the second military regime, the Ashikaga shogunate (1333–1567), the *shugo daimyo*, or provincial constables, early on performed a kind of alternate attendance to Kyoto, where they were given land grants to build residences. Before long, however, they tended to remain in Kyoto for long periods of time, leaving provincial matters to their subordinates.[1] During the period of unification (1567–1600), Hideyoshi commanded his vassals to attend him at Kyoto (Fushimi) and granted them subsidies of land and rice there. Tokugawa Ieyasu, his leading vassal, went almost every year, for varying amounts of time.[2]

In a number of ways, then, by the beginning of the Edo period the principles underlying the Tokugawa control mechanism in general and alternate attendance in particular already were being applied, although clearly on a limited scale. The Tokugawa as hegemons after 1603 transformed the system, making it a formal requirement for the outside daimyo in 1635 and the hereditary lords in 1642. However, in addition to the alternate attendance being practiced on a national level, the institution also continued on the local level as it was in its earlier form; that is, in a number of the larger domains, such as Saga, Satsuma, and Tosa, top retainers, the senior advisors, were required to perform a type of alternate attendance between their landed fiefs and the lord's castle town. Some were exceedingly mobile, performing a dual form of attendance between their fief and the lord's castle town and then accompanying the lord on his required journeys to Edo.[3]

The hostage system also had historical roots prior to 1603. It was in fact already a familiar custom by the Warring States period (1467–1567) and continued to be so during the early years of the seventeenth century, when, after the Battle of Sekigahara (1600), many of the most powerful daimyo offered close kin to the Tokugawa as guarantees of their own good behavior.[4] The case of Maeda Toshinaga's mother, who was offered as hostage by the Kaga lord, is often cited as the first such example in the Edo period, but other daimyo like the Mōri of Chōshū and Nabeshima of Saga also sent family members (sons in both cases).[5] Others, however, maintain that it was the suggestion of the senior advisor Ise Sadamasa of Satsuma that the daimyo leave his wife and children permanently in Edo as guarantees of loyalty, and many daimyo followed this advice.[6] The shogunate encouraged the lords to come to Edo by granting them land in Edo on which to build residences and giving a number of important lords travel expenses and sometimes reductions in corvee levies to those who left hostages in Edo.

Originally voluntary, the hostage system became compulsory as of 1635 with the institutionalization of alternate attendance. Long before this, however, it had become impolitic for daimyo not to leave hostages. One of the reasons cited for the confiscation of Katō Tadahiro's domain in 1632 was that he had taken his Edo-born son back to his domain without the permission of the Tokugawa.[7] The hostage requirement covered the hereditary lords as well in 1642, when alternate attendance was extended to them.

As a result of the hostage system, the wives of daimyo spent almost their entire married lives in Edo, with the exception of occasional trips to area hot springs such as Ikaho or to pilgrimage sites like Enoshima. These movements were putatively for therapeutic or religious reasons and were restricted to the area within the checking station (*sekisho*) system that ringed the Kantō region. These barriers were originally designed to keep daimyo wives from leaving Edo and to prevent the domains from importing excessive military hardware into Edo, a policy known as *iri-deppō ni de-onna* (inbound guns, outbound women).[8] The daughters of daimyo spent their entire lives in Edo, as did sons not designated heir to their father's position.

For a time it was also required that the top vassals of the daimyo leave their families in Edo, where as hostages they lived in a special residence (*shōnin ya-shiki*) within the shogun's castle under the administrative authority of a Tokugawa official, the magistrate of hostages (*shōnin bugyō*). The entire process was the suggestion of Tōdō Takatori, daimyo of Imabara (Iyo), in 1608, though he was not the first to actually order his officials to leave hostages.[9] Most domains maintained a small, fixed number of hostages (one to five) taken from the families of the daimyo's top vassals, usually senior advisors: Tosa, for example, maintained three, one of which rotated every two years from a group of four persons; in Kurume, the same fixed number were maintained in Edo, but the rotation occurred every year from among a group of six persons.[10] Apparently the system was deemed unnecessary if not troublesome and was terminated in 1665 on the fiftieth anniversary of Ieyasu's death. Its dissolution was touted as an act of beneficence, one that revealed the maturation of the system and the Tokugawa government's increasing sense of security. An official Tosa record attributed it to the continuation of peace and the daimyo's successful completion of a pilgrimage to Nikkō to commemorate Ieyasu's death anniversary.[11]

In the Edo period, the obligation of alternate attendance was part of the military preparedness expected of the daimyo; their domains were held, in theory at least, as a fiscal base to enable them to sustain those military obligations to the shogunate. Other military responsibilities included maintaining a standing army and using it when ordered to protect the shogun, guarding the coastline from foreign ships, assisting with the takeover of castles when a particular lord's domain was confiscated, providing guard duty at various gates around Edo castle, and contributing to the Tokugawa's military campaigns, as in Osaka (1615–1616) and Shimabara (1637–1638). In fact, the connection between alternate attendance and military service is most apparent when we consider that the reason daimyo asked for a relaxation of the requirement in the late Tokugawa period was so they could be more effective in guarding the coastline from the hairy barbarians. There were also nonmilitary forms of service, some of which were carried out in conjunction with alternate attendance or while the lord was in Edo, e.g., attending the shogun at court, making pilgrimages to the shrine of Tokugawa Ieyasu and Iemitsu at Nikkō, providing fire watch at the shogunal family mortuary temples of (Ueno) Kan'eiji and (Shiba) Zōjōji, repairing roads in the Tokugawa's official network, the Gokaidō, and carrying out riparian works designated by the shogunate.

During the first half of the seventeenth century the Tokugawa laid claim to a range of powers that made its government the strongest and most centralized in Japan's history. These powers are well known and require no lengthy elaboration here: the powers of attainder and transfer of daimyo domains; the one-castle per domain regulation and restrictions on castle repairs or expansion projects; a monopoly on foreign policy and foreign trade; a monopoly of the legitimate use of physical force within Japan; currency control; the creation of a centralized road network, built at local expense, that ran through the heart of the country and infringed on the sovereignty of those lords through whose territories it coursed; corvee labor requirements on the residents of those domains through which the roads passed, who were required to transport Tokugawa officials and cargo, thereby infringing on the daimyo's right or ability to tax the people in his own domain.[12] In sum, the Tokugawa usurped the discretionary powers of the daimyo by moving or disenfeoffing them in a number of ways. Domain governments "could no longer use domain income exclusively for their own needs, could no longer determine their own military requirements, could no longer conduct independent relations with neighbors or the world outside, and — given the exigencies of the *sankin kōtai* system — could no longer be masters of their own movements."[13] While analogies are sometimes drawn between the German states prior to unification in the nineteenth century and Tokugawa Japan, Germany had no institution analogous to alternate attendance. Nor was there a similar system in imperial China, whose much greater size would have made such periodic movement to and from the capital problematic.

Alternate attendance was part of the basic foundation of the Tokugawa system, but at two points it became necessary to alter it temporarily. The first reform came at a time of fiscal crisis for the Tokugawa government under Yoshimune during the Kyōhō period (1716–1735). Due to its dire economic straits the shogunate commanded the daimyo to pay a levy on the order of one hundred *koku* per ten thousand *koku* of assessed productivity (*kokudaka*), the first time it had imposed a direct tax on the daimyo.[14] It took this unprecedented step to prevent several hundred Tokugawa retainers from going hungry, and in partial recompense it allowed the daimyo to reduce the required period of residence in Edo by half. The reform, begun in 1722, ran for eight years before the system reverted to its original schedules. This course of action — a temporary reprieve from alternate attendance — was taken rather than a permanent reduction in frequency, to once every three or five years, a position which Yoshimune embraced at first. The shogun, though, was convinced by Muro Kyūsō's arguments that breaking with the tradition of biennial service would make the daimyo willful and less inclined to obey the shogun, which would lead to a disorderly realm.[15]

Indeed, that is exactly what happened when a later shogun, Iemochi, effected a reform similar to the plan Yoshimune first considered adopting. According to the American merchant Francis Hall, who was in Japan at the time, "[a] royal edict was indeed issued [in 1862] that the residency system of the daimio [*sic*] at Yedo should be broken up in a great measure. All the daimio [*sic*] were to retire with their families to their provinces and once in three years were to visit Yedo for 100 days, their families remaining in the country permanently."[16] One might be tempted to conclude from this that the shogunate finally gave in to a rising chorus of opinion from important lords, harking back to Ogyū Sorai's criticism of the early eighteenth century, that the system constituted an onerous economic burden. This criticism was not new, of course. It was only when faced with the growing menace posed by Western gunships in Japanese waters that the shogunate gave the daimyo some respite from their periodic migrations to save money for military preparations. In other words, without the arrival of Perry's black ships there would have been no impetus for reform. In one fell swoop the system was reformed radically, completely eliminating the hostage system and drastically reducing the period of residence. So much were alternate attendance and Tokugawa authority synonymous that once the requirement of residence in Edo was relaxed in 1862 the polity came apart at the seams within just a few years. Though the measure was only meant to reform, not abolish, the system, the shogunate was in such a weakened state that when it ordered a return to the old system three years later, few daimyo listened. Even a small domain such as Hachinohe (eighteen thousand *koku*) could ignore the Tokugawa order with impunity. The period between the institutionalization of the system and its reform in 1862, however, was more than two hundred years, during which time the daimyo paraded back and forth on the highways and byways of Japan with remarkable consistency and bravura.

Patterns of Movement

The physical movement of political actors is often key to the stability of regimes in various cultures across the globe. (The movements also have great cultural significance — a topic that will be explored in the Tokugawa context in chapter three.) In Morocco, for example, during the eighteenth and nineteenth centuries, the king tried to keep warrior-based tribes under control by moving around in his kingdom. His mobility was a central element in his power. He endeavored to hold the realm together "by a restless searching out of contact, most agonistic, with literally hundreds of lesser powers within it."[17] With an entourage of as many as forty thousand, the king's court was in almost constant motion. In Tokugawa Japan, however, we find almost an obverse image of this in that it was the lords, or daimyo, who were in constant motion while the sovereign, the shogun, remained at the center, in Edo. The shogun's power was manifested not in his regular movement, a court in motion, but in his ability to cause others to move.

There was, however, variation in the cyclical movement of the daimyo. The outside lords were divided into two groups, called "east" and "west" but in reality geographically mixed, half of whom alternated during odd-numbered years: fifty rotated during the fourth month, forty-five during the sixth, and sixteen were to appear in Edo during the twelfth and to return to their domains during the eighth.[18] The other half of the outside lords rotated during even-numbered years: thirty-nine during the fourth month, forty-seven during the sixth, and another fifteen were scheduled to arrive in Edo during the eighth month and to return six months later, during the second.[19] When the hereditary lords were incorporated into the system in 1642, sixty-nine of them rotated during the sixth month, while nine rotated during the eighth month. Another group of fourteen hereditary lords, all based close to Edo in the Kantō region, did the same on a semi-annual basis, half during the second month and the other during the eighth. In addition, some thirty-four or thirty-five of the Tokugawa's direct retainers, housemen known as *kōtai yoriai*, were likewise required to perform alternate attendance just like the daimyo.[20] Both the hereditary daimyo and the *kōtai yoriai*, like the outside lords, were divided into east and west groups which alternated in the timing of their Edo service.[21]

In this way both the movements of the lords and the timing of those movements were under Tokugawa control and, of course, daimyo were not to leave their domains without the shogun's permission.[22] Contiguous *tozama* domains, such as Tosa and Awa, often found themselves in different groups, east and west. Thus their lords were never in the same place, in the domain or in Edo, at the same time. This was also true for the Kyushu domains of Saga and Fukuoka. The grouping of daimyo into east and west groups may have been a conscious control measure to help prevent collusion. There was also a strategic defensive element probably involved as well; that is, it was not wise to remove the military leaders of entire sections of the country at the same time. For example, in the case of Saga and Fukuoka it was important that one of the two lords in charge of coastal defense in strategic northern Kyushu be in his domain at all times. Similarly, branch domains and the domain proper from which they split off rotated their alternations. In the case of Tosa and Nakamura (thirty thousand *koku*), Tosa made its trips to Edo in even-numbered years and Nakamura in odd-numbered ones.[23]

Some exceptions were made in the length of service required in Edo. In the case of the Kuroda of Fukuoka and the Nabeshima of Saga, who as noted performed coastal guard duty, the period of residence in Edo was reduced to one hundred days. The Sō, from distant Tsushima, were required to make the trip only every third year, and then only for four months, due to the domain's strategic role, which included managing foreign trade with Yi Korea. Matsumae of Ezo, for similar strategic reasons, was required to reside in Edo only four months every five years. Full exemptions were granted to certain daimyo either on a permanent basis, as with the related lord of Mito, who had the status of *jōfu* or "stationed in the (Tokugawa) capital," or those with a contingent exemption due to their holding office in the shogunal bureaucracy. The latter was true as well of the Tokugawa's senior councilors, junior councilors, and magistrates.[24] Temporary reprieves were given as well to compensate the daimyo when there was a foreign crisis. Saga and its three branch domains of Ogi, Kashima, and Hasunoike were all granted a five-year exemption from alternate attendance after the arrival of the Russians in Nagasaki in 1853.[25]

Even before the rotation of residences was institutionalized in 1635 and 1642, the daimyo had been traveling to pay homage to the Tokugawa rulers. The Laws for the Military Houses issued in 1629 were the first to designate Edo as the place to which the daimyo should travel; prior to this the lords also made trips to Kyoto, as in 1615, when the daimyo were ordered to Fushimi by shogun Hidetada during the Osaka campaign. While one might argue that the early movement of the daimyo was Kyoto-centered,[26] still the Yamauchi and other lords made numerous trips to Edo before 1635.[27] With the institutionalization of the system, the daimyo's movements became centered squarely on Edo.

The Laws for the Military Houses engendered several major flows of traffic, as noted above, but in addition to all this movement, there were less routine flows between Edo and the domains. The first of these involved retired daimyo, who sometimes, continuing the pattern of their years as reigning lords, alternated their residences between Edo and the domain castle town. A second and more routine flow consisted of the movement of the ruling daimyo's heir. These trips were not formally required by Tokugawa law — which perhaps explains why these movements have been overlooked by some historians; one, for example, has written that by the workings of the alternate attendance system, "future daimyo were born and raised at the metropolitan center and never visited their domain until they were invested as daimyo, after which they rotated between Edo and their fief."[28] According to another historian, it was not until Yoshimune's reform of alternate attendance in the 1720s that the heir apparent could go home to visit while his father was in Edo, but there is evidence that this occurred in Tosa from the early seventeenth century on. In fact, only seven of Tosa's sixteen daimyo were born in Edo, and it was essential that all future daimyo travel to the domain over which they were destined to rule to become familiar with it through personal experience — in the words of the day, *okokusei ominarai to shite* (learning to govern through observation).[29]

The movements of daimyo heirs, like that of retired daimyo, appear to have become customary, at least for the largest domains such as Satsuma, Kaga, and Tosa. The Yamauchi family's heirs routinely began traveling to the domain before becoming the lord. The third lord, Tadatoyo, for example, made his first trip to Tosa at the age of seventeen, thirty years before assuming the family headship in 1656. His successor, Toyomasa, was nineteen years old when he made his first trip in 1660, nine years before he became lord. In turn, his successor saw his future domain at the age of twenty-one, seven years before assuming his place as lord. This was true of later lords as well; Toyoteru embarked on his initial trip in 1828 at the age of thirteen, fifteen years before his accession. Another daimyo heir, Toyooki (1793–1809) made two trips to Edo at an even earlier age, the first in 1793 when he was an infant of only six months, and the second in 1802 at the age of nine, two years before he was designated heir and a full six years before he assumed the family headship.[30]

Thus, daimyo and heir both participated in alternate attendance. In fact, they each moved in opposite directions in a kind of shadow dance, and as a result the hostage element of alternate attendance remained in force, since when the heir was in the fief the lord was by the shogun's figurative side in Edo. Lord Yamauchi Tadayoshi (r. 1605–1656) and his son Tadatoyo (heir 1619–1656, r. 1656–1669) alternated periods of residence in the home domain. In 1644 Tadayoshi received his leave of absence, departing from Edo on 7/2; his heir, Tadatoyo, had arrived in Edo from Kōchi more than three months earlier, on 3/20. It was common for heir and lord to overlap periods of residence in Edo, but not in the domain. The following spring Tadayoshi arrived in Edo on 3/11. Tadatoyo was still in the shogunal capital, but took his leave for Kōchi on intercalary 5/9. This was the manner in which their movements brought them together and then took them on different trajectories.[31] When the heir Yamauchi Tadatoyo asked for a delay in his departure for Edo in 1640 due to a fire in the Tosa compound where he would be living, he was refused and had to make haste to get to Edo in time.[32]

Alternate attendance performed by the heir was not simply an informal requirement imposed, directly or indirectly, by an outside political power. It was also expected by top domainal officials as a recognition that the heir's participation was important to his education. Toyofusa, heir to the lordship of Tosa domain (heir 1689–1700; r. 1700–1706), refused to visit the domain for a prolonged period. Seven years after being formally adopted as heir in 1689, he still had not done so. Even after Lord Toyomasa arrived in Edo in 1696/4/18 Toyofusa showed no indication of requesting permission to leave for Tosa. In light of this, his chief retainer Asahina Genba remonstrated with him, telling him that most daimyo heirs of his status had already made several trips. The language of this document is polite yet unusual in its forcefulness:

> What I will write here is what others have wanted to say, but have been unable to do so. I have refrained from doing so until now, though, as it may seem that I am only recommending this course because I have been given leave to return to Tosa [hence as his close retainer would selfishly want Toyofusa to return as well]. You have not asked for permission for a leave

from your duties in Edo, but it is already past the time for returning to the domain. Since there will be no trip this year, I can now offer these words.

Two years ago you had the opportunity to travel to Tosa, but because you were sick, you did not request permission to do so. This year it is of course already too late. With great deference, I must say that the shogun has no doubt noticed this. Most daimyo heirs of your status [from province-holding daimyo houses] have already made the trip to the domain twice during the period you have been in Edo, but you have missed the opportunities and have not requested leave, even when you had gone for audiences to Edo castle. This may lead to rumors that your illness is grave or that there is some discord between you and the lord. People may also be wondering whether you have postponed making the trip to Tosa because you lack the ability to govern. Surely many think it is suspicious that you have overlooked such an important matter as this. . . .

If you continue to miss opportunities to return to the domain, people will think that it is because you lack the ability to govern. There could be nothing worse for a person of your status than if people from across the country begin to criticize you.

Claiming illness, you have not performed your duties for five or six years, and this has caused Lord Toyomasa great hardship. Nothing is of greater consequence to our domain than this problem. The lord does not know how this situation will resolve itself, but the future looks dark to him. [I repeat,] there is nothing of greater importance to the domain than this.[33]

The senior advisor Asahina Genba here remonstrates with his lord, underlining the political, economic, and social consequences of Toyofusa's inaction, not only for the domain as a whole and on the heir himself, but (in a later portion of the note) for those serving him most closely, his retainers. He argues that making the trip was important to the prestige of the domain, because not doing so would draw the negative attention of the shogun, other daimyo, and even the public at large, damaging Tosa's reputation. The perception of a daimyo's heir's illness could have negative consequences on at least two levels. It could lead to Toyofusa's designation as heir being rescinded. In a worst-case scenario, should Lord Toyomasa die suddenly and his heir Toyofusa be perceived as sickly and unable to rule, the domain could be abolished or penalized with a sizeable reduction in size and status. Given the unstable political climate of the late seventeenth century, when the shogun Tsunayoshi exercised the shogunate's right of attainder with vigor, this was a legitimate concern. While Asahina expresses deep concern that Toyofusa's failure to travel to Tosa would be interpreted as a sign of lack of leadership ability, one other concern seems to have been implied in his letter. It was considered important that the heir and lord not be in the same location — in the domain or in Edo — for strategic reasons in case of an emergency. For example, in the famous Akō Incident, both Lord Asano Naganori and his heir were in Edo, leaving only a senior advisor in charge in the castle town to confront the crisis facing the domain as a result of Asano's wounding of Lord Kira Yoshinaka in the shogun's castle in 1701.[34]

In Satsuma domain, Lord Mitsuhisa and his son and heir, Tsunahisa, both performed their own cycle of alternate attendance, trading places in Edo and Kagoshima almost without deviation until 1670, when Mitsuhisa's second son, Tsunetaka, received permission to travel to Kagoshima as well.[35] The dance now involved a third party. In 1670 Lord Mitsuhisa returned to the domain, leaving Edo on 4/15; Tsunetaka followed his trail, leaving Edo on 5/15. Before Tsunetaka's departure from Edo, heir Tsunahisa had arrived on 5/6. This pas-de-trois continued until Tsunahisa passed away in 1673. At this point, Mitsuhisa and the new heir, Tsunetaka, continued the two-person rotation until Mitsuhisa died in 1694. However, during that time Mitsuhisa retired (in 1687), and he and Tsunetaka, now the new reigning lord, switched schedules.

Yet another type of movement engendered by alternate attendance was the procession of domain senior advisors. In Tosa, a number of these officials led smaller but still substantial processions to Edo and back at certain times when a new lord succeeded or after the death of a lord who was on leave in the domain. These types of processions, it appears, were also extralegal. In the case of Tosa, a senior advisor of the Fukao family, which held a fief of ten thousand koku in Sakawa, led a procession to Edo as representative for the lord on seven different occasions. In 1843, 160 men accompanied him.[36] It is uncertain, however, whether other senior advisors were sent on different occasions, or indeed whether or not this practice was widespread in other domains.

The official domain diary, as well as the diaries kept by individual retainers, reveal that in addition to these various flows of men, a considerable but irregular stream of retainers headed in both directions throughout the year. For example, retainer Mori Yoshiki writes that on his trip back to Kōchi in 1801, accompanied by a total of ten other retainers and attendants, he met with other Tosa people on the Tōkaidō at Fukuroi, at Futagawa, at Yoshida, and at Fujikawa. Retainers like Yoshiki who completed their official duties in Edo were often given leave to return to the domain on their own.[37]

All of the various patterns engendered by alternate attendance created significant movement on the highways, movement which must have appeared constant to many, particularly those commoners living on or near a major thoroughfare. This is suggested in graphic fashion by some picture game boards that show a continuous line of processions along the highway from Edo to Kyoto or from a domain castle town to Edo.[38]

Preparations for Departure

The requirements of alternate attendance set in motion an almost continuous cycle of preparations as well as numerous rituals that led up to and included the actual departure and journey itself.[39] For daimyo making a biennial rotation, preparation for the next trip to Edo began less than six months after the lord returned to the seat of his power, demonstrating the degree to which *sankin kōtai* occupied domain officials. For the largest number of daimyo, who were on rotation during the fourth month, it was customary, usually in the early fall (eighth month), to send a letter of inquiry to the shogunate's senior councilors confirming the upcoming turn of service in Edo. Generally, by the eleventh month, the senior councilors issued a formal reply to appear in Edo the following spring, and this was relayed by messenger to the lord's castle town; for those daimyo due in Edo during the sixth month, notice was usually received four months earlier, during the second month. Though ritualistic in form, the daimyo were required to request permission to travel to Edo at a certain time and to notify the shogunate of any change in schedule.

Actual travel preparations began almost immediately upon receipt of the shogunal order. While the timing differed from locale to locale, over the following four-to-six-month period the administrative bureaucracies in the domains took similar steps in organizing and preparing for the trip. Personnel were designated to make the journey, and the list of those names, as well as the size of subsidies for travel preparation, were announced at the domain office. Particularly important was the designation of a senior advisor (or two in the case of larger domains) to accompany the lord and an inspector, who was general overseer of the procession. The length of individual notification given for Edo service tended to vary. For example, Mori Hirosada, a mid-ranking samurai from Tosa, received a full six months' notice in 1732, while Toyama Tamuro, a high-ranking samurai from Hachinohe domain, donned his formal attire on 1828/1/11 to receive the official notice of his appointment to Edo service only two months later.[40] Some of the designated personnel were also assigned travel-related duties, as will be explained below. In Sendai these announcements were usually made early in the eleventh month for a departure set for the following spring (third month).[41]

Preparations also involved numerous officials who did not themselves serve in Edo. Local magistrates had to be notified of the upcoming trip, as it was their offices that handled preparations for the passage of the lord's procession through the domain. These officials were responsible for ensuring that designated resting and lodging places were prepared and that villages along the road were notified to prepare food and lodging and clean the roads in preparation for the passage of the procession. Generally, post stations were notified six months before a daimyo's scheduled overnight stay, and lodging assignments were made for all members of the procession.[42] Gear to be used on the trip was inspected and necessary repairs ordered; any new gear needed was ordered at this time. Importantly, calculations had to be made for travel expenses, including the hiring of horses and porters at the post stations, lodging, and daily allowances. Finally, any foodstuffs to be brought along had to be readied for departure.

Domain officials selected the precise day of departure (e.g., on 1732/1/19 the date for the lord's departure was set for 3/3), often after receiving instructions from religious prelates attached to the lord's family temple, who picked an auspicious day. Later, on the day of the announcement, those retainers assigned to Edo duty dressed in their travel attire and proceeded to the palace for a celebratory audience. Prayers for a safe journey were read by the local clergy on a regular basis over the following period of roughly ten days before departure.

In addition to the other information listed above, a memorandum of travel orders for the retinue was posted at the domain office. This was also read to the troops (usually the middle and upper strata of the retainer corps), either before departure in the castle grounds or before crossing the border out of Tosa. Presumably, group leaders would read it to their subordinates and the instructions would in a similar fashion trickle downward to the valets, attendants, and other menials. The orders were meant to regulate the behavior of the members of the retinue, and as is true with any military troop movement, order, discipline, and efficiency were the goals stressed. For example, a statement of the senior advisor named Kirima Yoshitaka from Tosa was read to the retainers about to accompany the heir on his first trip to Edo in 1802. His comments reveal some particular concerns because it is the first such trip:

> Accompanying the heir to Edo is a serious duty and it goes without saying that all, regardless of rank, must perform their best. Retainers must strictly follow the rules that have been issued. Moreover, since this is the first trip to Edo for many of you as well, [the problems of] sake and women are of the greatest concerns. Retainers must behave according to regulations even when on their own time. All should take special care that these rules are followed.[43]

A sample list of these instructions, from an earlier date, in 1671, read:[44]

1. Strictly obey the laws of the Tokugawa government.
2. It is forbidden to have social intercourse with those from other domains.
3. Even when facing crowded conditions and delays at boat crossings, do not talk to those from other domains.

4. Do not act improperly with shopkeepers, when purchasing items, or with innkeepers.

5. It is forbidden to go to public baths, even if delayed at one place [due to weather or high water levels].

6. Lewd or other inappropriate behavior, gambling, and sightseeing are prohibited.

These regulations indicate a concern with order as well as with the avoidance of altercations with men from other domains and with commoners in general.[45] They also reflect a concern that procession members might try to use the reflected authority of domain for personal profit or gain, as with shopkeepers. Furthermore, because the road to Edo was difficult — physically challenging and tedious at times — there was heightened concern about disruptive or immoral behavior.[46]

Due to the physically taxing nature of the journey to Edo, retainers in some domains were directly instructed to get in shape beforehand. A memorandum from Lord Ikeda Mitsumasa to Okayama retainers from the mid-seventeenth century reminded them that "[t]oday's young people are not in as good condition as sixty-year-olds were in the past" and instructed them to build up their physical conditioning several months before the ten-day walk began.[47] Looking at the depiction of Kaga's procession making its way through a mountainous stretch on the way to Edo (Figure 1.1), one can well appreciate the sagacity of such advice. To rest up for the journey, retainers were released from their duties about a week before departure for Edo, and upon return to the domain were given a similar period of rest.[48]

Other practical travel preparations were made by officials charged with responsibility for arranging packhorses, porters, and lodging. A messenger from the castle town dispatched advance requisition orders for travel services to the post stations about five to six days before departure. Then, one to two days before departure, a list of lodging assignments for retainers was forwarded to the post station inns, along with the daimyo's placards, by a magistrate charged with that duty. The rectangular, wooden placards, which are preserved today in considerable numbers in local historical museums, were displayed at entrances to post stations and at the official inns where the lord and his top officials were to stay, thereby notifying all passersby of the elite status of the principal guest. Domain officials in charge of these services, acting much like travel agents, went ahead of the procession to verify that all the requisition orders and reservations had been received; they also inspected the inns to ensure that they had been maintained adequately for the lord.

On an individual, personal level, the days before departure could be filled with visits to friends and colleagues, as part of the custom of leave taking. In

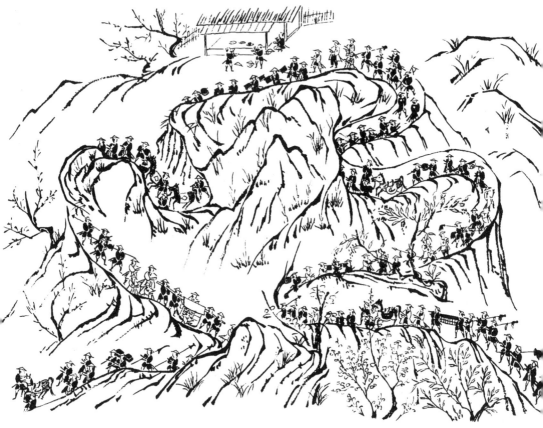

FIGURE 1.1. Procession of Kaga domain crossing the mountains. From "Daimyō gyōretsu zu" #5. Courtesy Kanazawa shiritsu Tamagawa toshokan.

fact, Tosa retainer Mori Yoshiki received invitations from so many people the week before departure that he was not able to accept them all. Some friends gave the departing member gifts, and, as will be discussed in chapter seven, retainers returning from Edo often came back with an abundance of presents. Yoshiki also made time for pilgrimages to several local temples.[49] His fellow retainer Miyaji Umanosuke received numerous farewell gifts of money and was hosted for dinner several times by friends. On one occasion he was offered celebratory red rice and whale soup, a local favorite.[50]

As the day of departure approached, the daimyo gave a farewell address to his near relatives and retainers staying behind. In 1689, for example, Toyomasa instructed those retainers to behave with decorum, to be diligent in preventing fires, to be assiduous in their study of both scholastic learning and the martial arts, and to follow the economizing measures in place without fail.[51] Celebratory meals were served to various officials, in groups, according to rank, including female attendants of the interior (*oku*).

As with most rituals involving *bushi*, the lord's departure was heavily scripted. This point is reinforced by diagrams that designate the placement of key retainers at the time of departure. Positions were commonly fixed by status; those of higher status were located inside the castle or in front of the main gate. Also, while not part of the official script, merchants and artisans, particularly those with ties to the domain and in some castle towns even sumo wrestlers, lined the streets in commoner districts while the procession passed.

The day of departure itself often began with a number of rituals, beginning with the lord's pilgrimage to the family temple, Shinmyōji in the case of Tosa, where he reported to the ancestral spirits his impending departure for Edo and prayed for a safe journey and for the well-being of the domain during his absence. Subsequently, he gave an audience for top-ranking retainers who were to accompany him, followed by tea, a simple meal, including soup and sake. On this day, departure time was usually set for late morning instead of the early dawn departure that prevailed during the remainder of the trip. In Nanbu the day of departure was similar to New Year's Day. Retainers came in full battle dress for an audience with the lord, an indication again that the alternate attendance procession was perceived as a military maneuver.[52]

Symbolically, a larger portion of the retainer corps accompanied the lord upon departure than would actually complete the trip to Edo. An indeterminate group of retainers saw the lord off by accompanying him just a short way on his journey. In Chōshū one group of officials not making the trip to Edo accompanied the lord until the point where the procession made its first rest stop at a teahouse designated for that purpose. There, a number of modest gifts from high-ranking retainers and the lord's concubines, customarily food, sake, or small handicraft items, were presented.[53] In Okayama, where the first leg of the journey from the castle town was made by boat, the main retainer corps lined the banks of the Asahi River, which ran through the castle town in a north-south direction, while the senior advisors accompanied him down the river as far as its outlet at Kojima Bay, in the Inland Sea. There they exchanged farewell cups of sake before the lord transferred to a larger vessel, which would take him as far as Osaka.[54]

Some of the rituals carried out after departure also had a religious element. After arrival at the first night's stop still within the home domain, representatives of the daimyo went to local shrines and temples, where they made donations and received protective charms. In the case of Chōshū, other representatives were sent to larger temples in the surrounding area as well. Local officials of all the shrines and temples visited sent representatives to greet the lord the following morning before his departure.[55]

At various points along the road and at subsequent official rest stops in the lord's domain, local officials from villages and the various magistrates' offices came to pay their respects and to offer small gifts. These troublesome, ritual exchanges were repeated at many stops, and the items received were meticulously recorded. Fresh fish (in the case of Chōshū), it appears, was particularly prized. A seemingly endless stream of messengers, gifts, and return gifts (usually clothing or money) brought the lord and his officials into contact with the local elite as they passed through the home domain.[56]

The rituals carried out on the journey to and from the shogun's capital included frequent communications between the procession, the domain headquarters, and the Edo compounds. Officials in all three locations dispatched messengers all along the route to update information on the progress of the retinue and on local conditions, especially after a checking station or some particularly difficult stretch of road was passed or body of water crossed successfully. Sometimes the information conveyed was more than ritualistic and could be crucial. For example, in 1657 the Shimazu lord was en route to Edo when he was informed of a great fire (the Meireki fire) in Edo, which destroyed the main compounds of Satsuma and many other domains. After receiving instructions from the shogunate to delay his attendance in Edo, the lord gave orders for the procession to turn around and head back to Kagoshima.[57]

The return to the domain followed the same pattern of predeparture procedures and accompanying rituals. There was understandably a more celebratory mood to the procession's return after the completion of a period of service in Edo. In Hachinohe, family members anxious to be reunited traveled to the first or second post station from the castle town, either fourteen or thirty-six kilometers away, to greet returning fathers, brothers, husbands, uncles, cousins, and friends. Apparently celebrations could occasionally get out of hand, as sake drinking at these times was prohibited periodically.[58] Toyama Tamuro's father, Heima, accompanied by a page, went to greet his son (at an unspecified location) in 1829 with a veritable feast of freshwater trout, flounder, loach, boiled vegetables, and rice. Once on his landed fief in Hachinohe, Tamuro received two hundred copper coins from the village head and three hundred from the farmers themselves.[59]

Still other, more formal rituals remained for retainers, as arrival in the castle town did not quite bring to an end their service on the return leg of the journey. Middle and high-ranking retainers had to report their arrival at the castle and make the rounds to their various superiors before returning home. It was dark before one middle-ranking retainer from Tosa, Gotō Seikō, could return to his home, where family and relatives had gathered to celebrate his safe return and the completion of his cycle of service in alternate attendance.[60]

Travel Expenses and the Local Economies

The costs of transporting large numbers of men on a periodic basis were stag-
gering. Travel expenses could, depending on the distance of a domain from
Edo, make up anywhere from five to twenty percent of its budget. These, together with costs incurred in Edo for the maintenance of domainal staff there,
typically consumed roughly half to three-quarters of a domain's total disposable income.[61] According to the political economist Kaiho Seiryō, Edo-related
expenses were greater than domainal government ones, and the available statistics bear out his statement.[62] These outlays of cash made the requirement a
tax by another name — and a heavy tax at that. The requirements of alternate
attendance meant that the daimyo could no longer use domain income exclusively for internal needs, and therefore it also limited the resources they could
afford to go uncontrolled within the fief. In short, alternate attendance was perhaps the most significant external factor the domains had to take into account
when managing fiscal policy. As the work of Luke Roberts on Tosa domain
has shown, it was a challenge with which samurai policymakers continuously
grappled.[63]

On the road, the retinues relied upon the local economies of the post stations for lodging.[64] The lord and his top vassals were housed in special inns
designated for their use (*honjin*, "daimyo inns," and *waki-honjin*, or "auxiliary
daimyo inns"). On the Tōkaidō, the most heavily traveled road, there were a
total of 179.[65] Ordinarily no more than sixty people, the lord and his top ranking officials, could stay in a large facility.[66] The remainder of the procession
found bedding in commoner inns or in households in the post station when the
other facilities were not sufficient. All available space in commoner inns was
put to use when a large retinue came through; not only tatami-matted rooms,
but any wooden floored area, including hallways. In some cases, when the procession was large or the facilities at a post station underdeveloped, men had to
be spread out into the surrounding community and were lodged in commoner
homes and in shrines or temples in nearby villages.[67]

The processions were also dependent to a varying degree upon the local
economies of the post stations for food, though it is difficult to obtain a clear
picture of this.[68] The general trend, as one might expect, seems to have been
that early on, in a continuation of the pattern of the wartime mobilizations of
the late sixteenth century, daimyo processions were largely self-sufficient; that
is, necessary foodstuffs and cooking implements were brought along from the
home domain. This is in line with the meaning of the term for the daimyo's
inn, *honjin*, or "battle-time camp." Alternate attendance was, after all, a type
of travel for military purposes. Therefore, it was natural that the procession be

self-sufficient to the largest extent possible. This is made clear in case of Maeda Toshitsune (1593–1658), lord of Kaga domain, a vigorous man who liked traveling at night and wading across rivers (rather than being carried across them in a palanquin). His cooks were instructed to gather certain edible greens (*hakobe*, or stickwort) from the roadside for his soups. A retainer, who apparently did not think this was appropriate for the lord and his retainers, said, "Recently all the lords are buying their meals at inns, but only men in Kaga's procession cook their own food." To this the lord replied, "In times of war there are no inns." To the lord, being self-sufficient was a question of military preparedness.[69]

As the threat of war subsided and the size of processions grew during the course of the seventeenth century, and as facilities on the highways improved, there was a greater reliance upon the local inns by the lords. The issue is clouded, though, by the fact that there were great differences among the daimyo. Some traveled light and relied upon the inns for nearly everything. Others brought along their own foodstuffs and utensils for its preparation. In the latter case, domainal kitchen officials built a place to prepare food near the official inn and used the labor of cooks in the domain's employ, and sometimes local commoners as well, to assist in the preparation of the food, perhaps not an efficient way to provide for the procession. Moreover, by consigning all food preparation to the inns, domain officials did not have to negotiate directly with villagers. Even late in the Tokugawa period, however, not all daimyo relied on the inns. Minor daimyo heading small processions were particularly likely to prepare their own food. Or some domains might bring along foodstuffs to cook for the lord and his top officials, but consign to the inns responsibility for providing for the others in the procession. This allowed the processions to travel much lighter, as heavy foodstuffs and utensils used in their preparation and serving could be left behind. Such seems to have been the case with Tosa's procession in 1688: nineteen cooks were a part of the main group (1,474 men) to cook for the lord and probably his closest retainers, but none were included in the forward and trailing parties (471 and 586 men, respectively).[70]

Even those domains which relied on the local inns for food seemed to bring along many articles for the daimyo's personal use, all bearing his family crest: food trays, tableware, tea box, dessert box, not to mention some local delicacies from the castle town for him to eat, such as the Nabeshima lord's pickled eggplant. In fact just about everything the lord needed — his bedding, some furniture, bathtub, toilet, washbasin, helmet and armor, clothing, medicines, and writing box, among other items — was brought from home. The Maeda lord of Kaga (see Figure 1.2) was even said to have had his own bathwater carried all the way from Kanazawa. The lord of Matsue, who was an adherent of the Sekishū school of tea, always traveled with a prized tea caddy carried beside his palanquin. Others brought along caged birds.[71]

FIGURE 1.2. Lord Maeda (on horseback) of Kaga domain. From Hishikawa Moro-
nobu's "Daimyō gyōretsu." Courtesy Museum für Asiatische Kunst, Staatliche
Museen zu Berlin.

Sometimes the procession members would be provided with boxed lunches
by the daimyo inns. At other times the procession would stop for lunch at other
post station inns. For example, the members of the procession of the Uwajima
lord (one hundred thousand *koku*) on the way to Edo in 1788 took a reprieve for
lunch at Ōiso post station on the Tōkaidō, where they were fed a light meal of
boiled rice soaked with tea.[72] In contrast, most of the men in the Sendai retinue
in 1863 had a more substantial lunch of white rice, miso soup with potato and
tofu, and pickled eggplant. Full samurai ate slightly better, also receiving some
pickled melon.[73]

The official and auxiliary official inns where the daimyo and his highest-
ranking retainers ate were also the largest and most impressive buildings in the
post towns. Befitting the status of their guests, they were centrally located in

the station and the only buildings allowed to have gatehouses marking their entrances. To mark the arrival of a daimyo, a conical heap of sand was constructed
on each side of the gate as a sign of courtesy,[74] and a purple crepe curtain was
hung across the inn entranceway. Several days before the daimyo's arrival, advance men from the domain delivered wooden placards bearing the name of
the lord, which were erected on a wooden post in front of the inn and at both
ends of the station. One foreign guest noted that the inside was as impressive as
the outside: "Seen from the outside they could not be distinguished from palaces. Inside they were beautifully laid out; fine mats on the floors, golden leather
finishings. The bathrooms most tasteful, towel racks and fixtures black lacquer
with gold. In short, everything tastefully done."[75] Because many daimyo traveled at the same time, there was keen competition to stay at the official inns.
Given that they were limited in number, usually two *honjin* and *waki-honjin* at
each station, a priority system based on status and rank was employed. Those
for example who were bumped from the main official inns were forced to find
lodgings at the auxiliary inns or to go on to the next station. A river stoppage
could tie up traffic and wreak havoc with the reservation system.[76]

Early on the lords competed to see who could spend the most, but before long
many got the reputation of misers at the inns and teahouses as they tried to cut
expenses wherever they could.[77] For example, a humorous poem said of the lord
of Kōriyama:

> Yamato Koriyama is his domain
> As much as 150,000 *koku* in size
> But for tea, he gives a mere 200 coppers.[78]

Daimyo were forced to economize any way they could because of the large
number of people in the entourage, who had to be fed and housed all the way to
and from Edo. Domain officials could reduce costs by pushing the procession
to travel long days and thus keep the number of days on the road to a minimum. This meant waking up before dawn, as depicted in Hiroshige's "Tōkaidō
gojūsan tsugi" series print of Kameyama station, where we can see some of the
troops, shrouded in semidarkness, beginning to assemble outside the inn. It
also meant traveling until dark—*kure muttsu tomari no nanatsu tachi*, "Up
at 4 [a.m.] and stop for the night at dark," according to the expression of the
time—but processions sometimes walked at night as well.[79]

Domain officials also tried to economize by negotiating prices for lodging
with inn officials, as Tosa representatives did in 1848.[80] Sometimes they even
tried bargaining for discounts on the spot.[81] Daimyo inns derived income from
two sources, lodging fees and gratuities, and prices were standardized and artificially low. There were usually other *honjin* available at the post stations, which
allowed some leeway for negotiation when domain officials made preliminary

inquiries about reservations months before departure. Financially hard-pressed daimyo naturally cut back on gratuities (hence the type of critical poems cited above) and this practice gravely damaged inn business.[82] The inns petitioned the Tokugawa authorities about this, complained about their ignoring previous petitions, and asked for financial assistance because they claimed they had to take out loans to survive.[83]

Some daimyo also sought to reduce expenditures by avoiding the customary exchange of gifts with the *honjin* operator.[84] The exchange of gifts, however, could result in the circulation of local specialty products, as was the case in 1802, when the Tosa lord gave an innkeeper some of Tosa's high-quality paper.[85] This was just one of the ways in which the alternate attendance acted as a mechanism for the circulation of material culture in early modern Japan.

Other funds inevitably had to be spent to pay for local services and to purchase various commodities to be used on the road, such as straw sandals, inexpensive items (four to sixteen *mon*) that had to be replaced every four to five days. Money was also dispersed along the roads at teahouses, where porters were given tips for refreshments. As will be discussed in some detail in chapter seven, members of the retinue could also make personal purchases, such as for souvenirs, at the post stations.[86] In a variety of ways, then, income produced in the domains was circulated along Tokugawa Japan's main arteries via the alternate attendance and local material culture carried across the country.

By far the majority of money expended at the local level was for transport charges. Daimyo on alternate attendance were allowed to use certain numbers of horses and porters provided by post stations on the official Tokugawa road network, the Gokaidō, at a partially subsidized "fixed rate." The numbers allowed varied by road (e.g., one hundred men and one hundred horses per station on the Tōkaidō, fifty men and fifty horses on the Nakasendō, and twenty-five men and twenty-five horses on other roads) and were sufficient for a time, but as procession sizes grew larger during the seventeenth century they proved inadequate, prompting the development of an extensive network of corvée villages charged with supplying the extra horses and manpower needed.[87] Corvée labor was remunerated, but at a rate insufficient to cover the costs of food and transport or to make up for lost time and labor. It could be commuted to a cash payment, but that posed a different set of problems. Additional numbers of horses and men could be requisitioned beyond these limits, but they had to be paid for at the market rate (*aitai chinsen*). In Morioka domain, the lord's procession of about three hundred men in the early nineteenth century required four times the allotted number of men and horses.[88] Tosa's large processions of the late seventeenth and early eighteenth centuries required a massive mobilization of the countryside; for the procession of 1,799 men in 1718 as many as seven thousand villagers were requisitioned from four different districts in Tosa to engage in road upkeep as well as to meet the transport needs of the retinue.[89] Demands for such levels of corvee labor in Tosa and elsewhere "promoted frequent resistance."[90]

As the size of processions increased, so did the demand for laborers provided by the post station, both the regular workers as well as corvee labor. Additional sources of labor therefore had to be found and paid for. Labor contractors supplied porters, palanquin bearers, and other laborers for daimyo processions. Yoneya Kyūemon was one such contractor, and he handled the labor needs of eight domains, including Numazu and Kuwana, in the late 1850s. In 1859, for example, he supplied 103 laborers — 57 percent of the total number of men in the procession — to carry baggage for the retinue of Kuwana domain on the trip to Edo. For Kaga domain's procession in 1827, 35 percent of the personnel were hired laborers. Unlike post station porters, who worked the distance between two post stations, these contract laborers worked the entire distance.[91]

For the various expenses incurred on the road, for transport services, lodging, river crossings, rest and lunch breaks, and miscellaneous purchases, cash was required. All domains had to carry cash boxes along the routes to and from Edo. The weight of these boxes, according to a humorous poem, could make its carriers' legs bowed. With Tokugawa Japan's multimetallic monetary system, a domain such as Kaga had to carry both silver and gold as it passed on its alternate attendance route from the Kansai-based silver region to the gold-based Kantō.[92]

Encounters on the Road

During the busiest months for alternate attendance, the fourth and sixth, daimyo processions sometimes encountered the processions of other domains, imperial envoys, or representatives of the Tokugawa shogunate while traveling on the road or at the post stations. Since these meetings could cause diplomatically awkward situations, not to mention delays, an effort was made to avoid them.[93] When that was not possible the proper protocol had to be followed even though it often put one lord in a subordinate position, and travel schedules had to be adjusted. Occasionally, conflict occurred between members of different processions or between members of a daimyo procession and commoners who refused to give way. Daimyo usually gave precedence to imperial envoys. For example, when forced unexpectedly to lodge at the same post station, the Tosa daimyo in 1799 occupied the auxiliary official inn while the envoys occupied the regular official inn.[94] Two daimyo overlapping by chance at the same post station could be accommodated, each in his own official inn, if the post station was large enough to have two of them. In such cases, though, not all the men in the two processions could be lodged at the station, and neighboring villages would be called upon to provide service. In general principle, however, those daimyo of lesser status were required to defer to their social superiors, even if it meant finding lodging in another post station.

Small changes in schedule due to weather or the lord's illness could result in the disruption of service along a stretch of highway. As a result, for example, an official inn might not be able to accommodate a request for a procession to take a lunch break there.[95] Or, as occurred on the return trip in 1808, the procession of the Hachinohe lord was required to take an unscheduled rest break at a post station outside of Edo because all the post horses were being used to transport the baggage of Sendai, a much larger domain.[96]

Many daimyo tried to avoid meeting another on the high road, especially when they received information that the other lord was of higher rank. However, when a meeting was unavoidable there was certain protocol to follow. If one of the lords was from the Tokugawa's Three Related Houses (*gosanke*), then the other lord had his palanquin stopped, got out, and gave a greeting. The higher-ranking daimyo remained in his palanquin but opened his door and gave a light greeting.[97] For daimyo other than the *gosanke*, the daimyo of lower status would dispatch a messenger to the other lord. The greetings were not always simply a relayed verbal message; they could also include a gift. Daimyo of equal status would each send messengers. If they shared the same audience hall in Edo, both might greet the other personally from inside their palanquins with the door open. Retainers accompanying the lords' palanquins would be expected of course to remove headgear and prostrate themselves. The processions would each keep to one side of the road in passing by the other. Such simple etiquette was paid when the retinues of Okayama and Kaga encountered each other on the road in 1848.[98] Foreigners attached to the Dutch mission, which performed a kind of alternate attendance, report that when they encountered high-ranking daimyo, the Dutchmen's procession would move out of the way, but ordinary daimyo would open up the road and allow them to pass.[99]

The samurai's sense of relative social standing and social deference was well-developed, which meant that daimyo processions generally dealt with encounters, both chance and unexpected, without problem.[100] However, confrontations did occur occasionally when one party perceived a slight to their lord's prestige. For example, an incident occurred in 1810 when the processions of Lord Hachisuka of Tokushima (257,000 *koku*) and that of Nagai Yamato no kami, who was returning to Edo after a tour of guard duty at Nijō castle in Kyoto, met at Ōiso post station on the Tōkaidō.[101] A number of Nagai's officials instructed the men accompanying the Tokushima lord to remove their sedge hats, which they refused to do. Nagai's men then proceeded to block off the road, preventing the other procession from moving forward, and his officials repeated their earlier order to remove hats. Their commands were no more effective the second time, and so some of the members of Nagai's procession began a physical altercation with the men from Tokushima. Further details on how the impasse was resolved are not available. The case did, however, come before the Tokugawa government, which decided that Nagai's officials had been guilty of an offense, described variously as *burei* (disrespectful [act]), *furachi* (insolence), *fuhō* (illegal [act]), and *gasatsu* (violent [act]). The shogunate ordered a sentence of light banishment for Nagai, which meant he had to shut himself up in a kind of domiciliary confinement for a time. According to the shogunate's resolution, some deference should have been paid to Nagai, most likely in the form of a messenger sent by Lord Hachisuka, since Nagai's force was traveling from a post where he had to perform a specific duty for the Tokugawa (guard service at Osaka castle), but Nagai's officials had no right to demand that Hachisuka's men remove their hats and prostrate themselves. Moreover, Nagai's men's actions in blocking the road was illegal.

An infamous incident involving the issue of right of way occurred in 1862 on the Tōkaidō between Kanagawa and Kawasaki, a beautiful stretch of highway many foreigners referred to as "the Avenue" and which afforded a pleasant view of Mt. Fuji through the pine trees lining the road. Known as the Namamugi Incident, it involved four British and a retinue of Satsuma warriors accompanying Shimazu Hisamitsu, the daimyo's father. There are conflicting accounts of the events leading up to the murder of C. L. Richardson, a Shanghai merchant, and the wounding of Woodthorpe C. Clarke and William Marshall, Yokohama merchants. Marshall was accompanied by Mrs. Borrodaile, his cousin, the only person to escape from the incident relatively unharmed. According to Sir Ernest Satow, a British diplomat in Japan at the time, the train of Satsuma retainers ordered them, all on horseback, to stand aside. The four,

> passed on at the edge of the road, until they came in sight of a palanquin, occupied by Shimadzu [sic] Saburō, father of the Prince of Satsuma. They were now ordered to turn back, and as they were wheeling their horses in obedience, were suddenly set upon by several armed men belonging to the train, who hacked at them with their sharp-edged heavy swords.[102]

This basic account is repeated in Francis Hall's journal for September 14, 1862.[103] A Dutch diplomat, however, reported a different story. He wrote,

> Marshall later told me it was entirely Richardson's fault. They could have let the procession pass, but Richardson paid no attention to Marshall, who called "For God's sake, let's not have a row! Turn back!" Richardson, a great braggart, cut right through the escort and was cut down immediately."[104]

Given that Marshall recognized and called out the identity of the procession, Richardson, who was at the head of the party, would have certainly been foolish not to pull to the side or to turn back. However, there were also certain circumstances that converged at that particular location which exacerbated this volatile confrontation between the fierce Satsuma warriors and the hated representatives of the imperialist powers.

Richardson and the others, who only moments earlier had passed by a different group of samurai without violence, were not as lucky with the Satsuma retinue.[105] They managed to pass safely by the first few groups at the head of the procession, after which there was a break, but then approached a curve in the road, where they encountered the main part of the procession. The road was quite narrow at this point, with no space to pull to the side without being forced up onto the embankment. According to Japanese accounts, Richardson's horse, feeling pressed in by the main part of the procession, became excited, reared up, and headed into the middle of the highway.[106] Some samurai in the musket group ordered them to pull to the side or to get down. Mrs. Borrodaile's horse also became excited. At this point a samurai guard for Shimazu's palanquin came running up and ordered them to turn back. Apparently Richardson began to reverse direction when he was cut from behind in the back. Marshall hollered to Mrs. Borrodaile to escape alone, as there was nothing they could do to help her. Marshall and Clark were both wounded, though Marshall not as badly. Richardson was surrounded and received multiple cuts, but somehow managed to ride away a distance before he fell. A number of samurai then set their blades upon him, with devastating results: "His head was nearly severed from the trunk, one shoulder was cleft in twain, there was a spear wound over the heart, one hand was severed, the other partially so, while the bowels protruded from a deep gash in the side and back."[107] Finally, his throat was slit and his corpse wrapped up in a straw mat and placed behind one of the roadside pine trees. The result of the incident, as is well known, became a major diplomatic crisis for the Tokugawa. While there is no evidence that bloodshed ever resulted during an encounter between the processions of two lords on the road, this evidence does suggest the great importance daimyo and their representatives attached to honor and decorum, even while traveling.

2

The Road to Edo (and Back)

THE REQUIREMENTS OF alternate attendance continued largely unchanged for more than two centuries, leading us to believe that the daimyo's performance of them did likewise. In this chapter it will be argued that this notion is patently false. Like so much involving Tokugawa Japan, the long life of many of its institutions belies significant change in practice — changes that are evident only when one reads broadly and across the long expanse of the historical record. The seeming uniformity in practice also masks the fact that this institution, while in theory imposed uniformly on all the daimyo, could impact them and their domains quite differently. Reading across time reveals that the routes taken by individual daimyo to and from Edo could vary for a number of reasons, and that while the daimyo were required in principle to maintain a regular schedule of alternating residences, the reality could be quite different. As a result of these and other factors, no two cycles of alternate attendance were ever the same. To reveal some of the variation in practice, here we will examine the experience of one of the largest domains, Tosa, located in southern Shikoku. Since the performance of alternate attendance by Tosa involved travel by sea as well as overland, its experience is representative of many domains from Shikoku, Kyushu, and parts of western Honshu. Moreover, after its arrival in Osaka, Tosa's procession traveled on the same routes taken by most daimyo from all points west of that city.

THE ROAD TO EDO was long and hard. Depending on the route taken, the trip for Tosa's retinue could require one month each way.[1] As a result, daimyo living at some distance from Edo, like the Yamauchi lord, actually spent more time outside their domain than in it. This reinforces the legalistic notion of the period of residence in the domain as a leave of absence. The trip was also physically taxing. The discomfort involved in such a long journey is intimated in Kobayashi Issa's poem: "Even the lord / Soaked to the bone / I sit by the hearth" (*Daimyō mo nurete tōru o kotatsu ka na*). One can easily imagine Issa sitting in front of a charcoal brazier at a roadside teahouse sipping a warm beverage while observing a daimyo procession passing by, its members drenched by the rain. In some years unseasonable weather certainly must have made the trip seem even longer. In 1791, Tosa retainer Gotō Einosuke, observing the rice fields still not planted in the fifth month, felt the cold northern winds, even with two layers of overcoat on, and took ill during the procession's two-day stay in Osaka.[2] Those taken seriously ill were allowed to ride in palanquins at the tail end of the procession, but others had to manage the discomfort, like Einosuke, who also complained of recurring foot pain. Mori Hirosada, also of Tosa, injured his foot prior to departure but managed with a makeshift cane all the way up the Tōkaidō.[3]

The difficulties experienced on the journey, however, must have been mitigated to some extent by the opportunity to observe conditions outside of, and to speak with people not native to, the home domain — features of the cultural experience of alternate attendance that will be explored in more detail in chapter seven. For example, Tosa retainer Gotō Seikō asked about local planting conditions in Kakegawa, observed groups of retainers from many different domains going up and down the road, and in Odawara noted that the bells in the castle were rung in the same fashion as in Kōchi. There was some pleasure in observing nature, too, at least when it was hospitable. Seikō, for example, noted that skylarks, which had built nests in the fields of winter wheat, took off in flight singing with the movement of the procession passing by. In Hakone he had a good view of Mt. Fuji, the top half still covered in snow.[4]

Nor was the trip easy for the daimyo. The lord was the symbolic axis of the domain, and in the procession he occupied the physical center as well. Given this twofold centrality, his well-being was of utmost concern to the retainers around him. From procession scrolls and popular depictions of alternate attendance we think of daimyo as riding to and from their domains in palanquins. In many cases this was the primary mode of their transport, but sitting in such a contained space, even one luxurious compared with palanquins used by commoners, was uncomfortable.[5] To help ease the boredom and discomfort, daimyo were supplied with a number of items in their palanquin, such as a pipe, tobacco pouch and tobacco bowl, travel guide, stationery, medicine box (for motion sickness and other minor maladies), a blanket for the lap, lantern, flower vase, a lacquered snack box, which might include a favorite food item, such as the pickled plums of the Nanbu lord mentioned earlier.[6] When even these material objects were not sufficient, some daimyo chose to use other means of transport as well. According to a vassal assigned to stay by the side of Edo-born Yamauchi Toyotsune (lived 1711–1725/9/2), who was making his first and last trip to Kōchi as daimyo in 1725, the lord usually walked or rode a horse, only very rarely electing to ride in a palanquin.[7] The same was apparently true of the last Tosa lord, Yamauchi Yōdō, who was said to have ridden his white horse on his first trip from Edo to the domain.[8]

The palanquin was a place to which the lord could retreat when it rained, yet not all lords were anxious to use one even in inclement weather. Toyotsune, perhaps because of his youth, felt great empathy for his men when the retinue was met by a sudden downpour as it approached Mt. Suzuka en route to its scheduled stop for the night at Kusatsu on the Tōkaidō. Raingear had been sent ahead to the post station, so all the protection the retinue had were their helmets; those worn by upper samurai just covered the head, thereby offering less protection that the wide-rimmed helmets lower samurai donned. The lord, seeing that his people were getting drenched, suggested that the retinue stop for the night at a station before Kusatsu. However, since the gear for preparing and cooking the lord's food and the baggage of the low-ranking retainers had already been sent forward to Kusatsu, where preparations for their arrival had been made, the procession went forward. The rain refused to let up, and about five miles down the road, the lord again suggested that they stop for the night, particularly since it was beginning to get dark. Yet again the lord's suggestion was deflected. Showing the marks of good stewardship, however, Toyotsune ordered his palanquin bearers to stop, got out, and mounted a horse. Wearing a woolen jacket and small helmet just like the men around him, he likewise became thoroughly drenched.[9]

While the lord might have sympathized with the difficulties experienced by his men, there were limits to how he might demonstrate those feeling, for social propriety dictated that no man could ride while the lord walked. The future Lord Toyoteru (r. 1843–1848), making the trip to Kōchi in 1837 while still heir as part of his apprenticeship in governance, saw how distressed his retainers were becoming due to the strong winds and heavy rain the procession encountered on the Tōkaidō at Hakone, and he decided to walk as well. After a short distance, one of the attending samurai, seeing that the lord's clothing was getting wet and muddy, suggested that Toyoteru get back into the palanquin, but Toyoteru continued walking. The attendant asked him more forcefully to stop walking when they encountered horse dung in the road, but Toyoteru did not relent. Changing tack, Toyoteru's attendant told him that his men were grateful for his actions, but that because Toyoteru was walking everyone riding in a palanquin, including a number of elderly persons, had to get out and walk. A number of the elderly people were having great difficulty walking, he pleaded, and only then did Toyoteru yield and return to his vehicle.

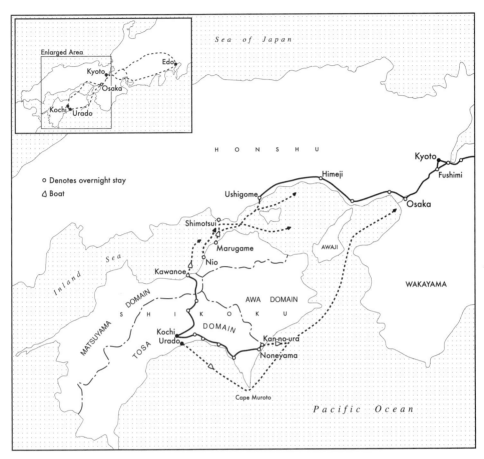

FIGURE 2.1. Main routes used by Tosa domain on alternate attendance. Courtesy of
Cartographic Services Laboratory, University of Maryland, Baltimore County.

How much a lord might walk or ride in a palanquin (see Figure 2.1) depended
to a large extent upon the route selected by Tosa domain officials, and, as noted,
the reasons for that selection varied: weather conditions, the personal predilec-
tions of the lords, and the relative cost and safety of sea versus land travel. There
were substantial differences between travel in early modern and in modern
times. It might seem counterintuitive to us today that the daimyo, from the late
seventeenth century on, came to rely increasingly on overland rather than sea
transport even though travel on land could take longer.[10] Also perhaps coun-
terintuitively, by some accounts going overland was also less expensive.[11] While
comparative statistics are not available, the sea route, as noted, indeed may have
been far more expensive than the overland option, particularly when there were
delays due to poor weather.

FIGURE 2.2. The Tosa lord on alternate attendance. "Tosa han gyōretsu ezu."
Courtesy of Kōchi kenritsu rekishi minzoku shiryōkan.

One scholar posits that the use of boat transport decreased after the mid-Tokugawa period because of uncertainty and delays caused by unpredictable winds and tide, consequent problems securing adequate food and water, and the improvement of post station and road facilities in Kyushu and western Honshu.[12] Evidence from Tosa, to be discussed below, will clarify some of these points, but it is worth considering here the proposition that the expense and manpower necessary to maintain a large fleet of vessels became increasingly difficult to cover as domain budgets came under more pressure from Genroku times onward.[13]

What is certain, however, is that by the late eighteenth century the shogunate was concerned enough to enjoin the daimyo, in 1791, to use sea transport more often: "Many daimyo who formerly employed boats are now opting for overland routes.... Daimyo should use sea routes more often when traveling to perform alternate attendance, as facilities for sea travel are well developed."[14]

Encouraging the daimyo to use sea transport, however, was not an exhortation to all daimyo to come to Edo in boats. For strategic reasons, the daimyo were permitted to travel by boat only as far as Osaka, which meant that only the western daimyo were affected. For the remainder of the journey an overland route was required. This was apparently one of the unwritten laws of the shogunate, like the requirements that traffic move on the left side of the road or the prohibition of carts on the Gokaidō network. The restrictions on sea travel also applied to foreigners, for even the Korean embassies only traveled as far as Osaka by boat.[15]

The Kan-no-ura Route

The decision to follow an overland course to the east coast of Shikoku, the Kan-no-ura route, from which the retinue traveled by boat to Osaka — rather than a direct boat trip from Urado (Kōchi's port) to Osaka — was made during the rule of the third Tosa lord, Tadatoyo (see Figure 2.2). Unlike his two predecessors, Tadatoyo made frequent use of this overland route from the time of his first trip to Edo in 1640 on alternate attendance as heir.[16] This was done apparently because of the difficulty of sailing around Cape Muroto at the southeast tip of Shikoku. Even today it is a stormy area, known as the "Typhoon Ginza." By the time of his successor, Toyomasa (r. 1669–1700), who according to a contemporary record did not care much for sea travel, the Kan-no-ura route had become the standard choice, though it would not remain so for long.[17]

The reason for the virtual abandonment of the direct sea route is dramatized by the experience of Miyaji Umanosuke, a Confucian scholar. The son of Miyaji Nakae, who himself made three journeys to Edo in the same capacity, Umanosuke was a member of the advance party and departed from Urado on 1832/2/25, two weeks before Lord Toyosuke (1795–1872). Due to numerous delays getting around Cape Muroto, however, he arrived in Osaka two days after the lord. The bulk of the forces heading to Edo traveled with the lord and had made their way on foot to Kan-no-ura; the advance or lead party and the trailing party of the entourage might still take the sea route from Urado, as was the case with Miyaji Umanosuke. Miyaji's boat tried a number of times to round the craggy cape at Muroto. After failing the first time, the sailors dropped the vessel's sails and tried rowing around it, but the headwinds were too strong. For some reason they changed the rudder, hoisted the sails, and tried again, but they were no more successful. In fact, the powerful headwinds nearly threw the boat on the shoals. Seeing that they were making no progress, a decision was made to call for six or seven corvee boats, which were apparently waiting nearby. Finally, after being pulled around the cape, Miyaji was elated and relieved that "the danger he found difficult to express" was over.[18]

Miyaji's experience of delays was not unusual, even for boats departing from Kan-no-ura. If the weather there was poor, a wait of one or two weeks was not uncommon. The most unusual case of delay, however, involved the eighth lord, Toyonobu (1712–1767), who arrived in Kan-no-ura on 1758/3/4. There, strong winds, rain, and rough seas made it impossible to set sail. A pilgrimage was made to a nearby shrine in hopes that supplications to the deities might have a calming effect on the weather, but there was no change. Still in Kan-no-ura on 3/19, Toyonobu's eye malady worsened, so on 4/1 he departed not for Edo, but back to Kōchi again. The majority of those with him returned by boat, the rest going on foot. Toyonobu recuperated at home and was well enough by 9/25 to try again from Kan-no-ura. Not having much luck this time as well, the lord's party was forced to wait three days for good weather before setting sail, only to be pushed back again to Kan-no-ura. It would take almost a month before Toyonobu would see Osaka, a trip that normally required two or three days of good sailing.

Yet because the seas around Tosa were not always hospitable, even if the bulk of the retinue traveled overland to Kan-no-ura, rough waters often meant that people were kept waiting there for ships from Kōchi that were to take them to Osaka. Such was the case in 1688, when the retinue was forced to wait almost two weeks at Kan-no-ura for the seas to calm.[19] The Kan-no-ura route may also have been less desirable because of the large number of sailors required to man the ships. The trip in 1682 required as many as 1,357 sailors and forty-six boats.[20]

The Kan-no-ura route spared the bulk of the retinue from the uncertainties of sea travel around Cape Muroto. It followed along the coastline east of Kōchi as far as Nahari, and generally involved four overnight stays at Akaoka, Aki, Tano, and None, where local domain and religious officials waited to greet the lord.[21] From Nahari the procession followed the Noneyama road for forty-four kilometers through the mountains to None.[22] From there, it was barely a day's walk to Kan-no-ura, the northernmost point along the eastern coast in his domain, near the border with Awa domain, and the port from which boats would depart for Osaka.

Taking the overland route to Kan-no-ura also reduced the distance at sea to Osaka from 100 to 70 *ri* (from 244 to 171 miles). From Kan-no-ura, if the weather was good, the ships could pull up sails in Osaka Bay in two to three days. Together with the overland trip to Kan-no-ura, the overall trip from Kōchi to Osaka could be accomplished in roughly a week.

The Northern (Kitayama) Route

The high probability of delay in arriving in Edo (the *tozama* lords were to report to Edo in the fourth month), and the costs associated with it, were significant factors in the decision to make a second major change in the travel route taken to Osaka. The sixth Tosa lord, Toyotaka, made the decision in 1718 to use a northern route, or Kitayama dōri (known as the Tosa kaidō in other parts of Shikoku), across the mountains that border Tosa and Iyo. This required about the same number of overnight stays, five, as the Kan-no-ura route, and the Kitayama route brought the procession to the much safer Inland Sea. By the mid-eighteenth century this became the preferred route for the remainder of the Edo period, which meant almost a complete abandonment of the use of boats, except for those used to cross the more protected, calm stretch of water across the Inland Sea.

The northern route was opened expressly for use by the domain on alternate attendance. Later, in 1763, when commoners were allowed access, it developed an important role in commerce between Tosa and central-northern Shikoku, particularly in Tosa's trade in *goishi-cha*, a type of fermented tea, and paper mulberry. Hundreds of trees were planted along the road to provide shade on a stretch of the Kitayama-dō leading north from the edge of the castle town.[23] Here, as in many domains across Japan, the requirements of alternate attendance encouraged economic development in the form of new and improved roads and ports.

Long delays — e.g., in 1756, one month — due to using the sea route from Kan-no-ura to Osaka only reinforced the tendency to travel overland. The risk of accidents on the seas, which were costly in both human and economic terms, also must have been compelling evidence in the decision to switch to the Kitayama route. In 1715, for example, at least ten people were lost at sea in a storm off the coast of eastern Shikoku.[24]

Transporting the daimyo and his entourage had real economic costs for the commoners who were required to bear that burden. While the rising demand for corvee labor and post horses, and the hardships it posed on farming communities, has been well documented for some of the major thoroughfares in the Tokugawa's official road network, the Gokaidō,[25] sources are scarce for Tosa domain. Still, the heavy nature of corvee obligations in Tosa "provoked frequent resistance . . . [and] was blamed for the poor care of crops by peasants, unsuccessful commerce by shippers and bad catches by fishermen."[26]

The journey itself began of course at the castle town. Due to the fortuitous availability of documentation we can reconstruct the choreography of this ritual of departure on the northern route.

On the day of departure the central ranks of the retainer corps lined the main street leading east from the central gate of the castle. Heading east for about a kilometer, the procession passed through the townsman area of Hasuike machi. As will be explained in chapter three, this was done largely to display the lord's power and authority before his subjects. Turning left at Shinbori, the procession headed north toward Yamada machi, the location of one of the three guard posts or checkpoints into the castle town. There, at the Yamada Bridge, other middle-ranking samurai, higher-level officials (*chūrō*, or junior advisors, who were ranked below the senior advisors), and doctors in the domain's employ greeted the lord. This was the starting point for the Kitayama road, which would take the procession north, into Iyo province, roughly following the course of present-day National Route 32. One last group of officials, including a senior advisor, accompanied the lord as far as the edge of town, at Hijima. Continuing north about another kilometer, the procession passed by Kakegawa shrine. Serving a function similar to Enryakuji temple in Kyoto, the shrine was erected to the northeast (in Chinese geomancy the direction from which evil is directed) of the castle town. It was built in remembrance of the clan's origins in Kakegawa (Tōtōmi), the domain of sixty thousand *koku* that the Yamauchi controlled before Tokugawa Ieyasu bequeathed the much larger Tosa domain to Kazutoyo, the first Yamauchi lord, for his contributions to the Tokugawa victory at Sekigahara in 1600. There, the deity that Ieyasu had become, Gongen-sama Tōshōgū, was enshrined. On his way to Edo, the Yamauchi lord would acknowledge this historic debt by stopping at Kakegawa shrine, getting out of his palanquin, performing ablutions at the water basin engraved with the Tokugawa hollycock symbol, and worshiping the deity of Ieyasu.

After the first night's lodging, usually at Motoyama, the Kitayama road quickly became strenuous. Having hiked over a portion of what remains of the overland route, near Tachikawa, the last overnight stop in Tosa province, I am convinced that the decision to use that route had more to do with the difficulties of sea travel rather than a strong desire to hike over the steep, narrow paths (one to two meters) that the retinues took in crossing mountains that make up the backbone of Shikoku.[27] It was because of the difficulty of the route north that Lord Toyochika noted that he reduced the number of people in the procession.[28] There were several particularly demanding stretches traveling north before Umatate: Kunimi tōge ("View the Province Pass," 1,020 meters), near the border between Tosa and Iyo domain (Ehime), the last place traveling north from which the lord and his retinue could see Tosa Bay and home; Sasagamine, the highest point

(1,027 meters) on the Kitayama route and the spot where local officials would meet the procession on the return leg of the journey to Edo; "Waterless Pass" (*mizu nashi tōge*, 904 meters); "Remove Your Hat" Pass (*kasa tori tōge*, 904 meters); and "Stomach Knife" (*hara bōchō*). The road at Stomach Knife was so steep apparently that when samurai descended the pass they had to push the handles of their long swords down, away from the stomach, to prevent the tip of the sword from hitting the ground.[29] Near Umatate there was a river crossing where temporary floating bridges erected by stringing boats together and laying boards across them were built for the Tosa procession's use. At Kawanoe (Iyo province), a port in Tokugawa territory under the administration of Matsuyama domain, the lord said prayers at the local Hachimangū shrine for good weather to cross the Inland Sea, though the procession continued overland to the east along the northern coast of Shikoku for another day to one of several ports, Nio or Marugame (both Sanuki province), from which a shorter crossing to Honshu could actually be made.

The boats needed to transport the procession across the Inland Sea still had to be dispatched from the domain. If the seas were friendly and the overland party remained on schedule, then the ships from Kōchi would be ready in Marugame or some other designated port in northern Shikoku for the procession when it arrived. It was the job of the magistrate of boats to do all he could to see that this happened. In the 1840s this job befell Tosa samurai Yoshida Tōyō, who supervised the fleet of 134 domain boats. In 1847 Tōyō accompanied the fleet to Marugame, arriving there on 2/23, well ahead of the departure on 3/5 of the lord and his entourage, who traveled overland from Kōchi. After arriving in Marugame on 3/11 the lord boarded the waiting boats, accompanied by Tōyō, and crossed the Inland Sea to Bizen Ushimado. The job completed and with ships on time, Tōyō could then return to Kōchi, relieved and content with the monetary gift that he received from the lord.[30]

Coordinating the timing between the main procession traveling overland and the boats dispatched from the domain to meet it in northern Shikoku did not always go smoothly, however. Unexpected delays in schedule, particularly on the relatively backward Kitayama road, could complicate the trip and cause problems. For example, in 1802, just three days out of Kōchi on foot, the young heir Toyooki, who was not yet nine years old, fell ill.[31] Due to the illness, which was exacerbated by motion sickness caused by riding in a palanquin, Toyooki threw up repeatedly and asked to return to the castle. Mori Yoshiki, Hirosada's son, who served as the heir's protector and companion during the trip, comforted the heir and got him to rest. So that Toyooki might sleep more comfortably, Yoshiki removed the "implements," perhaps toys or other objects placed there to distract him or to help relieve the tedium of travel in a closed palanquin. While the heir slept, his top retainers debated whether to turn back toward the castle and stop at Motoyama. Supplies of rice at nearby Kawaguchi station, where the retinue was not scheduled to spend the night, were insufficient, and at the next station heading north, Tachikawa, there was only enough food for one night's stay. Finally, it was decided to take whatever food was available at Kawaguchi and continue on toward Tachikawa, on the border of Iyo Province, hoping that the heir's illness would be short-lived. Due to the delay, however, the procession was forced to walk through the night with torches, pulling into Tachikawa at dawn.

Debates about whether or how best to proceed erupted repeatedly. As the young heir's illness worsened, his aides tried to nurse him back to health with potatoes. Toyooki, however, was unable to keep any food down or to sleep in his palanquin. Mori Yoshiki picked him up and carried him for a while until he fell asleep in his arms, then placed him back in the palanquin. Fortunately his condition improved enough so that he was feeling able to make the boat crossing from Marugame, and the Inland Sea was calm. Later, while traveling on the Chūgoku road, the retinue met with a severe rainstorm and the lord's doctor argued they should stop for the day at the next post station rather than go on to their scheduled stop, which was some distance beyond. It is interesting that in his note to the senior advisor, the highest ranking official under the heir in the procession, the doctor cited his concern for the men in the retinue who would become drenched in the downpour, rather than for the health of the heir. Yoshiki did not agree with the doctor's recommendation, which would have caused a day's delay in the schedule, and dispatched his own memo to the senior advisor. In it he argued there was no guarantee the storm would cease before the next day, so that it was best to continue a while longer until they arrived at their scheduled stopping place. Secondly, he asserted, there was no evidence that anyone was sick yet. And lastly, he argued most strongly, the doctor's responsibility lay only with the young heir and not the men in the retinue, so he should refrain from overstepping the limits of his authority; whether or not the retinue should stop was solely the senior advisor's responsibility, not the doctor's. Despite Yoshiki's protestations, however, the official decided in the doctor's favor. The stress of this trip must have been great for Yoshiki, for this year, unlike in previous trips, he was able to sleep while riding in a palanquin while off duty.[32]

The route across the Inland Sea was not apparently fixed. Sometimes, as was the case with Mori Yoshiki and the young heir Toyooki in 1802, the crossing was made from Nio, but Marugame seems to have been the most frequently selected. After landing on Honshu island, the procession marched up the Chūgokuji to Osaka. In the eighteenth century, the Kitayama-Chūgokuji course gradually became the preferred one, and after the end of that century only rarely did the Yamauchi daimyo travel by sea from Kan-no-ura.

Despite the frequency with which the Chūgokuji was used, because it deviated from the earlier routes taken, Tosa still had to obtain shogunal permission. To have done otherwise could have incurred the displeasure of the Tokugawa, as happened to Shōnai domain in 1811.[33] In their letters of request, the lords usually cited the same basic reasons for wanting to use the mainly overland route: (1) the lord's sickness (the term *shakki* was often used to describe his "illness" —more on the issue of illness, real and feigned, below), which implied that it was less taxing than other routes; (2) the roughness of the southern (*Nankai*) seas, which made sea travel dangerous and caused delays; (3) the lord's unfamiliarity with sea travel; and (4) precedents for taking the Chūgokuji. The requests normally covered the return trip as well. In 1781 a draft of the lord's letter of request was shown to the senior councilors informally, and after they assured Tosa officials that there was "no cause for fear," they submitted it formally.[34]

As the discussion above makes clear, the route to Osaka varied for a number of reasons, but not everyone in the procession traveled together nor did they all travel the same route. The retinue was often divided into two or three groups (see Table 2.1), and for logistical and sometimes economic reasons it was not uncommon for each to take a different route. The forward group often left before the main group, which accompanied the lord. Since much of the baggage was transported in the vanguard, it usually went by boat. Some of the baggage was necessary for the overland trip from Osaka to Edo, hence it was important that it arrive in Osaka in time for the main group. In 1680 the forward group consisted of 320 people (23 percent of the total); the bulk of the procession, 1,413 people (77 percent), accompanied the lord. When the procession was particularly large, as in 1688 (2,531 people), as much as 40 percent of the total traveled in the forward and following groups to mitigate transport problems.

Some of the dynamics of a trip, scheduling in particular, are evident from an examination of the entourage of which Mori Hirosada was a part in 1732. Traveling overland to Kan-no-ura with the main group, Hirosada departed on 3/3 (see Table 2.2).[35] The forward group, traveling by boat to the same preliminary destination, boarded boats on the same day (usually it was customary for it to leave at least a day earlier). The boats were able to make it downriver from Kōchi to the port Urado, but poor weather impeded their further progress until 3/17. Just before departure, Mori Hirosada sent off a letter to his family, informing them of his situation. At every extended stop he similarly dashed off letters for home, a total of four times while still in Tosa domain. Hirosada also had time to engage in a favorite activity not normally associated with samurai—sumo wrestling. Unfortunately, he injured his foot in one of the matches and later required assistance walking. Nonetheless, he bragged, "With a cane I am walking the fifty-three stages [of the Tōkaidō] and feel strong enough that I could walk all the way to China."

TABLE 2.1. Tosa Domain Processions*

Year	Forward Group	Main Group	Following Group	Total
1645 (Shōhō 2)	—	—	—	1477
1676 (Enpō 4)	278	1249	—	1527
1680 (Enpō 8)	320	1413	—	1799
1682 (Tenna 2)	291	1375	—	1666
1684 (Jōkyō 1)	436	1269	320	2025
1688 (Genroku 1)	471	1474	586	2531
1690 (Genroku 3)	430	1592	753	2775
1697 (Genroku 10)	—	—	—	2813
1698 (Genroku 11)	644	1525	446	2615
1718 (Kyōhō 3)	—	—	—	1799

*Based on information from Hirao n.d.; ms. YKS, vols. 18, 43, 58, 65, 78, 86, 89. In 1688, the forward group left on 3/1, the main group on 3/10, and the following group on 3/27.

In contrast to the advance party, the main group made great speed overland, arriving in Kan-no-ura on the fourth day, one day faster than normal. In fact, the procession traveled thirty-five kilometers in one day, about ten more than usual. Perhaps its speed was related to the economizing measures in effect due to a blight that hit all of western Japan that year; a quicker journey meant that fewer nights' lodging were necessary.[36] The accompanying group had been waiting at Kan-no-ura for almost ten days by the time the "advance" party arrived on 3/25. Delayed at Kan-no-ura, the lord occupied himself with hunting, snagging a wild boar, and making an excursion to the seashore at Shirahama. The main group could not go on to Osaka independently of the preliminary group, as the boats necessary for the trip, including the lord's boat (see Figure 2.3) sailed in the latter group.[37] Both groups departed together from Kan-no-ura on 3/26 and pulled into Osaka three days later, Hirosada's boat leading the way into Osaka Bay.

From Osaka to Edo

The journey the rest of the way to Edo was often routine, but it still involved considerable difficulties. It entailed a forced march of ten or eleven days, and there were potential trouble spots that any procession had to pass through, particularly the numerous rivers that had to be forded. Moreover, as the road between Osaka and Edo was the most heavily traveled in the realm, a proces-

TABLE 2.2. Mori Hirosada's Trip to Edo, 1732*

Date	Travel Note
3/3	Board boat in Kōchi; anchor for night at Urada port (Kōchi)
3/4–3/6	Delay at Urado due to inadequate winds, bad current, hard rain; send letter home
3/7	Depart Urado; anchor for night at Tsuro† (Tosa domain); send letter home
3/17	Delayed in Tsuro due to poor weather (rain); send letter
3/24	Home on 3/21; sightsee at local temples; visit friend
3/25	Arrive in Kan-no-ura; send letter home
3/26	Depart Kan-no-ura; anchor for night at Ōsaki (Kii)
3/27	Anchor for night at Tanigawa (Izumi)
3/28	Overnight in Sakai
3/29	Arrive in Osaka; lodge at Tosa's compound at Nagabori
4/1	Depart from Osaka with full procession; overnight in Fushimi; free time in Fushimi on 4/2; depart on 4/3
4/4	Cross Yokota River (dry) via temporary earthen bridge
4/7	Free time in Yoshida
4/8–4/10	Delayed at Arai due to winds blowing in wrong direction (for boat crossing to Maisaka). Dispatch subordinate via Honzakadō to check on water levels at Tenryū River, further north on the Tōkaidō‡
4/10	Cross Tenryū River; Hirosada receives report of water level rising at Ōi River (procession accelerates pace)
4/11	Most people in Tosa's procession cross Ōi, but horses must wait until 4/12 (due to high water, people given priority)
4/13–4/15	Cross Okitsu, Fuji, and Banyū Rivers
4/16	Arrive in Edo, thirty-four days late

* Mori Hirosada 1732, fols. 1–13.

† The port of Tsuro was developed by the famous domain senior advisor Nonaka Kenzan as a place of refuge for the domain's boats on alternate attendance because of the great difficulties of the eastern route around Cape Muroto.

‡ To avoid similar delays at Arai or Maisaka, which were quite common, travelers sometimes used the longer Honzakadō around Lake Hamana. Vaporis 1994a, 188–190.

FIGURE 2.3. The Yamauchi lord's boat. Courtesy of Kōchi kenritsu rekishi minzoku shiryōkan.

sion could have its schedule thrown into disarray by chance encounters with another.

In Osaka, the various parts of the procession assembled for the trip up the Tōkaidō to Edo, and communications were made with officials in several cities regarding its progress as well as the health of the lord. As noted above, the advance party usually came from Kōchi or Kan-no-ura by boat and met with the main group at the domain's residence in Osaka at Nagabori, where members of the retinue could rest for two or three days for the upcoming trip. Officials dispatched messengers to Edo to report the lord's arrival there to the shogunate's senior councilors as well as to Kōchi. Greetings were also dispatched to the keeper of Osaka castle, another shogunal official.

While in Osaka the lord or heir pursued numerous leisure and religious activities. He made a pilgrimage to the Inari shrine in the Tosa compound, rested, and received visitors, including merchants with whom the domain had relations of one sort or another. Occasionally he also viewed Noh theater, dance, and acrobatics at the compound, most often performed by artists from Kyoto. For example, in 1802 the young heir Toyooki visited the merchant Kōnoike Zen'eimon, with whom the domain had close commercial connections and at whose residence the boy looked over the merchant financier's collection of Chinese books. He was also shown a variety of art objects and some items from overseas, including a "Dutch-style" toy. Kōnoike further entertained the heir with a performance of Noh and Kyōgen.[38]

From Osaka, the lord's entourage might take riverboats up the Yodo River to Fushimi or go directly to Kyoto and connect to the Tōkaidō (125 *ri* (305 miles) to Edo). It was not uncommon for the lord to visit Kyoto, often on a day trip from Fushimi, for sightseeing at Kiyomizu, Chion-in, the Gion area and, while it was still standing, the Great Buddha statue. He might also pay courtesy visits to shogunal officials, such as the Kyoto deputy or the aristocratic Sanjō family, with whom the Yamauchi had familial ties, and dine at the Tosa residence at Kawaramachi.[39] Messengers bringing greetings (or returning greetings) from families of the court and religious aristocracy came as well to Tosa's residence. Apparently because of shogunal restrictions, only on rare occasions did the lord spend the night in Kyoto. For example, in 1679 Toyomasa stayed four nights on his way to Kōchi and received many messengers from court nobles and religious prelates.[40] Permission from the Tokugawa's senior councilors to stop in Kyoto was a necessity, although in at least one case, as will be detailed below, the daimyo went there without permission, in disguise.[41] Even when the lord did not stop in Kyoto, visitors came to see him in Fushimi, and a stream of gifts arrived from others not able to visit. Moreover, actors occasionally came from Kyoto to perform, though this occurred more often in Osaka.[42]

From Osaka or Fushimi there were several possibilities for the overland trip to Edo. The most frequent choice for Tosa, as for most daimyo from western Japan, was the Tōkaidō.[43] While it was the most developed in terms of travel facilities, this route had some large rivers that had to be forded and which were subject to seasonal flooding. Flooded or not, crossing large rivers like the Ōi was costly, as related in the *senryū*: Gold coins rain / Alternate attendance in spring / Shimada [post station].[44] On the return leg to the domain, some of these costs might be avoided by taking the Nakasendō, permission for which was required from the shogunate. Using the Nakasendō — twenty-seven kilometers longer, more mountainous, and less developed than the Tōkaidō — was attractive because there were no major rivers, there was less traffic, and transport costs were cheaper.

With the exception of the first day of travel, when departure from either Kōchi or Edo was around midday, the procession set out on the road generally by 6 or 7 a.m. While this might seem relatively late, preparations for departure actually had to begin three hours earlier. In some domains, signals regarding the various stages of preparation were given with wooden clappers, but for Tosa a series of circulars was sent around. Based on Mori Hirosada's account, at 3 a.m. the first notice, a wake-up call, was circulated, and after breakfast a second notice went around. An hour after the initial notice, at 4 a.m., by which time the lord had completed his bath, a third one was dispatched. Not all retainers had assembled even after the third call, however, so an urgent notice was sent around at 6 a.m. Shortly thereafter, a little more than three hours after the first notice circulated, the procession was ready for departure.[45]

Once on the Tōkaidō, a number of rivers had to be forded, and heavy rains sometimes caused river stoppages and financial hardship. In 1832, Miyaji Umanosuke's party was forced to wait at the Ōi River for four days until the water level dropped to an acceptable level. On that day, Miyaji reports, the riverbank was "like a battlefield." When river-crossing porters did not come to service them immediately, Miyaji, who was in charge of the baggage, was forced to pay a hefty tip, equal to fifty percent of the regular charge, since even lesser daimyo were doing so. Although it grated him to do so, he felt "it could damage the lord's prestige (*goikō ni mo kakari*) if the baggage was late." Protecting the lord's reputation clearly had a price, and the river-crossing porters took advantage of it.[46]

Given the potential problems faced by travelers at river crossings, responsibility for overseeing the procession's passage across them was one of the most important administrative assignments given to retainers on the trip.[47] Mori Hirosada, for example, was one of several Tosa officials in charge of river crossings on the Tōkaidō heading toward Edo in 1732. Mainly this involved investigating whether the water level was low enough and the water flow slow enough to allow for a safe crossing. From his diary we know he was also in charge of the financial ledger kept for river crossings. Hirosada was of such rank of course that he sent subordinates to investigate and report back to him, as happened while the procession was held up at Arai due to poor weather. The subordinates went ahead, probably by the Honzakadō around Lake Hamana, to investigate conditions at the next river, the Tenryū, after making the crossing. The Tenryū was rising, so Hirosada consulted with a local official in charge of the river crossing, who informed him that it would be closing soon that day. The information was then relayed up the chain of command to the lord.[48]

Timely information gathering and rapid decision making were necessary for smooth progress through trouble spots on the Tōkaidō, particularly river crossings such as at the Tenryū. On this occasion, the procession was able to cross the river in boats before the service was closed. Hirosada's vessel went before the lord's and landed at the spot designated for the lord's boat to check the conditions there. To avoid the same problem at the following crossing, Hirosada sent a subordinate ahead to investigate the condition of the infamous Ōi River. There he learned that water levels there were rising and that a river stoppage would begin in the early afternoon. As a result of this information, Tosa officials made the decision to push to make the crossing before it closed.[49] At the crossing, people were given priority over horses; the procession therefore had to hold up at the post station on the other side of the Ōi until the horses could be crossed the following day, if conditions allowed. Taking turns with another official, Hirosada rode ahead of the procession as it progressed to check on conditions at successive rivers while traveling up the Tōkaidō.

Even though the water level had not risen sufficiently to close down the Ōi, crossing it was still dangerous due to its strong currents. On the banks of the river, Hirosada inspected the platform upon which the lord's palanquin would sit, and he followed the lord and his bearers into the water on horseback. To ensure the lord's safe crossing, twenty men carried his platform while another twenty men stood upstream in a row with locked arms to help break the current for the lord's passage. Another twenty men were held in reserve, far more than usual, in case of an emergency. All told, the labor of at least sixty-one men was necessary to oversee the lord's crossing. This brings to mind the river crossing of the Moroccan sultan's caravan in the late nineteenth century. There, the sultan's horse was "surrounded by negroes on foot, while a line of expert swimmers were held in readiness, linked hand in hand, stretched from bank to bank."[50] In Tokugawa Japan, a retainer like Hirosada followed behind the platform, watching for any mishaps. Once the lord's bearers were safely back on land, he rushed ahead and inspected the area where the palanquin would be set down.

Hirosada worked hard during the trip to Edo but, as noted, when not on duty he had several options. On the trip from Osaka to Edo, Hirosada was off duty for at least parts of four days. He could rest or sleep in a palanquin or break from the procession and go forward on his own. In his diary he records the order: "You are free to go ahead [of the procession] as you see fit."[51] Of course he and his fellow retainers were required to rejoin the procession when back on duty, but this allowed for some sightseeing along the road, an activity that will be discussed again in chapter seven.

In returning to Kōchi, the procession basically retraced its steps from the previous year, though job assignments were not necessarily the same. Hirosada, for example, was not given river-crossing duty, probably much to his relief. Instead, he was assigned to walk at the side of the lord's palanquin. On the last leg of the journey, at Akaoka, where the procession lodged for the final night before entering the castle town, four friends came to greet him. Others too no doubt received friends and perhaps family with much enthusiasm. Certainly Hirosada had to feel some comfort being so close to home, and he must have looked forward to the time off — about three weeks — he was about to enjoy.[52]

Arrival and Departure from Edo

Arrival in and departure from Edo followed a certain routine and was marked with ceremony. As will be argued in the next chapter, alternate attendance was a form of theater or public performance, so Tosa's procession usually lodged at a post station close to Edo the night before arrival so that its grand entrance into the city could be made in broad daylight, in full view of as many people as possible. The procession stopped on the outskirts of the city, at Shinagawa, at one of the domain's compounds. There, members of the retinue fixed their hair and changed into new clothing; in the case of retainers, this meant putting on formal attire. After the lord himself changed and was greeted by officials there, the retinue proceeded from Shinagawa through the streets of Edo to the domain's main residence at Kajibashi, close to Edo castle.[53]

At Kajibashi, all upper samurai (those who had just arrived from Kōchi changed yet again into a different set of formal clothes) proceeded to the main audience hall, where a ceremony of arrival and greeting was held. Once this brief ritual was completed, all were excused and allowed to go their own way.[54] Those retainers, subretainers, and menials who made the trip to Edo were assigned to one of Tosa's numerous compounds (a major topic of chapter five), and those with assignments other than Kajibashi were permitted to head there.

At the official level, messengers were dispatched to the shogun's castle to report the Tosa lord's arrival to the shogun and a number of shogunal officials, including the senior councilors. Domain representatives also presented them with gifts; in Tosa's case this typically meant a long sword, one hundred pieces of silver, and sheaths of crepe silk, black satin, or sometimes orangutan hide for the shogun; twenty pieces of silver and ten rolls of crepe silk for the shogunal heir.[55] Nanbu domain often presented some local specialties such as *katakuriko* (a type of starch), iron kettles, horses, and hawks, in addition to the more standardized gifts of a sword, silver, and rolls of cotton.[56]

On different occasions during the year the domains bestowed other gifts on the shogun and his officials. As one would expect, larger domains gave more frequently than smaller ones. Satsuma, for example, offered gifts at eleven different times during the year; a smaller domain such as Matsue gave on seven occasions. The gifts were largely token and were perhaps a remnant of the ancient practice of subjects presenting local produce to the sovereign as tribute. The shogunate did not gain monetarily by the tribute, as it gave the daimyo gifts of equal or greater value upon departure. Official gift giving in all its various forms provided a mechanism by which local material culture was circulated around the country. The shogunate sold the gifts bequeathed by the daimyo and others to merchant agents who specialized in these goods.[57]

Much the same procedures were followed when a daimyo prepared to depart from Edo. In the case of a distinguished lord such as the Yamauchi, a senior councilor (rather than a messenger sent by the official, as in the case of a lesser lord) came to the main compound to relay the shogun's order granting him a leave of absence and informing him of the date on which his predeparture audience with the shogun would be held. Gifts from the hegemon were presented at this time, most commonly twenty rolls of silk gauze, thirty pieces of silver, and a sword.[58] Similar gifts from the shogunal heir were presented as well. All retainers at the main compound assembled, dressed in formal attire, to receive these items.[59] On the actual day of departure, a horse from the shogun was delivered to the main compound, though occasionally it was presented at Edo castle itself.[60]

When departing from Edo on the return to Kōchi, the attendance of all retainers was required as far as Shinagawa, the point of egress on the Tōkaidō for Edo, which made for a grand display. The procession stopped for a break at the domain's compound there, and all retainers ate celebratory red rice in honor of the lord's successful completion of his tour of service in Edo. After Shinagawa, retainers could travel independently when not on duty, as on the trip to Edo the previous year.

The return trip seemed much more relaxed than the journey to Edo, no doubt particularly for the lord. On his way back in 1733, Yamauchi Toyonobu took the time to inspect the grounds of the checking station at Hakone after asking permission to do so the previous year on his way to Edo, and he appears to have met with more local notables than on the trip to Edo.[61] On at least one occasion, the advance group appears to have broken up, with individual groups of varying sizes traveling together. During a six-day period, groups of three, eight, four, fourteen, and forty-five people trickled home.[62] This allowed for some freedom to visit places of interest.

Once safely back in the domain, a high-ranking vassal was sent to Edo as messenger to report his lord's arrival and to thank the shogun for the leave of absence. On this occasion, too, gifts from Tosa, which usually included dried bonito, abalone, and silk crepe, were presented to the shogun and his heir, with more modest gifts delivered to top shogunal officials as well. In the next couple of days after arrival, the lord made a pilgrimage to his family temple to report to his ancestors on his service in Edo and to give them thanks, thus drawing to its conclusion one cycle of alternate attendance.

Journeys Delayed or Not Taken —
Daimyo "Illness" and Bakufu Aid

Alternate attendance worked too well as a control device, for it kept the lords in debt to the merchant moneylenders. Yet despite the oppressive nature of many of the Tokugawa control measures, the Tokugawa did not want to crush or to eliminate the other daimyo. As the Confucian scholar Ogyū Sorai (1666–1728) advised the shogun (Yoshimune),

> In the early days of the bakufu [shogunate] it was the best policy to
> weaken the daimyo and to encourage expenditures. Now since the daimyo
> are in severely straitened circumstances, the wisest policy is to see that
> they are kept solvent so that they can continue to perform the alternate
> attendance.[63]

Despite Sorai's thoughts, there is the tendency to see the shogunate and the domains locked in perpetual opposition, when in fact the political system was "firmly based on the full cooperation between the two levels of government."[64] The political arrangement of Tokugawa times was in many respects advantageous to the domains because it protected them to a far greater degree than their predecessors in the Warring States period had been.

The relationship between domain and shogunate, rather than being one-sided, involved give and take. The shogunate saw itself as having national responsibilities as a government, and this included responsibility for the well-being of the domains. This sense of obligation led it to respond to calls for assistance from the domains, and that assistance assumed a variety of forms, the most obvious being loans to rebuild mansions that had burned down. However, it should be stressed that by no means was assistance always proffered.

Other forms of assistance granted the domains by the shogunate were exemptions from the alternate attendance or permission to deviate from established routines, when for example they performed some service for the Tokugawa. Tosa was charged with dredging the moats of Edo castle in 1765 and performed riparian work in the Kanto region in 1822. As a result, the Yamauchi lords were granted a six-month and a four-month delay, respectively, in their departure dates from Edo.[65] Toward the end of the Edo period, exemptions for coastal defense became more frequent, leading one scholar to assert that the daimyo "began to use their responsibility for coastal defense as an excuse to avoid appearing in Edo and to flout the authority of the bakufu [shogunate]."[66] These requests for exemptions, however, should be seen as cost-cutting measures, particularly important for coastal domains as they sought to strengthen military defenses in light of the growing Western threat, rather than conscious acts of defiance.

Exemptions from duty were often given under different circumstances, such as a major fire in either the domainal castle or in the main residence in Edo. In 1809 the shogunate granted Kaga a three-year respite after a fire burned down the palace in the domainal castle; the Maeda lord, however, chose to resume his duty in Edo after only two years. A two-year respite was given due to famine in 1785, but in this case too the Maeda lord opted not to take full advantage of it and appeared for duty in Edo the following year. Perhaps not wanting to even give the suggestion of shirking his responsibilities to the shogun, the Maeda lord refused on both occasions to excuse himself. Exemptions were routinely given during a change in lordship brought on by death. Delay in the performance of duty was also granted in the case of a lord who assumed his position in his infancy or during his minority.[67]

While exemptions were only infrequently granted, the Tokugawa government, as noted above, did under certain circumstances allow domains to deviate from the fixed schedule for arrivals and departures. In some cases the intent behind the requests to economize is clear. One scholar states, however, that the Tokugawa were reluctant to permit deviations from the system and cites an example from Aizu domain in support. In 1721 the Aizu lord was denied permission to leave Edo early even though the main residence burned down, and "when permission to leave Edo was requested, the bakufu ruled that only if all three of the han *yashiki* were destroyed and there were absolutely no other quarters available could leave be granted."[68] Without more information it is difficult to evaluate this case. Perhaps the Tokugawa government had some urgent need to keep the Aizu forces in Edo to perform some service, or there might have been a problem with the manner in which the request was made. Regardless, Aizu, being a sizeable domain, had many other residences to which the population of the main residence could be distributed, and it was possible to send home some men to reduce the overcrowding. Indeed, this very thing happened when Tosa's main compound at Kajibashi burned in 1780; some staff members were sent home and the rest were distributed among two other compounds (Shiba and Shinagawa), while some high-ranking retainers were sent to the Azabu compound of Tosa's branch domain, Kōchi shinden.[69]

While the shogunate may have been reluctant to allow exemptions or deviations from the schedule when a residence burned, it did grant them with some frequency when a lord was too sick to travel. The daimyo recognized this and as a result some complained of illness in order to extend their stays in Edo and, less frequently, in the domain. The Tokugawa, in turn, felt compelled to instruct the lords not to extend their periods of residence in Edo by complaining of illness.[70] Sometimes when the illness was too transparent, the shogunate censured the lord in question. Such was the case in 1744, when the lord of Hasuike, a branch domain of Saga, requested the main branch to petition the shogunate to allow it to suspend performance of the alternate attendance. When the main house refused, Hasuike sought to delay the next round of attendance by pleading illness, inviting the censure.[71]

Certainly illness was not always a pretext, as the lifestyle of the lords seems to have rendered them frail and prone to sickness. On at least two occasions, in 1758 and 1798, the lord had to turn around en route from Kōchi to Edo due to illness, an eye ailment in the former case and fever and chills in the later. In the 1798 case the procession turned around after four days, and a second, successful, attempt was undertaken the next month. No doubt the lord's illness was not an excuse, for such a development was costly and extremely troublesome. Toyoshige (1827–1872), the fifteenth Tosa lord, requested and received a two-month delay because of illness a month before his scheduled departure from Kōchi.[72] Earlier, in 1799, Lord Toyokazu (1773–1825) was granted permission to leave Edo about two months early due to illness. While in Kōchi he had to request permission from the shogunate, through Tosa's Edo liaison, to go for walks for recuperation so as not to give the appearance that his illness was merely an excuse to go home early.[73] Later, in 1800, in asking to be allowed to remain in Edo, Toyokazu noted that he had returned to Edo, even though he had not fully recuperated from his illness despite the therapy in the hot springs and seawater baths, because he did not want to inconvenience the shogun. He complained of his ill health and continued pain in his feet, both of which prevented him from stopping in Kyoto on the way to Edo. Once in the capital, he felt unable to visit the senior councilors and dispatched a memorandum stating that he would not be able to fulfill his duties — i.e., attend at the shogun's court at Edo castle "for a while" — and took up residence in the more spacious residence at Shiba.[74] The following year, in his request to remain in Edo, which importantly cited a recent precedent for his request, the lord noted:

> Since last fall I have been sick and on top of this I have suffered dizzy spells and pain in my feet. Although my foot is slightly better, it still hampers my movement, and my general condition is much the same.[75]

In fact Toyokazu was allowed to remain in Edo almost three years (he arrived in Edo 1800/4/1 and did not return again to Kōchi until 1803/3/2), the longest delay in Tosa's participation in the alternate attendance. Officially on leave even though the lord remained in Edo, Toyokazu was instructed to reduce his staff in the city, and some men were sent home, including at least one of the two senior advisors who had accompanied Toyokazu to Edo.[76]

After completing his leave in Tosa and having fulfilled his regular period of residence in Edo, Toyokazu again requested to prolong his stay in the Tokugawa capital, which he did, from 1804/3/15 to 1806/5/25. Whether "sick" in Edo or back in Kōchi, the lord's activities had to be circumscribed and official permission obtained for him to leave the castle or Edo residence for any reason. Of course he was unable to attend ceremonies at the shogun's castle on New Year's Day, excusing himself with a note to the senior councilors explaining that his head hurt due to his illness and sending messengers with the customary gifts.[77] Whether real or feigned (and there is no evidence that it was feigned), the lord's illness allowed the domain to skip one cycle in the alternate attendance and to send staff members home, both of which resulted in great savings.

Let me emphasize that the desire of the Tosa, or any other lord, to cut costs should not be interpreted, *prime facie*, as a sign of ambition to flout shogunal law. While some may have had those sentiments, it is apparent that in numerous cases lords had a difficult time raising sufficient funds to leave Edo or to make it all the way back home, which no doubt would have brought great shame to the lord and domain had it become public knowledge. To cite two such examples, the daimyo of Dewa Shōnai, on his way home from Edo, made it as far as Fukushima before running out of funds. Money then had to be sent from Shōnai before the journey could be completed. The second example (also undated) involves the Date of Sendai, who had so little money that his entourage had to sleep outdoors and hunt for their food. Apparently hearing of his plight, Tokugawa officials granted him money to make it home.[78]

Requests to leave Edo early were expressed in terms of the lord's illness. The type of illness and the therapy suggested by domain officials often became code words used to receive the shogunate's permission. The Tosa lord's sickness was usually described as *shakki*, with pain extending to his limbs. A 1780 request stated that the lord wanted to return to Kōchi in the middle of the second month of the new year to take the waters at the hot springs "near the castle." The request stated that were the lord to leave Edo according to the "regular" schedule, by the time he reached Kōchi the hot summer would be approaching and he would not be able to take the waters as freely, but that conditions would be much better in the spring.

Despite the inference made in the request that there were hot springs in Kōchi near the castle, there is not any documentary evidence that they ever existed. While the lord's official letters to shogunal officials spoke of his pain, he felt well enough to stop his journey to make pilgrimages in Kamakura to Hachiman-gū and Benzai-ten (Benten) in Enoshima. His actions further down the Tōkaidō in Kyoto support the interpretation that the lord's illness was simply a pretext for leaving Edo early. While contemporary official records make no mention of the fact, the official domainal record, a private house record, reveals that the lord also stopped in Kyoto. In the ancient capital he went sightseeing, paying a visit to the lower Gion Shrine, where he ate a packed lunch, and then went flower viewing in the area before returning to Fushimi by nightfall. It further reveals that he did so in disguise.[79]

The real reason for wanting an early departure from Edo apparently was a fire at the main residence in 1780/10/14. The official domain record reports that the fire forced the residents at Kajibashi to move to the secondary mansion at Shiba, creating cramped conditions there. The timing of the disaster and the lord's "illness" are crucial here: The fire struck Kajibashi on 10/14 and the official request from Tosa to the Tokugawa's senior councilors was delivered on 11/22. In between those two dates, a small number of retainers were sent home early, including a senior advisor, an acupuncture doctor, a tea master, and a Confucian scholar. In fact, an entry in the domainal official record for 11/17 explicitly links the two events, revealing that by that date a decision had been made to request early leave from Edo because of the fire.[80]

Certainly the Tokugawa were aware of the fire and its consequences for Tosa's Edo population. Why did requests have to be coded? Was fire not a sufficient reason? Perhaps this was problematic because it put the shogunate in the position of having to act as fire inspectors and insurance adjustors, that is, to assess both absolute and relative damage and to determine publicly which domain(s) suffered sufficiently to warrant delay.

In another case, from 1788, there is evidence that the shogunate was not only aware that the illness was not real, but actually advised the domain's officials to phrase their request for a delay in those terms.[81] This incident relates to the point made earlier about the cooperative nature of early modern governance. Tosa domain began an economic reform program in 1787 and did not have the money to depart from Kōchi at the usual time, early in the third month. Tosa's Edo liaison inquired informally of the shogunate's officials whether it was possible to delay departure. The informal, off-the-record, response from the Tokugawa's senior councilor was that there was a recent precedent for doing so because of a lord's illness, implying that a request couched in those terms would stand a good chance of acceptance. The official request, when phrased in those terms — i.e., that the lord was too sick to travel and needed to remain in Kōchi to receive treatment, which included taking the hot spring waters — was accepted, and departure from the castle town was delayed four months.[82] This might seem absurd to us today, but Tokugawa society was a world where precedent and face were paramount.

In another related case, Lord Toyokazu decided in 1806, after being allowed to skip a turn of leave in Tosa, that he needed to return home despite his continued illness. His decision to reverse his pattern of extending his stay in Edo was no doubt related to the large fires that ravaged the two principal compounds at Kajibashi and Shiba. His letter of request to return to Tosa noted the cramped conditions at the lower compound at Shinagawa, to which he had escaped, and complained that he could not convalesce there easily: "My illness has been getting worse and this has caused me great distress. If at all possible, I would like to request a leave to return home to take the waters." Before submitting a formal request, of course, the lord's Edo liaison had already discussed the matter with the senior councilor on duty and received his verbal assurance that a request would be looked upon favorably.[83] His illness apparently was real and is confirmed by the private diary of one of the domain elders,[84] but the ailments which had kept him in Edo provided the pretext to request leave when conditions in Edo were not optimal.

From these and other similar cases one can conclude that when daimyo were pleading illness, many were doing so falsely, and various edicts telling them to adhere to fixed schedules indicate this as well. Nevertheless, in one respect deviations that kept the lords in Edo actually served the original purpose of the system, which was to keep them under surveillance in the shogun's capital. From Tosa's documentary histories I have found, in sum, evidence of only eleven requests for delays in performing either part of the alternate attendance —hardly a sign of insubordinate behavior. In fact, most of the requests were simply a matter of a month or two. In allowing the lords some flexibility when "ill," whether real or feigned, the Tokugawa could be seen to be acting in a benevolent manner. To be sure, a certain amount of deviation in leaving for Edo on time could be allowed so long as it did not threaten the continuation of the system and the lords did not question their duty to carry it out. After all, no daimyo remained ill and unable to perform the alternate attendance for more than several years.

3

The Daimyo Procession

THE MOVEMENTS OF THE daimyo, who were in a sense portable lords, and their entourages to and from Edo were not done haphazardly. They were a type of group activity that assumed certain distinct forms that marked the cultural landscape of early modern Japan. Alternate attendance was in essence a military exercise, and because of this basic fact, the various elements in the daimyo procession originated in the order of battle. It will be argued here, though, that with the onset of peace, the form of the procession came to mimic rather than replicate those earlier military movements. Once the memory of warfare faded during the course of the seventeenth century, daimyo processions came to assume a more parade-like character, in a sense subverting their origins. They assumed notable theatrical elements and became a type of cultural performance. The road became the stage; the members of the retinue, particularly the infamous *yakko* footmen, became the players; the implements carried, the props; and the people lining the road, the audience. These images were captured in "still frame" in woodblock prints, in printed books, and in written descriptions by foreigners and Japanese alike. They became the background of imaginative journeys played by children on picture game boards as well as part of a narrative journey that played itself out across picture scrolls as they were unfurled. It is no wonder perhaps that the images of daimyo processions — part military exercise, part theater — described by the Englishman Lord Mitford in the introduction remained vivid in his mind long after he left Japan.

While the regular, parade-like embassies from Korea and the Ryukyu kingdom have received scholarly attention, the more routine movements of the daimyo, who plied the highways of Tokugawa Japan from their castle towns to Edo and back year after year, generally have not.[1] This is even though the relationship between political elites and theater has been examined in a number of other societies. For example, in Morocco during the eighteenth and nineteenth centuries, the king tried to keep the hundreds of warrior-based tribes under control by moving around in his kingdom. The mobility of the king was a central element in his power.[2] With an entourage of as many as forty thousand, the king was in almost constant motion, his throne like a saddle, "the sky his canopy."[3] In Elizabethan England, the queen's regular progresses around the country during a forty-four-year reign (1558–1603) gave her "a public stage on which to present herself as the people's sovereign" and provided the settings in which she crafted her royal authority.[4] Movement here too was central to the government in question. In Tokugawa Japan we find almost a mirror image of the situation in these two other countries: the lords, or daimyo, were in constant motion while the sovereign, the shogun, remained at the center in Edo.[5] The shogun's power was manifested not in his regular movement, a court in motion, as was the case in England and elsewhere in Europe. The year of the queen's death, the Tokugawa government was founded, and once its power was consolidated by the middle of the seventeenth century the shogun rarely moved. The lords, and not the hegemon, were rendered portable.

The shogun's authority derived not from movement and public visibility but from his stasis, his relative inaccessibility at the center, and his ability to cause his subordinates to move in orbit around him. Much as Elizabeth's visits to hundreds of local elite "created a dislocating confusion that reminded courtiers, citizens and hosts of the queen's centrality in their lives," the Tokugawa, through an interplay between structure (a settled existence) and antistructure (lives on the move), created disorder—a chaos that facilitated their ability to rule.[6] The daimyo's periodic movements on the highways made that authority concrete for all who went to see the retinues and to all who were unable to witness them firsthand but were able to hear about them through word of mouth, to see images of them, or to read about them in contemporary fiction or books of heraldry (bukan). Their movements to and from Edo made it clear that the Tokugawa capital was the political center of the realm and the shogun the sovereign power. They were reminders of the "august authority" (goikō) of the shogun.[7] In other words, through the ritual of alternate attendance, the daimyo processions made the people conscious of the Tokugawa's political authority.

The daimyo spent most of their adult lives in Edo or traveling to and from the center. Preparations for the trip to and for life in Edo consumed the time and energy of many officials, and expenses for both were quite taxing. Given the importance of these movements to understanding the nature of alternate attendance and its relationship to political authority, this chapter will explore what is perceived to be the dual nature of the daimyo procession and the significance of the interplay between those two elements: first as a symbol of authority, both of the individual daimyo as local rulers and also of the Tokugawa shogunate as national hegemons; and second as performance or theater. I examine both elements through the use of popular cultural forms, such as woodblock prints, picture game boards, horizontal scrolls, contemporary accounts, and oral literature. Since the processions were minidramas, theaters of power, this chapter will also examine the processions as sites of competing production — daimyo and shogunate — with multiple levels of performance and audience.

Reception of the Procession

In Tokugawa Japan's castle towns, certain preparations were carried out in anticipation of the departure of the lord's procession. Generally, the streets were swept clean, water buckets and brooms placed in front of households facing the road, and decorative sand (known as *morisuna*) heaped into a conical shape, often one on each side of a building or gatepost. This practice dates from the Muromachi period and has been commonly interpreted as a symbol of welcome or "hospitality" (*gochisō*) for a guest of high rank. It also has religious overtones, as salt, which was spread on top of the sand pile, connotes purification. Together with the placement of the buckets and broom, these various practices, carried out in the castle towns and post stations through which the processions passed, symbolized the cleaning of the road.[8]

Hospitality connoted public signs of deference to rank, and as extended to daimyo processions as they passed through post stations could assume a number of forms. From the records of the Ishii family, operators of the official inn at Yagake station in Okayama (Niwase domain), we know that it could also consist of (1) greeting domain officials and post station officials, especially the head official of the daimyo inn, meeting and welcoming travelers at the entrances to the post station; (2) village or post station officials leading the way for the travelers through their village, calling out "*Shita ni (iro), Shita ni (iro)*" "Down!" often preceded by two men, brooms in hand, clearing the way and signaling symbolically that the road had been cleaned; (3) guard service, mainly the establishment of temporary guard posts in front of the official inn, manned by domainal footsoldiers; (4) the sending off of travelers by domainal officials at the borders of post stations and the domain and by post station officials at the borders of their settlement; and (5) physical symbols or marks of cleaning or purification, namely the decorative water buckets, brooms, and sand piles. All these were basic duties, signs of respect and public deference that were owed by local officials and those under their authority to the lords who passed through their settlements.[9]

This great variation in the degree of hospitality extended was consistent with the general pattern in Tokugawa Japan of calibrating most everything to status

(*mibun*), and it was part of the natural, accepted social order. Hospitality therefore depended on the identity of the traveling party and its relationship to the
domainal as well as shogunal authority. Accordingly, officials of the Tokugawa
generally received the highest level of hospitality. From the records of the official inns at Yagake post station, it seems that most daimyo formally received no
special treatment except for their reception by post station officials, the courtesy of freshly swept roads, and the hanging of decorative curtains in front of
the *honjin*. A few lords had water buckets and brooms arrayed for their passage.
These courtesies represented hospitality as shown by the post station. At other
stations, hospitality might also include the placement of torchlights or lanterns
for the lord's convenience.[10]

Hospitality sponsored by the domain, rather than by the post station, typically was extended only to Tokugawa officials, like the Nagasaki magistrate,
and to lords with whom there was a direct connection of some sort. It was up
to the domain lord, in the final analysis, to determine the level of hospitality
beyond what the post station offered. Most of the fourteen or fifteen daimyo
who passed through Yagake post station annually did so without any greetings
from the local daimyo, but occasionally as a courtesy, a low-ranking official
of the domain might send his name placard with instructions to the itinerant
lord to contact him should any need arise. As other examples of this type of
irregular hospitality offered by the local daimyo, the Mōri lord of Chōshū was
treated to tea and sweets at a rest stop near Yagake post station at the expense of
the local lord of Niwase domain; the Hōjō lord sent a messenger with greetings
and a small box of dried sea bream to the lord of Hagi as he passed through
Odawara; and, for the early morning (4–5 a.m.) passage of the Satsuma lord
through Nagoya, lanterns were lit on both sides of the road.[11]

A number of contemporary commentators noted some of the various signs
of hospitality. In the early 1860s, at Goyu station on the Tōkaidō, Sir Rutherford Alcock witnessed the sand piles and the road-clearing exercise that was
routinely carried out:

> We met a cortege, with some Daimio [*sic*] of unusual importance, appar-
> ently; for a train of little sand-heaps marked the road for several miles, in
> testimony of respect, signifying that the road was freshly swept and sanded
> for him especially. So, even with ourselves, there generally ran before us a
> couple of little ragged urchins, dragging their brooms after them, and shout-
> ing as they went, for an advertisement to all whom they might meet, the
> magic word which brings every Japanese to his knees, "Shitanirio!" [*sic*] or,
> rather, this was the word which should have been articulated; but, in their
> mouths, it was transmuted into a sort of monotonous cry or howl, which we
> often took occasion to leave far behind us by pushing our horses on.[12]

On a later day he wrote with incredulity how within a few steps of a "dense mass of swaying bodies and excited heads," a wide path suddenly opened up in front of them, "as if by magic," with the wave of an official's fan and the command of "Shita ni iro."[13]

Francis Hall's account of life in the closing years of the shogunate also relates important information about the reception of processions. He wrote in 1860 that he was "desirous to see what I might of the cortege of a man whose traveling train is said frequently to contain five thousand."[14] While the reputation of the size of the lord of Owari's procession far exceeded its reality, it was nevertheless a spectacle. To observe, he and his party watched from a bluff in Kanagawa, overlooking the Tōkaidō. On his hilltop position with a Dr. James Hepburn, a Dr. Simmons, and Dr. Simmons's wife, Hall and the foreigners were themselves spotted and the herald shouted for them to get down. Hall reported, "The Japanese went down as if shot and Dr. S[immons] followed suit, Mrs. S[immons], Dr. H[epburn] and myself continued standing, though presently Mrs. S[immons] sat down beside the Dr."[15] The lord of Owari saw them observing him in his palanquin, and he ordered his vehicle stopped, slid the door open, and gazed back at them through an opera glass. Hall later noted that the lord took a long look at them, especially Mrs. Simmons, whom he presumed "was the first foreign lady he had ever seen."[16] Hall, his legs perched over the edge of the cliff, bowed back. This mutual cross-cultural investigation went on for several minutes before the train moved on. Hall's Japanese guide later informed him that the incident on the hill had created quite a stir among the Japanese, and he related what a "great breach of Japanese etiquette" Hall's behavior had been. They should have "gone within some home and looked out unseen," he said. Not to have done so was in fact dangerous; another daimyo "less friendly might take such displeasure as to order his soldiers to shoot at us," Hall learned. He was instructed that the "mark of politeness would be to 'turn your back towards the royal cortege.'"[17]

The misbehavior or lack of proper conduct of a Japanese toward a daimyo procession might be corrected on the spot. As Hall reported when he encountered the train of the daimyo of Fukui on the Tōkaidō, all went down on their knees except "one poor fellow who was not quite quick enough. [He] had his wide straw hat knocked over his eyes and was hustled very much as men in a crowd are sometimes hustled in a home mob."[18] Other contemporary accounts indicate that those who failed to move quickly enough might be pushed out of the way. A peddler selling sweet bean soup in the middle of the road was taken unawares by the procession of the Sendai lord one night and, though he tried to move his things out of the way, apparently he did not do so quickly enough, for "without saying a word, one of the men at the head of the procession kicked over the cart, sending its contents flying." When he squatted down to clear up the mess, someone kicked the hot pot, sending it flying. It struck the man on the left side of his face above the eye, burning him.[19]

Domainal officials felt the need to instruct residents how to behave during the passage of the daimyo's procession. In Chōshū, for example, commoners were commanded (1) to remove hats and other head coverings; (2) to refrain from playing musical instruments; (3) to keep children from being a nuisance; (4) not to hang wash outside or place unsightly things by the roadside; (5) not to spread manure in nearby fields the day before the lord's passage; (6) not to argue or make loud noises; (7) not to hold funerals the day of the passage; (8) to listen to the instructions of officials; and (9) to clean the road, make sand piles, and put out lanterns should it grow dark while the procession was passing by.[20] In short, they were to act respectful and not impede the progress of the retinue.

In addition to these written accounts, pictorial representations also inform us to some extent about the issue of reception. In the scroll "Kishū han sankin kōtai gyōretsu zu," an anonymous artist has reproduced the procession of the lord of Kii (Wakayama), with some 1,320 men in the retinue and about five hundred spectators gathered along the travel route, which runs through parts of present-day Sakai and Osaka cities.[21] How are we to read the implicit narratives as we unroll the scrolls, pictorial representations without written text?[22] "A parade is not an instantaneous 'event,' but a 'process' that develops over time and space," Ronald Toby reminds us.[23] In the Kishū scroll, which dates from late Tokugawa times, we can observe the people along the route going down on their knees, and others simply squatting, only when the section centered on the lord approached (see Figure 3.1). The approach of the lord and the main section of the procession were marked by a large gap, followed by road clearers. The concentration of bodyguards around the lord further highlighted his presence. The people before and after the main force are depicted as casual spectators, going about their business seemingly oblivious to the event unfolding nearby. Given the length of the procession and the slow pace dictated by the dignity of the lord, one can understand perhaps why people are seen kneeling only for the passage of the main portion of the retinue. Yet this flies in the face of the popular image of commoners lying prostrate before entire processions. As the main segment of the parade approached and people went down on their knees, they are respectful, but their faces are relaxed and definitely not buried in the ground. Once the lord passes people are up on their feet again. Just before the road clearers in this main segment we observe a humorous scene. A man, broom in hand, has apparently finished sweeping the road, but below him in the foreground a boy has spread some of the contents of a water bucket in a manner which has angered a samurai nearby, who scowls in response.

The passage of another lord is depicted in much the same fashion in the "Sunpu jōka gyōretsu byōbu," a screen painted in the first half of the seven-

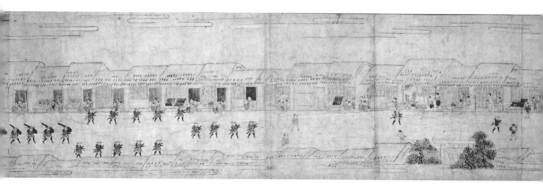

FIGURE 3.1. Procession of Kii Wakayama domain. Sections from "Kishū han sankin kōtai gyōretsu zu." Courtesy of Sakai shi hakubutsukan.

teenth century. People are out of their homes and on their knees before the lord's palanquin; elsewhere, people are on their knees, while others are standing but bent over in a bow.[24] On the other hand, the Swiss consul Rudolph Lindau, in the closing years of the Tokugawa period, reported that,

> With the call "shita ni iro" the entire area went quiet, as a sign of respect. Work was temporarily halted; windows were shut, and many people quickly returned to their homes. . . . Travelers went down on their knees, foreheads to the ground, until the lord's palanquin passed.[25]

While accounts vary, it is clear that at least the portion of the procession that centered on the lord was treated with great respect.

The passage of daimyo processions was part of the regular cycle of yearly events experienced by people living in castle towns, including Edo, and in settlements along the alternate attendance routes in domains, as well as along the Gokaidō transport network. That single-sheet guides were not ordinarily published for them by commercial artists, as they were for processions of foreigners from Korea and Ryukyu, might seem to suggest that daimyo retinues were viewed by the populace as routine. They certainly occurred on a regular basis, unlike the far more episodic foreign missions, and the marchers were Japanese rather than alien. Therefore for most Japanese they did not remain "in the realm of fantasy, heard about but unseen," as did the parades of foreigners.[26] One was far more likely to see a daimyo procession than a parade of foreigners.

Nevertheless, daimyo processions were often grand spectacles that attracted much attention and often formed the backdrop of woodblock prints and picture game boards, which demonstrates their hold on the popular imagination. For example, in Utagawa Hiroshige's "Hōeidō Tōkaidō" series, in at least four of the prints, beginning with the first, the members of the retinue are the major or only human figures in the work and are thus the focal points.[27] The popularity of game boards with travel themes reflected the boom in travel that occurred in the late eighteenth and early nineteenth centuries. The games were a favorite pastime of children at New Year's and during festivals.[28] Parts of daimyo processions were routinely depicted in the blocks apportioned for particular stops (post stations) on the highway; in others, processions wind their way back and forth across the board. Moreover, almost without fail Nihonbashi in Edo, the zero point for the Tokugawa official road network and the starting point for the game board, was associated with alternate attendance through the visual representation of a procession crossing the bridge, as in "Nihonbashi, Morning View (c. 1833–1834) Odawara-chō," by Hiroshige, from his series "Fifty-three Stations along the Tōkaidō," where the retinue is depicted just beginning the journey home.[29] In this way, then, alternate attendance became synonymous with shogunal authority through these artistic representations.

Some oral histories taken in the early Meiji period relate the attraction of the daimyo procession to commoner spectators. One woman who lived in Osaka remembered that people intentionally sought out processions as one would seek out a parade. Just over the bridge from her house in Kyōmachi were the compounds of the lords of Satsuma, Higo, and Marugame. She recalled how "when lords or young princesses arrived from the provinces large numbers of people came out to pay their respects" (*taigai ogami ni itta mon dasu*). The gates to the compound wide open, a curtain hanging across them, and all around the ground swept clean signaled to her and others that someone important would be arriving that day. "The spectators," she said, "would be on their knees from early on, when they heard '*Shita nii, shita nii.*' Sometimes the lord would not arrive until evening; we'd be hungry and our eyes had gone dizzy, but we had to wait patiently."[30] This recollection, incidentally, conflicts with the notion that spectators observed the courtesy of kneeling or bowing only for the passage of the main segment of the procession.

Remembering seeing a daimyo procession in Edo one night, a former townsman remarked, "It was really something (*jitsu ni taishita mon de*) — there were around 300 men accompanying the lord. It was so quiet that all one could hear was the sound of horse bridles." This was true even when the procession was just a small unit accompanying the lord within the city. For example, upon seeing the procession of the Saga lord at Kandabashi returning to his main compound at night, the same person remarked, "There were more than fifty men in two rows, like a cluster of stars. They were uniform in height, not even an inch difference among them. . . . The procession passed by quietly, not so much as a cough coming from any of the men. Thanks to working at night, I was able to witness this grand spectacle, which has been engrained in my mind."[31]

Samurai, too, had occasion to comment on daimyo processions. Mutō Hiroki, a Sendai retainer who created a written and pictorial record of his lord's first procession to the domain in 1842, observed that the streets of Edo "were so crowded with sightseers that the procession could barely move."[32] Maki Yasuomi, a Kurume retainer, viewed the retinues of several daimyo while traveling on the Tōkaidō in 1843 and noted:

> I rested at Mitsuke [post station] where I had encountered the retinue of the daimyo of Kumamoto on his way back to the han. Both in accoutrements and in the number of men and horses, it is probably the finest in Japan. I also met with that of the daimyo of Chōshū, and observed it while resting in a house by the side of the Road. His cortege, if one compares it with that of Kumamoto, was only half as large; however the samurai were extremely well disciplined and the effects of the daimyo's reform is a sight to behold. I also met with the daimyo of Fukui, Ōtsu, and Kurushima, none of whom are worth looking at.[33]

Maki had clearly rated these various processions in his mind and on paper, revealing the keen status consciousness with which samurai viewed their society. Similarly, the Tosa samurai Mori Yoshiki noted in 1801 that the retinue of the Ikeda lord, Narikuni, of Tottori domain (325,000 *koku*) was smaller than that of the Tosa (240,000 *koku*) lord, of which he was a part.[34] Samurai were highly competitive and strongly aware of the hierarchical order of which they were a part.

Samurai apparently were also aware that daimyo processions were viewed by commoners as a form of theater. According to the recollections of a former retainer from Satsuma domain, the most popular forms of sightseeing (*kenbutsu*) in Edo were: "one, watching the daimyo processions in front of Edo castle (*geba*); two, sumō; and three, the theater," all of which were types of spectatorship.[35] Moreover, some samurai viewed them the same way, as Mori Ōgai reported that Tsugaru domain doctor Shibue Chūsai would rush out of his house to watch a procession go by.[36]

Processions as Theaters of Power

Processions are a group activity that exists in most if not all cultures, yet they do not consist simply of a group of people walking in the same direction. There are certain principles that define them.[37] For one, a procession consists of a group organized in columns that proceeds forward on a set course to a predetermined destination. Second, people wait along the route for the group to pass, watching the procession while obeying certain rules of an audience. Third, the group marching, while being watched by the spectators, also observes them. Fourth, the arrangement of the procession and the behavior of the spectators are both regulated or controlled by some underlying authority or power. Put differently, parades are political acts. Those in the procession move with the understanding that they will be seen and move fully conscious of the fact that their movement is a demonstration of power and authority. In sum, the procession functions in four ways: to see, to show, to be seen, and to cause to be seen.

As the various observations noted in the section above implied, processions as political acts are dramatic representations, performance, or theater.[38] Drama and power have, of course, long been closely linked. In ancient times as well as in medieval and early modern Europe, "the wielders of authority — the church and the state — developed expertise in the techniques of display; the relationship between theatre and monarchy, processions and power, was intimate."[39] While the bakufu had its own processions, shogunal processions to Kyoto and Nikkō in particular, it will be argued here that the daimyo parades were a reflection of both domainal status and Tokugawa authority.

Daimyo processions used a system of signs and emblems, the latter having several functions. First of all, they distinguished one political power (daimyo) from another. Second, they were meant to make a good impression on the spectator — to awe the ruled with the power and authority of the lord — as well as to impress other spectators not of the same domain with the prestige of that lord. Third, the emblems clearly translate the principles upheld by the lord, including the notion that the daimyo's authority was based on military might.[40]

More concretely, there were many elements to the theatrical or dramatic character of the daimyo processions, elements that heightened their political impact: size, forms of movement, attire, military gear and other accoutrements, color, and sound. The first, size, consisted of the sometimes awe-inspiring sheer number of men and horses that moved together, generally in a stately manner. Prestige required numbers. As Kaempfer noted, "the train of some of the most eminent among the Princes of the Empire [daimyo] fills up the road for some days."[41] On his second trip to Edo, Kaempfer's group encountered a portion of the Kii lord's procession: "We counted eighty led horses, more than fifty *norimono*, one hundred or more ordinary pikes, thirty-six pikes with feathers

and drooping bushes or horsehair, thirty to forty men carrying bows, excluding those men who were still inside the houses, thirty boxes with the gilded
emblem of the shogun and other gilded coats of arms, and many many more."[42]
Francois Caron, in Japan in the 1630s, was so impressed by the numbers that he
took to exaggeration, writing that some of the lords traveled "to and from with
one, two, three, four, five and six thousand men."[43] More than two centuries
later (1865), the German archaeologist Heinrich Schliemann, visiting Japan in
1865, estimated the largest daimyo procession at fifteen thousand men.[44] Siebold, too, was taken to exaggeration by the large numbers: "The trains with
which the princes of the empire visit Yedo amount in number to ten thousand
men for those of the lowest rank, and twenty thousand for those of the highest."[45] The largest of the domains' processions were actually in the range of two
to three thousand men. Regarding the number of horses included in the procession, Kaga, for example, brought almost four hundred from the domain, and as
many as a thousand animals from villages in areas around the roads traversed
in the domain might be required for a substantial procession.[46]

Foreigners were not the only ones impressed by the size of many daimyo
processions. The Japanese geographer Furukawa Koshōken traveled around
the country in 1787 with a group of shogunal inspectors. His party exited Edo
at the same time as the lord of Sendai, and the two groups met on the roadway
after that. He noted,

> Despite hearing of the economizing measures being practiced in recent
> years, with attendant reductions in daimyo processions, from the various
> implements carried to the number of men in the retinue, the procession
> of the Sendai lord is large and resplendent (*bibishiki taninzū ni te*), by far
> superior to that of the lord of Satsuma's. The display of not only the Senior
> Advisors [and their men] but of all the samurai, and the various imple-
> ments they are carrying is astonishing (*me o odorokaseshi tomomawari
> nari*). The family crest is a nine-star pattern on a vermillion background.
> The men, all dressed in sleeveless, long overcoats that look like formal
> wear, hold their implements upright, against their shoulders. I have seen
> many province-holding daimyo's processions, but none as fine as this.[47]

This account is even more remarkable given that it was written during the Tenmei famine, which centered on the north of Japan and affected Sendai. If the
procession Furukawa saw was similar in scope to the one from 1842 that a Sendai retainer painted, a retinue with 1,577 men headed by fifty gunners and fifty
bowmen, one can well understand his admiration.[48]

While the numbers of men a lord brought with him were tied to prestige, and
the large numbers lent to the theatricality of the corteges, the practical military
rationale behind the numbers should not be overlooked. The processions were

military exercises — planned exercises in mobilizing and moving large numbers of troops and attendant war materiel. As such, daimyo needed to have an
adequate number of men appropriate to their status should the shogun require
their military services. This requirement of military service also dictated that
adequate military hardware and materiel be brought along. To protect the lord
at overnight stops, for example, a metal sheet was placed under the tatami matting in his bedroom at the inn where he was lodging.

Daimyo processions had the reputation of being excessively large, as was
suggested in the haiku by Kobayashi Issa:

Ato tomo wa	The rear of the procession
Kasumi hikikeri	vanished into distant mist
Kaga no kami	The lord of Kaga[49]

These men accompanied the daimyo to Edo, where they were to assist them
in the performance of their duty to the shogun. In practical terms this meant
they were to guard the gates of the shogun's castle, provide fire prevention
units at various locations in the city, and attend to the lord on his way to and
from formal audiences at the shogun's palace or the Tokugawa family's mortuary temples. Given the nature of these duties, which did not require a large
force, it is not surprising that the Tokugawa government tried to regulate the
number of men the lords could bring to Edo. This was due not only to military
considerations — the shogun did not want a large buildup of potentially hos-
tile forces in his capital — but also because of concerns about overcrowding in
Edo and overburdening the official transport network.[50] Warnings concerning the large numbers of men being brought to Edo were issued from early
on, in the Laws for the Military Houses of 1635 and 1653, and again in 1701 and
1712.[51] Whether or not these instructions were repeated to all daimyo at their
audiences before returning to their domains is uncertain, but the lord of Tosa
was directed in 1679 both to carry out the religious inquiry census registers
(*Kirishitan shūmon aratame*) diligently and to reduce the numbers in his procession when he returned to Edo the following year.[52] In particular, criticism
was directed at the practice of hiring commoners (*machi no yakko*) to fill out
the processions; these people were of "no use" since the processions were by
nature a military exercise.[53]

The number of men a lord could bring with him to Edo was based upon
the officially assessed domainal productive output (*omotedaka*). The larger the
domain, the more men allowed — and at least through the beginning of the
eighteenth century, the daimyo greatly exceeded the limits established.[54] They
did this despite the financial burdens because in times of peace, the size of one's
entourage, like the number and size of the lord's mansions, were indicators of
status and thus of utmost importance in the world of the samurai.

The great lords at times far exceeded the numbers set by Tokugawa regulations. For example, according to regulations issued in 1658, the Tosa lord should have brought about eighteen hundred men with him to Edo. Available records for Tosa show (see Table 2.1) that around this time the lord was bringing slightly fewer than the prescribed number of attendants, around fifteen hundred, with him. The record reveals, however, that at the height of the period of conspicuous consumption at the end of the seventeenth century, this figure was routinely exceeded, sometimes by almost a thousand men. In 1690, for example, 2,775 men accompanied the lord to Edo. Among the personnel who traveled to Edo, some only accompanied the procession to Edo and then returned home. Others came and went with the lord, while still others remained as long-term staff. The same was true of Kaga. Even though, according to regulations issued in 1721, all domains of more than 200,000 *koku* should have had no more than twenty mounted samurai, 120 to 130 footsoldiers and 250 to 300 menial attendants—a total of 385 to 450 men—Kaga domain routinely had between two and three thousand men in its processions. Even if one were to hypothesize that the regulations applied only to those in the main body of the procession or to those directly attached to the lord, Kaga's numbers still far exceeded those stipulated in Tokugawa regulations (Table 3.1).

There is evidence for a decrease in the size of procession after the early eighteenth century. Available data for Tosa domain, for example, shows a drop to 1,799 persons in 1718, which was just one person shy of the 1,800 standard for Tosa prescribed by shogunal regulation.[55] There, as elsewhere, fluctuations in the domain's fiscal condition, rather than the centrally issued edicts of the Tokugawa, probably account for the reduction in numbers, particularly evident in the eighteenth and nineteenth centuries.[56] This was no doubt also a factor in the decision to change the course for alternate attendance to the overland route across Shikoku initiated in 1718 (the Kitayama route).

Despite the apparent decrease in the numbers accompanying the Yamauchi lord, the size of Tosa's processions was still a target of criticism and reform during the Tenmei period in the late eighteenth century. For example, one scholar from Tosa reported that:

This summer [1787], on the return trip to the domain, at Kusatsu post station, we saw the procession of the lord of Aki province [lord Asano of Hiroshima], and people were saying that its size was not even a third of ours. In other places people were saying that, at present, there is not another daimyo in all of Shikoku and the Western provinces with a procession as large as that of the Tosa lord's, while noting that the lord of Awa [Tokushima Hachisuka] had reduced the numbers in his retinue by one-half.[57]

TABLE 3.1. Procession Figures for Various Domains*
(K = *kōtai*; unless otherwise noted all figures are for *sankin*, i.e., the trip to Edo)

Domain	Size (koku)	Seventeenth Century (year)	Eighteenth Century (year)	Nineteenth Century (year)
Akita	105,800	1,350 (1616) 1,020 (1682)		173 (1855)
Fukuyama	100,000	1,121 (1688)		
Hachinohe	20,000		188 (1797)K	210 (1822) 202 (1854)
Hiroshima	426,500	2,169 (1663) 1,628 (1698)		
Hitoyoshi	22,165		203 (1730)K 193 (1781) 252 (1799)K	
Honjō	20,400	260 (1677)		
Ichinoseki	30,000			218 (1831)
Kaga	1,022,700		3,000 (1724) 2,500 (1745) 2,184 (1764)	3,500 (1802) 2,144 (1816) 2,238 (1860)
Kii	550,000			1,322 (1833)
Komatsu	10,000		57 (1719) 47 (1797)	58 (1800)
Kumamoto	540,000	2,720 (1645) 2,563 (1680)K	546 (1777)	694 (1812) 3,000 (ca. 1826)K
Kurume	210,000		804 (1706)	
Morioka	200,000	1,660 (1634) 800 (1677)		500 (1818)
Nagaoka	74,000			
Okayama	315,000	1,628 (1698)	640 (1720) 710 (1722)	139 (1843)
Ōmura	27,973			
Satsuma	770,800	1,240 (1635)	920 (1749) 507 (1765)K 559 (1790)	1,282 (1842)K
Sendai	625,600	3,480 (1675)		
Tahara	12,000	223 (1696)		
Tosa	200,000	1,477 (1645) 2,775 (1690) 2,813 (1697)K	1,799 (1718)	94 (1860s)
Ushiku	10,017			539 (1800)K
Usuki	50,000			470 (1840) 299 (1842) 276 (1862)

TABLE 3.1. *(Continued)*

Domain	Size (koku)	Seventeenth Century (year)	Eighteenth Century (year)	Nineteenth Century (year)
Uwajima	100,403			84 (1833)K
Yoita	20,000			

*The table on procession numbers is based on the following sources: Aizu: *HDJ* vol. 6, 340–341; Akita: *HDJ* vol. 1, 365–366; Ōta Kōtarō 1965, 32; Fukuyama: *HDJ* vol. 6, 291; Hachinohe: Miura Tadashi, 1994, 19; *HDJ* vol. 1, 97; Hiroshima: *HDJ* vol. 6, 315; Hitoyoshi: *HDJ* vol. 7, 318; Maruyama Yasunari 1987; Honjō: *HDJ* vol. 1, 387; Ichinoseki: *HDJ* vol. 1, 150; Kaga: Chūda 1993, 58–59; Kagoshima: *HDJ* vol. 7, 552; Maruyama Yasunari 1979, 81–82; Kii (Wakayama): Ishikawa kenritsu toshokan 1991, 56; Komatsu: *HDJ* vol. 6, 488; Kumamoto: Maruyama Yasunari 1987, 25; Kanagawa kenritsu rekishi hakubutsukan 2001, 59, 103; Kurume: *HDJ* vol. 7, 53; Miharu: *HDJ* vol. 1, 184; Nagaoka: *HDJ* vol. 3, 90; Okayama: *HDJ* vol. 6, 192–193; Neville 1958; Ōmura: *HDJ* vol. 7: 212; Sendai: *HDJ* vol. 1, 184; Takakura 1987, 22–23; Tahara: *HDJ* vol. 4, 266. Ushiku: *HDJ* vol. 2, 125; Uwajima: *HDJ* vol. 6, 552; Usuki: Ego 1999, 25–26; Yoita: *HDJ* vol. 3, 76.

In the context of the times, this connoted criticism, because Tosa, unlike the other domains cited, had not reduced the size of its procession.

Among some domains, however, the drop in numbers could be more startling. The Hosokawa of Kumamoto domain reduced their numbers from 2,720 (1645) to 2,563 (1680) to 546 (1777).[58] Sendai han, among others, did the same. A key part of the domain's program in its own reform, launched in 1789 in response to massive crop losses caused by an extended period of cold and rain, was to reduce the numbers in its retinue by "two-thirds."[59] Still, as mentioned earlier, the geographer Furukawa Koshōken noted in 1788 that despite these measures, Sendai's retinue was startling, far greater than any of those of the large, province-holding daimyo he had ever seen before, even that of Satsuma.

Apparently the reduction in numbers for Sendai domain did not last long, for according to the "Rakuzan-kō" scroll the numbers were still substantial in the 1840s, with as many as 1,282 people in 1842. For some domains it was a matter of local pride that even in dire economic times the procession remain large. According to Sendai retainer Mutō Hiroki, "[f]rom the beginning of the Tenpō period [1830–1844] . . . all the great lords like Kii, Mito, Kaga, Satsuma, Hosokawa [Kumamoto], Aki, Kuroda [Fukuoka], Aizu, Echizen, Saga, Mōri [Chōshū] have made reductions below what their status dictates (*bungai no shōryaku*) in the amount of men, arms and military accoutrements. The Sendai lord alone has strictly maintained them all as before."[60] Perhaps Sendai, like Aizu, felt it could not reduce the size of its procession because of the need to protect the reputation of the domain. In explaining the domain's decision in 1721 not to reduce the size of the procession, a senior advisor asked rhetorically, "What will happen to our domain's reputation if it becomes known that our numbers have been reduced?"[61]

Since size imparted prestige, even when daimyo reduced the official numbers in their processions, many hired temporary laborers for departures and arrivals to swell the ranks. The Tokugawa caught on to this gimmick and prohibited it, apparently to no avail.[62] The daimyo expanded the ranks artificially for local consumption as well. One of the senior advisors of Sendai, the castellan of Shiroishi, welcomed the lord at the border of the domain, adding 295 men to the 1,282 already in the daimyo's procession in 1842 for the final leg home to the castle.[63]

Like Sendai, Kaga, for reasons of prestige, did not cut back on the scale of processions over time (see Figure 3.2).[64] Particularly large numbers of men were dispatched after the succession of a new daimyo, as in 1802 when Maeda Tsunanori made his first entry into Kanazawa as lord.[65] This was also an occasion for careful documenting of the size and progress of the retinue as well as making a visual record in scroll form; many procession scrolls were made to mark such occasions.[66]

Kaga, Hiroshima, Tosa, and Okayama were among the largest domains and were therefore most likely to send large numbers of people to Edo. For domains of middling size, producing 50,000 to 200,000 *koku*, we have the examples of Yonezawa (150,000 *koku*), which typically had more than 700 men; Kurume (210,000 *koku*), 804 men in 1706; Uwajima (100,403 *koku*), 539 men in 1800; Miharu (50,000 *koku*), 150 men in 1807, and Nagaoka (74,000 *koku*), 500 men in 1818.[67] According to Maruyama Yasunari, in Kyushu, a daimyo of about 100,000 *koku* would bring roughly 280 men with him, while one of 75,000 *koku* would bring 190. Outside of Kyushu, he holds, processions were in the 150 to 300 range.[68] Falling within these general ranges, Morioka domain (100,000 *koku* until the early nineteenth century) varied from 300 to 600 men.[69] On the far end of the spectrum, however, small branch domains such as Hachinohe (20,000 *koku*), which was one of 161 domains in 1732 producing between 10,000 and 50,000 *koku*, had from fifty to several hundred people in its retinues.[70]

In accounting for the size of Kaga and other domains' processions, we must first look to the large number of hired laborers and others needed to transport the many goods necessary for the procession to make it the mobile fighting force it was intended to be. Almost half of Kaga's procession in 1827 consisted of such men: 35 percent were hired in the domain, the remaining 15 percent hired at post stations from local labor pools, thus helping to support local economies along the highways.[71] Besides the food, drinking water, sake, and soy sauce that were carried in wooden barrels, raincoats, clothing, ammunition (powder,

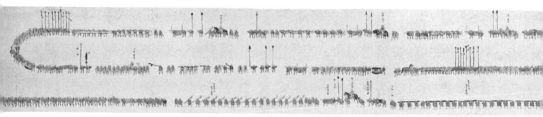

FIGURE 3.2. Procession of the Maeda lord of Kaga domain. "Daimyō gyōretsu emaki." Courtesy of Kanazawa shiritsu Tamagawa toshokan.

balls, fuse cord), portable chairs, and torches and lanterns were needed. For raincoats alone, one retainer of 550 *koku* status, who brought twenty-five men with him to Edo, required two of them to carry rain gear.[72] A number of doctors were needed as well, and in the case of Kaga this included not only a surgeon and acupuncturist but also a veterinarian for horses.[73] According to the Sendai scroll, in addition to the man leading each horse, one man was necessary to carry, in a box suspended on a pole across his shoulder, feed for each horse. Also required in the Kaga procession were five to six carpenters to inspect and/or repair the lord's rooms at official inns; workmen to repair flags, curtains, and carrying cases for guns; cooks; and scribes to keep records and to look up precedents in log books. Finally, the lord always traveled with a portable toilet and bathtub. Some daimyo brought animals, including pets, along with them on the journey as well, and these had to be carried, in the case of the Ōgaki lord's birds, or walked by an attendant, as was the case with the Arima, Sendai, or Matsue lords' dogs.[74] The dogs were often used for hunting and working in conjunction with falcons to retrieve downed birds. Consequently, at least several falconers, together with their animals, were a part of most processions, though some of the birds were meant as gifts for the shogun.

A second element to the spectacle was the attire the men wore, usually coordinated and colorful. To an official in the Kyoto City magistrate's office, the "luxurious display" of the Owari lord's procession was "startling" (*me o odoro-kasu*).[75] Kaempfer, as noted above, remarked that everyone except the palanquin bearers was dressed in resplendent black silk. Though writing of nineteenth-century Philadelphia, Susan G. Davis's comment applies to Tokugawa Japan as well. She noted, "Uniforms reduced variety and effaced individualism, heightening the image of order created by concerted movement. At the same time, costumes caught the eye with a gorgeous and colorful organization of detail."[76] Depictions of the men in Sendai's procession scroll are not individualized, but the painter closely details the clothing and implements carried. The lead

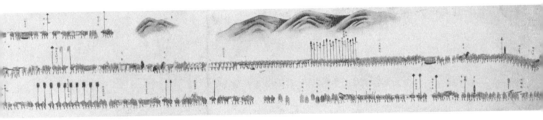

group of gunners is divided into two units, one outfitted with dark blue cotton waistcoats (*haori*) marked with an abstract white, nine-star crest, their guns enclosed in scarlet cloth bags; the other group wears black cotton tops with red seals and carries guns wrapped in black woolen cloth. Similarly, the dress of one lance-carrying unit in the Nanbu domain scroll — formal black waistcoats with a light blue undergarment and black-and-white striped leggings — was a particularly riveting sight. Another remarkable unit consisted of a group of men each carrying two boxes of arrows connected by a wooden pole and covered in red cloth, each decorated with one of the domainal crests, two sparrows surrounded by bamboo leaves. The red of the arrow boxes is contrasted nicely with the yellow color of their leggings and sedge hats. Their formal blue attire is dramatically accented by thick white lines, bent like lightning bolts, down the sleeves. In Kaga domain's procession, members of individual units all wear the same type of clothing, particularly the topcoat and sedge hat; for the latter, a sedge hat from the local Etchū Kosugi area (*sugegasa*), which had a little slope to it, was favored. From a distance, a line of these made an impressive sight. Uniformity seems to have been important even in the rain. If someone in the main body of Kaga domain's procession forgot his rain gear, he was required to drop back to the following group.[77] The spectacle was increased further in Edo, as the members of the processions usually changed into formal attire before entering or departing the city. The various visual and textual sources reveal that there were substantial differences in attire among the domains. From this one might conclude that this was one way daimyo proudly displayed the local culture of their domain to those from other political entities.

Although the attention to appearance and decoration might tempt one to conclude that it was only during the Tokugawa peace that the daimyo became preoccupied with display, this is incorrect. Such concerns were not new to this time and reflected military considerations as well. In the late Sengoku period, the Go-Hōjō of Odawara domain, for example, "ordered their retainers to deco-

rate ornately their weapons and armor and to dress their *matamoto* [subretainers] in colorful costumes," especially when they were to accompany the lord. To have one's followers dressed gaily, as if on parade, "was a means not only for stirring up the fighting spirit of one's own forces but also for intimidating the enemy and winning over the people."[78] In other words, dress had a clear military function.

A third, related, element was the weapons and other implements carried (discussed below). These, together with the numbers of marchers, constituted a demonstration of military power that was meant to awe, to display the lord's status and authority. But the procession was also, in effect, a demonstration of Tokugawa authority, since it was known to all that the shogunate was commanding these processions to move to Edo and back.

FIGURE 3.3. Procession from Sendai domain. Rakuzan-kō ogyōretsu zukan. Courtesy of Sendai shiritsu hakubutsukan.

The implements carried either had a military function or served as status markers, but there were other objects carried in some processions that seem to have had both religious and theatrical elements. In the Sendai scroll (Figure 3.3), this is evident from the very beginning of the procession, which was marked by four sets of porters carrying long containers, each covered in red cloth and topped with a combination of purifying Shinto wand and mask. The masks are representations of Ebisu, *kami* of good fortune, Okame (on two containers), a folk symbol of fertility, and the humorous *hyottoko*. These various religious and folk objects, which were often used in local festivals, heading the procession presented the lord's arrival as a festive occurrence, one that would bring happiness and good fortune and drive away evil. In a case such as this, with a lord making his first appearance in the domain as ruler, these symbols conveyed an ideological message from him that his rule would not be harsh, but rather would bring prosperity to all.

Related to this political message is an exotic object that appears toward the middle of the same Sendai procession. It is a combination of thickly padded saddle on the bottom, like those used on the roads near Ise shrine for pilgrims, and a black chair used by monks (*kyokuroku*) on top. The lacquer frame perched on top of the red and green padding is open in the rear and would offer no back support. All in all, it seems quite unwieldy and uncomfortable, and therefore it is unlikely that it was actually used by the lord for riding. Behind the lacquer frame, on opposite sides, appear two short decorative sheaths (*keyari*), topped with bird feathers. Kaempfer actually viewed the object in the procession of the lord of Kii, though he made no association with a monk's chair. He noted that the object was on the last of a group of four horses, "which carried a black chair placed on a black seat with two large pike-tufts at the back and three or four black and white feather standards at the side, in front, and behind."[79] In the Sendai scroll, where the black chair is without the sheaths, the object together with the horse are referred to as *otsuzura uma* (*tsuzura* can refer to what is usually a wicker basket for transporting goods or a wicker seat/saddle for a rider). In each of the processions the horses bearing the seats are in line with the lord's horse or his spare horses, which indicates that the device was also meant for the lord's use, at least in a symbolic sense. Whatever its origins, it was an object of display. The Nagoya retainer known as Enkōan (Kōroki Takenobu) remarked that the example in the Aizu procession that passed through his domain was of "unparalleled beauty."[80] Perhaps this was merely another exotic object that marked the lord's high status, but the association of the lord with a wise Buddhist monk who lectures his followers was probably intentional.

Two other elements of the theatrical performance involved the form of movement, that is, the way the men in the retinue made their progress and the sounds that accompanied them. Kaempfer wrote that the men attending the lord of Kii marched in strict formation so that "they somehow seemed to be crouching together and marched in total silence."[81] The order to "fix the line" (*gyōretsu o tateru*) occurred just before a procession arrived at a castle town or a major post station, including a checking station, revealing the daimyo as political actor who wanted to impress the audience, checking his appearance before stepping foot on stage. In practical terms this meant aligning the queue, adjusting helmets, synchronizing steps, raising lances (from a resting position on the shoulder), and mounting horses.[82] From what Heinrich Schliemann witnessed in Japan in 1865, this was also highlighted by the bravura performance of the retainers he saw in a number of processions, who looked sideways at the people in an intimidating fashion.[83]

Numerous observers made comments about the quiet through which the procession passed. In contrast to Elizabethan England, spectators in Tokugawa Japan were hushed, a sign of respect and hospitality. Moreover, the retinue moved with little sound, giving the procession an air of effortlessness, solemnity, and grandeur.[84] Likewise, the closed formation and silent mode of progression made the procession an exercise in self-discipline and martial vigor.

The silence of the procession, however, was punctuated at certain points by two types of sounds — sounds that added greater weight to the silence that preceded and followed them. It was first broken by the local officials who walked ahead of the procession when it began its passage through post stations or castle towns, calling out "*Shita ni iro, shita ni iro.*" To this was later added another theatrical element of sight and sound, as the *yakko* footmen (Figures 3.4 and 3.5) toward the front and at various other locations in the procession walked with a slow, unique step, moving side to side and raising their arms and legs. Doing so made the fringes, feathers, or animal hair on top of their decorative lances swirl gracefully. The cycle of the performance also included the men tossing these objects into the air to partners, who would catch them and continue. This male posturing added an element found in parades in nineteenth-century Philadelphia, where "all participants assumed the masculine posture, stepping high, chest expanded, as they marched into the public ceremony."[85] This was theater, meant for an audience. Having marched hard, on average ten *ri* (about forty kilometers) per day, the men in daimyo retinues reserved the performance for short stints when the procession would have the largest audience and hence the maximum impact.

Like their counterpart across the ocean, the Tokugawa daimyo processions were "almost exclusively male affairs," adding a different sort of affinity with the theater, the kabuki version that by the end of the seventeenth century was a strictly male production. In this skewed gender scheme, women, when they were a part of the procession, were always few in number, came toward the rear of the procession, and were not visible to the observer; indeed, they were withdrawn into closed palanquins. None are visible in any of the numerous procession scrolls and images I have viewed. Displaying their femininity to the public eye would detract from the martial character of the procession.[86]

Dance added to the theater that was the daimyo procession. In one scene from the "Kishū han sankin kōtai gyōretsu zu," mentioned above, a young boy points at one of the decorative lances being held high by a carrier; in conversation with her son, the mother smiles. Here and elsewhere in the main body of the procession we can discern, by the raised position of the feet and the footmen's body position, that a dance on the part of the footmen is taking place. Several men have their free hand held straight out, just as Kaempfer critically described it in the early eighteenth century:

FIGURE 3.4. *Yakko* footmen in Nanokaichi domain procession. Nanokaichi hanshu Osaka tōjō zu. Courtesy of Gunma kenritsu hakubutsukan.

It is ridiculous to see how the bearers of pikes and *norimono* have their clothes tucked in high at the back to publicly display their bare buttocks with only a narrow loincloth down the gap. Also how the bodyguards and bearers of pikes, the sun hat, parasol, and boxes put on a swaggering gait when they pass through inhabited areas and meet other processions. With every step they kick up their heels nearly to their backsides and at the same time thrust the opposite arm forward, so that it looks as if they are swimming in the air. Adopting the same rhythm, the bearers with each step twirl around their pikes, the hat, and the parasol a number of times, and the *hasamibako* are kept in constant motion on men's shoulders. The *norimono* porters bare their arms, tying up their sleeves by threading a string through them, and carry their burden one moment on their shoulders, the next on one hand raised above the head, while the other arm is held stretched out horizontally palm up. The gesturing of this spare arm in combination with their short steps done with stiff knees make a ludicrous display of fear and caution.[87]

The "swimming in the air" Kaempfer described can be observed in the *yakko* depicted in the "Tōkaidō dōchū fūkei byōbu" and is similar to the movement

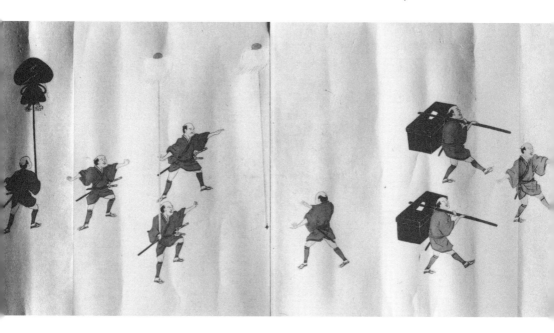

in kabuki known as *idaten hashiri*; the element of foot stomping in synchrony with arm movements is likewise similar to the *roppō furi*.[88] Matsudaira Sadanobu's son Shinkō and Confucian scholar Dazai Shundai also found the theatrical element a bit excessive, the former ridiculing the artificiality of the high stepping manner of the spear-wielding *yakko* and the latter describing these movements as "displaying arrogance" (*bōjaku bujin naru tei o nasu*).[89] While these observers were put off by the theatricality of the processions, it may have been this very quality that accounts for their serving as the background for, or the subtext of, numerous woodblock prints and picture game boards.

Another obvious theatrical element was observable in the processions of only some of the most prestigious daimyo houses, like Sendai, whose gunners were allowed to light a segment of fuse cord, which gave off a bluish white smoke, while walking through castle towns. This only added to the display of the procession. It was also an indication that the implements being carried were indeed weapons, though safety and economics did not allow them to be fired while the procession walked through populated settlements.

This theatrical scenario was, to be sure, more restrained than in many other parts of the contemporary world. In early modern France, for example, processions often "opened with a burst of color and sound from the ceremonial

FIGURE 3.5. Boy playing with *yakko* doll. "Sōhitsu gojūsantsugi. Nihonbashi."
Courtesy of Kumon kodomo kenkyūjo.

guard" and included "a trumpeter in a red costume with silver lace, who cleared the way for dignitaries behind him with a blast of music."[90] The restraint exhibited in Tokugawa processions, observable in the slow manner in which they passed through post stations and castle towns, reflected the stately manner in which authority was ideally exercised. Tokugawa processions were more restrained than those in France perhaps, but they still were drama—colorful displays of marching men whose silent passage was punctuated only by the road clearers and the theatrics of the *yakko* footmen. They were theater enough for the roughly five hundred spectators depicted observing the Kii lord pass through the area of Anryu post station near Osaka. A crowd of spectators at an unidentified post station on the Hokkoku kaidō watched the procession of the Kaga lord, amazingly, from the comfort of covered reviewing stands, which protected them from the elements (Figure 3.6). The commoners there appear to be on their knees, while in contrast two officials in formal attire are on all fours with their faces toward the ground.[91] According to an unidentified source that Sendai retainer Mutō Hiroki quotes in the textual comments accompanying his procession scroll, "[c]rowds of people, young and old, lined the road from the domain compound at Shiba [in Edo] all the way to Senjū [on the outskirts of the city] to view the procession, with its variety of unusual objects."[92]

Various visual texts were available to help spectators read the processions. Although it is a rare example, *surimono*, a type of woodblock-printed newssheet, were made and presumably made available for purchase to help spectators interpret the three-thousand-man procession of Kumamoto domain. Supporting this interpretation is that in the top portion of the paper are headnotes that list the various parts of the procession.[93] More commonly, viewers apparently used books of heraldry to identify and read processions. These books, which were widely available by the early eighteenth century, also reveal an element of sport to viewing daimyo processions, as the owners "checked off species [in their books] as if building lifetime lists of sightings."[94]

The theatrical element of daimyo processions is also revealed in the integration of these events in commoner life through imitation. This imitation can be seen in the behavior of young boys and sometimes even adults mimicking daimyo processions in their play, as captured for example in Kitao Shigemasa's print "Yatsushi hakkei Seta no sekishō" (Figure 3.7), in which three children are imitating a daimyo procession crossing the Seta bridge (Ōmi province), thereby recognizing, if only implicitly, the procession as a site of power and status.[95] Certain forms from daimyo processions also found their way into local festivals, as evidenced in places such as Niimi and Yagake (both in Okayama Prefecture), Iwataki (the northern part of Kyoto Prefecture), Ōi (Shizuoka), Hagi (Yamaguchi), Yuzawa (Akita), and Kōchi (Kōchi Prefecture). In all but the latter, this

FIGURE 3.6. Crowd viewing procession of Kaga lord. From "Daimyō gyōretsu zu." Courtesy of Kanazawa shiritsu Tamagawa toshokan.

practice continues even today.[96] In Niimi in particular, old cultural forms have been maintained but at the same time transformed and put to new uses. For at least 250 years local residents in Niimi have taken part in a festival in which part of the form of the daimyo procession has been maintained. Referred to variously as the "Goshinkō buki gyōretsu matsuri" ("festival of transporting the kami and the procession of arms"), "daimyō gyōretsu matsuri" ("daimyo procession festival") or "dogeza matsuri" ("kneeling festival"), it is a fall festival of thanksgiving for the harvest, which also has its origins in the support of the local daimyo, the Seki lord of Niimi, whose domain was established only in 1697.[97]

The procession festival in its current manifestation is said to be a "faithful" recreation of the Seki lord's first entry into his new domain, consisting of sixty-four men in formal period attire, including road clearers and men holding lances, decorative spears, guns, bows, and various containers for footwear and baggage. Occupying the center of the procession is a white horse, symbolic of

FIGURE 3.7.
Children imitating
a daimyo proces-
sion. "Yatsushi hak-
kei Seta no sekisho."
Courtesy of Kumon
kodomo kenkyūjo.

the lord. The men in arms act as a military guard for the local deities in portable
shrines being transported on a set course through the town.[98] Part of the "authenticity" of the procession festival is also said to lie in the custom of "hospitality" for the procession. Local merchants and residents along the course build
sand mounds, topping them off with purifying salt. Observers are required to
get down on their knees before the procession, though in its current interpretation this means simply to be seated on the ground or to squat, not necessarily to
prostrate oneself. Those who remain standing even after the road clearers call
out "*Shita (ni), Shita (ni)*" are ordered to get down, as this researcher observed
in 2003.

The daimyo procession, as practiced in Niimi, demonstrated the town's important links to its early modern past. It also revealed how for many Japanese,

daimyo processions are emblematic of the Tokugawa period.[99] It is perhaps because the Japanese, like the "Indians and perhaps all peoples, think of their culture encapsulated in such discrete performances, which they can exhibit to outsiders as well as to themselves," that the people of Niimi took their festival to France in 1992.[100]

In 1860 the American merchant Francis Hall observed a festival similar to Niimi's taking place in July in honor of Benten, the deity of the sea, which he likened to Carnival. The festival was divided into a number of different sections, the eighth such unit a representation of a daimyo retinue passing through the streets of Edo. The lord's palanquin "was preceded by pike and standard bearers, armor bearers, weapon bearers who wound along with a peculiar slow and mock dignified step, for this scene was evidently a half caricature." Inside the palanquin rode not a lord but a fox, and on each side of the vehicle "walked three men clad in female attire, their faces painted and colored like so many harlequins."[101] In this festival we see both gender and social inversion, commoners imitating if not mimicking their social superiors, while at the same time the target of their humor reveals the importance of that social practice as a symbol of warrior authority. One cannot help but wonder how widespread this imitation was in other festivals across the country. As a result of such manifestations, though, one can argue that the political and cultural impact of the daimyo processions, like the foreign embassies, "was felt far beyond the confines of the prescribed route, to a greater social and cultural depth, and over a much longer chronological span than the ephemeral, 'event' quality of the historical . . . [events] would suggest."[102]

It is important to remember that depictions of daimyo processions in woodblock prints and in scrolls are in one sense simply images reflecting the biases of the artists and their patrons. Documentation produced by artists under domainal patronage, reflecting the perspective of the samurai leadership, presented images of processions proceeding in a grand, stately manner. The formal processions evident in these media were only seen in castle towns, in post stations, and in Edo, when the procession was a unified body. Nonofficial artists, including woodblock artists like Hiroshige and the artist of the Kishū scroll, were more likely to capture the real-life, slightly less grand images. Since daimyo processions routinely covered thirty-five to forty kilometers or more in a day, they did not always proceed in an orderly fashion. The tail end of the Wakayama lord's procession depicted in the Kishū scroll is far less orderly than the earlier sections. In it one can observe that some men are holding their lances across a shoulder rather than straight up. Small numbers of men throughout the procession have turned the upper parts of their bodies back, no doubt to talk with someone behind them. Understandably, boredom — and physical exhaustion — would not have been uncommon. Sometimes nature called; the anonymous creator of the "Ōshū kaidō ezu" depicted one man in the procession — apparently toward the rear of it, as the formation is rather sparse at that point — standing, his back to the viewer, apparently relieving himself in a rice field.[103]

The samurai ideal of respectful commoners bowing before daimyo processions was similarly not always a reality. There is evidence that some commoners in the late Tokugawa period were less respectful of daimyo processions than before. This is not surprising given the general trend of questioning or disrespecting authority noted by many observers.[104] Examining local documentation from Chōshū domain, Taniguchi Shinko has discovered an increased incidence of commoners not prostrating themselves as processions went by. She found twenty-one occurrences reported between 1744 and 1789. The punishment in these cases could be either a monetary fine or banishment, although we are not told how the cases were resolved. In one case in Edo, a commoner, who was drunk, cut in front of a daimyo procession at Edobashi. He was warned by a retainer but talked back and consequently was cut down.[105]

In certain parts of Edo the passage of daimyo processions was probably too common a sight to interrupt the patterns of life. For example, in the image of Kasumigaseki in the *Edo meisho zue*, the artist depicts a scene in which two daimyo processions are about to pass one another. Commoners in the scene continue going about their business in a seemingly carefree manner; none of them stop and drop to their knees. Two peddlers continue walking parallel to the retinues, though staying at the edge of the road, and one of them turns the upper half of his body to observe the processions. One group of two men in the middle ground stops to observe the procession while another pair talks, oblivious to the men walking by. Near the head of the procession closest to the viewer a samurai with an attendant bows to the procession, but two commoner women, under a parasol and directly in the line of the procession, are standing and watching.[106]

Composition of the Procession: People and Regalia

The composition of the processions can be examined using a variety of written and graphic sources. While there is a dearth of commercial art work in which the daimyo processions are the main subject matter, daimyo ordered that scrolls be created depicting a procession from their domain, most often it seems to commemorate his first entry to the domain. These scrolls most often consist of a static depiction of the retinue members without any geographic or other background visual detail or a depiction of the procession moving through time and space in its journey across Japan. These supplement various written accounts by foreigners as well as the occasional comments made by native observers. From these various sources we can determine that the processions, while different in matters of size and the type of equipment carried, also shared significant common features that reflected both their military character as well as the pacific nature of the times.

Kaempfer was one foreigner who had occasion to watch numerous processions. He described in detail the passage of an "ordinary daimyo . . . whose processions are no different and fit the same description [as those of important daimyo from Satsuma, Kaga, Owari, etc.], except for their special pikes, personal crests, number of led horses, bearers of hasamibako [a rectangular box for clothing and other items, attached to a pole and carried on the shoulder], porters of sedan chairs and their companions, as well as some arbitrary variations in the order of marching."[107] As this is the only contemporaneous, extended description of a daimyo procession, it is quoted at length. Kaempfer noted that there were:

1. Several advance parties consisting of quartermasters, scribes, cooks, and their assistants, who prepared the inns for the dignified accommodation of the lord and his courtiers [attendants].

2. The lord's personal luggage, some items transported in packs on horses, each marked with a small personal flag and the name of the owner, some carried in large boxes covered with lacquered leather and painted with the lord's personal crest. Each piece is accompanied by various attendants to add to the grandeur.

3. A long trail of lesser retinues of the lord's most senior servants and nobles, accompanied by men carrying pikes, scythes, parasols [a ceremonial umbrella wrapped and tied up], and small boxes, and grooms leading horses, all according to each man's birth, rank, and proper station, with the principals in *norimono, kago,* or riding horses.

4. The lord and his personal escort, marching in unusual formation, as well as various troops of soldiers, each led by a marshal and consisting of:

   i. Five horses, some less sprightly than others, each with a groom at the side and two servants following behind;

   ii. Five, six, or more burly porters walking in single file with *hasamibako,* or small lacquered boxes, some also with rather delicate, lacquered baskets on their shoulders, containing clothes and other items kept in readiness for the lord, with each porter being accompanied by two attendants walking behind;

   iii. Ten or more men bearing arms, walking in single file with scythes, pikes, valuable small swords, and guns in wooden, lacquered cases, as well as quivers with bows and arrows. Occasionally the size of this party is made larger by placing porters of *hasamibako* and led horses in between the men.

iv. Two, three, and more personal, ornamental pikes, with bunches of black cock feathers at the top, dressed and covered with certain rough skins or other ornaments specific to the lord. These are carried in single file and each is followed by a servant.

v. The sun hat covered in black velvet with two officials walking behind.

vi. A sun parasol, covered and accompanied in the same fashion.

vii. Various additional *hasamibako* and personal luggage covered with lacquered leather and with the golden imprint of the lord's coat of arms, each piece accompanied by two attendants.

viii. About sixteen bodyguards in rows of two as advance party of the lord's *norimono*. For this task the tallest men available are searched out and employed.

ix. The *norimono*, or palanquin, in which the lord sits, carried by six to eight uniformed men, who are often relieved by an equally large party of men. The palanquin is accompanied on each side by two or three valets to hand the lord whatever he desires and assist him in getting in and out of the palanquin.

x. Two or three saddled horses with saddles covered in black, the last one carrying a large armchair covered with black velvet on a *norikake* that is also covered in black velvet, with each of these horses led and accompanied by the appropriate number of attendants. These personal horses of the lord are often led by men from his bodyguard.

xi. Two pike bearers.

xii. Ten or more people each carrying two incredibly large baskets, one in front and one behind, suspended from a pole over their shoulders. Their function is to enhance the usual display rather than to be of any practical use. Sometimes these men alternate with porters carrying cases and *hasamibako*. The lord's personal party is followed by:

   a. Six to twelve horses with their grooms and attendants.

   b. A large rear guard of the lord's servants with their official valets and pike and *hasamibako* bearers. Some are carried in *kago*, or there might only be one *norimono* at the head with the lord's highest minister or steward.

In his lengthy description, Kaempfer first makes note of the men in the procession, the retainers, the lord, and the menials who provided support for them. In reading it one should not forget that alternate attendance was a form of military service whereby the daimyo and his small army traveled from the seat of his administration to a point of service, the capital of his overlord in Edo.

The march was a type of military maneuver, with forced progress of upwards of forty kilometers a day over whatever distance the retinue had to cover to and from the domain. This is graphically depicted in the "Ōshū kaidō ezu," where we see the retinue from an unidentified domain moving at a fast pace through a hilly area in Shimotsuke (Tochigi).[108]

The composition of the retinue replicated the form of a military force setting out for battle, but with certain important modifications. The retinue can be considered in most general terms in two or three parts. First came the vanguard, or attack force, led by a domain senior advisor. He acted as general, and in the case of attack was trusted with complete authority by the daimyo to direct battle. The senior advisor contributed substantial numbers of men to the procession; in the case of a large domain such as Chōshū he brought along 260 retainers and 496 subretainers, as much as 40 percent of the total.[109] Second came the main body, sometimes referred to as the "inner procession," which consisted of a group of retainers whose duty it was to protect the lord. Lastly, there was the "rear guard," which was deployed at the back of the procession to protect against attacks from behind. This group was frequently headed by a senior advisor as well. Oftentimes, however, only the main body is depicted in procession scrolls.

In battle an army was led by an advance force. For example, according to the Shimabara Battle screen, which depicted the last major battle of the Tokugawa period, the advance force was far larger than the lord's and contained a significant number of mounted warriors. During Tokugawa times it was unusual to have a large number of horses in the procession. This was no doubt a cost-saving device, but it was also indicative of the changed character of the procession in peacetime. Similarly, the advance group tended to be abbreviated, making the main segment of the procession, the portion in which the lord was located, more central.[110] Symbolism was thus emphasized in the pacific display that characterized the modified procession of the era.

As the lord was paramount, he occupied roughly the central position in the procession. In the "Kishū Wakayama han" depiction of a daimyo procession, the second group, centering on the lord, does not begin until the fifteenth of forty segments of the scroll. The main body of the procession, like the *hatamoto zonae* force in a wartime army upon which it was based, was primarily defensive in nature.[111] The lord traveled in his palanquin, which was itself a great symbol of status with a myriad of variations in construction and finish, surrounded and protected by a compact group of samurai designated for that purpose.[112] In Kaempfer's words, the lord "was traveling in closed formation with his courtiers."[113] More than a century later, Francis Hall noted: "The procession had been filing along slowly in this manner for nearly an hour when the train began to move in a more compact mass, for the lord of Owari himself was approaching." The bodyguard around the lord, by his account, "contained seven hundred men."[114] In the Kishū scroll (Figure 3.3), the lord was backed up by some seventy double-sworded men; for Chōshū, seventy-five men were clustered around the lord.[115] These were men of high rank who formed an elite bodyguard while the lord traveled.

The vanguard of the first group, the attack force, made it clear that the daimyo procession was a relic of the military formation.[116] It consisted of men carrying three types of weapons. Their function was to clear the way in a military sense for the main body of the procession. The lead and principal weapon was the musket. Typically, a unit of twenty to thirty gunners was followed by spearmen and archers, though the order of the latter two was sometimes reversed. Each unit was led by a unit commander. A mounted warrior, accompanied by several men before and after him (subretainers or menials), was interspersed between units. The social ranking was not as clearly laid out as Kaempfer suggests. Marius Jansen, reading Kaempfer, notes that the warriors were "arranged from low to highest rank as the daimyo palanquin nears, and then tapering off again in reverse sequence."[117] In fact, while relatively low-ranking men led the procession, each group of twenty to thirty men was led by a higher-ranking unit commander.

The dominant position of the musket in the vanguard reflected changes in the nature of military warfare that took place during the sixteenth and early seventeenth centuries. This is evident in depictions of the Battle of Shimabara in 1638. In the two famous six-paneled screens of the Akitsuki lord's military force heading for battle, archers are not visible until the end of the second of six rows, which move back and forth across the screen, revealing their secondary position in the hierarchy of Tokugawa weaponry.[118] The order of guns, bows, spears, and cavalry (though abbreviated in the daimyo procession), prevailed among the domains "because strategists envisioned a battle plan in which, reflecting the nature of the weapons, the order of combat would proceed from muskets to bows to spears and would culminate in a cavalry battle."[119]

In the Shimabara screens, the lord sits on his chestnut-colored steed, as befitting a leader on his way to battle, with a bright red covering on the horse under the saddle, close to the center (absolute center would have placed part of his body across two different panels). The division between the attack force and the main force is conspicuously marked by tall black-and-white banners. In alternate attendance processions the two groups are more subtly yet, to the informed observer, clearly separated by physical space, the beginning of the main segment with the lord marked by the presence of road clearers. The clearers, like the daimyo's frequent use of the palanquin, are indicative of the modifications made to the form of the processions in peacetime.

Following the main unit centered on the lord came the rear guard, or *shin-*

gari, in which doctors, spare horses, and palanquins bearing retainers who worked the night shift or who otherwise required relief could be found.

While the shogunate attempted to regulate the numbers in a procession, fixing numerical figures based on *kokudaka*, we noted that these numbers appear to have referred only to those in the main body of the procession, that is, those attached to the lord. The majority of the men in a procession were not under the direct authority of the lord, but rather retainers of his vassals (subretainers). In the case of a small domain such as Ichinoseki (thirty thousand *koku*) there might be rough parity (48 retainers and 49 subretainers in a procession of 218 in 1831), but in the case of a large domain such as Okayama the gap could be quite pronounced. In 1698, for example, there were 756 subretainers in contrast to 115 direct retainers of the lord; and for Kaga, 830 subretainers and 185 direct retainers.[120]

Looking at the procession more specifically in terms of status, as befitting a military force, samurai (*shi*) made up the core of the procession — roughly 20 percent of the retinue in many domains, though in some the figure could be much higher.[121] For Hachinohe in 1854, there were 37 samurai out of 202 people (18 percent). Numerically, pages (*komono*) were the single largest group (47, or 23 percent), followed by subretainers (37, or 18 percent), and footsoldiers (25, or 12 percent). Hired workers necessary to support the movements of their social superiors (46) made up another 18 percent. The remaining personnel were doctors (2), tea specialists (2), *sōji bōzu* (1), palanquin bearers (9), horse grooms (5), and carriers of small implements (15).[122]

Returning to Kaempfer's description of the daimyo procession, it is clear that he emphasizes the accoutrements carried in the procession. These various implements and paraphernalia were "tokens of identity" and like the badges, sashes, ribbons, and banners carried in parades in America, "unified marchers and separated them from their audience."[123] In Tokugawa Japan the richness of color and material, together with the artifacts carried, were intended as displays of wealth, rank, military power, and authority. Just as the size of the procession and the attire of the men in it were indicators of a lord's status, most of the regalia displayed, which was precisely dictated by shogunal regulation, publicly proclaimed the lord's place in the political universe. These were visual elements of political power, reflections of a lord's position in the daimyo hierarchy, his relationship to the Tokugawa, and the family's past military achievements. These status distinctions were well known and recorded in the warrior books of heraldry, which included drawings of some of the implements and were widely available from commercial publishers since the seventeenth century.[124] A form of serial publication, like calendars, the books enjoyed the tacit approval of the Tokugawa. They were constantly updated, and this "was some indication of their functional value in the complex bureaucratic world of Edo."[125] Thus the processions were texts that could be read, more or less precisely, by observers who could then rank the lords.

The procession in its entirety can be read as a status symbol. The implements carried, like the overall size and sartorial makeup of the procession, were of great significance. The number of spears and *hasamibako* and their placement in the procession were also markers, as was the presence (or absence) of halberds, the type of vehicle in which the lord rode, the type and shape of umbrella used, and so forth. That a number of the implements carried were highly ornamental led one scholar to criticize the processions as "a decadent survival of the warlike columns of armed men who accompanied their lord to battle or attended him on his journeys in the days before the long Tokugawa peace."[126] Certainly in a time of prolonged peace great attention was paid to status distinctions in many sectors of Tokugawa life, and it is not surprising therefore that this would be the case with such a visible symbol of authority as the daimyo procession. But, as noted before, samurai believed that colorful displays of clothing and decorated weaponry had a definite military function.

Of the various implements, lances or spears were one of the most important status markers. As a Tokugawa-era poem declares, "A daimyo's spear / Without speaking / Announces the lord's name."[127] Germane here were not only the number and type of lances but the pattern of their arrangement and their position in the procession. The number of spears before and after the lord's palanquin was dependent on his status. Members of the related Tokugawa families were allowed four (two in front, two behind), Satsuma and Sendai a total of three, two in front and one behind. Lesser lords might have only one or two. Having two across was a mark of distinction and required shogunal permission. Great stock was also put in the spears' decorative covers, the distinctive shapes of which identified specific lords. A red handle, symbolic of blood spilt on the battlefield, was a sign of a family's ancestors' military valor and of loyalty to the shogun.[128] Given the importance of the lance as a marker of the lord's status, attention was paid to the physical stature and looks of the men. Good looks and tall stature, rather than skill with the lance, were the key attributes. Theatrical imperatives warped military prerogatives and skills.

Hasamibako were another important accoutrement, as it was a site where the daimyo displayed the family crest; it was a particular mark of distinction to be allowed to have one embossed in gold. As with the lances, a further indicator of high status was the privilege, allotted to only twenty daimyo, of having a pair of men, rather than a single one, carry *hasamibako*. Fukuoka domain, for example, was allowed to increase the number of spears and *hasamibako* (from one of each to two of each) in front of the lord's palanquin after receiving an heir from the Tokugawa house of Hitotsubashi.[129] They were positioned before and after the lord's palanquin. These boxes were small, so most of the lord's possessions, not to mention most of the luggage for the members of the procession, were carried in rectangular chests called *nagamochi*.

The mere presence of certain objects indicated a lord's high status. A *naginata*, or halberd, for example, was allowed only for thirty-one daimyo houses. It is said that the fifth shogun Tsunayoshi would not allow even Yanagisawa, his top advisor and paramour, to use it. Portable tea kits — an iron teapot, tea cups, and brazier — were likewise restricted to certain daimyo, about thirty in number, all with holdings in excess of one hundred thousand *koku*.[130]

While many objects carried were practical in nature — rain gear, other clothing, food, armor, powder, money, the lord's bathtub — some were highly ornamental and highlighted the theatrical character of the procession. In the Morioka procession scroll, a man holding a *daigasa*, a rain helmet mounted on a pole, was followed by a man holding a *tategasa*, a regular umbrella with a long handle, both of which might in other cases have been covered with black velvet or some other type of cloth and tied up with a purple or black cord. These men were followed by two others carrying decorative lances topped with swan feathers. Black swan feathers, black or white bear hair, or monkey hair were other possibilities. A monkey hair–covered decorative lance and a spear sheath covered in sea otter skin (i.e., a foreign object) were distinguishing markers of the retinues of the lord of Morioka and Sendai, respectively.[131] In Tosa a special type of fowl (*onaga dori*) was bred to produce unique feathers for the decorative lances that made the Tosa procession immediately recognizable.[132] While alternate attendance affected Japanese culture in myriad ways, this may be the singular case in which it impacted local practices in animal husbandry. In any case, the decorative lances gave daimyo another way to display the local culture of their domain.

Closer investigation into some of the accoutrements as revealed in a procession scroll of Morioka domain reveals the political relationship between the Nanbu lord and the Tokugawa. The family crest of the Nanbu family, two cranes facing center, was embossed in gold on objects carried in the procession with shogunal permission only. It stood out brilliantly on the red-lacquered leather material covering the *hasamibako* and chests. Also symbolic of the relationship between Tokugawa and lord were two tiger skins, which were used as covers for the daimyo's spare horses. The skins were obtained as gifts from the first shogun, Ieyasu, to the second Nanbu daimyo, Toshinao, early in the seventeenth century. They therefore symbolized the historic relationship of lord and subject between the two houses. The same was true of the scarlet leather bags, used to cover the lord's musket, given by the second shogun, Hidetada, to

Nanbu Toshinao. Also in the procession, but intended as gifts from the current daimyo to the current shogun, were several hawks and Nanbu horses, known for their speed. These gifts, too, demonstrated the historic and ritual ties between daimyo and shogun.

That these markers of status were important to the lords is revealed in the lengths to which daimyo went to acquire them. One domain, for example, tried to bolster its visual status by using gold seals when it was not qualified to do so. Hachinohe, a small domain of eighteen thousand *koku*, masked this deception by covering up the gold seals until the procession passed beyond Senjū, beyond the city limits of Edo.[133] Daimyo could and did petition the Tokugawa for the right to use and display certain objects. Aizu, for example, made a request to use a lacquered palanquin (for the lord), to have three spears accompany the lord's palanquin (two in front and one in back), and to have a tiger skin saddle cover on the lord's spare horse. The application was made after the lord had successfully completed a period of duty as the shogunal messenger to the imperial court, and that permission was granted for all three items in the request might be interpreted as the government's sign of appreciation for the Aizu lord's service. A year later, though, another request from Aizu, to emboss its *hasamibako* with gold seals, was not accepted completely. The lord was allowed to display them only outside Edo![134]

This discussion of the regulation of the panoply of regalia brings to mind Philip Brown's notion of the Tokugawa as a "flamboyant" state whose leaders "employ displays of the state's nominal authority to serve important symbolic functions."[135] All the pomp that the term implies was certainly present in early modern Japan, not only "fully marshaled on behalf of the hegemons in the political use of Noh drama, monumental castle architecture, and tea ceremonies,"[136] but also quite visible in the daimyo processions which paraded on the highways leading from all corners of the country to Edo and back. During those migrations, the shogunate was in effect parading daimyo past other daimyo and infringing upon the authority of daimyo as domainal rulers by commanding them to allow others through their domains both on and off the official Gokaidō network of highways, which was Tokugawa territory. The annual movements of the lords were in this regard nothing more than a performance that expressed the supreme position of shogunal authority. Moreover, the Tokugawa's regulation of the accoutrements of the parade set daimyo in competition with each other. The special gold seals, lances, tea boxes, and other status markers all reminded the daimyo that they held their domains at the pleasure of the shogun. Peter Kornicki writes that "it remains remarkable" in the light of the prohibition on foreigners purchasing *bukan* "and the insistence on censorship edicts on avoiding reference in print to contemporary officials, that the Bakufu [shogunate] tolerated the exposure of its personnel to the public gaze in this way."[137] The shogunate wanted this information — about *all* daimyo — made publicly available, as it reinforced its sovereign position, which included its powers to regulate the symbols of authority and status. These two points — competition and the subordinate position of the daimyo — were made clear in all the paraphernalia regulated in the daimyo procession, but also by those things that more directly revealed ties to the Tokugawa, for example, the tiger skins bequeathed by the first Tokugawa shogun to the Nanbu lord or the routine gifts of horses and hawks presented to the shoguns.

Daimyo clearly had different agendas in displaying the variety of objects regulated by the Tokugawa. They were probably less interested in elevating the shogunate's position than in performing their own status. They revealed to informed observers the position of the lord in the hierarchy of Tokugawa society. The parading of the physical manifestations of historic ties to the shogunal family was meant to elevate the position of the daimyo through association with the hegemonic power. The comments of Furukawa Koshōken that the Sendai lord's procession was "far superior" to that of Satsuma, Kurume retainer Maki Yasuomi's comparison of the retinues of Kumamoto and Chōshū, and Hachinohe's illicit use of gold seals suggests that there was a competitive dimension to alternate attendance. Daimyo were, in other words, performing for each other up and down the highways of Tokugawa Japan and in the shogun's capital of Edo. When they could afford it, and sometimes even when they could not, many tried to exceed their status by bringing to Edo larger numbers of men than shogunal regulations allowed.

Daimyo had multiple agendas, though, in staging these displays of power and authority, and they were concerned with multiple audiences. While in public (that is, Tokugawa) space, daimyo competed with one another in their performative movements before spectators from whatever domains through which their processions passed. But the daimyo were also concerned about the processions as displays of their authority when in private (their own domainal) space. Many lords boosted the numbers in their processions when they reached the borders of their domains, either by employing temporary laborers or by adding the substantive retinue of a senior advisor who joined the lords' as they paraded through the home territory, no doubt anticipating the crowds that would witness their passage through the domain and arrival in the castle town. These dual agendas overlapped of course, and this was particularly evident when a lord made his first entry into the domain as ruler, when the numbers in the procession tended to be much higher. Witness the impressive size, three thousand men, in Hosokawa Narimori's entourage on his first trip to Kumamoto as lord around 1826, as compared with the 694 men accompanying his predecessor in

1812. The impetus to display the daimyo's authority through the sheer numbers of men in the procession was probably even greater when the man in question was adopted, as was the case with Narimori. No doubt it was also because of the larger numbers involved that a first entry was documented for posterity in print or scroll form.

Symbols of political authority, the parades also reflected the social hierarchies and conditions of the time, reinforcing the centrality of the lord and his samurai, around whom the social structure was constructed. The lengths of the trains of men were generally diminished by the financial exigencies that developed from the early eighteenth century, but their basic nature as spectacle and symbol of authority remained unchanged for the remainder of the period, even to be recreated by later political entities seeking to link past and present.

4

Assignment
Edo

ALTERNATE ATTENDANCE affected the lives of a broad spectrum of people in Tokugawa Japan: peasants who paid taxes to support the lord's travel, transported the baggage and men in his procession, and maintained the roads; members of the samurai status group who participated in the system and the support staff who attended to them; and all the members of the daimyo retainer bands and their families. The families' economic lives were directly impacted by the forced "loans" the lord collected from their stipends, which were largely due to financial exigencies caused by the economic burden of alternate attendance. In addition to the economic impact, families were also affected in numerous ways by the physical absence of one or more of their male members.

This chapter begins a transition from a focus on movement to an examination of a type of stasis — the lives of the domainal retainers in Edo. It begins with a basic question, one which has not yet been asked, let alone explored, in the secondary literature in either Japanese or English: Who went to Edo and why? By what mechanisms did retainers and their attendants elect to, or were selected to, serve in Edo? What motivated them to serve in Edo? In part the answer to the latter question lies with the attractions of Edo as a city and as an intellectual and artistic center, a subject that will be taken up in subsequent chapters. Using diaries and other materials from Tosa domain, in this chapter we will attempt to piece together a picture of the mechanism of and rationale for Edo service. In doing so it will be argued that Edo service involved compulsory elements, common in military draft systems, but that it also reflected the feudal nature of alternate attendance.

Moreover, domain officials sought to have some continuity within the forces dispatched to Edo by mixing inexperienced men with veterans. It will also be argued that the system was to some extent flexible and even allowed for a degree of volition. Lastly, the chapter will briefly explore the administrative apparatus for service in Edo.

Edo Service

The movement of officials at the behest of a higher political authority occurred, of course, in places other than Japan. Since early imperial times in China, for example, the state mobilized its elite through a system of court-designated appointments of scholar-officials. Successful in the examination competitions, these educated men were constantly being relocated throughout the vast Chinese empire. They also traveled to the capital for appointments, evaluations, and imperial audiences. The principle of avoidance, which prevented an individual from serving in his native area and limited service in one place to a three-year term, made transfers and trips to the capital routine.[1] In Japan a smaller elite, the daimyo, were mobilized by the Tokugawa state for service, not in "some unpredictable destinations"[2] but in its capital of Edo. *Sankin*, like the Chinese practice of *huanyou*, to travel for the purpose of taking up an official post, was a system of elite mobility imposed by the state. In Japan, of course, because of feudal and other obligations, large numbers of domainal retainers were also drawn into the system along with the lord. Roughly 25 to 30 percent of Edo's population—about 250,000 to 300,000 people from the early eighteenth century—traveled from the domains to take up residence in the more than six hundred domain compounds found across the city, and their numbers were continuously replenished from the castle towns through the migrations of alternate attendance; as many as one-third to one-half of these numbers accompanied the daimyo on their periodic trips in any given year.

To explore the nature of the Edo experience for those retainers who traveled on alternate attendance, it would be useful to have an understanding of the selection process. Unfortunately, the mechanism for selection is not transparent and, as noted, the issue has been completely overlooked. Moreover, to date I have found no documentary evidence that clearly illuminates the process in any domain. Nevertheless, I will present here some of the limited data available and offer some preliminary explanations and hypotheses regarding the system.

For the selection of personnel to serve in Edo, as in most other matters, there was no doubt some variation from domain to domain, yet some type of rotation system for the selection of at least a portion of the retinue was almost certainly in effect. It is improbable that the choice of who would accompany the lord on his important tour of duty in Edo was left to chance. In the larger domains at least two (out of twelve, in the case of Tosa) senior advisors usually accompanied the lord on his travels.[3] For the selection of the bulk of the forces, a likely scenario was that each group leader in the retainer band — Tosa's was divided into fourteen groups (*kumi*) — was charged with designating a specified number of people for Edo duty. Retainers of some means would then designate their own men (subretainers) to accompany them to Edo. Despite the compulsory element in the selection of retainers, there was some flexibility in the system, as revealed by the experiences of the Mori family, discussed below. Retainers assigned duty were able to find substitutes on some occasions when for whatever reason they did not wish to go. In other cases, retainers were able to avoid service at least temporarily without finding a substitute.

We know that retainers and their attendants were in Edo for different lengths of time and for different reasons. There were at least four categories of service: the first of these, *tachikaeri*, signified accompanying the lord to Edo and then immediately returning to the domain. The second, *otomo*, involved accompanying the lord to and from Edo. The vast majority of the men who traveled with the lord stayed with him for the year of his service and were known as *Edo kinban mono* (people serving in Edo). All these men came to Edo without families, just like many modern salaried men. The third category was *jōzume* or *jōfu*, men on long-term posting in Edo. This designation allowed them to bring their families to Edo. Their movement to and from the Tokugawa capital could be independent of the lord's, and the diaries of retainers who did so suggest that it was the rule. Some of those on long-term status came from families that were hereditary Edo-based retainers, but the others returned home after an indefinite period, when the domain's personnel needs in Edo changed or the retainer in question asked for leave; the latter was the case with the father of Matsuyama domain's Naitō Meisetsu, who asked to be reassigned to the domain after twelve years of service in Edo.[4] The fourth category involved retainers sent as messengers to Edo. Like *tachikaeri*, they would return after a brief period of rest in Edo. Lastly, though not a type of service but actually a leave of absence, some retainers received leave from their duties in the domain and were given permission to travel to Edo for study at their own expense (*jiriki*); they would in most cases reside in one of the domain's compounds.

There were also retainers whose hereditary positions naturally sent them to Edo, Osaka, or Kyoto for service. In other words, there appears to have been various tracks in terms of where a retainer might serve. An examination of the chronologies of Tosa retainers, as with the Mori below, reveals that those assigned to duty in Edo tended to go repeatedly. The same applied for service in Kyoto and Osaka. For example, the Befu family worked in Osaka as low-ranking officials dealing with the sale of Tosa lumber and later as purchasing agents in Kyoto.[5]

Rosters exist of samurai (*shi*) from Tosa selected for service, either for the trip to or from Edo, for certain years in the late seventeenth century. We have no way of knowing how complete these lists are, as it was common for samurai to travel in either direction on their own or in small groups, and at any time of the year, distinct from the main procession. Even given the limitations of this data, some useful conclusions can still be drawn. The lists exist for the return trip in 1670, 1671, and 1676 and for the 1676 leg to Edo, totaling 274 people-units.[6] Certain names appear on more than one roster, meaning that only 190 individuals are represented. Of the 190 individuals, 124 are listed only once. A small number might have died in Edo, but it is probably safe to say that all 124 completed one cycle of alternate attendance (having returned from Edo one can assume that they made the trip there from Tosa). Sixty-six individuals, then, made more than one trip. Forty people made two trips, twenty-four made three, and two made four trips. In sum, then, more than a third (35 percent) were repeat participants during the eight-year period from 1669 to 1677. For a given year, 1676 for example, almost half of the samurai (39 of 85) were making their first trip, while the rest were veterans. The same pattern of multiple service is evident from *sankin* rosters for 1682, which reveal that 29 *shi* (out of 79) had served earlier in 1671 or 1676. Similarly, the *sankin* roster for 1690 reveals 22 repeaters (out of 128 *shi*) from the years 1671, 1675, 1676, or 1682; nine of them served twice, nine served three times, and four served four times.[7]

We cannot know to what extent individuals elected to serve multiple times. The disparity in the number of times different people served suggests that some amount of volition may have been involved. Combining inexperienced men with veterans makes sense in any military institution: newer men are able to benefit from the knowledge of those who have gone before. If this pattern was typical—and there is nothing in the record of these years to indicate that it was not—introducing such a large number of men to Edo service spread the experience of alternate attendance widely through the retainer corps.

It is clear that there was some element of both compulsion and volunteerism involved. For example, in Tosa domain there were a small number of footsoldiers, known as *jō otomo ashigaru*, assigned the regular task of accompanying the lord on his biennial journeys.[8] That retainers were able to avoid Edo duty, or at least postpone it, due to medical problems suggests that some compulsion was involved. While perhaps an extreme example, there is the case of a Tosa retainer named Komori Kihachirō. Ordered to accompany the daimyo heir to Edo in the spring of 1828, he attempted to avoid service, complaining to his superior that he was suffering from hemorrhoids. Perhaps thinking that his story would be taken for a ruse, Komori offered to show him his bottom. Despite his superior's protestations, it is reported that Komori insisted on exposing himself.[9]

Some were no doubt reluctant to leave family and the comfort of home. Mori Masakatsu of Tosa appears to be such a man. While neither he nor any other diarist I have read went on record to express reluctance or distaste for Edo duty, after traveling to Edo as a messenger in 1683, he avoided making another trip. When subsequently ordered to serve in Edo on two occasions, he found a replacement.[10] At least one document records that the substitute was paid a fee.[11] Sometimes that replacement was a son — one who had passed through the rites of manhood — as in Mori Masakatsu's case in 1694. Known as *daikin*, or "replacement service," this appears to have been quite common in the lower end of the retainer corps, particularly when the father was in poor health but had not yet turned over the family headship to the son. Of course, that it was possible to find a replacement also reveals some flexibility in this draft-like system.

As in Song China, it was common for a son to accompany a father in his official duties[12] to get important life experience and on-the-job training, preparing him for when he would assume the family headship or perhaps simply to expand the boundaries of his known physical world. For example, though he would never himself be posted to Edo, Kusunose Ōe, a lower samurai from Tosa and later student of famed Confucian scholar Tani Mashio, as a young teenager accompanied his father to Edo and Suruga before succeeding to the family headship.[13] In such cases as Ōe's, the son would be "attached" (*fuzoku*) to his father (and in some cases to an uncle); that is, he would be the father's responsibility, live in his father's residence in the compound, and travel at his own expense. Gotō Sakoemon requested and received the permission of Tosa authorities for his son Yoemon to accompany him, at the equivalent status of steward, at his own expense.[14] Contemporary Japanese referred to this experience as *minarai*, or learning through observation. In this manner the trip to Edo for the son of a *bushi* fulfilled the same function as a trip to Ise for a commoner. The aphorism "send a cherished child on a trip," in effect, was embraced by both commoner and samurai alike.

Some families, like the Mori, served repeatedly in Edo; others lived out their collective lives in Tosa; while still others had members who served the domain outside of Shikoku. For example, of the five generations of the family line stemming from Okuda Shin'eimon in the mid-seventeenth century, only two served in Edo. Second-generation head Shinsuke worked back and forth in Tosa and Edo for a decade (1724–1734), and after this his son Shinshichi served in his place, although the father did not formally retire until 1751. Shinshichi then served in his own right at least five times during the years 1740–1760, mostly in the capacity of a scribe, and received rewards for good performance.[15] Despite this record of Edo service of Shinsuke and Shinshichi, the following two generations, for reasons that are not clear, lived out their lives entirely in Tosa.

Looking at the lineages of Tosa men from the lower end of the retainer corps reveals the uneven way Edo service was distributed. We can see a varied pattern of service outside Tosa, for example, for five generations of the Odate family stemming from Gōhachi (served 1685–1708) in the late seventeenth century.[16] Gōhachi served as a footsoldier for seventeen years beginning in 1685, though it is not certain whether he made a trip to Edo before 1699. His second and final trip to Edo came in 1708, when he replaced a retainer serving on the domain boat that operated between Kōchi and Edo. His son, Bunkurō (served 1722–1770), completed tours of duty in Edo in 1724 and in 1726 as a footsoldier in the domain's fire brigade. He went to Edo as a messenger in 1729 and on two tours, in 1759 and 1762, performed miscellaneous functions related to the reconstruction of the main compound in Kajibashi. Third-generation head Magobei (served 1770–1786) held the important post of the keeper of the lock to the inner (women's) quarters at the middle compound in Shiba for one tour, in 1772, and held the same post at the more important main compound from 1778 until an undetermined date. (He either stayed in Edo from 1778 until 1785, or he returned for a tour in 1784, was ordered to go yet again in 1786 but became ill, delayed his departure, and ultimately died before he could leave.) His successor, Gengo (served 1786–1798), traveled to Edo on a temporary posting in 1796, but then was given a job supervising construction at the lower compound in Shinagawa for a year. The following year he worked in procurement at the domain's compound in Edo before dying at what was probably a young age. The fifth-generation head, Tatsuji (served 1833–1855), made at least five trips to Edo during the years 1834 through 1850, holding a variety of financial positions, including bursar for river and other water crossings on the alternate attendance trip as well as a low-level supervisory position for construction at the domain's warehouse compound at Tsukiji. For this last position he received an increase of one *koku* in stipend for his role in saving money in the construction of the main residence there. On several other occasions he had supervisory positions for transporting the daimyo procession, but only as far as Marugame on the northern shore of Shikoku, returning home once that job was completed.

Of the eight generations of the Heiuchi family beginning with Gonpei, half experienced service outside of Tosa.[17] The founder, Gonpei (served 1664–1707), spent fifteen of his forty-three years of service outside Tosa, six as a scribe in Edo and nine as a constable at the domain's Kyoto compound. The next three generations of heads of household worked entirely in Tosa, before Tadagorō (served 1787–1798) made one tour of Edo, where he acted as a supervisor of pages. The next-to-last generation head, Jungo (served 1820–1846), traveled to Edo on at least five occasions, the first as a messenger. On his third tour in 1835 he was praised for his service and assigned to regular duty accompanying the lord.[18] From these few examples it is evident that service varied greatly, even within the same household, and even amongst those assigned the hereditary duty of accompanying the lord to Edo.

The Mori Family

The experience of one branch of the Mori family of Tosa gives us some further insight into the question of who went to Edo and under what circumstances. There were more than ten families bearing the surname Mori in the retainer band of the Yamauchi family. The family line (see Table 4.1) of which Mori Masana (1803–1873) was a part descended from the third son of Kazuhide, a man named Mori Seiju. The male households of this line were of *umamawari* (mounted warrior) status, which was the most active, integral part of the retainer corps and generally had fiefs and salary supplements that reflected their utility. Fourth-generation househead Mori Hirosada, for example, had a fief of two hundred *koku*, supplemented with what could be an equal sum as salary for specific assignments given.[19]

At least two points concerning the Mori family tree need be raised here. First of all, Mori Masana's grandfather, Hirosada, produced no heir with his wife and consequently adopted his younger brother's son, Hirotake, as his own son and heir. He did however have a son with a concubine, whom he named Yoshiki. Yoshiki was important to the family line because he was adopted by his cousin (Hirotake) as son and heir since Hirotake had no male issue. Thus, Yoshiki (family head number 6) did eventually succeed his father (family head number 4), despite his maternity, after being adopted by his cousin, who served for a short time as family head (number 5). Three generations of Mori — Hirosada, Yoshiki, and Masana — were all impressive, extensive diarists whose personal accounts form an important backbone of this study. A second point that should be highlighted about this samurai lineage is that Mori Masana was Yoshiki's fourth son and, like his two immediate elder brothers, adopted into other branch families of the Mori family. In this way "excess" male offspring of one branch were absorbed by other branches.

Masana's branch of the Mori family had a close connection with Edo. As far as the documentary record allows us to know, seven of the nine generation heads (excepting the first and ninth) made the journey to Edo at least once. Some members made multiple trips: the third, Seiju, five times; the fourth, Hirosada, four times; the seventh, Yoshiki, three times; and, Mori Masana, who as noted was the fourth son of the sixth generation head, Yoshiki, five times.

The nature of their service on these trips to Edo varied. The second, third, and fourth householders each made one trip as a messenger. Seiju, the third househead, made two immediate round trips — that is, he accompanied the lord

TABLE 4.1. Family Line of Mori Masana*

	Name	Date(s)	Notes
2	Masakatsu	1683–1664	Messenger to Edo castle to deliver greetings to shogun (two-month stay in Edo)
3	Kyūemon Masatoshi	1694	Traveled to Edo for duty in his father's place.
		1704	Traveled in lord's procession to Edo but returned home directly afterward.
		1706	Same as above.
		1715	Due to some undetermined offense, he is ordered back to Tosa (travel dates unknown).
		1720	Sent to Edo as high-speed messenger upon the birth of a son to the daimyo.
4	Kanzaemon Hirosada	1727	Edo duty (*Edo kinban*).
		1732	Edo duty; river-crossing duty on trip.
		1737	Accompanied lord.
		1767	Messenger sent to Edo castle to deliver thanks from lord after safe arrival in Kōchi.
5	San'emon Hirotake	1778	Died in Edo.
6	Kanzaemon Yoshiki	1788	In Edo; presented a memorial to the lord and received a letter of commendation. Edo duty as *oshioki yaku*; left Kōchi 1801/1/21; departed Edo 1801/4/8.
		1801	Accompanied heir to Edo as *omori yaku*, *osoba goyō yaku*.
		1802	Arrived Edo 4/18; left Edo 1804/5/8.
		1828	Left for Edo 5/2 (still there in 1829 according to younger brother Masana's "Mori Masana Edo nikki"); departed Edo 2/27.
		1844	Left Kōchi 2/7 to serve in Edo as *goyō-ooku muki goyō, Edo gunbi goyō*.
7	Kanzaemon Yoshie	1828	Left for Edo 5/2 (still there in 1829 according to younger brother Masana's "Mori Masana Edo nikki"); departed Edo 2/27
		1844	Left Kōchi 2/7 to serve in Edo as *goyō-ooku muki goyō, Edo gunbi goyō*.
	Saihei Ujihide	1829	Died in Edo 1830.

TABLE 4.1. *(Continued)*

	Name	Date(s)	Notes
	Shirō Masana	1828	Traveled to Edo for "*gakumon bugei*" (scholastic and martial studies); attached to elder brother Yoshie. Arrived in Edo 5/2. Left Edo 1829/3/27.
		1829	Arrived in Edo 11/17; departed 1830/8/26.
		1834	Arrived in Edo 5/27; accompanied by family; *Edo jōzume* (long-term status); 1837/9th month, given leave to return home. Began compiling his biographical work *Tosa jinbutsu shi* in Edo.
		1854	Arrived in Edo 3/17; 12/24 appointed to help build cannon emplacements in Shinagawa. Departed Edo 1855/3/3.
		1856	Arrived in Edo 9/18. Still there 1857/int. 5/3.
8	Saihachi Yoshisada	1859	Sent to Nikkō (from Edo as messenger; returned to Edo 5/26. 1861, commits indiscretion (*kurashikata furachi ni tsuki*) and is ordered into seclusion / house arrest (*enryo*).
		1862	Genealogical entry puts him back in Tosa.

*The information here on the Mori family is largely based on "Osamuraichū senzogaki keizu chō" n.d., vol. 24; Mori Yoshiki 1793–1807, 12 vols.; Mori Masana 1828–1856, 10 vols.

to Edo and then returned home to Kōchi immediately. The third-generation head substituted on one occasion for his father and was assigned guard duty in Edo. Seventh-generation head Yoshiki, who had just returned from Edo the previous summer, was charged with caring for the young heir on his trip to Edo in 1802. Hirosada (number 4) left Tosa on five occasions. With the exception of one trip he made accompanying the lord to Arima hot springs, all these were to Edo, beginning with his first at age eighteen and his final one at age fifty-eight.

For Masana, too, with the exception of a visit to Arima hot springs in 1860, all five of his other trips outside of Tosa were to Edo. These journeys spanned most of his adult life. His first experience was in 1828, at the age of twenty-four, when he was given special permission to make the trip to the Tokugawa capital for martial and scholarly studies (*gakumon bugei shūgyō*) and was attached to his elder brother Yoshie.[20] His fifth and last was made some twenty-eight years later, in 1856, when he accompanied Lord Yamauchi Yōdō. Perhaps feeling conscious of his fifty-two years of age, he boasted in his diary that he walked across Shikoku rather than ride a horse or ride in a palanquin. On his fifth period of service, in 1834, he was stationed in Edo on long-term posting. Masana was the only member of his family line to serve in this capacity, but he remained in Edo only from 1834 to 1837.[21]

Financial Incentives

From an examination of the experience of the Mori family above we can get a sense of the range of attitudes samurai held toward Edo service. Some sought to avoid it, perhaps because of the lengthy separation from home that it entailed, as was the case of Mori Masakatsu, who twice found substitutes. Others, such as Mori Masana, saw service in Edo as an opportunity and sought out an assignment that would take them there. As argued in chapter seven, for the domain's cultured elite — the Confucian scholars, doctors, painters, poets, tea masters, potters, and other high-class artisans — as well as those who aspired to those positions, service in Edo was highly desirable, because it was there they could come into contact with their peers from other domains, as well as teachers from whom they could improve their skills. Service in Edo may also have been more attractive to some, like Tani Tannai and Sakai Banshirō, because of financial incentives involved, namely travel and maintenance allowances.[22] Kii domain samurai Sakai Banshirō as well as Tani Tanshirō and his son, Tannai, of Tosa were able to save a considerable amount of money during their stays in Edo. Specifically, Sakai was able to return to Wakayama with 15.6 *ryō* of his Edo allowance of 39 *ryō*. Sakai's service in Edo was, in effect, a way to stabilize the family finances at a time when consumer prices were rising. His stipend of 30 *koku* would not have been enough for his family of five to live on had he remained in Wakayama.[23] An examination of Tannai's correspondence with the merchant Saitaniya Naomasa (1705–1779), to whom he was in debt, reveals that the special stipends given Edo-based retainers helped him to repay those loans.[24] For this reason, Saitaniya encouraged Tani to serve in Edo a second time, in 1754. This probably goes far in explaining why Tannai, one of Tosa's Confucian scholars, went to Edo so often — a total of ten times between 1746 and 1788.[25] As will be discussed further below, Tosa's subsidy program was hardly unique.

The financial impact of alternate attendance on a retainer's finances is important here, because to a certain extent money determined whether he could afford to eat out or drink at restaurants, go to see plays, or become the student of a teacher not employed by his domain. It also determined the amount of goods he could purchase for personal consumption and for gift giving. More-over, it probably made retainers more amenable to participating in the system. In other words, it is imperative to consider subsidy programs, in addition to a retainer's status (hence his income), when considering the Edo lifestyle of domain retainers.

Some retainers were anxious to serve in Edo for personal and financial rea-sons, and they were able to fulfill their wishes. Mori Masana, for example, was able to use the mechanism of alternate attendance to travel to Edo, as he did in 1828 when he received permission for scholastic study and martial training. Others sought out posts in Edo with the notion that they could pursue indi-vidual interests in their ample free time. Some commoners as well were able to travel to Edo by securing employment as pages or other menial positions in service to retainers. Such was the case, for example, with Kōchi townsman painter Hirose Dōi, the son of a hairdresser. Known more commonly as Ekin (1812–1872), he traveled to Edo on alternate attendance as a page and spent three years there studying with the Kanō artist Dōeki.

In many domains, retainers assigned a tour of duty in Edo were given travel and maintenance allowances, which were pegged to status and size of fief or stipend. In Tosa in 1627, for example, the Edo subsidy for a retainer of *umama-mari* status with a fief of less than forty *koku* was ten *koku*; someone of the same status with a one-hundred-*koku* fief would receive a subsidy of thirty *koku*.[26] Tosa retainers on long-term postings in Edo were well taken care of, at least from the perspective of domain officials.[27] Elsewhere, in Sendai, a subsidy pro-gram was initiated in the early eighteenth century. Retainers of samurai rank received seven *ryō* per year for themselves and five *ryō* for each subretainer. In addition, all received a rice supplement pegged to the size of fief or stipend.[28] The subsidies, it must be noted, came largely from a general tax on the retainer corps, known as *dashigin* in Tosa, and also from mutual-aid (*moyai*) systems into which retainers periodically paid funds.[29]

In a recent study of the financial condition of the Inoyama household of Kaga domain, the author, Isoda Michifumi, seems to draw conflicting conclusions regarding Edo service. On the one hand he states that it "was an honor for a low-ranking *bushi* and could also present an important career opportunity."[30] At the same time he also concludes that such service was "fraught with danger of bankrupting a house if mistakes were made," but he does not specify what type of mistakes. In fact, his subject, retainer Inoyama Kinzō, a purchasing agent, received a salary supplement while serving in Edo, which was followed one year later by a raise for diligent service. Two years' duty there were followed by three years in Kanazawa, with promotions in rank and salary, before reap-pointment for Edo duty in 1827. This time he was given a job as bursar, which put him in a supervisory position for the preparations for the wedding of the heir to the shogun's daughter. This important job, unfortunately for Kinzō, required a great outlay of money for entertaining and gift giving, and as a result, Isoda concludes, Edo service was the cause of the Inoyama family's debt.[31] While this particular job assignment, and not Edo service per se, was one of the causes of the household's debt, an examination of the author's own evidence also reveals another source, namely, excessive consumption, both the acquisition of material goods as well as entertainment.[32] In an attempt to get a handle on their debt, the Inoyama household sold off goods including clothing, books, furniture, and implements for the tea ceremony.

Given the disparity in domain size, not to mention retainers' rank and stipends, it is not surprising that participation in alternate attendance could impact individuals in different ways. What was an opportunity for some could be a hardship for others. Sakai Banshirō and Tani Tannai were able to save money as a result of their assignment to Edo, but without detailed financial ledgers similar to those left by the above two men it is difficult to draw broad conclusions about the impact of a tour of duty on samurai households. Nevertheless the diaries kept by numerous retainers suggest that they were able to live well while serving in Edo and contain no comments about experiencing poverty or being prevented from doing things because of inadequate funds.[33]

Sakai and his Edo experience will be discussed in chapter six, but Tani Tannai (or Mashio, 1727–1797), one of the original four professors at the Tosa domain school in Kōchi, was a Confucian scholar of outstanding lineage who repeatedly sought service in Edo because of the stipends that accompanied such service. This is apparent from an examination of a collection of financial records from the years 1748 through 1754 that Tani kept, "Record of Daily Necessities" (Nichiyō beien roku, lit. "Record of the daily necessities of rice and salt"), in which he also reproduced some correspondence between himself and the merchant Saitaniya Naomasa (1705–1779).[34] A close examination of Tannai's long-term fiscal crisis likewise reveals that his dependency on Saitaniya was fostered by a number of factors, such as variable rates for the conversion of rice to cash, the nature of the multimetallic monetary system, the domain's forced borrowings and twice-yearly stipend payment method, not to mention the attitude of samurai toward money and arithmetic. Tannai's example is significant because he is representative of the many retainers who fall into the category of lower samurai in terms of income. His "Record" is of further interest because it chronicles the difficulties faced by a samurai at an important point in the economic history of the Tokugawa period, the mid-eighteenth century, a time by which most domains had resorted to imposing forced loans upon their retainers. Furthermore, while it is well-known that many retainers resorted to taking out loans from merchants and turned to a variety of side employments to cushion the blow of those forced loans, this account reveals that Tannai and his father adopted different strategies. Attracted by the subsidies provided by the domain to retainers for Edo service, they became dependent on those funds and apparently repeatedly sought appointments that would allow them to accompany the Tosa lord to the shogunal capital on his biennial trips of alternate attendance. In this context, then, Edo service, as well as participation in mutual-savings associations, should be recognized as significant strategies that samurai might employ to combat their chronic financial difficulties.

While the Tani household's financial problems predated the compilation of the "Record," his first letter to Saitaniya already hints at political and economic conditions undermining his household's financial health. This first piece of correspondence was written only the day after his father, Kakimori, set out for Edo on alternate attendance with the Tosa lord to serve as a lecturer in Confucian studies:

1750 (Kan'en 3)/6/6

To: Saitaniya Hachirōbei:

I am writing this letter seeking your advice. My household has benefited from your assistance for many years and thus somehow we have managed to get by. Our gratitude is such that I know I need not express it here now.

As you know, however, our expenses have gone up in recent years, forcing us to use the following year's income in advance. If this state of affairs continues, the future looks bleak — and I believe that you will suffer loss as well. This is truly regrettable.

The members of my household live frugally; however, because our numbers are great, it is inevitable that our living expenses will be high. I am grateful for the increase in income received from the lord in recent years,[35] and should in principle, be able to live on this amount for the entire year; yet when this proves not to be the case, as now, we are forced to live day-to-day. Moreover, if by some chance I am unable to continue to accompany the lord on his periodic trips to Edo, the household will be unable to function. All of this is clear to me. Somehow we must make do with our present yearly income.

Being unfamiliar with these [financial] matters, however, I am uncertain whether or not this is possible; but I would like to try. Please write and inform me in detail as to how much my yearly income is in man-allotments (*fuchi*) of rice and rice certificates (*kippu*), and how much is being "borrowed" (*kariage*) by the lord. Also, please inform me how much the remaining income is once converted into silver and copper coins. Then, I will request that you prepare a monthly budget for my consideration. Both my mother and wife are in agreement with me about all of this. [His father, Kakimori, was in Edo.] Once you have done this, I will know what I can spend in one year, and will not ask you for more money. If I do, please do not lend it to me. Should there be particularly unforeseen circumstances, however, then a decision should be made on a case-by-case basis.

Please advise me whether I should do as I have written above, and feel free to let me know whether there are other things that might be done.

Tani Tannai

Several issues that Tannai raises should be underscored here. First and foremost, the forced paybacks to the lord represent one of the most regular and pressing problems faced by retainers; this issue will be explored at some length below. Second, when Tannai writes that he must "make do" with his present yearly income, he is saying that he must not be dependent on the extra income received for Edo service to support his household in Tosa. Later in the log, he records two pieces of advice to himself: (1) Do not mix Edo and Tosa budgets, and (2) do not take out other loans.[36] His own records, however, reveal his inability to follow either of these precepts.

Later, Saitaniya responds by drawing up a budget for Tannai, but before this, Tannai himself outlines the basic elements of his household's financial condition. Central to the Tani budget was a stipend of twenty-four *koku* in rice certificates. Most retainers, rather than holding a fief (*chigyō*) which yielded tax rice, received stipends and support rice; one *fuchi* of rice was supposed to support one man for a year. In Tosa during the mid-eighteenth century, domainal retainers received their stipends in two equal portions, summer and winter (year-end) payments. But due to the forced loans to the lord, retainers were required to return one-quarter of their base stipend. In Tannai's case this meant that his stipend ordinarily would have been reduced to eighteen *koku*. Unfortunately for retainers, the payback was deducted in one sum, from the summer payment. In Tannai's case, this meant that he received only one-half, or six, of his nominal twelve *koku* payment in the summer, leaving him with insufficient funds to cover his expenses until the end of the year. Of course the real value of that eighteen *koku* fluctuated with the market exchange rate for rice, e.g., forty-five *monme* per *koku* in 1750 versus only thirty-one and a half *koku* in 1753, which added to the instability of samurai finances.

The second key source of the Tannai household's income was the support rice received from the domain. This consisted of a ten-man allotment of rice (equivalent to eighteen *koku*/91.8 bushels), seven for Tannai's father Kakimori and three for himself. As the householder (until 1752), Tannai's father received more rice support than Tannai. The rice allotments, each one equivalent to 1.8 *koku*, were generally awarded to retainers for performing certain specific services or for some meritorious service. In Tannai's case, since he was from a scholarly family and designated his father's heir, those funds were no doubt intended to support his studies. Because the two men belonged to one household, however, the two allowances can be considered as one.

The domain's twice-yearly stipend payment system forced Tannai to live on credit and thus pushed him to seek the assistance of a creditor like Saitaniya to remain solvent. The winter stipend payment was quickly used to cover the bills for staple items like rice, miso, tea, vegetables, sumi, firewood, paper, and lamp oil.[37] This meant Tannai had to borrow money to live until the following summer payment, which, as noted, was reduced by one-half due to the forced loans. Even if the principal was paid back, interest payments tended to pile up and further eat into his meager income. In short, the forced loans, not to mention the twice-yearly payment method, induced a state of indebtedness.

Frustrated by his inability to get out of a cycle of debt, Tannai wrote Saitaniya asking for his advice, probably knowing that there was no easy solution to his difficulties. A week later, as requested, Saitaniya delivered the budget he had drawn up for Tannai, as follows:[38]

1750/6/13
MEMORANDUM (Income Statement for Tani Tannai's household)
    Article. *Fuchi*: seven-man allotment [father's portion]
    Article. *Fuchi*: three-man allotment [Tannai's portion]
    Article. 24 *koku kippu* [base stipend in rice certificates], six *koku* of which are "returned" to the lord leaving 18 koku.

    The above-listed basic stipend [eighteen *koku*], converted to silver [using a poorer quality silver, it was converted here at a lower rate of one *monme* silver = 70 *mon* copper rather than the normal rate of conversion of one *monme* silver = 80 *mon* copper and 45 *monme* silver = one *koku* rice] comes to 925.7 *monme*
        (–) 114 *monme* interest
        (=) 811.7 *monme* yearly income available

According to this budget, Tannai's yearly income of 811.7 *monme* left him with a monthly budget of 67.6 *monme*. This was to cover miso, soybeans, firewood, clothing, the dyeing of clothes, servants' salaries, and other miscellaneous expenses, including a year-end thank-you payment customarily given his regular pharmacist-cum-doctor, from whom he obtained medicines. Interest payments consumed approximately 14 percent of Tannai's real income of eighteen *koku*, and together with the forced borrowings left him with a significantly reduced monetary inflow. Despite the high interest rates, Saitaniya claimed that the budget he fixed for Tannai would meet "most unexpected expenses." Nonetheless, he allowed for the possibility that there might be "exceptional cases."[39]

In an effort to gain control over his expenditures after writing Saitaniya, Tannai compiled a list of payments made during Obon and New Year's for expenses incurred during 1750.[40] Together, these expenses of 144.93 *monme* equaled more than twice the monthly budget of 67.6 *monme* that Saitaniya had drawn up. To remain solvent, Tannai would have had to pay for these expenses out of his monthly budget, but this was difficult. Tannai's accounting did not have any perceptible effect on his ability to keep within the budget. His expenses for the sixth through twelfth months, including the Obon and New Year's bills, totaled 781.5 *monme*, which left him with a deficit of 308.3 *monme* (33 percent of his income).

How this deficiency was resolved is not spelled out, but six months later, early in the new year (1751/1/8), Tannai wrote another letter to Saitaniya, complaining of his difficulties. This letter began:

> Our household has tried hard to economize and live on 18 *koku*, as I wrote in my letter of 6/6 last year, but I am ashamed to say that there has not been a month since then in which we have not spent more than our budgeted income. The reason for this is that my household is large, and even the rice allowance (*fuchi mai*) is not sufficient to meet our needs. As there is no way to follow the plan I wrote earlier, I must consider other measures if we are to make do at the present income level."[41]

He went on to explain that there were seventeen people in the household supported by a ten-man rice allotment. With Tannai or his father serving in Edo, fourteen people would remain in Tosa, forced to live on a seven-man allotment. The three in Edo, Tannai or Kakimori, and two personal retainers each required a one-man allowance to maintain themselves there; the three, in essence, took their allowance with them to Edo. "No matter how much those who remain in Tosa economize," Tannai lamented, "the household is still short by a two-man allotment," that is, by about 3.6 *koku*.[42] Consequently, additional rice for consumption had to be purchased, and later, in 1754, he would have to purchase as much as five *koku*.[43] Tannai further explained, "With the present level of cash income, there will be a deficit of more than 200 *monme*," without taking rice consumption into consideration.[44] Adding on the extra expense incurred to meet the insufficient number of rice allotments, the total deficit would come to roughly 300 *monme*. (According to his calculations on fols. 4–5 the total deficit was actually 308.3 *monme*.) This deficit amounted to a full one-third of his basic stipend. He concluded, "If we continue as before, there is no way to make up this difference through normal economizing measures."[45]

In citing his financial difficulties, Tannai was preparing the ground for a proposal to Saitaniya to resolve them. He tells the merchant, "It is clear to me that we cannot continue to run up deficits year after year," and "While it would be beneficial to be able to economize more on food, this is not possible."[46] Consequently, Tannai admits, he must continue to rely on Saitaniya.

At this point Tannai unveils his plan. Rather than requesting an additional loan, he asks Saitaniya to restructure his debt load from past years by treating it as "old debt" on which no further interest payments would be due. The principal, he proposes, would be paid off over a ten-year period. He then asks Saitaniya to consider, retroactively, the twelve *koku* from his recent year-end stipend payment not as a loan, but simply the stipend due him (the stipend payment apparently was customarily released directly to the merchant). In other words, the year-end stipend payment ordinarily went toward paying his debts for that year, which meant that he had to borrow funds to live on during the first half of the new year. Seeking to avoid this, Tannai asks Saitaniya to count last year's debt as part of his "old debt," so that he would not have to borrow more funds. Exactly how much debt Tannai had accumulated by 1753 is not clear, but an entry in his log for 1750 indicates that the amount was two *kan* 953.11 *monme* in silver, roughly equivalent to 49 *koku* (at a rate of one *koku* = 60 *monme*) or two and a half times his annual income.[47]

This plan to restructure his debt was an attempt to break out of a cycle of spiraling debt by which Tannai was forced to make payments to Saitaniya and then take out a new loan to cover expenses until the summer payment. Still unable to discipline himself financially, he requests that Saitaniya act as his overseer and distribute his income to him in monthly installments. Perhaps fearing that he would simply spend the twelve *koku* if it were given him in a lump sum, Tannai requests that Saitaniya hold the money and give him an allowance on the first of each month until the sixth month. For Tannai's allowance Saitaniya was to use only nine of the twelve *koku* of the year-end stipend payment, with the remaining three *koku* added to the six *koku* due Tannai from his summer stipend payment (the other six *koku* were returned to the lord), thus giving him a budget of nine *koku* to sustain his household for each of the two halves of the year.

While Tannai proposed repaying the principal over a period of ten years, he does not seem confident of his ability to do so, telling Saitaniya, "It will be very difficult to repay my old loans to you as long as forced loans to the lord continue." His dependence on Edo subsidies is made clear, however, when he continues, "If we (my father and I or one of us) are assigned to accompany the lord to Edo, any extra funds which remain from the allowance for service there can be applied to the loans."[48]

To impress upon Saitaniya his intent to live more frugally, Tannai tells him of his idea to move his residence from its current location at Kita-Hōkōnin-chō, just north of the castle, a short distance farther away from the urban center, to the vicinity of Kuma, Mama, and Jinzenji, closer to the mountains that ring Kōchi in the north. The purchase of a house in this area — his self-styled *yama yashiki* or "mountain residence" — would cost five or six *koku*, he informs Saitaniya, perhaps testing the ground for a loan. Such a move, Tannai claims, would be beneficial for a number of reasons. First of all, there would be less risk of fire than in the crowded inner city. Second, it would improve his household economy (for example, his manservant could gather firewood in the mountains). Third, the quiet would be good for his scholarly work.

Tannai was not unusual in seeking a respite from urban life. The high cost of living in castle towns led samurai across Japan to find refuge in the countryside. In Chōshū domain, as early as 1669, those with holdings under two hundred *koku* were given permission to reside temporarily outside the urban settlement. Laws were enacted to prevent continued residence, and although the number of those absent from Chōshū remained fairly steady, "there was a constant turnover within their numbers."[49]

In Tannai's case as well, a move to a mountain residence would have required a formal request to his overlord. Tosa samurai like Tannai could petition to be declared officially "poverty-stricken" (*hissoku*), which allowed them to live temporarily on the land, outside the castle town, and to withdraw from official duties and contracts to allow a retainer's household to try to recover its economic health.

Saitaniya did not look favorably upon Tannai's plan to restructure his debt by counting last year's loans as "old debt." Although he did not object to Tannai's proposal to move, he was not particularly enthusiastic about it nor did he offer to advance any funds. This left the retainer with little choice. Tannai wrote Saitaniya again on 1/30, apparently the day after he had enjoyed the merchant's hospitality, asking for another loan on the order of the 270.68 *monme* to carry him over until his summer payment.[50] In his letter he detailed how important his family's Edo subsidies were to the repayment of Tannai's loans:

> When my father Tanshirō returns from Edo sometime in the middle of the Fifth Month, he should bring back five or six *ryō* [gold, equivalent to 300 or 360 *monme*], and from this the above-stated loan will be repaid. If he does not bring back enough money, I will repay you from my Summer payment of 6 *koku*. . . . In this case, I would require another loan until the end of the year.
>
> At the end of the year I will be appointed for Edo duty, and will use the 22 *koku* [Saitaniya, below, gives the figure as 20 *koku*] service allowance (*Edo watarimono*), which at a rate of 50 *monme/koku*, converts to one *kan* 100 me, for repayment of my various new loans of 598 *monme*. . . .
>
> Given the above, I will not be able to pay back the old loans next year. Moreover, although I will receive a subsidy for Edo service next year, those

funds will be needed to maintain myself there. However, should some money remain from them, it can be applied to the loans — but it probably will not be very much.

If Tanshirō returns from Edo the year after next with some funds, that money can be applied to my old loans. Should I be appointed again at the end of the year for Edo service, the entire advance payment of 10 *koku* can also be applied to the loan. I am resolved that things will work out in this manner. Moreover, if the forced loans cease, those funds can all be applied toward repayment.

Financial affairs do not ordinarily proceed as planned, but I have nevertheless laid out my ideas above. If my thinking is mistaken, please let me know. Since tomorrow is a fortuitous day, I hope that you can do as I have written and dispense 60 *monme*, one-third of the loan, at that time. (signed Tani Tannai)

Tani's letter reveals his household's dire financial straits. Saitaniya's refusal to treat Tannai's outstanding loans as old debt or to treat his year-end stipend payment as earned income rather than a loan meant Tannai had no easy way out of his cycle of debt. As a result, Tannai was forced to act contrary to his memo to himself by relying on income for Edo service that his father might bring back as well as what might later be paid to Tannai himself, and by taking out additional loans to support his household in Tosa. The many hypothetical elements that his calculations depended upon further indicate the severity of his indebtedness. His lack of financial discipline and his dependence on Saitaniya is revealed when Tani, afraid he will spend the 270.68 *monme* all at once, asks Saitaniya to divide his income into equal halves and to dispense the funds to him over a period of several months.

Saitaniya's response included some minor corrections to and emendations to Tannai's calculations.[51] He also informed Tani that he thought Kakimori should be able to bring back (save) seven *ryō* from Edo in an average year, a figure higher than the five or six *ryō* Tannai estimated. Also, with the advance payment due on Tannai's subsidy, Saitaniya argued that Tannai could make do on his earnings and did not need another loan.[52] Indeed, Tani was already in debt. As noted earlier, his outstanding loans, as of the first month of 1751, amounted to roughly three times his annual income of eighteen *koku*, the sum that remained after the forced borrowing was deducted.[53]

The forced borrowings by the domain, caused to a large extent by the daimyo's forced participation in alternate attendance, figured large in the Tani household's financial difficulties. Although occasionally imposed before the mid-eighteenth century, the practice had become routine and widespread by the time of Tannai's financial record. First exacted in Tosa in 1704 at a rate of 10 percent, the reductions became more severe toward the middle of the century, when the domain's financial state worsened.

Tosa's economic difficulties were in large measure a result of natural disasters. In the countryside, poor conditions induced peasant disturbances in 1751 and 1754. The urban center of Kōchi also had its own problems. Before repairs were completed on the castle from a fire in 1727, another fiery disaster struck in 1746, consuming more than 2,600 households. Of course it did not help the domain that during these years of natural disasters there were no exemptions from demands by the Tokugawa shogunate for contributions to public works, particularly for riparian works on the Tenryū River.[54]

In response to these economic difficulties, the forced exactions grew more demanding. The rate varied from 25 percent (1748 to 1751) to 40 percent (1752), and then was temporarily cut back down to 10 percent (1753 to 1756) before returning to a varying rate of 25 or 50 percent during the 1760s and 1770s.[55] Tannai's first letter to Saitaniya came during the third year of reductions at the 25 percent level, by which time he had obviously grown greatly disturbed by his financial straits. This level of exaction was widespread, hardly unique to Tosa. In Chōshū, for example, the domain borrowed back from its retainers in twenty of twenty-one years, 1742 to 1762, at a rate as high as 50 percent.[56] In Yonezawa, the domain borrowed back 50 percent in the years from 1749 to 1789.[57] Forced loans were a continuous feature of Tannai's life, and he was never able to use funds from his stipend to repay his old debt.

The forced loans compelled many retainers to find alternate sources of income, especially side employments such as handicrafts. In Yonezawa, for example, the domain encouraged the production of silk cloth in samurai households.[58] There is no evidence from Tannai's ledger, however, that the Tani household adopted this strategy. Instead, Kakimori and his son Tannai appear to have adopted a different scheme for economic survival through the benefits that accrued to them by accompanying the Tosa lord to Edo. If it was not a conscious plan at first, certainly the Tani came to rely on the subsidies received for that service.

Special subsidies were necessary because of the high costs of service in Edo. Many domains, such as Ogaki, Hachinohe, Morioka, Tsugaru, and Tsushima, used them to counteract some of the negative effects of forced borrowings on retainers going for Edo service. In Mito, too, retainers in Edo were exempt from contributions to the domain's military expenses and were also given supplementary allowances. Fief holders received "Edo rations," equivalent to three *fuchi* per fifty *koku* of holding, while those with stipends less than twenty *koku* (and whose office allowance was also less than twenty *koku*) were recipients of an extra supplement itemized as "firewood expenses."[59] In Tosa as well, retainers serving in Edo received a subsidy, in the form of a rice certificate, which was a return on the domain's forced borrowing. In Tannai's case, this amounted to 0.87 *koku* (14 percent) of the six *koku* borrowed back by the lord.[60] Furthermore, those stationed in Edo long-term had the amount of their forced loans reduced by one-half.[61]

Additional economic incentive to serve the Tosa lord in Edo came in the form of other special allowances, the amount of which varied according to the size of a retainer's stipend or fief.[62] In Tannai's case, the allowance amounted to twenty *koku*, ten *koku* support rice and another ten *koku* service grant; apparently Tannai was mistaken earlier when he noted that the figure was twenty-two *koku*.[63] Allowances of this magnitude were probably received on each of Tannai's ten trips to Edo between the years 1741 and 1788.[64] Tanshirō also made a number of trips, and the "Record" shows that he received a subsidy for his service in Edo in 1749 and 1750.

In later entries from Tannai's account,[65] we can see that he was still struggling with his debt, difficulties exacerbated by his father's death in 1752. In addition to the expenses of the funeral (150 *monme*), Kakimori's death caused problems in that while Tannai's succession as househead was permitted, at the same status as his father, he was granted a stipend of only twenty *koku* plus a seven-man allotment of rice. This was a decrease of four *koku* in base stipend and three-man allotment of rice from the amount received while Kakimori was househead. With a forced borrowing of 25 percent, in actual terms Kakimori's death meant a reduction in stipend of three *koku*, from eighteen to fifteen *koku*. His death reduced the number of mouths to be fed, but the household still had to purchase additional rice for consumption. As a result, early in the first month of 1753 Tannai sent Saitaniya what appears to have been a hurriedly written letter, briefly reviewing how his income was spent and requesting Saitaniya's assistance with another, substantial loan.[66] This time the loan was for 650 *monme*, a sum roughly equivalent to his annual income minus the forced borrowing. Because of Kakimori's death, no member of the Tani family went to Edo in 1752, but beginning with the next cycle of alternate attendance, Tannai made the trip frequently (eight times in over a twenty-year period).

At a reduced level of income and with continued forced borrowings, there was little hope of Tannai gaining financial solvency, even with subsidies received for Edo service. According to a memo he kept, Tannai was not able to pay all his year-end bills in 1752–1753; in 1752, 33.82 *monme* of his bill for medicine (63.52 *monme*) and 1,112 *mon* of his bill for miscellaneous goods, including rice (3,942 *mon*), went unpaid.[67] No mention is made, however, of what provisions might have been made for that remaining debt.

Tannai was repeatedly forced to break the second precept he set for himself by taking out additional loans from other merchants, including a pawnbroker. (He was able, however, to collect his pawned sword later after making a payment of 48.9 *monme*.) A notation from the end of the following year, 1753, lists loans of 150 *monme* from a nonmerchant source (from a Yoshimoto dono), 54 *monme* from a pawn shop, and incompletely paid bills to four individuals, for a total of 56 *monme* and 486 *mon*.[68] The situation showed no improvement in 1754, with Tannai requesting a loan of 100 *monme* from Saitaniya shortly before leaving for Edo on the alternate attendance. He tells Saitaniya, "I probably will be able to pay it back when I return from Edo next year," but he does not promise anything, for "the future is unknown" (*un wa ten ni ari*).[69] There is evidence that about this time Tannai had been seeking a different solution to his financial problems, joining a mutual savings association (*kō*). An entry for 1754 shows that he received the sum of 60 *monme* from an unnamed association, which he applied to the loans he owed Saitaniya.[70]

More than two decades after his "Record of Daily Necessities," Tannai was appointed to a number of important positions in the domain bureaucracy that came with a sizeable stipend (two hundred *koku*) and office salaries, but his written account stops in 1754 and thus gives us no clues as to how his life might have changed.[71] This late career path was exceptional, however, and the segment of his life covered in the account ledger was by far more typical of the existence of a low-ranking retainer in the middle of the Edo period.

The Administrative and Support Staff

Alternate attendance resulted in a bifurcation of domainal government, with the main headquarters in the castle town and a secondary branch in Edo.[72] Given the dual structure of early modern government, the administrative structure of the Edo branch largely mirrored the one back home. The obvious exception was that there were no domain officials in Edo in charge of urban, rural, or shrine and temple affairs for the domain. Ordinarily three senior advisors were stationed in Edo while the lord resided there, and one of them served on long-term status as the *Edo rusui karō*, the highest authority of the domain during the lord's absence.

An inventory of jobs performed by retainers in Edo differs little from a list of the same jobs in the domain. Officials supervised, and their subordinates carried out, secretarial and budgetary tasks, personnel management, oversight of shipping, rice stocks, purchasing and storage of general supplies, and guard duties in the interior of the compound as well as at its several gates. There were numerous positions surrounding the needs of the lord, such as bodyguards, food servers, cooks (including more specialized fish cooks), a miso master, food taster (*gozenban*), doctors, furniture cleaners, tea master, hairdresser, and stable master. Some of these officials interacted with merchants with whom the domain had an ongoing, established relationship to acquire the commodities and supplies necessary to support the compounds and their populations. They also had to deal with commoners who were hired on a contractual basis to maintain the gardens there.[73]

Since the purpose of alternate attendance was service to the shogun, many retainers carried out tasks in support of that. Tosa, for example, was responsible for fire-prevention duty at Zōjōji temple, an assignment usually given within a couple of weeks of the lord's arrival in Edo. It was a duty often shared with Arima. In the case of fire, Tosa men protected the main hall while Arima men were dispersed throughout the remainder of the precincts.[74]

One position of great importance to the domain that was unique to Edo was that of the Edo liaison (*Edo rusui yaku*). Earlier, in chapter one, we noted his role in requesting permission for the lord to deviate from the fixed schedule for rotation or to deviate from the designated route. Not to be confused with the *Edo rusui karō*, the liaison's main function was to maintain smooth diplomatic relationships with the shogunate and with other domains. The significance of this position is highlighted by the fact that problems between two domains, even when they occurred outside of Edo, were not dealt with by officials in the domains. Negotiations were carried out by the liaisons in Edo, as when, for example, border disputes occurred between two neighboring domains, such as Tosa and Uwajima.[75] The liaison's roles as a public relations man, lobbyist, information officer, and agent for the delivery of official gifts from the domain to the shogunate necessitated an unusual degree of mobility, and they were free to come and go at the compound without permission from an overlord. The liaison would make contacts at extravagant parties and outings in and around Yoshiwara, during visits to theaters, and through frequent attendance at *haikai* and other literary meetings.[76]

Created early in the period at daimyo initiative, the position of Edo liaison signified a reaction to unstable conditions, particularly the Tokugawa's frequent use of confiscation and transfers.[77] His key responsibility was to assure that his domain was fulfilling its obligations to the shogun and acting according to precedent. Carrying that out involved simple communications, transmitting newly issued Tokugawa laws and ordinances to the lord or notifying the shogun of the lord's whereabouts, as when Tosa's liaison delivered the following note from Lord Yamauchi Toyonobu: "This morning a fire broke out nearby and soon spread to my residence, destroying it completely. This is to inform you that because of the fire I have evacuated to the middle compound at Shiba."[78] It could also be for more weighty matters, such as when Tosa, as part of its reform program in 1787, sought permission from the shogunate to perform its ceremonial duties and gift giving at half-status. Tosa's Edo liaison conferred with his counterpart from Kumamoto domain, since officials there had already successfully applied for the same. In response, Tosa "changed the request to be more similar to the precedent."[79] Tosa's liaison called on the representatives of the shogunate's senior councilors every day for twenty days until the request was approved.

With more than 250 domains, it is not surprising that smaller groups of representatives formed cooperatives based largely on status, personal relations between daimyo, or the physical proximity of compounds in Edo. Tosa was a member of the second of the two most important groups, the "Nine House" Cooperative (*kyūke kumiai*), whose other members included Kuroda, Fujito, Hachisuka, Nabeshima, Satake, Date, Sō, and Tachibana. The representatives communicated most often outside one another's compounds, meeting in person at teahouses or, as suggested above, sometimes at the Yoshiwara, as well as via circulars and regular two-way correspondence.[80]

The written communications sent between Edo liaisons reveal their many concerns. They worried about issues of behavior and etiquette related to the daimyo's procession; public incidents, particularly those involving bloodshed by people from their domain; etiquette vis-à-vis the shogunate, including gift giving; and, most broadly, the interpretation of Tokugawa laws and ordinances. The liaisons also gathered information for future use. By consulting one another, they were able to respond to the shogunate's demands in a unified manner, at times to deflect demands deemed unreasonable from the domains' perspective, as when Tanuma Okitsugu made an unprecedented attempt to impose what amounted to a regular form of taxation on the daimyo in the late eighteenth century.[81]

The importance of the position of Edo liaison is indicated by its high level of remuneration (usually in the two- to three-hundred-*ryō* range, but even higher in some large domains).[82] As one Confucian scholar from Tosa recorded in his diary account of the domain's economizing program, "The Edo liaison's work involves the shogunate, so for this special reason his stipend will continue as before."[83] They were also given generous allowances for entertainment and bribes and were known to misappropriate funds. The diary of Tosa's Mori Yoshiki makes note of the poor behavior of Satsuma's Edo liaison, whom he reported stayed only five days a month in his domain's compound, sleeping routinely at teahouses, spending money frivolously, sometimes even dipping into the domain's construction funds for personal use.[84] Retainer Mori Masana's relation, Mori Oki'emon, served as Tosa's Edo liaison and held frequent parties for his counterparts from elsewhere. Masana referred to these parties as "extravagant" and noted that it was customary to have an "after party" for the benefit of the host's friends with any leftovers that remained. So many of his Tosa friends came for the party that Oki'emon had to ask them to stop by in two shifts.[85] The

Tokugawa repeatedly prohibited the debauched behavior of liaisons, yet the fact that they were tolerated reveals that the shogunate thought them important to the efficient functioning of the realm.[86]

The Edo liaison needed to be a skilled interpreter of the political scene, to be able to comprehend the meaning of subtle changes in the wording of shogunal regulations (or, when they were unclear, to run to Edo castle to seek clarification), to investigate how other domains were interpreting the law, and to gauge the domains' reaction to these instructions. He also had to craft proposals for the domain that were most likely to be accepted. This involved extensive research, since precedent was of the greatest consequence in samurai society. These communications were essential for such matters as petitioning for a change in schedule for alternate attendance, to ensure a smooth succession or marriage for the lord, to request permission to repair the castle, to print paper money, or to hold musket practice in a daimyo compound in Edo.[87] In this way the representatives kept each other informed and helped their domains steer a safe course through the political waters of the time.

Another area of responsibility of these officials involved keeping the lord informed of procedures and etiquette for his periodic audiences with the shogun, as well as to accompany him to those events.[88] Actually, the liaison preceded the lord to the castle to make sure there were no troublesome surprises. Though he could not enter the audience hall with the lord, the representatives used this time to meet with various low-ranking officials in the government to keep abreast of recent developments.

While the Edo liaisons and many other important positions were filled by Tosa retainers, the smooth functioning of the domain's compounds also depended on the local population and surrounding rural areas. This local service population was usually employed on a contractual basis. In fact, it has been estimated that up to 10 percent of the city's population consisted of servants of the samurai and that perhaps one-quarter of the "samurai" population of Edo were servants.[89] This trend, within the daimyo compounds at least, developed largely as a result of the rising costs of participation in alternate attendance. Retainers on long-term posting in Edo were instructed to reduce the number of attendants they brought to Edo and to hire help locally when needed.[90]

This was particularly true for the inner quarters of the compounds. Explaining why such employment in warrior households was desirable for commoner women, the American merchant Francis Hall wrote that the "palaces of the hereditary nobles, employ a large number of female servants and each mistress of such Yashki [sic] is surrounded by a bevy of maids whose idle and luxurious life is the coveted position to which many a simple country maid aspires, knowing in what arts and accomplishments she will there be educated, to the better adornment of her position."[91] In the case of daimyo households, however, officials were looking not only for "simple country maids" who could clean, cook, and sew, but also young ladies to fill positions as female pages, attendants, and personal assistants of high-ranking women. The lord of Oshi domain (one hundred thousand *koku*) and his wife, for example, had twenty-four women serving them, and the wife of the retired lord had eighteen. Some of these women, however, were hired directly by the people they served and received their salaries directly from them, not from the domain.[92] Many fathers of merchant status or from elite village official or entrepreneurial families were willing to bear the substantial costs involved in service (mainly clothing and gifts) because a woman's refinement became "an index of the family's economic and social status."[93] In this way, many commoner women were exposed to samurai culture. Other women like Inoue Tsūjo, though, were appointed to their positions while in the domain and traveled to Edo to serve their own, largely voluntary, tour of duty.

There was a hierarchy of posts in the inner quarters of the compounds filled by women indispensable to its smooth functioning.[94] The woman filling the post of *orōjo* (female senior advisor of the inner quarters) for Tosa, for example, helped maintain communications between the lord, Toyokazu, and his nine-year-old son. Although Mori Yoshiki, the man who carried the heir when he was ill en route to Edo, was supposed to be in charge of his upbringing, relations between the son and his father were so poor that the *orōjo* had to intervene to keep them talking to one another, for instance by urging the boy to apologize to his father.[95]

All of the people discussed above—the women staffing the inner quarters, retainers such as Mori Yoshiki, Tani Tannai, among others, and a large support staff—fulfilled their varied duties in direct or indirect service to the lord in Edo. There they found a city unlike any other in Japan—in Tannai's time, probably the largest in the world. This urban center was shaped by the demands of alternate attendance, which drew tens of thousands of people annually from domains across the country and necessitated the establishment of elaborate networks of secondary administrative headquarters to house them. In the following chapter we will examine the physical world in which they lived.

5

Daimyo Compounds
Place and Space

THE MOBILIZATION OF the daimyo elite through alternate attendance changed the face of what had been up to 1603 simply the castle town of one of the most powerful lords in the country. Unlike Paris, London, and St. Petersburg, cities with which it has sometimes been compared, Edo was built in a frontier region, backward in political and economic terms. Yet with the Tokugawa's establishment of the shogunate in 1603 and the imposition of numerous controls on the daimyo, including most importantly alternate attendance, the city of Edo was transformed into a national center. Alternate attendance drew tens of thousands of residents annually from across the country and necessitated the establishment of an elaborate network of secondary administrative headquarters for the domains in Edo, where retainers like Tani Tannai could reside. While Edo was not the capital of a unified nation-state, alternate attendance gave the city a high degree of centrality through the forced movement of population to it from across the realm and the mobilization of resources required to support them.

This centrality generated growth in population to more than one million in the early eighteenth century, leading Englebert Kaempfer to opine that "one might rightfully call her [Edo] the largest in the world."[1] Almost a century and a half later, the Englishman Laurence Oliphant remarked that "the capital of Japan must take a first-class position, in point of extent and population, among the cities of the world."[2] Such was its reputation that a number of Western visitors to Japan claimed that its population topped the two million mark.[3] Its size and centrality led Japanese authors as well to refer matter-of-factly to Edo as Tōtō, the eastern capital, to contrast it with the former capital of Kyoto in the west.[4]

This chapter will examine how alternate attendance changed the face of Edo through the establishment of a network of daimyo compounds across the city. It will also explore the nature of the compound as a social microcosm: how space was utilized within its borders and how it related to the larger area outside. Most discussions of Edo in English-language sources focus on commoner sections of the city or the shogun's castle, leaving the broad sections of the city defined by the daimyo compounds largely unexplored.[5]

The Network of Daimyo Compounds

Cities may function as both politicized and politicizing entities. Edo, under the Tokugawa, became the supreme metaphor and mechanism of shogunal authority.[6] With the submission of the daimyo to Ieyasu and his investiture as shogun in 1603, Ieyasu was able to call upon the daimyo to transform his castle town into one more befitting a power asserting national hegemony. While there was no enclosing wall around the city, a monumental castle was constructed at the center with a donjon that stood almost seventy meters high, the tallest in the land. The city was laid out with an eye to internal threats, and accordingly it followed basic geomantic principles to align with the cosmos. It also was laid out to maintain strict segregation of the social estates by residential area. The city formed a clockwise spiral pattern; it passed through the social hierarchy as it led outward from the castle, through the residences of the daimyo, the bannermen and housemen, and finally the townsmen area at Nihonbashi. The spiral, which was probably not a preconceived design, was defined not by roads but by the wide moats and canals that served two purposes, defense and transport of goods in the city.[7]

Not only did the shogun compel the daimyo to rebuild the Tokugawa's castle town, he then forced the daimyo to build residences in the city and live there. The vassal daimyo were mostly located to the northeast of the castle, offering it the most protection from a geomantic perspective. The outside daimyo, including Tosa, were likewise mostly placed to the southwest (see Figure 5.1), especially along what became known as Daimyo Avenue (*Daimyō kōji*). The direct vassals of the Tokugawa were placed in a wide swath running from the southwest to the northeast. Lastly, townsmen occupied an area outside the secondary moat, running from the northeast to the south.[8]

In these areas the shogun bequeathed land to the daimyo on which to build residences (*hairyō yashiki*) close to his castle, first to those who began coming to Edo after 1600 to curry favor with the Tokugawa family. Of course, once a few lords came, others felt obliged to follow, much as the French nobility in Louis XIV's time felt compelled personally to attend the king's court.[9] Some Japanese warlords even transferred their families to Edo on their own initiative,

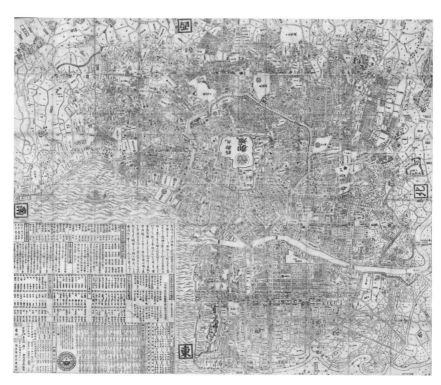

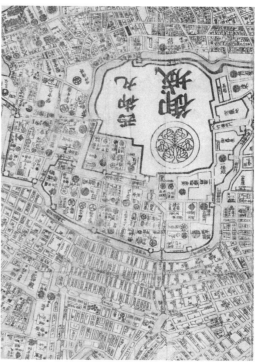

FIGURE 5.1. Map of Edo (above) and detail of area around Daimyō kōji (right). From Kanamaru Hikogoro publisher, Bunken Edo oezu, 1803. Courtesy of the East Asian Library, University of California, Berkeley.

although the lord of Tosa was not one of them. With the institutionalization of alternate attendance by 1642, all the lords required land on which to build their compounds. These made up more than half the warrior land, meaning the land in Edo granted by the shogun to his direct retainers, the housemen and bannermen, as well as to the daimyo. Warrior land in turn occupied almost 70 percent of the urban area.[10]

There were by most accounts between nine hundred and a thousand daimyo compounds.[11] While their numbers varied over time, at least two plots of land were granted to each lord, on which they built primary and secondary compounds. This grant was for use only and did not amount to ownership. The shogunate could in theory repossess it at will and dispose of it as desired, to grant it to another domain, to create a firebreak, or even to put in a medicinal herb garden for its own purposes. On the land grants closest to the shogun's castle, the daimyo built compounds referred to as the "upper" residence (*kami yashiki*). These were the main residence of the lords (also known as *i yashiki*, or place of residence) and their immediate families, chief officials, and many of their retainers. They also came to function as the official administrative center or headquarters of the domain in Edo.

Strategic factors may have affected the distribution of land for main compounds, part of a larger defensive strategy adopted by the shogunate in planning its capital city, where the easy flow of military forces was hindered by devices such as T-intersections, moats, and gates. One other precaution was that just as neighboring rulers, such as the lords of Tosa and Awa, were on different cycles of alternate attendance, they were also not to be in Edo at the same time. In the shogunal capital their main compounds stood side by side, recreating in miniature the political map in Shikoku. The arrangement of compounds could be manipulated at times by the shogunate in the same manner as the larger political map of Japan: a powerful domain such as Kaga, for example, found its main compound surrounded by those of Mito and Fukuyama, who were more trusted by the Tokugawa and hence could maintain some measure of surveillance over the activities in the Kaga compound.

Warrior land, including the daimyo compounds, occupied the high ground in the city, the so-called High City, or Yamanote as it is known today.[12] In fact, Edo, like Rome, was largely divided by rivers into a number of valleys and seven hills. Poised on the hilltops, the compounds took advantage of the natural beauty of the Musashino uplands. In contrast to the tightly packed commoner areas in the Low City, "the samurai—and especially the daimyo—residential areas in the High City enjoyed vast garden settings unimaginable in a [contemporary] western city" of the time. Wherever possible they faced highland ridge roads and used any natural spring to create a pond, which became the center of a landscape garden. The resident portion of the compound, whenever possible, was placed on high level ground in the northern part of the lot, with the garden on south-facing slopes.

The daimyo compounds were part of a city of green, again in contrast to the Low City, which was a densely occupied area, originally largely landfill, to the east of Edo Castle, occupied by commoners. Although living conditions in the barracks at the main residence were usually cramped, "the large surrounding gardens gave Edo the overall appearance of a great landscape park, particularly in the quarters of the most powerful lords."[13] From the top of Mt. Atago George Smith remarked, "[t]he whole surrounding aspect is that of a succession of Hyde Parks or Kensington Gardens — a city of green slopes and overhanging groves." This and other observations made by foreigners are also confirmed by a variety of pictorial sources, including *doro-e*, oil paintings dating from late in the period.[14] In the Jōnan area between Akasaka and Shirogane, daimyo compounds actually occupied the entire hillock, and through its woods "Mount Fuji could be seen to the west, and the sea to the east, while gentle pastoral scenes extended over a richly varied landscape."[15]

Strolling gardens were part and parcel of every principal compound, but it is not as commonly known that many of these contained flower gardens, which fulfilled multiple purposes in addition to the obvious aesthetic one. At Kii domain's residence in Akasaka, there were two different flower gardens, a chrysanthemum field and orchards for plum and peach trees. The garden in Owari's Ichigaya compound appears to have been a place to stockpile plants for use as needed in the rest of the compound. Potted plants and flowers were grown here for official gifts as well, and plants were grown for medicinal purposes.[16]

The daimyo quarter was not only green but spacious. Rutherford Alcock noted that circling between the broad moats around the castle "are fine open spaces . . . not less than fifty feet in width, lined on one side with the outer buildings and great massive-looking gateways of the Daimio's residences."[17] Moving from the commercial part of the city into the daimyo quarter, he found the vast dimensions of all the daimyo residences striking.

Secondary or middle compounds (*naka yashiki*) were built at some distance from the castle, and their function was more fluid relative to the upper and lower compounds. They were to be used when the main headquarters were being repaired or as the residence of the recognized heir of the current daimyo, the retired lord, or the mother of the current lord. It was not unusual for larger domains to have multiple middle compounds, as was the case with Tosa. Typically they were larger than the main residence since they were not constrained by proximity to the castle, where land was at a premium.

After the Meireki fire of 1657, which left more than a hundred thousand persons dead, the shogunate instructed the daimyo to build residences on the outskirts of the city to alleviate crowding, to serve as a refuge in case of fire in the city center, and to provide temporary housing when the main residences burned down. These were known as "lower" or supplementary compounds (*shimo yashiki*). They were not built up as extensively as the other two, and they assumed the characteristics of a vacation retreat or villa. Given their location, they were often surrounded by townsman areas or farmland. The largest of the three principal residences, the lower compounds often contained extensive strolling gardens, with ponds and teahouses. At least one (Hirado) had a stable of sumo wrestlers. Daimyo like Matsura Seizan of Hirado lived in their domain's lower residence during their retirement. There they were free of their former responsibilities and had time to stroll in the gardens and to meet with friends and a cultured elite.[18]

The recreational character of these residences is evident in Owari domain's lower residence in Toyama-chō (present-day Shinjuku ward), which was four kilometers from the main compound. It was the most spacious and certainly the most unusual of the domain's holdings. Dating to 1669, it spanned an area of 136,000 *tsubo* (450,160 sq. m), the majority of which was taken up by the garden. Within this space a pond of 20,000 *tsubo* (66,200 sq. m) was dug, the dirt from which was deployed to recreate in miniature mountains such as Hakone-san (44.6 m) and Atago-san (25.6 m). Odawara post station (located near Hakone) was faithfully reproduced to scale, its thirty-seven buildings running to more than two hundred meters in length. A river coursed through the compound, and three pre-existing shrines and temples were incorporated into the grounds.[19]

The more relaxed atmosphere of the lower residence is evident in that a number of lords, including Mito and Owari, had kilns constructed in the gardens. Owari's Toyama kiln was staffed by potters from Seto and produced ceramics in the style of Seto-Mino. Similar to many of his fellow daimyo, "he [Owari] apparently thought that the addition of a small operating kiln would add to the ambience of the garden, as well as afford him the opportunity to create his own ceramic utensils."[20] In this way, regional culture (i.e., of the domains) was produced in Edo and sometimes circulated elsewhere as well through gift exchanges.

Many domains built multiple lower residences but did not house substantial numbers of people there. Accordingly, despite the proliferation of compounds, the Edo populations of the domains remained overwhelmingly concentrated in the main and middle residences, close to the lord. In the case of Tosa, for example, 93 percent of its population of 3,195 in Edo in 1684 was concentrated in these two residences. This made sense given that the ostensible purpose for retainers being in the city was service to the lord.

Most large domains had more than three principal compounds. There could only be one main residence (headquarters), of course, but these domains maintained multiple middle and lower compounds. The Ikeda of Tottori had ten of these three types of compounds, the Mōri of Chōshū nine, the Tokugawa of Kii and the Date of Sendai eight each, and the Nanbu of Morioka seven. The size of a domain's total holdings varied substantially. Both Sendai and Kii had eight compounds each, but Sendai's totaled only 80,000 *tsubo* (264,800 sq. m), in comparison with 230,000 *tsubo* (761,300 sq. m) for Kii domain. Moreover, Kaga's four compounds surpassed both of them with 320,000 *tsubo* (1,059,200 sq. m) in sum.[21] Tosa (see Table 5.1) was not in the same league as these domains, but in the early eighteenth century it was among the top thirty with total holdings (for the principal compounds) between 10,000 and 60,000 *tsubo*, its three compounds totaling 32,422 *tsubo*.[22]

In addition to the three main residences, most domains purchased space along the waterfront of Edo Bay on which to build large-scale warehouses where commodity goods could be easily unloaded from ships and stored until needed. Some small domains without this type of compound instead used a part of the lower residence as a place to store goods from the home territory.

Many domains also purchased land in the outskirts of the city, often close or actually contiguous with the lower residences. Known most often as *kakae yashiki*, they were used for various purposes such as housing for various family members of the daimyo's family. One Western visitor to Japan in the early Meiji period described them as "smaller editions of the *bessō* [summer residences], being minor suburban residences in the country round Yedo."[23] They were also sometimes used as training areas, particularly for musket practice, and as an alternative safe haven in case of fire at the principal residences. Occasionally they were put to agricultural use; farmers living on the land taken into the domain's employ there helped to supply the principal compounds with foodstuffs.[24] Others were used as residences for retainers. By the closing decade of the period, *kakae yashiki* consisted of slightly more than a fifth (22.4 percent) of the total land under all domains' administrative control in Edo.[25]

Collectively, the compounds gave a distinctive look to the urban landscape. Felice Beato's famous panoramic view of Edo from Mt. Atago (Figure 5.2), looking north toward Daimyō kōji, captures a number of the compounds in the foreground, each enclosed by a wall of tiled barracks, broken in places only by massive gates. These compounds were described in the late 1870s by Thomas McClatchie, who was able to view them albeit often in run-down condition, as "present[ing] towards the street an almost unbroken frontage, save where a few large gateways, composed of heavy timbers strengthened with iron clamps, interpose to relieve the monotony of the general style of architecture. . . . They often differ widely as regards size, shape, mode of ornamentation, etc., but there is yet manifest a general likeness."[26] Some of this likeness came from the fact

TABLE 5.1. Tosa Domain's Edo Compounds

A. 1725

Compound	Location	Size (tsubo)
Upper	Kajibashi	7,052
Middle	Shiba Mita	8,479
Lower	Shinagawa Ōimura	16,891
Kakae	Shimo-Takanawa	5,875
Machinami kakae	Shinagawa Ōimura hama	869
Machinami kakae	Zōjōji orei-ryō	162
Kerai kakae	Shimo-Meguro mura Zōjōji orei-ryō	2,693
Kerai kakae	Shimo-Shitaya Kanesugi Tōei-zan ryō	653
Machi	Shimo-Takanawa Kita-chō	903
Machi (water supply)	Shiba Mita itchōme	367
Machi (warehouse)	Minami-Kon'ya	133
Machi (warehouse)	Minami-Hatchōbori ni-chōme	378
TOTAL (12)		44,455

B. 1842

Compound	Location	Size (tsubo)
Upper	Kajibashi	7,355
Middle	Shiba Mita	6,955
Middle	Hibiya	1,126
Rented Land	Shinagawa	200
Rented Land	Shinagawa	250
Rented Land	Shinagawa	200
Rented Land	Shinagawa	200
Rented Land	Shinagawa	100
Rented Land	Shinagawa	100
Lower	Shinagawa	15,851
Lower	Tsukiji	6,568
Lower	Fukagawa	4,000
Kakae	Fukagawa	606
Kakae	Shinagawa Hamagawa-chō	869
Machi nami	Shiba Mita	367
Machi	Imba-chō	136
TOTAL (16)		(44,883)

FIGURE 5.2. Panorama of Edo from Mt. Atago showing daimyo compounds in foreground. Felice Beato, ca. 1865. Collection Centre Canadien d'Architecture / Canadian Centre for Architecture, Montréal.

that the one seemed almost to meld into the next, as they were often in rectangular blocks of from four to six. This meant that many compounds typically had only two sides facing the street.

According to both written and pictorial evidence, the lords' mansions were quite a beautiful spectacle before the Meireki fire of 1657. The most startling visual evidence is the *Edozu byōbu*, panoramic screen paintings that depict the city in great detail, although the interior spaces of the daimyo compounds are much abbreviated (see Figure 5.3).[27] The freestanding gates were decorated in the extravagant style associated with Momoyama and early Edo-period architecture. Those of the highest-ranking (*kunimochi*, or "province-holding") daimyo mostly had two-story gateways with various sculpture and other embellishments. For example, the front gate of the residence of the daimyo of Hikone ran more than eighteen meters in length and was decorated with gilded sculptures of rhinoceroses. The generous use of gold leaf on the eaves and ridge tiles was a powerful political statement. According to *Ochiboshū*, the roof tiles of the main residence of the daimyo of Hikone was ringed by a *nagaya*, or barracks, with roof tiles decorated with "gold Chinese-bellflower crests from which light seemed to shine at night."[28]

One reason for the opulence of the compounds early in the period was that shoguns Hidetada and Iemitsu visited the daimyo frequently, which made the lords feel compelled to make major renovations.[29] They spent lavishly, particularly in building special ceremonial entrances as well as audience and entertainment facilities. These extravagant gates contained cusped gables of a type that could also be found only on castle donjons and above the entrance of palaces.[30]

The Meireki fire "effectively dampened the enthusiasm of the shogun and

daimyo alike for costly, rhetorical building projects."[31] The repeated fires encouraged this restraint, and the shogunate continually reminded the daimyo, even those of province-holding status, that "rebuilding in an elaborate way is a waste [of resources] — it should be done as simply as possible."[32] The construction of two-story gateways was prohibited, and the daimyo replaced the freestanding ceremonial gateways that had burned with more modest entrances built into the walls of the barracks that defined the boundaries of the compound. This type of gateway had formerly been used early in the period as service entrances to the compounds, but "were now elevated to a role of the highest symbolic importance."[33] Given their importance, it is not surprising that gates were pegged to status and subject to minute regulations regarding size, number of guardhouses, and general style, including whether or not the guardhouse gable was cusped.

Although rebuilt in a less resplendent fashion, Daimyo Avenue was still a remarkable sight. The massive timbers of the entrances of the compounds "and flanking guard houses, or *bansho*, became a substitute for the polychrome grandeur of the earlier gateways . . . [and] spelled out in a quieter symbolic language the identity and rank of the daimyo for whom they were built."[34] They were a must see for pilgrims and other travelers passing through Edo on their way to Ise and other destinations. A village headman in Edo to present a petition in 1865 used the adjective "beautiful" (*utsukushiki koto*) repeatedly to describe them.[35] Much earlier in the period, but still after the Meireki fire, Englebert Kaempfer, in Edo on his own type of alternate attendance with the Dutch, remarked that the compounds "are arranged along streets and are magnificently built, with heavy gates closing off the outer courtyard."[36] Indeed, a visit to the *nagayamon* located today outside the Tokyo National Museum at Ueno, its two

FIGURE 5.3. Main residences of Owari, Kii, Mito, and Echizen Fukui, at top, and Edo Castle area. From "Edo-zu byōbu." Courtesy of Kokuritsu rekishi minzoku hakubutsukan.

elaborate gatehouses all that remains of Tottori domain's main compound, gives the viewer a taste of its magnificence and visual power.[37]

After the Meireki fire, which wrought a path of destruction over about 60 percent of Edo, the city was redesigned in numerous ways and, with the bridging of the Sumida River, its population was allowed to spill over into Honjō. There was also widespread movement of the main and middle compounds. The Three Related Houses of Kii, Mito, and Owari were relocated out of the area within the inner moat of the castle to create a firebreak and give more spacious quarters. The middle compounds were largely moved to the inner side of the outer moat. Many shrines and temples were likewise transferred to the outskirts of the city, freeing more space in the inner core for redistribution of the daimyo compounds and the creation of wider streets and firebreaks.[38] After this forced movement and the establishment of lower compounds with shogunal encouragement (and land grants), the location of most of the main residences remained unchanged from the late seventeenth century onward, though land grants and transfers involving mostly smaller daimyo continued in other parts of the city until the mid-eighteenth century.[39] Moreover, as will be clear below, the static nature of the three principal residences for the larger daimyo belies other less apparent changes in land usage.

While most gates were rebuilt in a simpler style after the Meireki fire, colorful gates were not totally erased from the Edo landscape. A number of large domains were given permission by the shogunate to build red gates. These were visible, for example, in the compounds of the daimyo of Hiroshima (see Figure 5.4) and signified close ties to the Tokugawa; permission to build them was given only when a shogun's daughter married a daimyo.[40] The origins of the well-known red gate of Tokyo University lies here, with the betrothal of the daughter of the eleventh shogun, Ienari, to the Maeda Nariyasu in 1823. In apparent contravention of Tokugawa regulations, though, it was built as a freestanding gate. Despite its opulence, the *akamon* served as an entrance to the new bride's quarters in the compound and signified her symbolic importance as a link between her new family, the Maeda, and the shogun.

Tosa's Network of Compounds

Tosa's many compounds in Edo formed a network in which each played a distinct role. In 1684, the domain maintained five establishments: the main compound at Kajibashi and others at Shiba, Shinagawa, Hatchōbori, and Shindenjima. Interestingly, none of the compounds at this time were designated as "middle compounds."[41] Several decades later, the number had more than doubled to twelve, according to figures compiled at shogunal request in 1712 and 1725 (see Table 5.1).[42]

The large number of compounds, however, is far in excess of what is apparent from an examination of books of military heraldry, which usually only list the two or three principal compounds whose land was granted by the shogunate. The large number of compounds is also not apparent from an examination of Edo city maps, which often reflect only putative ownership — or more precisely, only rights to occupancy of plots of land — rather than actual land usage. As will be discussed below, the number and size of a domain's compounds varied over time, with officials purchasing and selling off land according to changing economic needs.

Tosa's network of twelve compounds in 1725 (Table 5.1A) consisted of one main headquarters at Kajibashi on Daimyo Avenue, just inside the gate for which it was named; one middle compound, at Shiba (Mita); and one lower compound at Shinagawa Ōimura. These three principal compounds were established on land granted the Yamauchi lord by the shogunate. The remaining parcels were found at various locations on townsman or farmer land, purchased

FIGURE 5.4. Main residences of Hiro-
shima (right and center-right) and
Saga (left and center-left) domains.
"Tōto meisho. Kasumigaseki zenzu."
Courtesy of Sakai Gankō, Ukiyoe
bijutsukan.

outside the city center. Tosa, like many other domains after the devastating
Meireki fire, formally requested of the shogunate, and also sought to purchase
on its own, land away from the congested central areas, and it was bequeathed
a land grant at Shinagawa three years later in 1660. It was the most spacious of
the compounds and grew from large (10,891 *tsubo* in 1712) to larger (16,891 *tsubo*
in 1725). Five other parcels of land (numbers 4–8 in Table 5.1A) were treated as
quasi–warrior lands, but came under the administrative authority of a Tokugawa intendant; consequently land taxes and various other exactions were applied to them. Two of the parcels (nos. 5 and 6) were on former agricultural land
and were treated as townsman land; that is, they too were under the administrative authority of an intendant, but for census purposes their inhabitants were
included in townsman figures.[43] Number 5, the parcel at Shinagawa Ōimura
hama, was located near the lower compound, and the back portion of it, which
faced the ocean, was used as an unloading and storage area for lumber. Number
6 was used to house retainers. Parcels 9 through 12 were purchased for the do-

main by commoner proxies and with one exception (number 9) were under the administrative authority of the city magistrate. Number 9, located at Shimo-Takanawa, was contiguous with the domain's other holding there (number 4) and the two together were treated as one. The water reservoir (number 10) was located across the street (Mita dōri) from the domain's middle compound at Shiba.[44] The final two parcels (numbers 11 and 12), at Minami Konya-chō and Minami Hatchōbori, were both warehouses.

Tosa, like many other domains after the Meireki fire, at its own initiative began purchasing farmland, classified as *kakae yashiki*, in villages outside the original boundary of Edo. At the time of the 1725 survey, it owned at least three such landholdings, which contributed to a drastic expansion of the informal city.

Retainers also lived in residences purchased by the domains in townsman areas, although it is not clear whether or not this was simply because the other residences were too crowded. For example, in the early eighteenth century, the mother of the Tosa lord, accompanied by a number of retainers, lived in in at a residence in Shimo-Takanawa, close to (probably adjoining) the lower compound at Shinagawa.[45] Some evidence for Satsuma domain suggests that these landholdings were used to alleviate crowded conditions in the main compounds when the lord was in Edo; retainers living in townsman areas were ordered to return to the main compounds after the Shimazu lord returned home. Elsewhere, too, some retainers requested to live in these areas, perhaps out of dislike for barracks life.[46]

Economic conditions directly affected the number of compounds a domain maintained. In 1768, forty-odd years after the previous census, Tosa domain was in possession of four fewer parcels of land, which reduced the overall area of its holdings by 11,000 *tsubo*, almost 25 percent.[47] The reduction in landholdings was no doubt due to the serious economic difficulties the domain was experiencing mid-century, conditions which led Tosa to undertake a reform program in the Tenmei period (1781–1789).[48]

The last survey figures available, from 1842 (Table 5.1B), show an economic recovery in the domain, as seen by the substantial increase in landholdings in Edo, slightly in excess of the levels of the early eighteenth century (44,883 vs. 44,455 *tsubo*). The domain sold or traded away its two small warehouses at Minami Konya-chō and Minami Hatchōbori, but acquired two large new ones (listed as lower compounds) from the shogunate, at Tsukiji and Fukagawa. Tsukiji was a substantial holding, nearly the same size as the middle compound at Mita. With the compound at Fukagawa, the domain acquired for the first time property on the eastern side of the Sumida River. It also acquired a small parcel (606 *tsubo*) of contiguous land, classified as townsman land, and then enclosed it with its shogunal land grant, a common strategy that domains pursued to increase the size of land grants. At first glance there appears to have been much activity in Shinagawa, with the domain leasing six small parcels of land totaling 1,050 *tsubo*. In fact, nothing about Tosa's landholdings in Shinagawa had changed since the earlier censuses of 1725 and 1802 except the manner in which they were reported to the Tokugawa. The six parcels had been part of the lower compound at Shinagawa since the early eighteenth century, but were recorded individually for the first time in 1842. The properties were listed as rentals for official purposes, since each was an individual land grant from the shogunate to other parties and therefore technically could not be alienated, but they were all joined to Tosa's official land grant of 15,851 *tsubo*.

Some scholars have assumed that the picture of land use with regard to the daimyo compounds, as least after the Meireki fire of 1657, remained largely static.[49] As the discussion above indicates, however, the situation was quite different. Records for at least twenty-five land transactions for Tosa in Edo reveal that the domain bought and sold property according to economic need and also for status considerations; it and other domains tried to expand individual plots whenever possible or to create large holdings through a series of purchases of smaller plots. Larger landholdings for the primary compounds improved the daimyo's status in a society that was obsessed with such social distinctions. They also ameliorated conditions at the densely populated main and secondary compounds.

While the land granted by the shogun could in principle be traded for another similar piece of land, it could not be sold. Yet an examination of Tosa's land transactions reveals that it only slightly disguised purchases of shogunal-granted land through fictitious land exchanges. For example, if one domain wanted to buy some of this land from another, on paper the two agreed to an "exchange" (*aitai gae*) of land. They did this to receive official permission for the transaction, but it is clear that the land was in fact sold. This is what happened with Tosa's lower residence at Shinagawa, which, as noted, consisted of one parcel of land granted from the Tokugawa and six (illegal) purchases.[50]

Tosa's main residence remained at Kajibashi for the duration of the Tokugawa period (and the area figures for 1802 and 1842 were identical at 7,052 *tsubo*), which might seem to indicate that the landholding was static. In 1698, however, significant changes occurred when the Tokugawa redistributed the land grants of a number of domains after a major fire inflicted substantial damage to the central part of the city. Tosa found three-quarters of its so-called Levee Residence and two-thirds of its middle compound confiscated by the shogunate. As dispenser of land to the daimyo, the shogunate reserved the right to take land back, and it exercised this right from time to time, as in this instance.[51] Both of these parcels of land were close to the main compound: the middle compound just to the east; and the Levee Residence, per its name, located on an embankment just inside Kajibashi gate just across the street to the east of the middle residence.[52] In exchange, Tosa was given land amounting to 7,041 *tsubo*, 800 *tsubo* more than the parcels confiscated. This was added to the main compound, drastically changing the configuration of that landholding and regularizing what had been an oddly shaped parcel into a shape close to a rectangle.[53] As a result of this change, the number of daimyo compounds on the block was reduced from five to two (Tosa and Awa), with Tosa occupying the northern portion.[54] After the alterations of 1698, however, the main residence at Kajibashi remained largely unchanged except for a minor redistribution of land in 1834 in which a small portion was confiscated from one part of the compound and a larger piece, in another section, granted, resulting in a net increase of 303 *tsubo*.[55]

The compound at Shiba Mita provides a good example of the sometimes substantial changes that could occur to a single landholding. Beginning in 1628 as a modest parcel of land of only 100 *tsubo* (331 sq. m), it became home to the young heir Tadatoyo three years later. Conditions there were cramped, however, so two parcels of land adjoining the original grant were purchased in 1669, increasing the area of the compound to 8,479 *tsubo*. This made it considerably larger than the main compound (then 7,052 *tsubo*). After two separate fires raged through the Shiba area in 1735, the shogunate decided to widen the road running between Tosa and Satsuma domain's compounds, confiscating a slice of Tosa's residence but giving it a corresponding piece adjoining another side; by this time Shiba had been designated the middle compound.[56] Fifteen years later (1750), the Tokugawa granted Tosa a second middle compound, at Hibiya, of 1,126 *tsubo*, and in exchange confiscated 1,519 *tsubo* from Shiba.[57] As a result, according to various records, conditions at Shiba became cramped and the domain's fire brigade, which performed duty for the Tokugawa at Zōjōji, was moved from Shiba to Hibiya.[58]

Tosa's compounds at Fukagawa and Tsukiji provide good examples of the way land granted by the shogunate was alienated late in the period, evidence that for most intents and purposes the daimyo were treating it as private property. Seeking to acquire the compound of a Tokugawa bannerman next door to its compound at Fukagawa, Tosa officials went through the required motions of trading one piece of granted land for another. In 1835, the two thousand–*tsubo* holding was acquired by "trading" it for a much smaller parcel of only one hundred *tsubo*. The internal Tosa domain record documenting this clearly notes that its piece of land was handed over in "name only." It was clear to all concerned, including the shogunate, which gave its sanction, that the transaction was a simple purchase. Such fictive exchanges increased significantly late in the Tokugawa period. These could involve multiple parties—witness the six-way transaction involving Matsudaira Sadanobu while he was serving as shogunal senior councilor—and money.[59]

The "Flowers of Edo"

Fires, like fights, were known by contemporaries as the "flowers" of Edo, colorful like fireworks (*hanabi*, or "flower-fires" in Japanese), which light up the sky. A major conflagration affecting a broad swath of the city occurred roughly once every six years.[60] This was a fact of life given the prevalence of wood as construction material and the high population density in the city, particularly in commoner sections.[61] In reading the Edo diaries of Tosa Confucian scholar Miyaji Umanosuke, one is struck by the frequency with which he mentions fires in the city. In much of his account, which covers the years 1839 through 1842, a notation about a fire occurs daily; on some occasions he records each of the four or five that had broken out in different areas, where and when the fire started, and importantly the time by which it had been put out, indicating just how much fires entered the consciousness of people living in Tokugawa Japan's largest city. These were not just distant fires of course. Residents in Tosa's Edo compounds had to deal with at least twenty-one major fires at the main residence and twelve at Shiba while the latter was the middle compound. Its other compounds in outlying areas were also affected, though not as frequently. Earthquakes, too, occasionally resulted in substantial damage.[62]

The spacing of the three principal residences of any domain took into consideration the frequency of fires in Edo. When there was a fire near the main residence, the lord and his entourage would be moved, depending on the direction of the fire, to either the middle or lower compound. The frequency of fires may have inured some people, including the lord, to them. From an upper floor at the main residence, Lord Toyosuke viewed the fire, which had already burned down the domain's compounds at Tsukiji and Hatchōbori, and gave instructions before he went to sleep to his attending retainer that he should be awakened if the fire came closer.[63] A warning of fire, with wooden clappers and bell, was sounded from the fire-watch tower at the main residence, but senior advisor Gotō Seijun recorded in his diary that the fire still seemed far away so he felt no need to report to the lord's residence.[64] On another occasion Mori Yoshiki was at the main residence at Kajibashi when a fire broke out in Shiba, and despite being on duty he was able to go with several colleagues to watch the fire, which burned one hundred homes. The following day he went "sightseeing" to witness the extent of the damage. On duty again four days later, fires struck closer to home. The watchman hit the alarm twelve times (indicating the fire's close proximity?) and called out that the fires could be spotted in seven different places, but in the end none reached the residence.[65]

The frequency of fires necessitated an escape plan, and most if not all domains had them. For Tosa, a fire in the vicinity of the main residence generally sent the lord and a small number of his retainers to the Shiba or Hibiya compound. When a fire struck close to the Shiba residence, the plan called for evacuation to the main residence or to nearby Zōjōji temple, which had a large amount of open space. If both the main and middle compounds were under threat, the contingency plan was to move essential personnel to the lower residence at Shinagawa, on the outskirts of the city.[66]

While the wide spatial distribution of a domain's principal compounds may have lessened the impact of major fires, the economic effects of Edo's many conflagrations was nonetheless considerable. The cost of rebuilding the main compound after the fires in 1772 and 1780 was a contributing factor in Tosa's dire fiscal conditional as well as its decision to apply to the shogunate to perform Edo-related duty at the reduced status of 100,000 *koku* (instead of the regular level of 200,000) for ten years. Tosa was not alone in this, of course, as the 1772 event was particularly devastating, leaving a path of destruction fifteen miles long and more than two miles wide. This reduced status would aid the domain in its program of domestic economic change, known as the Tenmei Reform. In practical terms this meant Tosa could reduce expenses in gift giving to the shogun and his officials. It also meant that while the lord would continue to perform duty at full status (e.g., continue fire prevention duty at Zōjōji) for the shogun, the numbers in his entourage could be reduced.[67]

While the fires that struck the main and middle compounds did not always result in complete disasters, the damage was often considerable and displaced many residents. When a principal compound burned down it often took years to rebuild. It took a full six years before the main residence at Kajibashi could be occupied again after a fire in 1756. Other major fires struck the main compound again in 1780 and 1784, and it was eight years before the lord was able to return. As a result, conditions at the middle compound became terribly cramped.[68]

When an Edo residence burned, it was not uncommon for other daimyo, Tokugawa officials, as well as religious prelates to assist the victims by sending emergency relief — "sympathy gifts" (*mimai hin*) — to the stricken domain. For example, in 1780, fire razed Tosa's main residence, and four hundred rice balls, a load of rice gruel, two barrels of sake, one thousand pieces of wood (to rebuild fences), steamed dumplings, and candlesticks were among the items received. That fire, one of three that broke out in its compounds and spread to a neighboring domain's, resulted in Tosa's being punished by the shogunate. In this case, the domain was put under orders of self-restraint (*ontashinami*) for eight days, which meant that social contacts at all of Tosa's compounds, not just at the offending main one, had to be kept to a minimum. Windows and gates in the barracks were shut and only unavoidable official business was permitted. Special fire watches throughout the night were also mandatory.[69]

When buildings burned in Edo, the flames could be felt, in a figurative sense, by retainers back in Tosa, who paid for reconstruction through stipend reductions. After the main compound burned in 1760, a 50 percent reduction was considered, but because of the severe consequences of such a drastic cut, stipends were reduced by a little more than 25 percent in 1761 and continued at that rate for an undetermined number of years.[70] Reductions of 50 percent did follow a major fire in 1772, prompting the domain to excuse retainers in Kōchi of less than two hundred *koku* from participating in the New Year's horse-riding competition, a major event in the castle town.[71] Edo-based samurai, in contrast, usually did not suffer these cutbacks, though they might lose valuable personal possessions in the flames. For example, Tosa retainer Hiraimiishi Motomasa had his menials toss his equipment into the moat below the main compound, but they burned nonetheless.[72] The shogunate recognized the tremendous burden these periodic fires imposed on the domain and occasionally offered the daimyo relief by allowing them to delay a cycle of attendance or even to excuse them from one, but these were only palliative measures.[73]

Tosa Domain's Other Compounds

The domain also maintained residences in Osaka, Kyoto, and Fushimi, which supplemented and in some respects supported the network of compounds in Edo. Of the three, Osaka was the most significant because the domain maintained warehouses there as well as residential space for a small permanent staff and a much larger cyclical, temporary influx of Tosa people. The Yamauchi lord and his retainers, like every daimyo of a western domain, passed through Osaka on the way to and from Edo, typically staying one to three days. The warehouses were for the storage of the domain's tax rice and other select domainal commodities — particularly lumber in the case of Tosa — until their later sale at central markets. Of course many of these goods were shipped for sale to Osaka not because there was no market for them in the domain but rather to satisfy creditors.[74] By the end of the seventeenth century, Osaka had assumed an important role as a transshipment node in both regional and national marketing systems. Large quantities of tax rice found its way to Edo and the Kantō area, as much as 8 to 10 percent of the rice consumed by Edo residents in many years.[75]

The practice of the daimyo maintaining residences in Osaka, unlike those in Edo, predated the imposition of Tokugawa rule in 1603. Many daimyo established residences in Osaka from the late sixteenth century, during Hideyoshi's reign. After the fall of his Toyotomi house in 1615, the shogunate confiscated all these residences and took the city under its direct administrative authority.[76] The daimyo could then only purchase land in Osaka using merchant proxies, and by the end of the seventeenth century nearly one hundred compounds had been constructed in a concentrated area known as Nakanoshima, newly developed by Osaka townsmen, with excellent access to the city's canals.[77] Tosa purchased a plot of land in 1617 across the river at Edo Canal that proved too narrow before moving four years later to a nearby location along the moat at Nagabori, where the compound would remain for the duration of the Edo period.[78]

These daimyo compounds in Osaka (known as *kura yashiki* or warehouse compounds) were smaller in scale (Tosa's was 4,500 *tsubo* compared to 7,052 and 8,479 for its main and middle residences in Edo) and per their name had the warehouse as one of their major structural elements. Nevertheless, Tosa's was one of the largest in the city and unusual in that it was bifurcated by a road. The eastern portion contained the lord's residence, numerous offices (for transport, rice, and paper) and rice warehouses. In the western section there was a boat warehouse, office and warehouse for retainers' stipend rice, a treasury, and a shrine to Inari.[79] To raise revenue, many domains also created rental housing on the property for townsmen, though these were physically separated from the rest of the compound.[80]

Given the centrality of the Osaka compound's economic function, it is not surprising that most of the few staff members permanently stationed there were financial officers, the highest ranked being charged with communicating with his counterpart in Edo regarding the market prices of key commodities. Other officials included supervisors of the rice warehouses, shipping and procurement agents, money officers, and inspectors.[81]

Osaka no doubt provided the lord and his entourage with a welcome rest break after the journey from Kōchi, whatever route was taken, before the almost two-week trek up the Tōkaidō to Edo. In Osaka the lord and his top retainers might relax by watching a performance of Noh or other type of theatrical performance at the compound.[82] Exactly how much freedom might have been given to the men in the entourage while in Osaka is unclear, but from the diaries of some retainers we know they were able to use the respite in Osaka to purchase goods, particularly on the return trip to Kōchi, a practice that will be discussed in more detail in chapter seven. On this leg of the journey, Osaka was the last stop before crossing over by boat to Shikoku and home, a time filled with anticipation and excitement.

Tosa and more than 130 other domains also maintained residences in Kyoto, mostly in the Shijō-Kawaramachi area.[83] These too, like the compounds maintained in Osaka, were purchased through commoner proxies. A long-term staff maintained the residence, where the lord might visit on his way to or from Edo.[84] The Tosa lord occasionally stayed overnight in Kyoto and, as noted in chapter one, had to petition the shogunate to do so legally.[85] Otherwise, the entourage would stop at Fushimi, where the lord and probably just a small number of his top officials would stay in a residence maintained by the domain.

The lord's activities in Kyoto reveal the important functions the city fulfilled in the cultural life of elite samurai even after the political capital had been moved east to Edo. While resting at his Kyoto residence, Lord Yamauchi would communicate with the permanent staff and give audiences to local aristocrats and Confucian scholars or other intellectuals or artists residing in the area. The top retainer in permanent residence at the compound, the Kyoto liaison (*Kyōto rusui yaku*), was in essence an intelligence and cultural affairs officer. He kept the lord informed of the goings-on in the area and communicated this to him personally, if the lord stopped in Kyoto, or, as was done more regularly, via correspondence. Another function was to help coordinate contacts for Tosa scholars and artisans who wanted to meet their counterparts, or to find teachers in the Kinai region to study under.[86] One of the most important officials posted to the imperial city was the Kyoto purchasing magistrate (*Kyōto kaimono bugyō*), who, as his title indicates, had the important job of overseeing the acquisition of high-quality goods, particularly handicraft goods, Nishijin silk, other types of cloth, arms, and armor from Kyoto for the domain residences in Edo and Kōchi. He worked together with merchant purveyors to acquire these goods.[87] In these various ways domains like Tosa remained connected, in economic and cultural terms, to the Kinai region, and alternate attendance acted as an agent in the flow of material culture across the country.

Spatial Organization within the Compound

Daimyo compounds were social spaces that reflected Tokugawa Japan's political and status systems. Reflecting the fractured nature of political authority below the shogun, the individual communities of the daimyo were walled. Describing a compound, Sir Rutherford Alcock wrote that it

> extends the greater part of its length on one side, with a large and imposing-looking gateway in the centre, from which stretches a long line of barred windows. . . . But these outbuildings are only the quarters of the numerous retainers attached, as in Europe in former times, to every baron and knight, by a feudal tenure. . . . In many cases, these extend for a quarter of a mile on each side of the main entrance, and form in effect the best gates, *entre cour et jardin*.[88]

The perimeter, in almost all cases, was defined by barracks, what Alcock refers to as "outbuildings," where the vast majority of retainers lived, and was broken only by the main and secondary gates.[89] The organization of the compound, with lower-ranking retainers ringing the perimeter, also mirrored the spatial layout of the castle towns, where their counterparts formed a protective zone around the castle and the lord's residence.

FIGURE 5.5. Schematic diagram of a daimyo compound. Courtesy of Cartographic Services Laboratory, University of Maryland, Baltimore County.

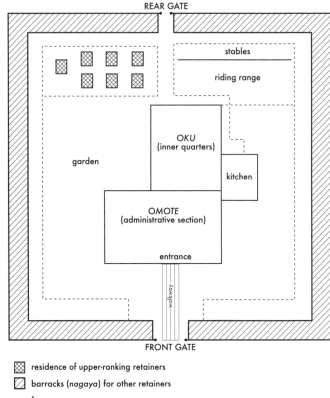

residence of upper-ranking retainers

barracks (*nagaya*) for other retainers

--- fence

Despite differences in scale between the various compounds, they also showed some common characteristics (Figure 5.5).[90] Space within the principal compounds of any domain, excluding the lower or warehouse compounds, was broadly divided into two sections: the palace (*goten kūkan*), itself divided into a subsection where the lord and his family resided (*oku*), and one where administrative and ritual functions took place (*omote*); and a section for his retainers, their dependents, and the support staff. On many contemporary maps the two sections are in different colors to make the division clear.

Given the daimyo's privileged position in the domain, as seen previously by his central position in the processions, it is not surprising that his living and working space and garden occupied the majority of the area in the compound. Consequently, retainers were packed together in a compressed space. Access to the lord's section was restricted to those working there or with official business. This inaccessibility further highlighted the lord's authority. To shield the daimyo's residence from his retainer's quarters, as Thomas McClatchie noted, a tall wooden fence was erected only a few paces from the barracks. Accord-

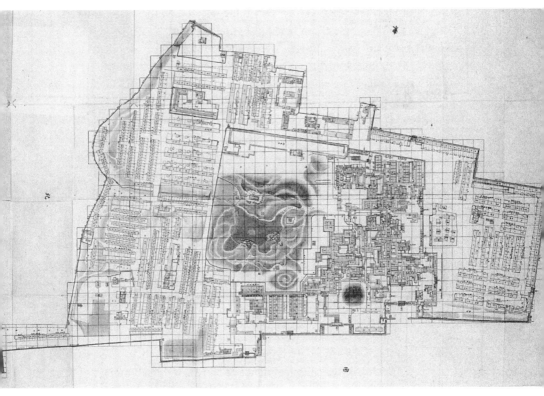

FIGURE 5.6. Kaga's main residence at Hongō. Courtesy of Kanazawa shiritsu
Tamagawa toshokan.

ingly, the entire inner face of the *nagaya* was "completely shut in as is the street
frontage."[91] At Kaga's main residence at Hongō (actual living conditions there,
in the barracks, will be explored in the following chapter), the living quarters
for retainers and their vassals were restricted to the northern and southern
portions, along with a strip along the eastern border (see Figure 5.6). Thus,
the normal route for retainers to move around the compound when on private
business would be to navigate around the lord's central space.

   To examine the interior space of the compound, we have a variety of sources,
including maps, diaries, and foreign observers' comments. Describing the space
just within the front gate, for example, Thomas McClatchie wrote that there "is
a courtyard, sometimes of very large size. In the case of the *yashiki* of a *daimio*
[*sic*] of high rank, it is paved all over with broad flagstones; in some instances it
is only partially paved, the remaining space being covered with large pebbles."[92]
This pebbled path led to the main part of the compound, which was divided
into official, public, and private spaces. Within the public space were rooms
where messengers brought news and rooms where the lord received guests or

granted audiences to retainers, the exact one selected on the basis of the status of the person or people to be brought before the lord. Leading farther away from the front of the compound were various administrative offices (for the senior advisor, inspector, treasurer, and supply chiefs, among others) where retainers discharged their duties. A number of small gardens divided the interior space as well as provided light to both the official and private portions of the residence. Other standard features of main compounds were a martial arts training center, watchtower, stables, and warehouses. Many other residences also had a holding cell, Noh stage, and, late in the period, a school for retainers. Those of larger domains might include riding grounds as well.[93]

Access between this official space and the private area of the compound was restricted by guards and a locked door. The private area was always oriented to the south for the most pleasant living conditions. The lord's sleeping quarters occupied the most remote portion of this area, and there were also living quarters for the lord's wife, with a separate sleeping area for when the lord spent the night, as well as for her female attendants. There was also a kitchen in the private area, manned usually by menials in the direct employ of the domain. Of course one or more gardens and a pond were essential features, and in some cases, depending on the lord's tastes, one could find a teahouse in the garden.

The compounds interfaced with the larger city of which they were a part. For example, a drawing of the main residence of Kururi, a vassal domain of thirty thousand *koku* in Kōzuke province, shows that it was bounded on two sides by four warrior residences: in the north by the main residence of Kurobane domain and the residence of a Tokugawa bannerman; and in the west by the main residence of Katsuyama domain. The other two sides faced roadways behind which rose other daimyo compounds. Two-storied barracks did not ring the entire perimeter. About two-thirds of the northern side, facing the daimyo and bannerman compounds, consisted of stockade fencing, leading to a barracks occupying the corner. About the same portion of the western side was similarly fenced. Since Kururi was a small domain, existing barracks probably adequately accommodated the men and therefore the stockade was an economical method of enclosing the perimeter.[94]

Use of Underground Space

Our knowledge of Edo has benefited greatly from the excavations of Tokyo that have taken place during the past twenty-five years, particularly during the economic heyday of the 1980s with its attendant building boom. One of the surprising discoveries in excavating Edo has been the extent to which underground space was utilized in samurai parts of the city — a necessity, perhaps, in a city with such a high population density and frequent fires. In some places there are many such chambers — more than a hundred at one of the University of Tokyo sites.[95] A few of these underground spaces — those in front of the palace — were indicated on compound maps, but most were not. They came to light only with the excavation of the various sites.[96] According to contemporary literary records, underground rooms first appeared after the Meireki fire of 1657 and became widespread by the turn of the century.[97]

Underground spaces (Figure 5.7) came in different shapes and sizes, often existed in multiple numbers with various configurations, and served diverse functions. Some were primarily storage spaces, particularly for valuables in times of fire.[98] Other, specifically designed underground rooms were used for making malt for sake, miso, rice vinegar, or even to raise bean sprouts, foodstuffs used for the compounds' residents.[99] Sometimes pits were created to obtain dirt to fill a depression elsewhere in the compound.[100] Also, on occasion underground rooms were converted to disposal pits when, for example, the caving in of a ceiling rendered the room unsuitable as storage space for valuables. Others, however, were intended from the beginning to hold refuse.[101]

Excavations have given us a concrete picture of how more surface or living space was created through landfill, sometimes using debris from a fire or natural disaster, and how building techniques were altered to compensate for soil conditions. At the Shiodome site — the location of three daimyo compounds — an elaborate wooden fence was constructed to brace the landfill in the compounds of the Sendai and Tatsuno domains. Thick wooden beams or layers of nonabsorbent materials such as tile or gravel were laid as support for the stone foundations of buildings at this and other daimyo compound sites constructed on the soft sediment of the Edo lowlands.[102]

The existence of disposal pits raises the question of how garbage was handled, whether goods were recycled, and more generally what kind of environmental consciousness those living in the compounds might have had. There is much to be investigated in this regard, as the mechanisms for the collection, transport, and disposal of *bushi* garbage are not well understood. Were disposal pits at the daimyo compounds intended as permanent repositories for refuse or were they temporary facilities for storing it until it could be discarded elsewhere, such as Eitai island?

Some scholars argue that a sophisticated disposal and recycling system existed in Edo from early on,[103] but the findings of archaeologists at Edo sites call this assumption into question. Piles of disposed materials can be found in the most unusual places: the middle of a garden or pond in a daimyo compound[104] or in the border ditch between two domain compounds. A large quantity of eighteenth- and nineteenth-century ceramics, particularly sake bottles and a small number of early Imari ware, for instance, were found in the ditch between the compounds of the Tosa and Awa domains.[105] Numerous wooden

FIGURE 5.7. Excavation of underground rooms of Hachinohe domain compound in Roppongi. Photos by author.

artifacts — unfinished wooden chopsticks, many broken into pieces, unfinished serving trays — and unglazed pottery, almost all made from molds, were found in a pond on the site of Kaga's residence in Hongō. It appears they were thrown away at one time or over a short period of time, probably after some ceremonial occasion.[106]

Spatial Consciousness

As daimyo compounds were individual social communities that interacted with the surrounding city, it is important to explore further the relationship between the two, particularly in spatial terms. In doing so our focus will be directed to the human activity along their boundaries, both within and just outside those lines of demarcation, deferring an examination of life inside the compounds until the next chapter.

The overwhelming domination by samurai of the physical space of Edo was a clear reflection of their dominant position in the Tokugawa social system. Given that samurai and commoner populations were roughly equal in numbers late in the Tokugawa period, population density for commoners was roughly four times as great.[107] As noted earlier, samurai privilege was further reflected in the type of land — the high ground — they occupied.

In considering the exterior space of the daimyo compound, the analysis offered here will begin with the main definer of the daimyo compound's boundary with the outside world and then move outward to consider the space farther away. The exterior walls marked the clearest border between the inside and outside of the daimyo compound. In most cases those walls were not free-standing but consisted of the exterior surface of the barracks, which often ringed the perimeter of the compound. In some cases they were two-storied, with two rows of lattice windows facing outward, like Akitsuki's compound at Shiba (Figure 5.8), or with just a single row of windows, as in the clapboard-sided compound of Satsuma at Takanawa. Given that the exterior walls of the barracks and the compound's gates represented the domain's social face, architectural form — e.g., the type and size of gates, as discussed earlier, and the type of finish applied to the walls — was of great symbolic importance. These forms had the visual power to mark the resident lord's status in the daimyo hierarchy. For example, outer walls covered with square tiles jointed with raised plaster was indicative of a substantial lord of two hundred thousand *koku* or more, as seen at the Hiroshima's main residence at Kasumigaseki (see Figures 5.4 and 7.1). A main gate with double guardhouses likewise marked a lord of the same status. The roof tiles of buildings visible from the road were also part of the domain's public face. While interior buildings were topped with wooden boards

FIGURE 5.8. Main residence of Kurume (Arima house), left, and Akitsuki (Kuroda house), right. Photo by Felice Beato. Courtesy of Yokohama kaikō shiryōkan.

or thatch, those facing the road or powerful neighbors were more conspicuous and therefore more likely to be tiled, as was the case with Kaga's barracks.

From the exterior the compounds seemed strictly closed to the outside world, but in reality they were far more permeable. Accordingly, domain officials, desirous of showing a dignified, stately face, fixed regulations for their retainers while in Edo, particularly those residing in the perimeter barracks. They were instructed, for example, not to expose "unsightly" (*migurushii*) things to the outside world through the first- and second-story windows.[108] Other prohibitions included hanging items, like laundry, in windows, throwing water out of them, or buying goods from itinerant merchants through them. Disruptive behavior in the outer barracks that might hurt the reputation of the lord, such as shouting or making loud music, were likewise banned. While not disruptive in a literal sense, retainers in the outer barracks were enjoined from "the misconduct of looking out the windows at the traffic going by," but the restrictions on life in the barracks, and the lure of activities going on outside them, made compliance difficult.[109] For example, Toda Kumajirō, the Kurume samurai and author of the text accompanying the "Kurume hanshi Edo kinban nagaya emaki" (Scroll of the Kurume domain retainers serving in Edo), wrote, "Sometimes when I put my head out the lattice of the barracks fronting the road, I can see many people standing around Akabane Bridge. A steady stream of palanquins goes by, their bearers calling out 'Ei ei, hō, hō.' Women come and go, the color of their attire rivaling the autumn tints of Tatsuta [near Hōryūji] and the cherry blossoms of Yoshino. It is almost as busy as the crossing at the Ōi River."[110] Alcock, too, noticed that "through these [barred windows] the faces of men, women, and children may be seen, eagerly or idly, as the case may be, looking at the passers-by."[111]

The concern about retainer behavior regarding windows was even more the case when the lord entered or exited the compound. Tottori officials noted, "When the lord goes out there are some retainers who peek from their barrack's window or keep their *shōji* open. This is truly a horrible sight." They were ordered to cease such behavior. Windows were to be shut not just when the lord left and returned, but the entire time he was absent, presumably since the time of his return could not be predicted.[112]

The perimeter barracks, while revealing the domain's social face, also acted as a shield to the outside world. Access to the location where authority resides connotes power, but the denial of such access, both physical and visual, also constitutes a type of power. Perimeter barracks often bounded a road or the compound of another domain. To avoid problems in such a situation, Chōshū and Sendai, for example, whose main compounds faced each other, reached an agreement in 1636 through an intermediary—a Tokugawa bannerman—not to put windows or doors in the side of their perimeter barracks which faced the other. Some retainers of Sendai, however, apparently made (cut out?) windows without permission. Chōshū, on the other hand, lived up to its deal, but ten years later, during a reconstruction of the compound, they discovered Sendai's infraction. To counter it, Chōshū made plans to top off the wall to be built on the boundary with a spiked, wooden palisade that would block Sendai's visual intrusion. An apology followed from Sendai officials, who, professing not to know of the existence of windows, denied using the windows to peer into Chōshū's space and agreed in principle to block the windows and doors that faced the other compound. Still, Sendai officials, arguing that the darkness of windowless living quarters caused hardship for its retainers, asked their Chōshū counterparts if it would be sufficient to board up only those windows from which the Chōshū compound could actually be seen, and they received a positive response. In the negotiations Sendai had also asked that Chōshū reconsider its plan to top the border wall with a fence, which they thought would be an eyesore, and they agreed to close up all windows deemed offensive by Chōshū. Chōshū's officials were also concerned with the doors, because with "men entering and exiting at the border some bad incident might happen."[113]

Chōshū also experienced problems with one of its other neighbors. Its officials had been approached by those of Kurobane domain, who complained that men from the Chōshū side were breaking an agreement to keep facing windows closed.[114] The windows had been boarded up with wood, but Chōshū retainers had torn the wood off and opened them again. Determined to try harder, the officials ordered the windows boarded up on the outside and wooden lattices constructed over the inside opening. Many other domains encountered similar problems.

This same concern with visual intrusions of the compound border can also be seen in Chōshū's general land-purchasing strategy. To cite one example, in 1641, its domain officials approached the shogunate's magistrate of residence lands, who oversaw the process of distributing daimyo and Tokugawa direct retainers' land grants in Edo, to put in a request for a large piece of vacant land to the north of its lower compound. They wanted this property to expand the compound to the east because without it, anyone, samurai or commoner, could look down into the compound from the road. If it was possible to purchase the parcel, the officials stated, they would expand the border walls to enclose the new portion, thereby shielding the interior of the compound from undesirable visual intrusions.[115]

The border between the Chōshū and Kurobane compounds was defined by a moat, and here too disputes occurred when Chōshū men exited their barrack's door, placed a board across the moat separating the two compounds, and crossed freely. Kurobane officials claimed that a woman from Chōshū's compound had used this route to seek refuge in their space. Chōshū's officials professed ignorance this time and agreed to remove the wooden board at once. They also took the opportunity, though, to ask Kurobane to board up one of its windows facing Chōshū's compound, which it found problematic.[116]

The perimeter of the daimyo compound presented an imposing face to the outside world, but it was not impenetrable — at least this is suggested by the case of one infamous thief. Nezumi kozō (Mouse Thief) Jirōkichi reputedly broke through small holes in the perimeter and climbed walls and fences. By the time the much-sought-after man was apprehended on the night of 1832/5/5 he had broken into more than 130 daimyo compounds over a ten-year period, stealing more than three thousand *ryō*, most often from the interior of the daimyo's residence. On six occasions he was able to heist more than one hundred *ryō*.[117] According to Tosa's Miyaji Umanosuke, not a single compound of the great lords in Daimyo Avenue had been spared, including the Yamauchi's.[118]

The area defined by the exterior barracks was protected by what amounted to a limited form of diplomatic immunity, like modern-day embassies. If a person under the administrative authority of a daimyo domain caused some incident or committed some crime within the same domain's compound, he or she would be dealt with according to domainal, and not Tokugawa, laws. This analogy of daimyo compound as embassy is also evident in that residents from the daimyo domains passing through Edo on pilgrimage could stop by the main residence if in need of legal or other types of assistance (or simply if they wanted to stop there to rest). Similarly, the instructions to retainers regarding behavior while in Edo read like advisories given travelers before embarking on a foreign trip.

There were limits, however, to daimyo authority in Edo. For example, a towns-man who entered a daimyo compound and committed a crime could not be punished according to the domain's laws. The case was to be reported to the shogunate's senior councilors, while the criminal was to be placed in the custody of the Edo city magistrate, who passed judgment on him. For example, in 1849 an Edo townsman who posed as a day laborer for Chōshū domain in order to steal gold and other valuables from its residence had to be turned over to city officials, even though it was his second time committing the same crime.

When a domainal samurai or his retainers committed a crime outside the daimyo compounds, a double-layered system of justice could be applied. Since the crime was committed outside the compound in space under the adminis-trative control of the Tokugawa, shogunal officials would first pass judgment on the case. After this, however, the domain would determine whether to punish the man independently as well. Typically, the retainer in question would be sent back to the domain, but more severe punishments such as banishment or con-fiscation could be added. In sum, the Tokugawa had authority over domainal people within *buke-chi* — land officially designated for warrior use — while out-side daimyo compounds. The domains additionally retained a level of authority over its retainers regardless of the administrative space they occupied when committing a crime.

Between the border walls and the road lay an area in which administra-tive authority was less clear. Early in the period, when confronted with several incidents of babies abandoned under the eaves of gates at its main compound, Chōshū domain officials had to query the Tokugawa whether the domain should treat the eaves as it would space inside the compound and assume re-sponsibility for the infants. By the middle of the Tokugawa period, however, the area under the eaves on roadfront property was referred to as *kōgi no jisho*, or public land. In other words, it was treated as part of the road and accordingly fell under the jurisdiction of guard posts located largely on street corners that were under shogunal administrative authority.[119] For example, several cases in which unidentified persons (presumably commoners) hung themselves with a rope tied around a tree growing over the wall from inside Chōshū's main com-pound were dealt with by the guard posts.[120]

It appears, therefore, that this kind of spatial consciousness on the part of the shogunate was lacking early in the period. Its later appearance might be interpreted as a clarification of jurisdiction. This is made clear by a notice sent both to Chōshū and to Tottori authorities in Edo in 1762 which informed them that while in the past it had been the responsibility of their officials to handle accidents and other cases which occurred under the eaves of buildings ringing the compounds, henceforth the guard posts, under Tokugawa authority, would handle matters in the space between the *komayose* (a wooden fence erected in front of the compound's gates to prevent the entry of horses and perhaps tourists from other parts of Japan) and the gates, or that involved the projecting lattice work on the windows of perimeter barracks.[121] In doing so, we see the Tokugawa refuting the notion that these spaces were private.[122]

In the space farther away from the border walls — the roads in front of the daimyo compounds — daimyo authority was even further diminished. In fact, this area was clearly under the administrative authority of the Tokugawa from the beginning of the period. However, early in the seventeenth century, when street violence was a problem, the shogunate charged the daimyo and the bannermen to act as its agents in maintaining law and order within that social space.[123] This was considered another form of duty the daimyo and bannermen owed the Tokugawa for the residential land grants awarded them. These agents of the Tokugawa were required to construct guard posts near many street corners, usually in the middle of the road (as in Hiroshige's print of "Kasumigaseki" in the Tōtō meisho series) and to patrol defined areas like a police beat.[124] There were no gated streets in the daimyo and samurai districts of Edo as there were in commoner areas, so the guard posts were the main mechanism for maintaining order.

More concretely, officials and their deputies were charged with a variety of tasks. Regulations from 1629 instruct that "if any violent, wounded, or suspicious person is sighted, men are to be dispatched from the guard house to apprehend them," and the appropriate administrative authorities were then to be contacted.[125] A manual for the treatment of incidents (1659) informs us that the guards' responsibilities in their area of patrol included: (1) taking into custody people involved in affairs of bloodshed; (2) assisting those who had fallen ill, had an accident, or collapsed from drink; (3) aiding lost or abandoned children; (4) disposing of abandoned corpses; and (5) collecting refuse or garbage left on the road. To give an example of the second function, assisting those who had taken ill or had had an accident, in 1671 a large crowd of people gathered throughout the city to watch the Ryukyuan embassy pass through the streets on its way to the Edo castle. Due in part, it seems, to the pressing crowd, a masterless samurai fell into the moat. Guards from Tosa and Kurume who were manning the guard post pulled him out. Unable to determine whether he was drunk or just mentally unstable, they were also unsuccessful in disarming him after he drew his sword and began to flail it about, inflicting himself with a serious wound. Given his status as a masterless samurai living in a commoner section of town, he was to be handed over to his Five-Man Group (*gonin gumi*). In other words, he was to fall under the administrative authority of commoner city government, but he died before that could take place.[126]

The Tokugawa also dictated the behavior and responsibilities of the guards when bloodshed was involved. For example, a shogunal notice to Tosa domain on the duties of its representatives in front of the compounds read:

> If a person is cut down with a sword in front of the compound, chase the assailant down. If he will not hand over his sword, you may kill him. Should he surrender his sword, however, hand him over to the magistrate's office.[127]

Even when a fight occurred directly in front of a daimyo compound, the parties involved in the fight were not to be taken inside the compound, regardless of whether or not there were casualties. They were to be brought to the guard post, which was likely manned by men from the same compound, and a doctor summoned.[128] These rules governing the guard posts make it abundantly clear that the administrative authority of the daimyo in Edo did not extend beyond their compound walls, even though their retainers were often the ones acting as constables outside them.

Despite the overall peaceful nature of Tokugawa society, martial conflict involving samurai or their retainers was a fact of life in Edo. This was inevitable given the large population of armed men constantly moving across the city, traveling between their domain's various compounds, performing guard duty for the shogunate, accompanying an overlord outside the compound, or on an outing while off duty. That Edo was not a violent city is largely because the samurai were, in Eiko Ikegami's words, "tamed," and the use of physical force was mostly confined to certain bureaucratic and procedural codes.[129] When warrior-related conflict did take place in Edo, it often occurred outside of warrior compounds. These cases of violence reveal the tension between customary law and legal statute. They also reveal aspects of the principle of warrior autonomy and hence point to the limits of Tokugawa political authority.

This tension is evident in different historical records concerning the military code of conduct. On the one hand, regulations such as the Laws for the Military Houses prohibited giving shelter to *bushi* seeking refuge after committing an act of bloodshed. Nevertheless, from cases as early as the mid-seventeenth century, we find that this was indeed taking place, as when a page in the employ of Ōkubo Tadayori killed his overlord and climbed over the wall into the adjoining daimyo compound. The officials there asked to have the assailant turned over to them, but they were refused.[130] According to the *Buke jūyōki*, an early eighteenth-century primer on warrior conduct, a samurai seeking refuge should not be handed over summarily to his pursuers, even if he has committed an "injustice," such as stealing or killing his master. Implicit here, then, is the notion that granting refuge should be automatic. That this was generally accepted in warrior society is even confirmed by an undated example (discussed in an early nineteenth-century source) in which the killer was handed over. Two men quarreled; a bannerman struck down the other *bushi* of undetermined status and fled the scene, seeking refuge in the main compound of Kii domain. The shogunate summoned officials from Kii and ordered that the assailant be turned over, but Kii's top administrative official, acting in the lord's absence, refused to comply. Later the lord admonished his official, saying "I understand that a bushi seeking refuge should not be turned over" but citing Kii's special relationship with the shogunate as one of the Three Related Houses as compelling them to obey.[131]

As a final example of refuge seeking, there is the noted case of Kawai Matagorō, who killed a fellow retainer of the Ikeda house and fled into the compound of a Tokugawa bannerman in 1630. The Ikeda lord demanded that Kawai be handed over to his authority and even appealed to the Tokugawa when the bannerman refused. The shogunate, however, refrained from involvement in the affair, probably because the murder involved persons from the same domain and because of the independence or extraterritoriality of the bannerman's compound.[132]

As to why assailants were given refuge, sometimes in spite of frequent prohibitions issued by the domains, we need to remember that the victor in a fight was not considered a killer or murderer. Instead, he was seen as upholding his honor and acting according to the warrior's code. The assumption that the assailant was being pursued was important; fleeing from a revenge seeker after achieving victory over an opponent was not considered cowardly. To shelter and assist such a person would be an act of sympathy, a response that demonstrated a "righteous spirit" (*giki*).[133] That many *bushi* may have acted improperly or committed some offense that led to the bloodshed was not relevant, at least in terms of the initial decision to grant refuge. As an early eighteenth-century text stated, "From early times, bushi seeking refuge were rarely turned out. This is the warrior's law (*bushi no hō*)."[134]

Here we have briefly examined life at and around the margins of daimyo compounds in Edo. The domains were concerned with projecting power by controlling the behavior of their retainers and by regulating the appearance of their compounds' face at the borders as well as by protecting both physical and visual access. These same concerns with power and prestige can be seen in the intense competition for land to expand or integrate landholdings in Edo by daimyo through fictive transfers (really purchases) of land from other daimyo, bannermen, townsmen, and even peasant farmers. In the physical space outside the daimyo compound, the evidence demonstrates that the area closest to the border was a site of shifting legal jurisdiction. Inside the compounds, the notion of sanctuary or extraterritoriality prevailed, revealing in part the multilayered nature of political authority in Edo.

Connections

While the compounds were each discrete social communities, it is important to remember that they were connected to the larger city in numerous ways: in economic terms as related to food supply, water supply, and waste disposal; in human terms by virtue of their population's movement around the city and social interaction with other residents; and through urban facilities or infrastructure, which included the guardhouses maintained in the daimyo compound areas, roads, and the water system. Some compounds also connected to the greater city by allowing the commoner population to enter their physical space at designated times to participate in religious observances at shrines and temples located within.

Of these various links between the compounds and Edo, water supply was particularly important. Alternate attendance necessitated the creation of a sophisticated system for provisioning water for drinking, for firefighting, and to feed the ponds and streams in the daimyo compounds. By the end of the seventeenth century the shogunate's engineering corps had completed two major (the Kanda and Tama) and four supplementary water systems for the city at great expense.[135] These various systems addressed first the needs of the shogun and samurai rather than merchant and artisan areas, reflecting once again the status-based nature of Tokugawa society. Tosa's main residence, for example, was connected to Edo's water supply via two lines that ran off from the Toranomon branch of the Tama system. That network began upstream on the Tama River almost forty kilometers from the shogun's castle.[136] The systems created to connect the domains to Edo's water supply are visible at any of the excavations of daimyo compounds in Tokyo that one might visit.[137] There, a variety of building techniques and materials—wooden planks, bamboo, and cut stone—were utilized to construct elaborate water supply and drainage systems (see Figure 5.9). As a result of this technology and the effective handing of human waste,[138] the water supply remained healthy. Edo residents are said to have been proud of the high quality of their water supply, which was reputed to have been so clean that it could safely be used for the first bath of a newborn baby.[139]

Compound Shrines and Temples

While commoners residing in the city must have found the walls and barracks that marked the outer boundary of the daimyo compounds imposing, they were sometimes allowed a limited form of access to what was otherwise to them

FIGURE 5.9. Excavation of drainage system at Sendai domain's residence (top) and section of water supply at Shiodome, with well in foreground (bottom). Photos by author.

a closed-off world. Of course commoners hired to work at the compound or merchants and artisans with official ties to the domain were routinely permitted entry through the rear gate, but late in the Tokugawa period large numbers of other people with no such connections were allowed, at designated times, to make pilgrimages to more than fifty shrines and temples at daimyo residences.[140] Typically these were located at a domain's more spacious middle or lower compounds rather than at the main residence. By making a pilgrimage, commoners gained access to spaces that were normally closed off to them, but these religious institutions were set off physically from the other parts of the compound. Commoner pilgrims were not able to gain access to the interior space where the lord and his retainers lived. Nevertheless they were able to get closer than would otherwise have been possible.[141]

A few domains began to open up the religious institutions on their premises in Edo to commoners as early as the eighteenth century. The reasons for this are not readily apparent but may very well have been pecuniary in nature. Konpira shrine, located in the residence of Marugame domain at Toranomon, is the most famous example from this period. In the nineteenth century, many more were opened to commoners and their deities became quite popular. Woodblock print artist Hiroshige was particularly fond of Konpira, in Edo, and captured the bustle associated with it in eight different images (surpassed only by the fourteen of Kurume's Suitengū, at the picturesque Akabane Bridge). One clue as to why the domains allowed this practice may lie in the considerable funds that were donated by pilgrims, many of whom were drawn to the shrine seeking divine assistance; at Suitengū this meant for aid in conceiving or for safe childbirth. The faithful made cash contributions: 100 to 150 *ryō* per year to Marugame's Konpira shrine (in Edo) in the late eighteenth century and as much as 1,700 *ryō* to Suitengū in the closing decades of the period.[142]

The vast majority of the religious sites open to commoners enshrined Inari, which was popular in large part due to its association with economic prosperity. For many domains, such as Tosa and Matsue, branches were set up in both Edo and Osaka.[143] The best known were the Toyokawa Inari at Akasaka, located in the Nishi-Ōhira domain residence, and Asakusa Inari, in the Yanagawa domain compound in the area behind the Yoshiwara. The shrines and temples established by daimyo in Edo, many of which became fashionable places to visit in the early nineteenth century, were part of a complicated system of popular belief in Edo, forming an important link between the daimyo residences and commoner inhabitants of the city.

Other Economic Links

While the daimyo compounds were social units, distinct from one another, they and the larger city of which they were a part had a number of economic connections to the localities, such as the water works and religious institutions discussed above. However, as it grew into a great metropolis, Edo became firmly connected to the Kinai and Kantō regions, which were necessary to provide for what became, by the early eighteenth century, the world's largest city, with a population of more than one million. Although it is impossible to know its exact dimensions, this dependency on the Kinai region, particularly Osaka, the "country's kitchen," continued well into the eighteenth century. These important economic linkages, known as *kudarimono* (goods that flowed "down" into Edo), were for critical commodities such as tea, oil, vinegar, soy sauce, sake, salt, household furnishings, pottery, military supplies, a variety of cotton and silk textiles, and a plethora of other goods necessary for daily living. Most of the cotton cloth available for retail sale in Edo during the seventeenth century probably passed through Osaka.[144] As daimyo in the eighteenth century began to promote local specialty products such as paper, candle wax, salt, sugar, indigo, and tatami-mat facing, these were also shipped to Osaka, but it is unclear to what extent they were transshipped to Edo or elsewhere rather than consumed locally in the Kinai region.

Despite the economic dependence on the Kinai, even during the seventeenth century Edo residents were reliant on the Kantō region and areas immediately to the north for a number of perishable foods, particularly fish, vegetable, and local fruits, as well as firewood and charcoal. Sizeable amounts of rice and rice bran were also drawn from the region into the city. During the course of the eighteenth century, then, a regional Kanto-based economic system developed.[145] Some locally produced commodities, particularly cotton cloth, came to compete with textiles produced in the Kinai. Yet despite fluctuations in the amount imported, Edo remained reliant on the Kinai in the early eighteenth century for as much as three-quarters of its oil and soy sauce.[146]

Given that alternate attendance was the major vehicle propelling population growth in Edo in the seventeenth century, it was responsible for fostering these economic linkages in two ways: first, to provide for the troops and support staff the lords brought with them to Edo; and second, to provide for the larger commoner population in the city, many of whom moved there to cater to the domainal samurai and their attendants. Intellectuals like Nakai Chikuzan complained that the high demand for food and other materials in Edo resulted in an unbalanced distribution of food throughout the country, which could cause periodic famines.[147]

In another way, of course, the samurai population in Edo contributed to the production of agricultural crops in the Kantō region: Domain officials contracted out rights to merchants for the night soil from the residence compounds, and in exchange, at least one domain received either cash or vegetables.[148]

These important economic links between Edo and the localities, particularly the Kinai, are visible at the level of both the domain and the individual.
While reserving a discussion of this issue from the perspective of the individual retainer for chapter seven, on the domainal level it is difficult to get a
precise picture of the degree to which the individual compounds of the various
domains were tied to their local economies. The daimyo probably first began
sending rice to Edo early in the seventeenth century, when men and material
were requisitioned to assist in the construction of Edo castle and surrounding
areas. Then, with the systematization of alternate attendance, the shipments of
rice and other commodities became regularized; while a national market for
rice developed in Osaka, many northern domains shipped directly to Edo. In
general, though, it is likely that the Edo compounds became less dependent on
the local domainal economies as the city developed into a center of a regional
economic network in the Kantō by the early eighteenth century. Nevertheless, some domains maintained small shipments of basic commodities from
the domain even after then. For example, Hachinohe domain periodically sent
shipments of rice, sake, soybeans, miso, and millet to Edo.[149] In fact, rice for
retainer salaries, in contrast with rice shipped to Osaka for sale, probably was
the primary food commodity shipped to Edo from most localities. In the case
of Kaga, the amount of rice transported to Edo fluctuated between 18,000 and
33,000 *koku*, compared with 73,000 to 132,000 *koku* that was sent to Osaka.
However, exactly what percentage of this was used to meet Kaga's substantial
population in Edo is not clear.[150] In Okayama, a percentage of the tax rice was
set aside for shipment to the domain's various residences in Edo, Fushimi, and
Osaka.[151] Tosa domain, late in the period, was shipping a minimum of 2,300
to 6,500 *koku* of rice to its residences in Edo and Osaka, with the vast majority going to Edo. It was also purchasing substantially larger amounts of rice
in Edo — roughly 7,600 to 16,500 *koku* — to feed its retainers and support staff
(refer to Table 5.2). Several hundred *koku* of rice also went toward the maintenance of the lord's family and the women in the interior, though whether it was
purchased in Edo or sent from the domain is not specified. Of course, all this
was in addition to funds sent regularly in gold and silver to support the network
of residences and their support staffs. In addition to rice, a number of domains
relied to varying degrees on local, domainal, sources of lumber to build and
repair their Edo residences.[152]

Wherever possible, domains transported these goods by water, which was
usually less costly than over land. For example, Edo and Kōchi were linked by
regular boat service, referred to as *Edo ōmawari*, which transported personnel
and commodity goods as well as private correspondence and official communications. Given this, the arrival and departure of the domain boats was routinely

TABLE 5.2. Tosa Rice and Funds for Edo and Osaka*

Year	Stipend Rice Sent to Edo/Osaka	Rice Purchased for Retainers in Edo/Osaka	Money Sent to Edo	Stipend Rice for the Interior in Edo
1799	4,390 *koku* (Edo)	7,930 *koku*	1,354 *kanme* 1,200 *ryō*	371 *koku*
1801	3,899 *koku* (Edo: 3,280)	7,651 *koku*		
1803	4,066 *koku* (Edo: 3,010)	9,395 *koku*		
1833	1,300 *koku*; 1,050 *koku* unhulled	16,458 *koku*		
1839	2,560 *koku*; 4,063 *koku* unhulled	10,662 *koku*	3,101 *kanme*	354 *koku*
1853	2,493 *koku*; 400 *koku* unhulled	16,149 *koku*		

*The year refers to the report's date of issuance. The statistics are most likely for the previous year. The rice purchased for those serving abroad specifies for those below the rank of "samurai." For 1799 only does the entry refer to all retainers and hired hands (*hōkōnin*). *Kanme* refers to silver and *ryō* to gold. Most of the rice purchased in Edo was of lower quality (*taimai*). Unless otherwise specified the *koku* figures are for hulled rice; a separate figure for unhulled rice is given where applicable. All figures, which have been rounded off, are based on "Tōbun oboegaki" 1788, 1801, 1839, 1845, 1853; Hirao 1965, 139–176.

noted in the personal diaries of many of Tosa's samurai diarists in service on alternate attendance.[153] In Edo, the goods were transshipped by smaller craft to one of the domain's warehouses.[154]

Excavations at a number of daimyo compound sites provide additional evidence for the circulation of commodity goods, including food, across Japan and the economic links between the local economies of the domains and their Edo compounds. These artifacts—what James Deetz has referred to as the "small things forgotten"—offer evidence about daily life not available from other sources.[155] For example, jars of refined sea salt from the Kinai region have been unearthed at numerous daimyo compound sites. The various producers' names imprinted on the vessels attest to the keen commercial competition for the lucrative Edo market.[156] Circular wooden containers and tubs identifying the source of the processed goods within — e.g., dried bonito from Arai (at the Tōtōmi Yokosuka domain compound), fermented soybeans from Odawara (at the Odawara compound), and large amounts of fish remains from the Hokuriku region (found in the barracks at Kaga's main residence) — suggest that a desire for familiar tastes from home led to the import of foodstuffs to Edo from various parts of the country.[157] In the case of Kaga, too, locally produced soy sauce, pickled vegetables, and miso were shipped from the domain for use in its Edo compounds.[158] Sendai produced miso in its lower compound for consumption by its retainers and support staff, but the reputation of the foodstuff spread amongst the city's commoner population, leading Edo merchants to handle the product for wide distribution.[159]

In addition to processed foods, in many cases manufactured goods found in the compounds had been produced in the home domain. For example, evidence has been found that roof tiles made in Kii, Kaga, Kamiyama, and Chōshū domains were used in their Edo residences.[160] In Nagoya domain's main residence, the roof tiles that fronted the road, and thus in a sense represented the face of the domain, were produced in the domain, thereby exhibiting a bit of local color.[161] Particularly after major fires, when supplies were short and therefore expensive in Edo, the domains might have to rely on materials acquired in the domain and in Osaka. After a two-day fire ravaged a huge swath of Edo in 1772, Chōshū domain sent twenty-seven boatloads of building products, including lumber, rope, 64,020 roof tiles, and more than two million nails.[162] As noted, a number of domains stocked their kitchens in Edo to some extent with ceramics produced at home and imported high-quality ware from different kilns across the country for ceremonial use there.[163] Hizen ware of *Kyoto-utsushi* type—i.e., ceramic ware made in Hizen, crafted in a Kyoto style, itself heavily influenced by Chinese and Korean potteries—was shipped to Edo from the second half of the seventeenth century for use in Takamatsu's compounds. This testifies eloquently to the cultural currents that flowed across early modern Japan, a phenomenon in which alternate attendance played no small part. Of course, Kyoto ceramics themselves were exported to both Takamatsu, for use at the castle, and to the domain's Edo mansions.[164] Ninsei wares (from Omuro, northwest of Kyoto), famous for their overglaze enamel decoration, were a highly desired item and have been found extensively in Edo sites, including Iidamachi.[165] Moreover, Takamatsu's own official ceramics, Rihei ware, have been excavated at the Iidamachi residence, and this has been cited "as evidence for the continued influence of Kyoto as a technique and design model for other centers in western Japan, especially Shikoku."[166] The existence of this local product in Takamatsu's main compound demonstrates the economic links between the home domain and Edo and the important role of alternate attendance as a mechanism for cultural cross-fertilization.

Excavations have also revealed the importance of ceramics in the Tokugawa economic life—a distinguishing feature of early modern times. The sheer volume of ceramic sherds—by far the most numerous items unearthed in daimyo and other sites—attests to the prevalence of ceramics in Edo daily life, to their nature as indispensable utensils, and to the fact that ceramics were commodities distributed throughout Japan.[167] In particular, exceedingly large numbers of ceramic sake bottles (*tokkuri*) have been unearthed (Figure 5.10), leading

FIGURE 5.10. *Tokkuri* excavated from Matsuyama domain's compound. Photo by Kobiki Harunobu. Courtesy of Tokyo Metropolitan Government.

some observers to interpret their vast quantity simply as a sign of the Edo-based samurai's affinity for rice wine.[168] However, we know that in Edo and in other cities these bottles were recycled and used for food oil, lamp oil, and vinegar. Of course samurai stationed in Edo were known to drink, and the store names found on many bottles indicate that they were initially purchased from liquor stores or delivered by restaurants.[169] *Tokkuri*, however, were multifunctional. Other liquids purchased at retail shops, or perhaps distributed within the daimyo compound, were measured out and poured into ceramic containers provided by the purchaser.

Ceramics excavated from the lord's residence at Nagoya's main compound likewise revealed extensive use of both distant Hizen ware as well as local Seto-Mino ware and secondary use of Kyoto and Shigaraki vessels. Large numbers of Seto-Mino wares of a common quality had distinctive markings, which have led some archaeologists to posit that these were meant for everyday use by Nagoya retainers in Edo. Many of this variety of sake bottles were found in Nagoya's main residence, but few at the castle in the domain, again leading to the conclusion that they were probably made largely for export use in Edo.[170]

Similarly, Nabeshima ware, produced by Saga domain, has been found at many daimyo compound sites, revealing that the Nabeshima lord gave it as gifts to his peers.[171] Tosa's Odo ware was also presented to the Yamauchi lord's peers, though it was not deemed of sufficiently high quality to bestow upon the

FIGURE 5.11. Clay whistles from Matsuyama domain's excavation. Photo by Kobiki Harunobu. Courtesy of Tokyo Metropolitan Government.

shogun and his top officials.[172] Moreover, as noted earlier, by the middle of the eighteenth century many domains, including some of the largest like Mito and Owari, had established kilns in their Edo residence gardens, using clays imported from the home domains to craft what were often elaborate, ornamental, nonutilitarian vessels referred to as "daimyo garden ceramics" (*oniwa yaki*).[173]

A different type of ceramic ware was produced not in the domain for shipment to Edo, but right in the daimyo residences. Large numbers of clay toys were manufactured inside numerous Edo compounds. For example, some one thousand items were unearthed from the Hakuō site where Matsuyama domain had its main compound, including clay whistles and unusual animal shapes (dove, sparrow, chicken, octopus) (see Figure 5.11).[174] Although it is not known what segment or segments of the population inside the compound manufactured the goods, no doubt they were produced for the same reason other domains engaged in commercial activities within their grounds, to increase income to improve economic conditions for the lord's retainers.

In this chapter we have explored a number of tangible and intangible ways the daimyo compounds were connected with the domains and integrated into the city of Edo, but perhaps the most obvious way was through the people who resided and worked in them. It is to them that we now turn our attention.

6

Life in the Capital

THE CONFUCIAN SCHOLAR Ogyū Sorai wrote, "For the period of each alternate year during which the daimyo live in Edo they live as in an inn (*ryoshuku no kyōkai*). Their wives, who remain in Edo all the time, live permanently as in an inn."[1] His comments were critical of the social effects of alternate attendance and were part of a broader critique of the policies that removed the samurai from the land. Sorai's notion of returning the samurai to the land and reducing the period of residence in Edo were never adopted by any shogun, and so the daimyo and their entourages plied the roads between their castle towns and Edo for almost two hundred more years. They continued, as before, their periodic, "inn-like" existence in the Tokugawa capital.

Edo was the "temporary abode" of Edo-based retainers, according to one samurai from Kurume who drew parallels between his existence in Edo and the medieval aristocrat-turned-monk Kamo no Chōmei's life in an impermanent residence, his famous ten-square-foot hut.[2] The literary allusion was apt in the sense that domainal samurai in Edo on alternate attendance were separated from home and family and living in temporary quarters. In another sense, though, the comparison was less accurate, for the retainers and their attendants in Edo were living in the largest and most exciting urban center in Japan, one of the grandest cities in the early modern world — hardly some grass hut far removed from the capital.

In this chapter our focus will shift from the infrastructure of the compounds to the population inside. Briefly surveying that population, we will then draw on visual and written records to reconstruct some of the experience of domainal retainers in Edo — their life at work and play. It will be argued that life in Edo drew them into an engagement with the commercial economy, much more so than was usually the case back in the castle town. This was of course because they were totally disconnected from family and home, where they could at least have grown vegetables or made basic foodstuffs like miso. Yet they also became engaged with the commercial economy because Edo had so much to offer. It was, after all, the largest city in the land and offered the greatest selection of stores, services, and opportunities for various diversions and entertainments. These opportunities, as well as the generally more permissive environment of the capital city, made life there less constrained, and therefore more attractive, for retainers on their tours of duty.

The Edo Population of the Daimyo Compounds

Alternate attendance played a key role in generating population growth at the center, as is evident from the fact that after the system was suspended in 1862, Edo lost half of its population of more than a million in less than seven years.[3] While there are no accurate figures for the population of samurai from the domains in Edo, estimates for the city as a whole in the early eighteenth century show roughly equal numbers of samurai and townsmen, about 600,000 each.[4] Working from a lower estimate of about 520,000, Sekiyama Naotarō calculates 23,000 direct retainers of the Tokugawa, who together with their families (estimated at five persons per family) comprised 115,000 persons.[5] Probably another 100,000 served as their subretainers and various types of menials. He further estimates that 20 percent of all domainal retainers, or 60,000 men, served in Edo on short- or long-term postings; of these, half maintained families, meaning roughly 150,000 persons.[6] Together, then, the domainal retainer corps plus families comprised 180,000 persons. Added to this were roughly 100,000 subretainers and menials.

The population of individual domains in Edo varied greatly, as one would expect. In general terms larger domains maintained a permanent population of at least one thousand, with some of the most prestigious lords as many as two to five thousand (Table 6.1). Medium and small domains varied, too, but were largely in the range of several hundred persons. For example, Izushi (fifty-eight thousand *koku*) maintained a population of five hundred during the early nineteenth century.[7] When the lord was in town the numbers increased significantly for many domains, although in the case of Tosa they could triple or even rise by a factor of six.[8]

For domains, the major Edo expense were the costs incurred in maintaining the large population of officials, administrative personnel, garrison troops, and menials in the domain compounds. This population constituted "at once the chief source of his [the daimyo's] expenditure," but at the same time it also provided "the evidence of his rank or power."[9] Given this, efforts to reduce the

TABLE 6.1. Edo Populations for Various Domains*

Domain (kokudaka)	Long-Term [year]	During Sankin Year
Chōshū (369,000)	2,171 [1750]	
Hikone (350,000)	5,000 [1688–1704]	
Hirosaki (100,000)	1,280 [1712]	
Izushu (58,000)	819 [1709]	
	509 [1828]	
	258 [1843]	
Kaga (1,022,700)	4,250 [1747]	
	4,500 [1754]	
	2,186 [1808]	
Matsumoto (70,000)	1,300 [1716–1736]	
Matsuyama (50,000)	1,000 [1852–1868]	
Wakasa Obama (103,500)	1,280 [1712]	
Okayama (369,000)	1,394 [1698]	3,022 [1698]
Satsuma (770,800)	2,000 [estimate, 1788]	
Shōnai (140,000)	435 [1667]	780 [1667]
Takata (150,000)	200 [1852–1868]	
Tottori (325,000)	117 [1758]	
	150 [1829]	
Uwajima (100,000)	881 [av. 1771–1803]	
	1,073–1119 [1859–1861]	
Kii Wakayama (555,000)	4,000 [1852–1868]	

*This chart is based on the following sources: Date 1935, 83–84; Date 1936, 83; Kimura, Fujino, and Murakami 1988–1990; Tōkyō-to Chiyoda-ku 1998, 421; Kanazawa shishi hensan iinkai 2001, doc. #17, 768–778.

size of domains' Edo populations, like similar attempts with the size of processions, met with only limited success.

Tosa's Edo Population

To get beyond the macro-data offered in Table 6.1, we can examine the evidence available for Tosa domain. While this information is still limited, used in comparison with data from other locales, it gives a clearer picture of the nature of the human population behind the compound walls and allows us to better understand the ways the network of residences was interconnected.

As many as 4,556 people (1694) lived in Tosa's various residences (see Table 6.2) when the daimyo was in Edo, but during his absence a much smaller staff remained behind. The available statistics for the size and percentage of long-term staff vary considerably, from 196 persons (11.7 percent of 1,673 persons) in

TABLE 6.2. Tosa Domain's Edo Population*

Year	Total No. Persons	No. on Long-Term Posting	Other Information
1645	1,673	196	*Sankin* year
1682	3,044	[1,380]	*Sankin* year
1684	3,048	[1,021]	*Sankin* year
1694	4,556		*Sankin* year
1696	3,945		*Sankin* year
1698	4,201	717	*Sankin* year
1718	2,905	1,106	*Sankin* year

* The figures for 1645 are from "Shōhō ninen, Tadayoshi sama ontomodachi narabini Edo jōzume hitodaka chō" 1645; for 1684 from "Jōkyō gannenbun jōge ninzū aratamegaki" 1684; for 1694 and 1696 from *TMK*, vol. 83, Genroku 11 [1698], fols. 55–57. Numbers in brackets were not contained in the original documents but represent calculations based on other figures given.

1645 to 1,380 persons (45 percent of 3,044) in 1682. It is difficult to explain the fluctuations, particularly given the fragmentary evidence. The low numbers for 1645 no doubt reflect that the system had only just become compulsory for the outer lords like the Yamauchi several years earlier. As the size of the processions grew, so too did the numbers who remained in Edo on long-term postings. However, it is important to keep these figures in perspective. Even when Tosa's numbers in Edo topped four thousand, this was still only about 1 percent of the domain's population.[10] These statistics are a reminder that while alternate attendance resulted in the circulation of many people, Tokugawa Japan was still a society in which samurai generally remained strongly rooted to their native places. Beyond the early eighteenth century, evidence from other domains (there is no data available for Tosa) suggests that domains tried to cut costs wherever possible, and this included some reduction in size of the Edo staff.

The main compound served as the domain's administrative headquarters in Edo, and accordingly, a majority (1,617, or 53 percent) of Tosa's Edo population resided therein (Table 6.3). Another 1,254 persons (41 percent) took up residence in the middle compound, leaving only 100 (3 percent) in the auxiliary or lower compound (the remainder were either distributed in the domain's other residences or their place of residence is unknown).

The statement that Edo was a man's world has often been repeated, and this was the case in Tosa's compounds, at least during the seventeenth century. This was because, as noted, only men on long-term postings in Edo were allowed to bring their families. At the end of the century (1697), men outnumbered women in Tosa's compounds almost nine to one (3,729 men and 472 women).[11] Almost

TABLE 6.3. Breakdown of Population Figures for Tosa, by Compound, 1684*

Compound	Location	Size (tsubo)	Population
Main	Kajibashi	7,052	1,617 (38 horses)
			66 female servants
Middle	Shiba	8,479	1,254 (17 horses)
			41 female servants
Lower	Shinagawa	16,891	100
			39 female servants
	Hatchōbori	378	11
	Shintaijima	—	5
	Others	—	61
TOTAL			3,048 (55 horses)
			146 female servants

*The document gives the incorrect total of 3,046, two fewer than the sum of the figures presented for the individual compounds. The figures for servicewomen are not included in the totals given.

a third (260 of 651) of the upper samurai population was female, most likely consisting of the wives and daughters of high-ranking samurai stationed long-term in Edo. The skewed sex ratio was not as high in Okayama's compounds at about the same time, or in Uwajima's in the late eighteenth century, but the imbalance was nonetheless substantial. This is what one would expect in a system of military service.[12]

Despite the trend toward gender parity among commoners in Edo late in the Tokugawa period, the city apparently retained a martial character even in the nineteenth century. As discussed in the previous chapter, bloodshed with swords did occur amongst samurai, and fights between hired menials belonging to different lords were not unusual. The large number of samurai and attendants, and the bravura that accompanied their movements in the city, surprised a painting student of Shiba Kōkan's (1748–1818) from the Kyoto region. "He thought," Kōkan remarked, "from all the daimyo and lesser lords with their swords and pikes that he was back in the times of civil war in ancient China."[13] Mori Masana almost got into a fight just for watching a confrontation in front of Arima domain's headquarters between a Tokugawa bannerman and a footsoldier from Mito domain. The Mito man confronted the bannerman, who would not get off his horse as his lord's procession was returning to its compound. This was despite the efforts of a road clearer, whom Masana heard screaming loudly, "get down" (shita ni). For some reason the Mito footsoldier, seeing Masana and at least several other people watching him, left the bannerman and came toward

Masana, shaking his sun umbrella as if to hit him. Masana told the enraged footsoldier that if he hit him with the umbrella he would have no choice but to draw his sword and kill him. Then Masana would have to commit seppuku. In short, they both, in Masana's words, would die "a dog's death" (*inujini*, i.e., a meaningless death). Given the great potential for conflict in the city with so many sworded men walking about, Masana concluded that "you must take care when walking the streets."[14]

Samurai played a prominent role serving the lord in Edo, but they formed a minority of the populations behind the walls of the compound, which were mixed social communities. This was true of the long-term population resident in daimyo compounds as well. Looking at Tosa's Edo population more closely, in 1645, just a few years after the outside lords like the Yamauchi were formally obligated to perform alternate attendance, a relatively small number (196, or 11.7 percent) of retainers were posted there long term. Of the 1,673 men in Edo while the daimyo was in Edo, roughly half of the total (810 men) were direct retainers, the remainder (863) being subretainers, meaning they were not on the lord's budget. By the end of the century, there was a substantial increase in the number of men brought to Edo (2,025 in 1684) as well as those stationed there long term (1,021), the latter of which comprised a full one-third of the total. More than nine-tenths of the total population in 1684 was stationed at the main and middle compounds (1,617 and 1,254, respectively). Indicative of the central importance of these two compounds was the fact that two senior advisors and one junior advisor were posted at the main compound; Shiba was supervised by one senior advisor, who was also in charge of Tosa's fire brigade, which performed fire-prevention duty at Zōjōji. One hundred people were posted to the lower compound at Shinagawa, where at this time the deceased former lord's wife lived. The remaining seventy-seven people were attached to the Tosa lord's relative at Azabu, living in unnamed auxiliary compounds or in townsmen quarters. Members of the various rungs of the lower samurai made up the majority of total population, followed by subretainers (37.5 percent). Upper samurai constituted only 5 percent. There was also a small population of women (sixty-six, forty-one, and thirty-nine, respectively) assigned to each for cleaning and other services.[15]

The 1684 census (Table 6.4) gives us a more detailed breakdown of the social composition of Tosa's Edo population. Much of the population of 3,046 consisted of the men (subretainers) retainers brought with them to Edo. The size of the daimyo's entourage was regulated by Tokugawa decree, and local (Tosa) ordinances dictated how many men the daimyo's retainers could bring. The latter was directly related to two factors, status and the size of the holding or stipend. Based on data from the mid-seventeenth century, a senior advisor of

TABLE 6.4. Tosa's Population in Edo (1684)*

Position	Number of Persons
Samurai below the rank of senior advisor	140
Mounted horsemen	9
Lower samurai (58 *goyōnin*, 65 *kachi*, 36 bowmen/musketmen)	159
Priests (*obōzu*)	30
Lord's cooks	26
Menials	38
Oashigaru (low-level retainers attached to lord)	420
Pages	973
Messengers	10
Subretainers	1,144
Female servants	148 (146?)
Carpenters	90
Women attached to Ohime-sama	66
Women attached to Yōryūin	41
Women attached to Honjō-sama	39
TOTAL	3,046

*"Jōkyō gannen bun jōge ninzū aratamegaki" 1684. The three titled women in the census are Ohimesama (Kunihime), the fourth daughter of fourth lord, Toyomasa, and wed to Toyofusa, the adopted fifth lord; Yōryūin, lord Toyomasa's sister; and, Honjō sama, the elder sister of Lord Toyomasa and Yōryūin. In sum, these three lines in the census are a rare reminder in the official record of the privileged life led by elite women around the lord; a world vastly different than that of the average retainer on a tour of duty in Edo.

one thousand *koku* could bring along thirty-five of his own retainers; a junior advisor with the same holding was allowed only twenty; and a unit leader of the same *koku* standing was allowed sixteen men. The numbers allowed dropped substantially with the onset of economic hard times, and especially as a result of the reform movement of the Kyōhō period (1716–1735). By this time, the number of men a senior advisor of ten thousand *koku* could bring dropped from ninety (1644) to eighty (1708) men and then to thirty-eight (1731). Interestingly, the regulations from 1731 also indicate minimums for each stipend category; that is, a senior advisor of ten thousand *koku* must not bring fewer than twenty men; those with 200 to 290 *koku* must not bring fewer than five (but no more than eight).[16] This reflected the need to economize, but at the same time highlighted the importance of maintaining status distinctions.

Views From the Barracks

Retainers were stationed in Edo to support the lord in the fulfillment of his duties to the shogun while he was present in the capital city and to maintain the residence compounds during the times when he was given leave. Yet because of the size of their social estate, samurai were almost by definition underemployed. Most retainers working for the domain in Edo found that their duties were not terribly demanding, occupying them only a limited number of times a month, and often for only a part of the day. According to samurai Naitō Meisetsu, retainers "did not work every day."[17] Sakai Banshirō, from Wakayama domain, related more precisely that retainers worked, on average, eight days a month and no more than thirteen.[18] Tosa's Mori Yoshiki, who held dual positions involving oversight of the young daimyo heir, was also underemployed, reporting for duty roughly ten days a month.[19] Hachinohe retainer Toyama Tamuro was off every third or fourth day, but a "day" of work typically involved only one of three shifts.[20]

While this light work schedule was not peculiar to Edo service, it left retainers with free time at their disposal.[21] Moreover, it appears to have been fairly easy to switch shifts to accommodate one's schedule, as when Toyama Tamuro found a replacement to take his overnight shift so he could go to Asakusa to watch the puppet theater.[22] Regulations on the number of times per month a retainer could leave the compound on personal business varied from domain to domain, but the evidence does not suggest that his life in Edo was restricted.

According to the text accompanying the "Scroll of the Life of Kurume Retainers in their Barracks while on Duty in Edo" (*Kurume hanshi Edo kinban nagaya emaki*), the "existence of retainers on duty in Edo involves pleasures and hardships."[23] The latter was particularly true in 1839, when during the fourth month, the lord of Kurume domain in Kyushu made his way to Edo Castle for what he probably thought was a routine ceremony. As discussed in chapter one, all daimyo on alternate attendance in Edo had to go through the formality of requesting leave to return to their domains after the period of required residence in the shogunal capital, and they were granted that permission during an official audience. In this case, however, the request was denied, and the Kurume lord was ordered to remain in Edo and continue his service to the shogun. Occasionally daimyo with responsibilities for guard service or fire watch duty at Tōei-zan and Zōjōji were required to extend their stays and continue that service when the lord assigned to take over the duty received permission to remain in his domain and miss a turn of alternate attendance. Tosa had the same experience as Kurume in 1829; at the time of the Yamauchi lord's audience no reason was given for keeping him in Edo, but it was probably related to the

FIGURE 6.1. Kurume retainers reacting to bad news. "Kurume hanshi Edo kinban nagaya emaki." Courtesy of Edo-Tōkyō hakubutsukan.

domain's duty to provide guard service at Zōjōji.[24] In the case of Kurume, this meant staying in Edo two more years to maintain the fixed cycle of alternate attendance. How the lord, Arima Yorinori, took this news is difficult to say, but apparently some of his retainers were extremely upset. At least one group got drunk, smashing sake bottles and tearing down doors in their barracks at the domain's main residence at Akabane in Edo.

This scene of drunken destruction and despair (Figure 6.1) is the climax of the Kurume scroll, the combined work of two Kurume domain retainers. The first was Kano Shōha (Mitani Masanobu), 1805–1869, who created the thirteen paintings that make up the visual text and who was employed as a domainal painter-in-attendance, like his father and grandfather before him. Like them, he also accompanied the Kurume lord on a number of journeys to Edo, and like many other retainers there studied under a master—a phenomenon which will be examined in chapter seven. Specifically, Shōha became a student of the Kobiki-chō artist Kano Isen, 1775–1828, and then Kano Seisen, 1796–1846.[25] A second retainer, Toda Kumajirō (1805–1882), wrote the scroll's text, which appears at the beginning and at various intervals throughout the remainder of the work.[26]

The Kurume scroll, which illustrates the life of a small circle of Kurume retainers associated with Toda Tomajirō in their barracks at the domainal residence in Edo, was created as a historical record. In the author's words, this was so that "people in Kurume can see what life in Edo was like."[27] Created sometime early in the Meiji period, it describes events that probably took place around 1839 and 1840. The scroll thus represents the selective memory of two persons, artist and author, looking back on a time decades earlier when they were obliged to remain in Edo, away from home and their loved ones. The nostalgic element is explicit, however, when Toda writes in the introduction, "The paintings will also serve as a reminder of the old days for those who were there."[28] As a result, the scroll offers a pastiche of images revealing the vicissitudes of life in Edo, the simple joys and pleasures as well as the loneliness and hardship sometimes involved when serving a tour of duty there.

The residence, near Akabane bridge in Shiba Mita-chō, served as Kurume domain's headquarters and occupied ten thousand *tsubo*, an area befitting a large domain of 210,000 *koku*.[29] According to a retainer from Owari, Kurume's was the fourth largest main establishment in Edo, after Wakayama, Mito, and Owari.[30] The compound has been captured in a well-known photograph by Felice Beato as well as in woodblock prints and *doro-e*.[31] It was also popular with both townsmen and samurai, many of whom made pilgrimages to Suitengū shrine, which was located inside.

The thirteen color paintings that make up the scroll focus on the living quarters in several of the barracks and show how a small group of samurai filled some of their leisure hours. The first two paintings take the viewer into the room of the surgeon Nakajima Bunshuku. In the first scene Nakajima is talking with his colleague, Takahara Otojirō, enjoying some sake and light food. The scene is devoid of any architectural detail, but the second scene provides a partial view of the room. Here, Nakajima is sitting by a *go* board with the same Takahara, while another doctor, Kuroiwa Ryūtaku, lying on the floor, looks on. As we know from diaries of other Edo-based retainers, *go* was a regular pastime, though in this scene the men are not playing it. Instead, in this and several other scenes the men appear to be playing a game called *rakan mawashi*, which entails imitating the hand and facial gestures made by each of the other participants. In Nakajima's room, books are stacked in the alcove, and on the wall behind them hangs a scroll depicting Shinnō, the Chinese god of medicine, a subject appropriate for a surgeon's room. Behind the desk, Nakajima uses an animal-skin rug, most likely an imported item, as a cushion. While only a part of the room is visible, it appears to have received ample natural light. In fact a bamboo blind is partially lowered in the window at the farthest right to shield the occupants from the sun. According to the text, the barracks were known as the *dengaku nagaya* (bean curd baked and coated with miso) because it became so hot inside.

The third scene takes us into the six-mat room of Inspector Toda Kumajirō, the author of the text. In the introduction Toda associates himself with a long tradition of hermits in Japanese history by referring to his own room as the "temporary abode of an Edo-based retainer" as well as by quoting from Bashō's *Genjūan ki* (A Record of the Unreal Hermitage). In this scene Toda sits at his desk facing out toward a small garden. Behind the flowers and miniature landscape scene, morning glories trail up the fence. Standing behind the right-hand portion of the fence, Kuroiwa, who served in Edo on multiple tours, peers in, perhaps to appreciate the beauty of the garden. Toda, pipe in hand, seems lost in contemplation and does not notice him. The wall in Toda's room is adorned with paintings and poetry. A bookshelf is suspended from the wall, on which a broom hangs. On the floor, against the wall, sits a hibachi with a teapot on top.

The fourth scene of the scroll moves to the room of Takahata Otojirō, who appeared in the first two paintings. Here the retainers are doing what they do most often in the scroll—drinking. Although it is still daylight, Nakajima Bunshuku is pouring sake for his host, Takahara. An unidentified figure appears to have already had enough (one emptied bottle of sake lies on its side) and is resting on his back, eyes closed. A painting of ships' sails decorates the wall behind Nakajima. We learn from the text that it is the work of Kanō Shōha, the Kurume retainer who was the official domain artist and creator of the present scroll's paintings. The sails, apparently also painted on another wall in Takahara's room (Scene 5), served as reminders of the distance separating the Kurume retainers from home. It was ships such as these that Takahara and his friends, at the end of their long sojourn in Edo, would board in Osaka for the final leg of the journey home. As Toda wrote, "Looking at the pictures reminds me of home; three years have already passed and still I have not been able to return there. Feeling the length of the passing days, I sigh, put down my brush, and lay my head down to sleep."[32]

In Scene 5 (Figure 6.2), in Takahara's room, a number of men are holding a poetry gathering, one of them recording the poems on a large sheet of paper. The poems on the sheet are not legible, but the text includes six dealing with the theme of coolness. Two in particular are concerned with cooling off in the company of one's friends or colleagues: "Coming to cool off / At the front gate / We put out the lanterns" and "The coolness / More than my gate, / Someone else's gate."[33] Four scrolls decorate the far wall. For the educated Edo-based retainer, play involved not only drinking sake but also "playing *shōgi*, singing songs, composing verse, and passing time in idle conversation,"[34] not to mention practicing the tea ceremony.

In fact, a tea ceremony in progress in Kanō Shōha's room is the sixth scene depicted. He is on the far left, serving three guests: Nakajima, Takahara, and an unidentified man. Retainers were not ordinarily allowed to remodel their rooms, but Shōha must have received permission to put in a sunken pit, into

FIGURE 6.2. Poetry gathering in Kurume barracks. "Kurume hanshi Edo kinban nagaya emaki." Courtesy of Edo-Tōkyō hakubutsukan.

which a brazier for the tea ceremony has been placed. As befitting the room of a painter, the closet doors behind him are decorated with his own work, a scene of a rising sun and a white plum tree. Along the wall to Shōha's left is an array of scrolls he has selected for display for this particular occasion.

The next two scenes (Scenes 7 and 8) take place in the second story of the barracks. In the first (Figure 6.3) we see both the inside and outside of Inspector Kakehashi Toyota's room, located directly above Shōha's. The pieces of paper that make up the *shōji* windows in the room, when lifted, reveal the rear of other barracks within the compound, facing away from the street; the roofs of these buildings are tiled rather than simply covered with wooden planks. Out the window on the right side, behind Kakehashi, we can observe the compound gate, beyond which lies greenery — perhaps part of Zōjōji's grounds. Also visible are two women talking to one another and two young girls dressed in red. The perspective out the left-hand window is quite different and allows us a view of the rear of the quarters. In fact, these offer the only view of the inside face of the barracks of which I am aware. Fortunately, Thomas McClatchie also described a similar scene, though he did not identify the compound: "That side of the *nagaya* which faces the interior of the *yashiki* is built like the frontage of ordinary Japanese houses or shops, and closed with sliding wooden screens

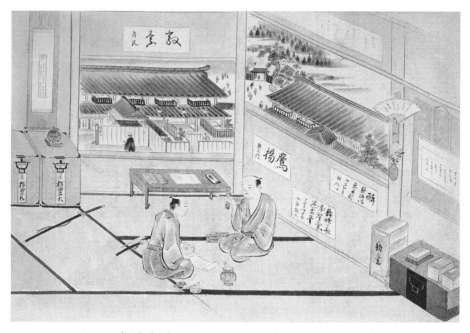

FIGURE 6.3. Room of Kakehashi Toyota, inspector of Kurume domain. "Kurume hanshi Edo kinban nagaya emaki." Courtesy of Edo-Tōkyō hakubutsukan.

running in a groove on a narrow verandah. In the case of a retainer of superior rank a small entrance porch is often added."[35] The furniture in the room consists of three trunks (Kakehashi's name is visible on two of them)—no doubt used to transport his personal effects to and from Edo—and a book box. As elsewhere, scrolls and flowers in a small vase adorn the room.

Scene 8 is also significant because it is the only one in which women appear. The main setting is the room of a retainer named Takahara Shinta, one of the two figures sitting next to a pot of cooking food, eating and drinking. A third, Hiraki Kensai, in Edo for studies, is at the window. Lifting the flap of paper designed as a *shōji* reveals the women. Kensai, who spent four years in Edo on his own (it is unclear whether or not he was married), looks "surreptitiously" at two women talking outside in the courtyard of a single-story residence. The text informs us that they are members of the family of a retainer in Edo on a long-term assignment. Since only such retainers were allowed to bring their families to Edo, the population in many domain compounds was overwhelmingly male. The sight of the women outside the barracks may have brought back memories of Hiraki's own family and a longing for home.

In the next three illustrations the viewer is able to observe the men entertaining themselves with drink and games. In Scenes 9 and 10, Toda, Kanō

Shōha, and their circle of friends eat, drink, and play *rakan mawashi*. In the final image, Scene 11 (refer back to Figure 6.1), however, the men were drinking for a different reason: despair. Expecting to return home soon, the men had just learned of the shogun's order preventing their lord—and therefore them—from going back to Kurume for another two years. The text tells us, "It is said that they drank heavily and carried on, whereby hoping to chase away their melancholy."[36] The drinking and bad news has turned some of the men destructive: sliding doors have been pulled out of their runners and are being trampled on; a sake jar lies broken in pieces; and one man is tearing up a porters' ledger, for it would no longer be needed for the journey home.

We see a return to normalcy in the final two images. With more time on their hands, the retainers have turned to leisurely pastimes, such as indoor archery (Scene 12), and they while away the evening cooling off in front of the entrances to their barracks (Scene 13/Figure 6.4). These are clearly single-story barracks, located in the interior of the compound rather than forming the perimeter. Behind the men, and in front of the entrances, are privacy fences, painted black, which left a small open area between the fence and the building. On the fence, to the right of the entrance, nameplates for the occupants are posted. These are not just artistic devices to allow the viewer to identify the men depicted. When Tosa's Mori Masana arrived at his residence at the Shiba compound in the western barracks, he found his nameplate posted and found this "comforting."[37] On both sides of the three men in the center, under the ground, run water pipes—the water being visible in a small open section closest to the gates. The water basin with its small ladle in the *genkan* area, for washing the feet before stepping up into the living area or for keeping the dust down in the earthen entrance, also indicates that there probably was a toilet to the side, but it is unlikely that there were such facilities in each residence of the barracks.

Considering the thirteen paintings collectively, they show a small group of retainers in the barracks at leisure, talking, eating, drinking, writing, and playing games. The men appear to be robust and healthy, and certainly do not appear to lack food or drink. While the barracks could be hot in the summer, the living quarters were well ventilated and received plentiful sunlight, making for healthy living conditions.

Given the nature of alternate attendance as a system of military service, the men, when deployed to Edo, found basic but adequate facilities waiting for them. Rooms were sparsely furnished, as was typical of contemporary dwellings. Retainers need not bring furniture with them, as rooms came furnished with desks, tables, night lamps (oil lamps and candle holders), and hibachi. One wonders about bedding, but no clue is offered here. At the end of a retainer's

FIGURE 6.4. Retainers cooling off in front of their barracks. "Kurume hanshi Edo kinban nagaya emaki." Courtesy of Edo-Tōkyō hakubutsukan.

tour of duty, domain officials inspected the physical structure of his dwelling, including the tatami matting and furnishings, and gave him a receipt for the goods. Such was the case even for a senior advisor.[38]

While retainers were deployed for military service in Edo, they lived in a time of great peace. Rooms therefore could be decorated to some extent according to personal taste. Samurai cultivated the "twin ways," the civil as well as the military arts, and so room decorations displaying their aesthetic taste were not out of character. Hanging scrolls or other artwork, purchased perhaps in Edo, and cut flowers in vases attached to wall posts, are found in most of the retainers' lodgings. In one of the rooms in the Kurume scroll we see several trunks used to carry personal belongings to Edo. One of them serves temporarily as a table for books, writing utensils and other implements. Later it would serve as a container to transport the retainer's belongings back home, no doubt including a fair number of presents and souvenirs bought in Edo.

Cleanliness was an important part of samurai values, but the Kurume scroll gives us few if any clues regarding bathing. The water pipes running into the residence depicted in the final painting may have also fed baths. It is clear from written sources that at least some of Tosa domain's high-ranking retainers had them in their dwellings. Given the expense of heating the water and the alternatives available, it is not surprising that retainers with these facilities would share them. Mori Masana, for example, frequently used the tub at his relative Mori Oki'emon's residence. His elder brother Yoshiki bathed repeatedly at colleagues' residences on his first tour of Edo. Invited by his friend Katsuji to bathe at his place, Yoshiki found him gone but took advantage of the facilities anyway. At other times, though, both Mori brothers and Sakai Banshirō used public baths in town.[39] According to a Kii retainer named Harada, there was some social mixing at the public baths, which usually reserved the second floor for those with swords and merchants of some status, so higher-ranking retainers may have wanted to avoid them.[40] During a later tour of duty, however, Yoshiki seems to have had his own facilities, for he invited numerous friends to his residence at different times to take a bath that had been prepared.[41]

The great majority of retainers going to Edo with their lord came to Edo without family, which gave them a certain degree of personal freedom. A married man away from home could, as the introduction to the scroll tells us, sleep late into the morning without worrying about "seeing a jealous wife's face" when he returned home. Long-term, Edo-based retainers with families resided with them in individual residential units within the compound. The scroll shows one such dwelling, a single-story detached residence. These family units were commonly grouped together within the compound. Other than these wives and female children, no other women were allowed into the residential quarters.

From the nameplates appearing in the last painting of the Kurume scroll and the written text, we know that a number of the men, of substantial rank and identified by name, lived in their own rooms. In the last painting we can also see two nameplates in front of one entranceway, indicating that the space was shared. Matsuyama retainer Naitō informs us that only men of "considerable status" (*yohodo taishin*) were privileged to have private living spaces. Specifically, he notes that this meant only those of *monogashira* status, men with job titles such as commander of the gunners and leader of the pikemen, selected from among the elite of *hirashi* status (the lowest ranking of the upper samurai).[42] Naitō also reports that the vassals or manservants of retainers lived above them, on the second floor, though this was apparently not universally the case, as evidenced by the Kurume scroll, where middle-ranking samurai occupy some second-story rooms.

The size and location of a retainer's dwelling, not to mention his general living conditions, were affected by the type of compound (i.e., main, middle, or lower) in which he resided, by the length of his posting to Edo and, of course, by his status. Given that a domain's main residence was usually the smallest, conditions there were the most crowded. Room conditions were noticeably better for retainers on long-term postings.[43] Available evidence indicates that such retainers were concentrated in separate barracks as well. At Tosa's middle residence at Hibiya, these quarters were located toward the back of the compound, away from the perimeter barracks, facing the embankment fronting Hibiya moat.[44] Room size was usually pegged concretely to status. Regulations from Wakayama domain, for example, explicitly listed room size by *kokudaka*. Those earning between twenty and thirty *koku* were assigned rooms about ten square meters in area; those between forty and eighty *koku* received an additional square meter.[45] At Kaga's main residence, the lowest rungs of the retainer band lived in shared rooms two to three *ken* (3.6–5.4 meters) in width, with common cooking, washing, and toilet facilities. Middle-ranking retainers enjoyed slightly larger rooms, ranging in width from four to eight *ken* (7.3–14.6 meters). These too were shared, but were likely made more crowded by attending subretainers and menials. High-ranking retainers (full samurai, with rights to an audience with the lord) had still larger rooms, from eight to thirteen *ken* (14.6–23.4 meters), but they had to be shared with a larger number of subretainers and menials.[46] Those at or near the top were privileged with more comfortable quarters. A senior advisor like Tosa's Gotō Seijun lived in a spacious corner suite of ten rooms, with an area of forty-five mats, on the first floor of a two-storied barrack in the northwestern portion of the main compound at Kajibashi. His living space included a large garden, hidden from others' view by a wooden fence.[47]

Beyond the basic information on interior living space, there is other information available about diet and personal consumption indicating that retainers across the ranks of the samurai status group enjoyed a generally healthy lifestyle while in Edo. In the Kurume scroll, for example, we can observe much eating and drinking going on in the barracks. In a number of scenes, various sizes of iron pots are visible, accompanied by sake and sometimes by sashimi. In one scene we actually witness a number of men cooking in their rooms, just as Sakai Banshirō, his uncle, and other roommates all took turns preparing the meals when they were not dining out in town. However, according to Naitō Meisetsu, manservants usually performed this service, often boiling the rice received from the domain with various vegetables.[48]

Evidence for diet and consumptive activities seen in the Kurume scroll can be supplemented with other sources, such as the account books of retainer Ogura Sadasuke or the diary of Sakai Banshirō, to give us a fuller picture of both. Sadasuke was a low-ranking retainer from Tosa, a footsoldier belonging to a family whose hereditary job it was to accompany the lord to Edo. He was of modest economic means, earning a salary of just over nine *koku*, but since alternate attendance made domainal retainers by definition consumers, he too became quite engaged with the market economy. During his sixth tour in Edo he kept a list of purchases for a half-year period from the seventh month through the end of the year. While we cannot know how exhaustive a list it might be, it does give us a good idea about the type of commodities purchased. Looking at the food items notated (Table 6.5), it is difficult to discern sometimes whether a particular item was a gift or for personal consumption, unless Ogura specifically made note of it. By "gift" I mean it was either taken to give to a host or to share at a social gathering. Tangerines, for example, were a popular gift item and probably served that purpose for Ogura. Fish was eaten frequently and taken as a gift as well. Whale and boar were no doubt tastes acquired from home, in Tosa. Soy sauce and miso were common food items used for flavoring, and the latter was used for soup as well. While he ate daikon frequently, the limited variety of other vegetables is surprising.

The diary of Sakai Banshirō (Wakayama) also reveals that even lower samurai (he had a stipend of thirty *koku*) in Edo consumed a plain but healthy diet in the barracks. Inexpensive sources of protein were regularly consumed in the form of sardines, either fresh or dried; tofu, which he ate in a variety of forms about once every five days; and miso soup.[49] This was supplemented with seasonal fresh, as well as pickled, vegetables. He and his roommates frequently pooled their rice allowances to make rice gruel, which was shared amongst them.

Archaeological remains from the daimyo compounds supplement this written evidence on diet, but also expand our focus to important issues such as garbage disposal and recycling, religion, and commodity distribution, to name a few. The question that has generated the most discussion in this area is how to assess the large amount of animal remains found in many sites. This evidence calls into question the common assumption that meat consumption was severely restricted, if not avoided, for religious reasons until after the Meiji Restoration in 1868. Given the martial values of the samurai, it should not be surprising that they ate meat, although they probably refrained from consuming it when important rituals or ceremonies were to take place. Dog was widely eaten in medieval times, and from literary sources such as *Ochiboshū* and *Ryōri monogatari* we know that this custom continued at least into the early Edo period. Stores selling game meat seem to have disappeared in Edo by the late seventeenth century, but curiously reappeared about a hundred years later. According to the contemporary source *Morisada Mankō*, such shops were popular from the 1830s in the three metropolises.[50] One domain, Hikone, even presented beef as a gift to the shogun.[51]

While the general consensus is that samurai continued to eat dog routinely throughout the Tokugawa period,[52] certainly not all these animals kept in the

TABLE 6.5. Food Purchases by Ogura Sadasuke, 1858 / 7th–12th Months*

Item	Note (number of items or quantity)
Soy sauce	2 *go*
Miso	
Salt	
Tea	
Sweets	
Drinking snack (*sakana dai*)	2 times
Shredded bonito (*katsuobushi*)	1
Sweet sea bream	4 times: 2, 7 (five as gift), 3 (gift), ? number
Tuna	
Whale meat	4 times, once as gift
Small grilled sea bream	5 times: 5; 1; 1; 2, as gift; 3, as gift
Grey mullet	8 times: 3; 1; 2, 1 as gift; 6 (large); 14; 6; 1; 3
Hatsu (fish)	2 times: ?; 50
Mackerel	2 times
Bonito	2 times (each time one)
Fish roe	2 times
Boar meat	
Daikon	5 times: 2; 2; 10; 3; 3 bundles
"Vegetables"	
Burdock	
Carrots	
Sweet potato	
Onions	2 bundles
Pears	5
Tangerine	3 times: ?; 10; 5
Hard candy	
Honey	

*Ogura 1858.

domain compounds were meant for consumption. For example, large dogs, probably Western ones or Japanese dogs that had acquired Western features through crossbreeding, were raised as pets at Sendai domain's lower compound.[53] Others clearly were prized as guard dogs, to be used in the hunt, as a source of meat to feed hawks, or even for dogfights (particularly Tosa's fighting dogs).[54]

Various other animals found in the excavations were put to different uses. Deer, wild boar, badger, and rabbit were found most frequently. Also present, although in lesser amounts, are otter, fox, horse, monkey, bear, marten/sable, cat, whale, wolf, and *kamoshika* (Japanese serow).[55] While these may not all have been consumed by humans, archaeological evidence—particularly the types of markings found on bones — confirms that boar, deer, bear, *kamoshika*, wolf, badger, fox, chicken, duck, and otter were eaten, but that ox and horse were not.[56] Many of the wild game animals were probably caught in the mountains west of the city and brought to the urban market via the Kōshū highway.[57] Other animals, though, were actually raised in the daimyo compounds. It is well known, for example, that late in the Tokugawa period employees of the Satsuma domain were raising pigs for consumption by its Edo population as well as to sell in the urban market.[58] Some other types of birds and reptiles, such as pheasants, peacocks, swans, cranes, ducks, chicken, geese, canaries, and snapping turtles, were found in the compounds.[59]

Some animals not meant as food or for display were put to other uses. Bone, antlers, and shells were used to craft hairpins, combs, and brushes. The hides of cows and horses likewise found a variety of uses. Whether or not people consumed cat is a subject of some debate, but it is clear that its skin was used (for *shamisen*) and its meat used as feed for hawks. Similarly, pigeons and sparrows were used as bait or feed. Exotic types of birds were kept as pets; monkeys and bears were probably used primarily for show.[60]

Fish played a more important part in a retainer's diet than did meat, and a great variety of fish was consumed, such as red sea bream, cod, *kisu* (a sillaginoid), sea perch, trout, sweetfish, bonito, yellowtail, tuna, flounder, flatfish, horse mackerel, mackerel, and sardines. The types of fish prized by Edo residents were not necessarily the same as those regarded highly in Japan today. Judging by the price, sea bream, salmon, flounder, and sea bass were regarded as of higher quality; cod, tuna, yellowtail, mackerel, and flatfish were less expensive.[61] From literary sources we know that eel was also eaten extensively, although few archaeological remains of it have been found.[62]

Local food products often made their way to the daimyo compounds in Edo. Accordingly, Kaga retainers, while in Edo, maintained to some extent their native eating habits by consuming large amounts of cod in their barracks at Hongō. Cod was the most commonly eaten fish at the time in the Hokuriku region, where Kaga domain was located. Shipped dried and salted to Edo, it provided the population at the main compound with a familiar foodstuff from home. Salted mackerel was also sent from Kaga to its Edo compound to supplement purchases made in the shogun's capital. By contrast, few remains of bonito were found at the site even though it was a popular fish at the time in Edo. Perhaps this again reflects the local tastes of Kaga people, who were not accustomed to eating bonito back home (it is not caught in great numbers in the Sea of Japan).[63]

Diet varied according to a retainer's income and status, and this is confirmed by garbage pits. In the official portion of the Kaga's main compound, where many banquets were held, a high incidence of red sea bream was found.[64] Here and at other headquarters and lower residences, expensive shellfish used primarily for banquets, such as ark shells, turbo shells, and abalone, were also commonly unearthed. In their barracks, upper-ranking samurai at Hongō ate a slightly different range of fish, higher-quality types such as sea bream and gurnet, but also clams, blowfish, and sardines, the latter three being fish ordinarily more associated with commoners.[65] The diet of lower samurai was far simpler, with dried sardines, tofu, *chazuke* (tea over rice), and soup being important staple foods. On days with banquets or other festivities their diet was more varied, often with sashimi, sushi, or some type of one-pot cooking.[66] To some extent the domain provided its retainers with food (rice and perhaps cod in the case of Kaga) to sustain themselves in Edo, and on special occasions they also enjoyed celebratory meals provided for them. For other foodstuffs as well as basic commodities necessary for daily life, retainers were forced to turn to the market to purchase them.

Alternate attendance, then, just like the daimyo's policies to draw their retainers into castle towns, created an instant class of consumers. From Ogura Sadasuke's pocket ledger we can get a sense of the purchases a retainer might routinely make (Table 6.6). In chapter seven we will examine the type of gifts Ogura and other retainers purchased to take home to the domain, but of items purchased on a more routine basis there are a few indulgences — tobacco, a New Year's decoration, and a few gifts — but otherwise it consists largely of daily necessities such as tooth powder, hair oil, lamp oil for light, charcoal for warmth, clothing, medicine, and ink and paper. The bamboo stilts were probably a gift meant for the amusement of a child.

"Hardships"

While many retainers no doubt looked forward to the opportunity to live in Tokugawa Japan's greatest city for a year, the mandatory time away from home could be a painful personal experience. This was undoubtedly even more the case when a stay of a year in Edo was extended.[67] The Kurume scroll touches on the human costs of the system of alternate attendance, which imposed on a large numbers of retainers a period of enforced residence in Edo, separating them from home, family, and friends. The text discusses the Edo experience of domainal retainers as one of pleasure as well as hardship. The visual images give some indication of both, but the image mentioned above of a man gazing out of a window at the family of a long-term retainer is a poignant reminder of the latter.

The Confucian scholar Nakai Chikuzan wrote that alternate attendance "was objectionable on moral grounds, since leaving behind wives and children as hostages in Edo was inhumane and cruel."[68] However, the ill effects of al-

TABLE 6.6. Non-food Purchases by Ogura Sadasuke, 1858 / 7th–12th month

Lamp oil (4 times)	Hair oil; cord for hair
Paper (2 times)	Ink stone and ink
Broom	
Thread (6 times, once dyed)	
Raincoat	Umbrella (for child)
Hand towel (4 times)	Striped cotton cloth, from Kansai (2); one time origin unspecified
Hakama	
Obi (Kokura obi)	
Leather *zōri* (2 pair), (2 pair), (1 pair) (1 pair)	Wet weather *zōri* (*setta*) for children
Zōri (4 pair)	*Bokkuri* (type of high *geta*)
Children's *geta* (2 times)	
Tobacco (3 times—two from Kansai region)	
Pipe	
Pair of bamboo stilts	
Sword guard	
Kinryūgan (medicine)	*Keishintan* (medicine)
Jitsubosan (medicine)	
Tooth powder	
Wooden bowl	Ceramic bowl
Sake bottle (*tokkuri*)	
Coal	
New Year's decoration (*kadomatsu*)	

ternate attendance were experienced throughout the lord's retainer band as well as by the men and women hired by its members. The degree of personal hardship suffered invariably differed from person to person, but systems of military service like alternate attendance rarely take into account personal circumstances. From personal diaries we get a sense of hardship experienced by people in Tosa. For example, Kusunose Oe's daughter, Suzu, was married for only two months before her husband was dispatched to Edo for a tour of duty.[69] Some retainers missed the births of children whom they had fathered, suffered the loss of a loved one while away, or came home to find their house burned down, as was the case with Miyaji Umanosuke's colleague Tani Kakimori. The wife of Sakai Genjirō, Mori Masana's roommate during his first stay in Edo, passed away while he was in Edo.[70] A son was born to senior advisor Gotō Seijun while he was en route to Edo, making it three children under the age of six at home without their father.[71] Sometimes bad news came by messenger. In one instance, the senior advisor Kirima received word that his young son had died, and in another, Mori Yoshiki recorded in his diary that "yesterday's official messenger brought news that Ichirōbei's son, age five, and Junchū's son, age four, died of measles."[72] Sometimes the misfortune was more widespread, as when a high-speed messenger brought news of a fire in Ino village, which burned down ninety-three households.[73] Whatever the bad news, however, a retainer could not cut short his tour of duty and return home.

The separation of retainers from friends, trusted colleagues, and loved ones could produce a sense of anxiety, evident from the focus on official messengers in numerous diaries. All the events surrounding them—expected and actual arrivals and departures—were noted with startling frequency. The approach of the official messenger's departure date seemed to spur a flurry of letter-writing activity, as retainers rushed to complete letters lest they have to wait for the next one in about ten days. On one occasion Mori Masana stayed in his room all day to complete a grand total of sixty-three letters to give the messenger before his departure.[74]

Written communications helped to keep retainers in touch with those left behind and thereby assuage feelings of separation. The arrival of letters from home, carried by official messengers or privately by retainers, normally took about three weeks from Tosa and brought relief for retainers like Miyaji Umanosuke whenever he received word that his family, parents, and relatives were all well.[75]

Similarly, written communications helped the people left behind deal with their anxiety over the departure of a colleague, friend, or loved one. When Mori Yoshiki arrived in Edo on 1802/4/18, he found twenty-five letters from Tosa already waiting for him, some of them no doubt expressing concern with how he had fared in the performance of his important duties on the road to Edo safeguarding the young heir.

The messenger service allowed fathers to stay in touch with their families and to continue to play a role, even if in absentia, in the upbringing of their children. Rai Shunsui, the father of Rai San'yō, and his wife, Baishi, maintained a steady correspondence during Shunsui's absence in Edo in which they discussed many issues facing the household, particularly the upbringing of their four children. Shunsui continually admonished his wife to be diligent in ensuring that San'yō apply himself to both his academic as well as his martial studies and asked for regular progress reports.[76] While this study focuses on the men serving in Edo, the diary of Baishi and other accounts of life in the domain suggest that a complete study of alternate attendance would have to consider more fully the effects of the system on those left behind. Here, however, some suggestive material will have to suffice.

The demands of alternate attendance could make it extremely difficult for a retainer to lead a normal life, particularly if he was called upon to serve in Edo repeatedly. Shunsui, a Confucian scholar, alternated residences along with his lord, the daimyo of Hiroshima, during a ten-year period. In between his seven tours of duty he was normally home for a period of roughly three to five months, though in one case it was as long as nine. While in Hiroshima, Shunsui was directly involved in his household's affairs, but given his repeated absences he had no choice but to entrust the education of his son to two uncles. Likewise, he relied on several male relatives and friends, rather than his wife, to oversee his household's financial affairs while he was in Edo. In this way, those serving in Edo were forced to rely on networks of friends and relatives to assist their household during their absence. Similarly, immediate family members relied on this network for support in a variety of forms during that time.

It is difficult to gauge the personal toll that the system exacted, but, depending on individual circumstances, it could be considerable. The letter of a high-ranking retainer, Asahina Genba, to the Yamauchi daimyo heir, whom he was serving, demonstrates how a prolonged period of enforced residence in Edo could profoundly affect the lives of retainers. When the future lord Yamauchi Toyofusa refused to make the trip to Tosa after becoming heir in 1689, Asahina was prompted to petition him to correct this situation. In doing so, the retainer underlined the political, economic, and social consequences of Toyofusa's inaction not only for the domain as a whole and the heir himself, but for those serving him most closely, his retainers.

Asahina wrote that the prolonged stay in Edo was not adversely affecting him personally, but other retainers were suffering hardship. His arguing thus may not have been genuine, for to complain of personal distress might have appeared selfish; by informing his lord of how his inaction was adversely impacting others, however, Asahina was the loyal retainer remonstrating with his lord. Whatever his actual situation and true feelings about his own circumstances, Asahina wrote:[77]

> I have been in your personal service here in this place [Edo] for five years. The income granted me is abundant and my domestic finances therefore have not been adversely affected by my stay in Edo. I have performed my duty without recourse to loans of rice or silver from our lord. I have had no concerns about the well-being of my wife and children in Tosa. There are others, however, who have been here for eight years [that is, since Toyofusa became heir], performing their duty night and day. They have been unable to look after their families' affairs in Tosa and have suffered financial difficulties.

Citing specific examples of how separation from Tosa was impacting the lives of various men, Asahina continued:

There is, for example, your retainer Nakayama Gen'emon, who has no heir yet and must therefore adopt a son. If other retainers such as Murata Shōhachi, Miyagawa Seijirō, Shibuya Jihei, Asada Ridayū, and Iwasaki Shōzaemon had been allowed to return home, they would already have married and had children, leading settled lives. They would not have to leave the care of their aged parents to their relatives. There is no limit to the number of such stories one hears about the lower ranks of the retainer corps as well. Those of low status (*karuki mono*) are unable to lead normal married lives. While they do not formally sever their matrimonial ties, they are forced to live apart from their spouses. This brings much grief to several hundred people, who face financial and other serious difficulties.

As a result, married lives were put on hold, new marriage unions delayed, family members were not cared for adequately, and children not sired — these were just a few of the negative effects of a prolonged period of enforced residence in Edo.

The tragic consequences resulting from the enforced absence of a husband is the subject of two works by the famous playwright Chikamatsu. The first, "Yari no Gonza" (Gonza the Lancer) is the slightly fictionalized account of a Matsue domain retainer, Sasa no Gonza, and the wife of his tea master Ichinoshin, against whom incriminatory evidence of adultery was collected. Although innocent, they had no defense and were forced to flee, only to be slain later, as required by custom, by the husband in a wife-revenge killing.[78] This case demonstrates that in the absence of their husbands, the wives of retainers had to be extra diligent to ensure that they were not put into situations where their virtue might be called into question. Another play of Chikamatsu's, "Horikawa Namino Tsuzumi" (The Drum Waves of Horikawa), was based on the actual adultery of the wife of Okura Hikohachirō and a drum teacher, Miyagi Gen'emon, in 1706. In this case the husband was informed of the adultery but did nothing about it, leading to his social ostracization. In a spiraling train of events, the husband's younger sister was divorced by her husband because of her connection to a man deemed too cowardly to punish his adulterous wife and her lover. Only when presented with incontrovertible proof did Hikohachirō slay the man, while his wife took her own life.[79] Of course adultery was a problem not restricted to the families of retainers serving in Edo, but the forced separation of couples no doubt made it more difficult to maintain close relationships.

"Pleasures"

While the text and pictures of the Kurume scroll may appear to tell a story of men idly whiling away their time, it hardly presents a complete description of retainer life in Edo. We should not be left with the impression that men on a tour of duty had nothing to do when not working but play games and drink. Socializing with friends and colleagues in the barracks was an important but not exclusive source of entertainment, nor did it constitute the sum and total range of activities for Edo-based retainers when they were off duty. The attraction of Edo to retainers from Tokugawa Japan's castle towns lay largely with the pleasures and the various opportunities uniquely available to them in Edo.

To a large extent, the "Edo experience" was what the individual made of it. It offered stimulating, new intellectual and experiential opportunities. As a result, the Satsuma samurai Saigo Takamori "was seemingly overwhelmed by this exciting and intimidating city [Edo]."[80] The diaries of the many men mentioned above reveal that a variety of different cultural, educational, and martial activities — lessons in Noh chanting and dance, the tea ceremony, poetry writing, not to mention various types of study groups — were available to them within the network of compounds. Mori Yoshiki, for instance, had plenty of time to participate in an informal reading group at the domainal residence and to receive lessons in Noh chanting and dance.[81] He also found time to join a study group focusing on the ancient chronicle *Nihon shoki* (Chronicles of Japan) in which, he noted, one retainer from Echigo and two Tokugawa bannermen also participated.[82] Saigō Takamori took part in a study group on Mito Learning with retainers from four other domains, including two from the northeast.[83]

As will be further explained in the next chapter, retainers like Saigō Takamori, Mori Yoshiki, and Sakai Banshirō could pursue new intellectual interests in Edo, develop new skills, and interact with scholars and fellow samurai from other domains. From the limited amount of information offered in the Kurume scroll, we know that the author of the text studied under the noted poet Yanagawa Seigan (1789–1858). Other sources of information about the men depicted in the scroll tell us that Kakehashi Toyota became a student of the National Learning scholar Tachibana Moribe (1781–1849) and that the artist Kanō Shōha studied poetry under Tagawa Hōrō (1762–1845).[84] If additional personal records were available for people mentioned in the scroll, they would no doubt reveal that many more of the retainers did not simply while away their time, but became active in Edo's cultural life.

Part of the attraction of Edo was that it was possible to engage in activities that were proscribed or looked down upon in the domain. That could involve a trip to one of Edo's licensed or nonlicensed pleasure quarters; Saigō Takamori noted that one of the first things new arrivals from Satsuma did was head to the brothels in Shinagawa.[85] Sakai Banshirō took lessons in *shamisen*, which would have been unthinkable back home in Wakayama because of restrictions on what were deemed frivolous activities. While the tea ceremony was banned in Mito in the mid-nineteenth century, the cultural climate within the compound in Edo was much less restrictive.[86] Moreover, as will be discussed below, when free to leave the compound, retainers could take in the sights of Edo, eat out at restaurants, make pilgrimages to temples and shrines and attend their festivals, watch plays, and view fireworks displays.

Despite the relative freedom of life in Edo, retainers in general did not have the right of unrestricted movement in and out of the domain's compound. Permission was required to exit through the gates when leaving on personal business. One Tosa retainer, for example, went out between five and ten times per month, a total of twenty-eight times in three months.[87] Sakai Banshirō took his meals outside the compound seven or eight times a month and, combined with outings for sightseeing, pilgrimages to shrines and temples, shopping, and other activities, usually went out on personal business ten times or more a month.[88]

A curfew existed, but it varied according to status and was enforced to varying degrees. Higher-ranking retainers from Usuki, for example, had an additional two hours beyond the standard time (6 p.m.) for everyone else. Those on long-term duty and those in Edo for individual study had two more additional hours.[89] On paper, the punishment for missing the curfew could be severe. The offender in principle could be sent back to the domain, where he would be placed under house confinement. However, in contrast with other forms of misbehavior, to be discussed below, this regulation does not seem to have been strictly applied. In some cases a small fine was imposed. In some cases, with the cooperation of the gate guards or the assistance of friends inside the compound, a tardy retainer might escape being caught altogether.[90] As clocks were available only in the lord's residence and the administrative center of the compound, the time was announced by menials who made the rounds throughout the compound, beating wooden clappers. The gate used for everyday traffic was apparently at the end of the rounds, and this gave the tardy retainers some leeway. Those who were on their second or third tour of duty tended to grow lax, it seems, and had to be saved by friends, who would bribe the man with the clappers to stop for a while midway on his course until the errant retainer returned.

While many activities did not require money, it was nonetheless an important factor in determining what a retainer could or could not do while in Edo; that is, whether he could afford to eat out at restaurants, go to see plays, visit the Yoshiwara, or become the student of a teacher not employed by the domain. Conditions differed from domain to domain and varied greatly depending on the retainer's status. While some samurai went without, others were able to save money during their tour of duty in Edo, as the discussion of Tani Tannai's experience in chapter four revealed.

If a retainer was not able to take care of all his personal business when outside the compound, he could avail himself of the services of merchants and book lenders who came by the compounds to ply their trades. Of course, retainers also left the compound on official business; while they were supposed to return immediately after the completion of those duties, they sometimes took their time doing so, making stops for personal pleasure along the way back. Mori Yoshiki, for example, wrote that he went sightseeing on the way back to his residence at Tosa's middle compound at Shiba after finishing his duties attending the daimyo heir at Kajibashi.[91]

The experience of Hachinohe retainer Toyama Tamuro is representative of many domainal samurai in Edo. With a relatively undemanding work schedule, he was able to go out nineteen times during a forty-day period. For leisure, he most often got together with friends, with whom he enjoyed tea or sake and conversation. His greatest passion, however, appears to have been the puppet theater in Kawarake, Shinbashi, and Akasaka, which he attended eight times in those forty days. On days off he followed a routine: first he had a bath at public facilities, then he had his hair dressed, followed by an evening performance of theater. On three occasions he went to public festivals at Kumano, Konpira, and Akiba shrines. Shopping was sometimes combined with one of the above activities, as when he stopped by Shinjuku on his way back from Konpira shrine to buy an unlined kimono.[92]

Similarly, the diary and financial ledger of Wakayama retainer Sakai Banshirō offers us an unusual glimpse into the social and economic life of a retainer posted to Edo.[93] Banshirō was twenty-eight years old when posted to Edo in 1860, where he shared a room in the barracks at the domain's middle compound at Akasaka with his uncle and another retainer whose relationship to them is uncertain. His uncle held the hereditary post of *okuzume goemon kata* in the interior, meaning he was responsible for instructing the women in the private part of the residence on all matters related to the selection and proper manner of wearing clothing. He was also responsible for the placement of screens in the interior. Banshirō was "attached" to his uncle to get on-the-job training by observing and assisting him. For Banshirō, then, service in Edo was a means to obtaining a better job, though his apprenticeship did not assure that he would be appointed to a similar post. There was also an economic motivation, for, as noted in chapter four, his allowance for serving in Edo was quite generous (thirty-nine *ryō* per year) and allowed him to save enough to support his wife, daughter, and parents back home. While Banshirō appears to have lived better in economic terms during his time in Edo, he was frugal in many respects, eating simply and not purchasing many gifts. He enjoyed a good time, but it pained him when he had to spend money unexpectedly. For example, when, after making a pilgrimage to Ekōin at Ryōgoku, Banshirō got caught in a rainstorm and had to pull in to a sweetshop and buy a snack, he grumbled in his diary, "I had no choice but to spend a hundred *mon*."[94] He complained about a friend who liked to smoke but never had his own tobacco, and noted that his uncle got very angry at him for correcting the uncle's miscalculation for a shared expense. His maintaining a pocket financial ledger while in Edo, with exclamations about high prices when he was forced to pay them, also indicates that he gave financial matters considerable thought.

Banshirō's actual duties were light, no more than half a day about every third day, which left him free time for his leisure activities, such as eating and drinking (both in the barracks and out on the town), sightseeing, going to the public bath, and taking music lessons. During his tour of duty in Edo he left the compound ten times or more a month on personal business, usually with three or four persons, including his roommates. On almost all these occasions he ate at local restaurants and drinking establishments, where he often partook of an inexpensive meal of soba. The noodles were usually consumed in conjunction with sake, sushi, or *nabemono*, a variety of one-pot meals that often included fowl or sometimes boar or pig,[95] and the meal usually ended a day spent shopping and going to shrines and temples. Visits to religious sites were most frequent during the summer and fall seasons, when many festivals were held. Banshirō visited most of the famous sites in town, including Sengakuji, the final resting place of the forty-seven loyal retainers, and some of the largest of the daimyo compounds. Less frequently he went to see plays, to listen to storytellers, or to visit the Yoshiwara.[96] In the pleasure quarters he and several of his friends viewed a procession of courtesans for the first time. Then, in the Ryōgoku area, they saw various freak shows, including one with ghosts or other scary creatures, young women's sumo (a Tokugawa version of women's mud wrestling), and several sex shows.[97]

Music lessons were also an important part of his outings. Apparently not fond of martial arts despite his position in the great guard unit, Banshirō's greatest pleasure, it seems, was the *shamisen*. These lessons with his teacher, Tokiwa Kinshun, who had two daughters and lived in a back tenement house, must have provided welcome relief as well from the all-male barracks; the same was no doubt true of the informal socializing that occurred afterward, particularly when the teacher's daughters taught him popular songs. His frequent instruction on this instrument highlights the fact that Edo offered opportunities not available elsewhere. *Shamisen* lessons would have been inconceivable back in the castle town, where such a pursuit would have been seen as unbecoming a samurai.[98]

Entertainment and miscellaneous expenses made up a substantial part of Banshirō's expenditures while in Edo (18.9 percent), surpassed only by clothing (27 percent) and food (20.2 percent). Whether on his days off duty or in the afternoons after work, Banshirō usually went out with three or four friends, including his two roommates. Tobacco was a regular expense, and occasionally he also purchased things for a child or children — probably for his three-year-old daughter, Uta, in Wakayama — such as *obi* and footwear. Lastly, he, like a number of his friends, paid his roommate Ōishi to do his hair, usually six to eight times a month.[99] Clothing costs were for the purchase of material for *hakama* and *haori*, tailoring, washing, and footwear. Banshirō bought a total of twelve pairs of footwear during the year (eight pairs of *zōri*, three pairs of *geta*, and one pair of straw sandals), though presumably some of these were intended as gifts.

He had other expenditures as well. Social expenses (16.2 percent) consisted of gifts to friends and social superiors, including his *shamisen* teacher, as well as social entertaining and mail service fees. Household expenses (4.9 percent) entailed the purchase of firewood and charcoal for cooking and warmth, candles, ceramic ware, and chopsticks for the brazier.[100] A small portion (2.9 percent) of his budget was for health and hygiene, which included trips to the public bath, where as noted he also drank sake and played *go* and the *shamisen*.[101]

Sightseeing was of course free, as were pilgrimages to shrines and temples and, in summer, fireworks displays, and many retainers availed themselves of these activities. Tosa's Mori Masana, Miyaji Umanosuke, and Mori Yoshiki, Hachinohe's Toyama Tamuro, Wakayama's Sakai Banshirō, and Owari's Kodera Kiyoaki participated in the popular culture of the city, attending festivals; watching fireworks displays, acrobatic and equestrian performances, as well as the puppet and other kinds of theater; flower viewing; visiting the pleasure quarters of Yoshiwara; going to the public bath; eating or drinking out; and shopping. Masana went to the Sannō festival with four other colleagues and commented that the festival floats there were not as nice as in Kōchi. Still, he noted, the clothes worn were "too beautiful to describe." Hachinohe's Toyama Tamuro frequented performances of *jōruri*. The others went to many of these shrines and festivals as well. Kodera, an Owari domain retainer serving in Edo in 1841, made pilgrimages to sixty-eight shrines and temples in Edo and the surrounding area.[102] Mori Masana also enjoyed visiting the gravestones of famous people buried in Edo, such as Arai Hakuseki and Ōishi Kuranosuke, whose grave at Sengakuji was routinely visited by retainers on tours of duty. Somehow, Mori Masana was able to take a guided tour of Edo Castle, two highlights of which were seeing the audience hall where the lords routinely gathered and touching the scar left in the pillar by Lord Asano's sword.[103] Wanting to move about the city inconspicuously, Tosa senior advisor Gotō Seijun left behind his normal entourage of five or six retainers and attendants and together with a colleague went sightseeing in a "stealthy" (*shinobi o motte*) manner to Edo Castle as well as to Zōjōji and Kanda myōjin temple.[104] Sakai Banshirō and Mori Masana enjoyed watching the daimyo and their attendants gathering in front of Edo Castle for their periodic audiences with the shogun. Taking in the event his first full day in Edo after a tour of Daimyo Avenue, Sakai found the sight "startling" (*me o odorokasu*).[105] Masana likewise went to watch the spectacle no less than three times during his first trip in 1828.[106]

Owari domain retainer Kodera Kiyoaki remained in Edo for nine months during his tour of duty in 1841, during which time he toured the city broadly but within well-defined limits.[107] A cultured man and prolific writer, his activities in the city and their geographic range can be detailed through his diary. Venturing out about seven times a month, Kiyoaki's activities tended to be concentrated in three zones, the bustling Ryōgoku and Asakusa areas as well the general vicinity of the domain headquarters at Ichigaya where he lived. In this, Kiyoaki was not unusual, because on days retainers worked they were limited in the distance they could travel and still make evening curfew. On days off, Kiyoaki and his friends and colleagues traveled more widely, in a radius of five to seven miles from the compound. On particular days they might visit Asakusa-Ryōgoku, Ryōgoku-Yanagiwara, or Asakusa-Yoshiwara as set courses. Ryōgoku, as noted, offered numerous pleasures, and this would be combined with a stop at Yanagiwara to shop at the antique stalls or used clothing stands; antique shopping and watching storytelling performances at Ichigaya near the compound were two of Kiyoaki's favorite pastimes. Similarly, while Asakusa offered many carnal temptations, Kiyoaki made frequent pilgrimages (seven in nine months) to the Kannon temple there. He also did likewise at Suitengū, Konpira (both located in daimyo compounds), and Bishamon temple, visiting these places on their festival days. On other days off he and his companions sometimes followed a course around the periphery of the city, which might include Fukagawa, Kamedo, Takadanobaba, Asakusa, Aoyama, Shibuya, Meguro, and Shinagawa. Still, as noted, samurai on tours of duty, unlike commoners, were limited in the geographic scope of their mobility due to curfews. Trips outside the city to popular spots such as Enoshima or Kamakura, for example, ordinarily were out of the question.

Given the range of activities in which retainers participated, it is evident they had a much less restricted lifestyle in Edo. After returning home to Wakayama, Banshirō, for example, continued his training, begun in the capital, at the Ujita house every third day and engaged in musket practice with some frequency (five to twelve times a month). His only leisure activity, however, seems to have been a monthly poetry club meeting. Given this, and the forced borrowing his household was forced to deal with, a tour of duty in Edo must have seemed like a pleasant dream to retainers like Banshirō.

Misbehavior and Illegal Activities

Upon arrival in Edo, those accompanying the lord or heir were read rules of conduct, which stated broadly that retainers were to obey the laws of the Toku-gawa government above all. Some of the more specific prohibitions issued by the domain regarding the activities of retainers in the outer barracks discussed in the last chapter give us some idea of the actual forms of misbehavior: keeping the *shōji* open and looking out from the windows at passersby; purchasing goods from itinerant merchants through open windows (even from the second floor!); throwing water out of the windows or hanging things from them; speaking in loud voices or playing music. While these were fairly innocuous forms of misbehavior, sometimes the temptations of Edo were too much and retainers got into serious trouble.

A more serious but common form of misbehavior was gambling. Punishment could also be severe. Retainers found guilty were often sent home as punishment, and a superior could be held responsible for the offense of his retainer, as was the case with Tosa's Teshima Kiroku.[108] Given this, one has to consider the possible implication that Edo service was seen by the authorities as a reward of sorts. Minor infractions, such as when Tosa retainer Yoshimatsu Kogorō failed to obey the gate guard's command to halt and exited the compound, could result in domiciliary confinement.[109] Minor dereliction of duty or disobeying some regulation could result in either domiciliary confinement or in a monetary fine. Early in the seventeenth century, fines were assessed when messengers, pages, or valets were not found at their post, were caught lying down on the job, or were caught sneaking out the back gate or entering the compound via the main gate, which was meant only for formal, official business. In the latter case the guard, of course, was fined as well.[110] Records from the nineteenth century indicate that three days' confinement was the standard punishment for a light offense, such as leaving a guard post while on duty.[111] Fighting had more serious penalties, as when footsoldier Okuda Otoji of Tosa was banished for his altercation with an individual identified only by name, Hagiwara Ihachi, at a sumo match. Okuda hit him with a bamboo stick, resulting in his banishment, loss of job, and loss of the right to wear a sword.[112] Though he did not engage in actual combat, Tosa retainer Sagara Sakichi claimed he had chased after and killed a townsman fireman who had pushed him under the water at the bathhouse. In actuality he told this story to several people to cover up a sword wound that was self-inflicted while drunk at a restaurant. His lies were quite apparent to all concerned, and the embarrassing case was resolved unofficially with his being ordered into domestic confinement for fifty to sixty days to recover from "illness."[113]

More serious crimes were committed of course by retainers and their attendants in Edo, though there is no indication that their frequency was any different than in the domain. For example, during the years 1671 to 1826, there were forty-three incidents of bloodshed or suicide in Edo involving Tottori domain retainers and their attendants, or less than one every three years. Many of these involved fights, and when one party was seriously wounded or left dead, the other usually committed suicide. In rare cases the killer absconded, as happened in 1750 when relations between two roommates went sour. Theft was punished harshly, as when a steward found guilty of the crime was decapitated at the domain's middle compound in Shiba. There appears to have been a holding cell in every main compound, and it was probably there that men were held in custody until *seppuku* could be enforced.[114] Negligence that led to fire in the compound was also strictly punished. The carelessness of one Tosa retainer with a hibachi caused a fire in the second story of the barracks at an unnamed compound where he was living. Though the fire was put out, he and one son were both banished.[115]

Of course only a small minority of retainers committed infractions of Tokugawa or their domains' regulations and had to be punished. Most retainers like Sakai Banshirō and Mori Masana performed their service in Edo without incident. They were able to expand their worldview by accompanying their lords to Edo, and while in the city by engaging in new social and cultural activities. Some retainers specifically sought out an Edo assignment for that purpose. Yet regardless of whether they were in Edo of their own volition or because it was a requirement of their military service, all retainers were exposed to new opportunities and experiences. Their participation in alternate attendance effected cultural change across the country, the subject to which we now turn our focus.

7

Carriers of Culture

TO SAY THAT ALTERNATE attendance influenced Japanese culture is a truism of sorts, but there has been little examination of how this actually occurred on either a macro or a micro level.[1] Moreover, in observing the functioning of alternate attendance, scholars in both Japan and America have misconstrued the process: Cultural flow is seen as unidirectional, spreading "Edo culture" from the center to the localities. For example, according to George Tsukahira the system "spread the culture of Edo . . . to the countryside"; an article by Nishiyama Matsunosuke, a leading Japanese cultural historian, titled "*Zenkoku ni hirogaru Edo no bunka*" (lit., "Edo culture, which spread all over the country"), develops the same idea; according to the editors of an exhibition catalogue on alternate attendance from the Edo-Tokyo Museum, "The culture of Edo spread to the local areas, and scholarship and the arts became uniform."[2]

In this chapter I will argue that in contrast with this Edo-centric model, the social processes involved in the production and integration of culture in the Edo period were much more complex. Rather than a unidirectional model, a more accurate paradigm of cultural change, as revealed by alternate attendance, consists of a number of currents by means of which people, ideas, and material goods and other culture flowed between the roughly 250 domains and the center (Edo), from the domains to the cities of Osaka and Kyoto, and from local area (domain) to local area, sometimes directly and sometimes via the center (Edo). Culture was, in other words, produced and transmitted all along the metaphorical road of alternate attendance. As a result, by the end of the eighteenth century Edo became a cultural nexus — the place where a spectrum of the samurai and other educated and artistic elite came together and interacted in numerous human networks. While Edo looms large in this cultural equation, the localities, the journey to and from the center, and the domainal compounds also played important roles. It is only through the study of the interaction between these various currents that we can understand the development of Tokugawa culture — and the role of alternate attendance in fostering a national identity — during Japan's early modern period.

A key aim here, then, is to advance the discussion, through an examination of the dynamics of alternate attendance, of how culture in early modern Japan was produced and disseminated. This will be done by focusing on the effects of the system on the daimyo's retainers, his vassal corps. The chapter also explores the role of retainers as "carriers of culture" by further developing some of the themes of the last chapter; that is, through a study of their consumption habits, use of material goods, and their cultural activities in Edo and at home. Such a focus is possible primarily because of the personal diaries kept by retainers from Tosa and a few other domains while participating in alternate attendance. Through these largely manuscript sources, it will be possible to examine the process of cultural production, diffusion, and integration set in motion by this political institution. While there was great variation from retainer to retainer, the overall documentary base strongly indicates that the requirements of participation in the system — not to mention the incidental travel between the domains and Edo made possible by the system — enriched the cultural life of the country as a whole and led to national integration and a population with a high level of shared culture and experience.

The Journey: Discovering Japan

The "Edo experience" of domainal retainers entailed more than a period of residence in the country's largest urban center. It also involved the trip to and from Edo, the focus of chapters one and two, which was an integral component of that experience. In the case of a distant domain such as Tosa, the trip ordinarily required between three to four weeks each way and would take the retainer from Kōchi, a castle town of about twenty thousand people, to the megalopolis of Edo. Personal diaries, such as those left by Tosa samurai Mori Masana, Mori Yoshiki, and the Confucian scholar Miyaji Umanosuke, give us some understanding of how the alternate attendance and the incidental travel made possible by the system impacted the individual lives of retainers. While that experience was hardly uniform, Mori Masana, whose world, like many retainers', had been confined to the borders of Tosa domain or the immediate area around Kōchi castle town, probably did not really understand what kind of domain "Tosa" was until he traveled to and from Edo in 1828–1829. The trip to Edo was a journey of discovery and through it he and others like him were able to place their localities within the context of the collectivity of domains and other territories that was known as "Japan."

Although our foremost image of alternate attendance is perhaps that of a procession of retainers accompanying the lord to and from Edo, as detailed in chapter three, a reading of numerous diaries written by retainers indicates that they were not always part of the retinue. Sakai Banshirō of Wakayama made his trip to Edo in 1860 in a group of five, which included his uncle. For Mori Masana of Tosa domain it was only on his fifth journey to Edo, in 1856, that he was an official part of a daimyo's retinue. While most of the retainers traveled in the three principal units of the procession, there also was an irregular stream of men heading in both directions during the remainder of the year.

On Masana's trip to Edo for studies in 1828, he was able to leave the procession, of which his brother was a formal part, and go off on his own when he wanted to stop somewhere not on the prescribed course.[3] He made a pilgrimage to Konpira-san (Kotohira shrine) with three others, perhaps in situations similar to his, and while there was able to see an exhibition of the temple art treasures and relics—something which according to Masana occurred "only once every thousand years." In Murotsu (Harima) he was able to see some theater; near Nishinomiya he visited a number of historical sites, including the graves of Taira no Kiyomori and Taira no Atsumori. In Osaka he was able to enjoy a marionette puppet show, which astonished him, as well as acrobatics and other street shows (*misemono*), all of which were probably not available in Kōchi. While in Kyoto he filled his days with sightseeing, visiting a number of shrines and temples, Nijō Castle, the Imperial Palace, and the pleasure quarters at Shimabara. At Shinnyō-ji and Nanzen-ji, he was again fortunate to be able to view exhibitions of temple art treasures. One day he made two trips to the lively quarters of the brothel district of Gion. He was so busy while in Kyoto, he quipped, that he "did not have time to count the images at Sanjūsangendō" (there are said to be 1,001).

For Tosa samurai, the trip to Edo, depending on the route, could involve passing by or through no fewer than sixteen castle towns.[4] Heading north from Kōchi, the first castle town Masana came upon in 1828 was Marugame (Sanuki province), on the other side of Shikoku (refer to Figure 2.1). Looking at the castle, he observed, "There is no keep. It does not look much like a place where a lord resides—it is a small castle." Walking though the town, however, he noted that "the townspeople appear prosperous, but the retainers are poor (*suibi*)." His brush never failed to record some comment when passing through other castle towns. At Okazaki, "The keep, the towers, walls, and gates are all spectacular. They do not appear to belong to a lord of a 50,000 *koku* domain"; at Yoshida, "It is small, but looks fine"; at Fuchū, "The castle walls and gates are big; since

I have not seen Nagoya, I would rank Fuchū the largest, and Osaka second largest, in the country" [after Edo]. At some castle towns like Yoshida, guards would not allow Masana to enter the inner area. At almost every castle town he passed through, the poor economic state of samurai compared with the townsmen was apparent.

By passing through these and other cities, Masana was able to see firsthand what it was like to live in other urban centers and domains, and he could make comparisons between them. He found Himeji castle "much grander than the castle in our domain. . . . It does not look like the castle of a domain of 150,000 koku." In contrast, at Numazu he found the situation similar to Marugame: the castle "does not look like the place where a lord lives." In this way, Masana was able to locate Tosa in the social hierarchy of domains.[5]

The so-called "three metropolises," Osaka, Kyoto, and Edo, made a great impression on Masana. Observing the differences between them, he commented,

> Entering Kyoto I saw that, as expected, the city was by far superior to Osaka; and men and women's fashion are twice as beautiful in Kyoto. After leaving Tosa, I was surprised by the prosperity of Marugame; continuing on to Osaka, that city appeared ten times more prosperous than Marugame; finally, Kyoto seemed still twice as much as Osaka.

A few days after arriving, Masana, like most retainers in Edo for the first time, climbed one of the highest spots in the city, Mt. Atago, and observed the sprawling urban center below him. From the top he observed a scene that must have been similar to the one captured by Felice Beato (as in Figure 5.1) and recorded, "This city is more than ten times bigger than Kyoto and Osaka."[6] He was surprised to find the area around Shitaya and Ueno "ten times more prosperous" than the other two big cities. According to his calculations, then, Edo was one or two hundred times as prosperous as Marugame and could not even compare with Kōchi. Sakai Banshirō also made the trip to Atago-san on his first full day in Edo. From there, he wrote that he could see one-third of the city. "Its great expanse," he noted, "is impossible to express in words, either spoken or written."[7]

For Masana and other retainers from the domains, Edo might have seemed a bit like a foreign country. During his first interview with the military scholar Hirayama Shiryū, Masana had problems understanding the man: "It is very difficult for me to understand the Edo dialect (Edo kotoba). I wrote down the gist of what I heard, but I was able to comprehend not even one-half. This is truly regrettable." While the teacher apparently had suffered a stroke, Masana felt that his own difficulties were due to his being unaccustomed to hearing Edo language. As he explained, "It was difficult to understand what he said next. Being in Edo for the first time, it is truly difficult to comprehend (the language)."

It was precisely for people like Masana that numerous dialect manuals, which usually compared local dialects and Edo language, became popular in the early nineteenth century. These aimed to instruct those living outside the Tokugawa capital city how to communicate in Edo in the Edo language.[8] Apparently Masana could not get his hands on such a manual or simply did not study much before setting out from Kōchi.

Despite the lack of evidence that Masana used a dialect manual, later in the same month as his interview with Hirayama, he attended his first class with the noted Iwamura domain (Mino) Confucian scholar Satō Issai (1772–1859). He found his "words were a little different, but Teacher Satō lectured in such a way that I could understand well."[9] Thus, just several weeks later, Masana was already adjusting to his new linguistic environment.

Masana's experience coincides with that of Aizu retainer Shiba Gorō, who found that "within two months or so" he knew the city well enough and "could go on errands on my own, understand the Edo dialect, and even reproduce it reasonably well."[10] Similarly, Shikitei Sanba's "The Women's Bath" makes it clear that it was possible for people from the Kamigata and Edo areas to understand one another without great difficulty. In that work, a number of women discuss language and cultural differences between their respective areas.[11] After a year in Edo, retainers probably went home able to comprehend Edo language but continued to use local dialect in the domain so as not to stand out. Were this not the case, Edo language would have spread much more quickly to the domains, and Masana's difficulty in comprehending Edo language, and the existence of dialect manuals, would be difficult to explain.

Masana's first trip to Edo gave him the experience and knowledge to begin to see his castle town, his domain, and probably himself in a wider context. He was further able to compare what he saw and experienced when he made his second journey in 1829, traveling from Urado, Kōchi's port, to Osaka by boat. When passing through Tokushima he noted that the buildings in the castle town resembled those that he had seen the previous year in Edo. His observations involved not only the physical landscape of the country, but the economic conditions around him and the customs of townsmen and samurai. In Tokushima, for example, he noticed that prohibitions on certain types of clothing for townsmen were not as well observed as in Kōchi. While traveling to and from Edo, Masana was also able to interact with persons from other domains, both *bushi* and commoner. On the return trip to Kōchi in 1829 he observed and inquired a great deal about the economic condition of *bushi* in Wakayama and heard, among other things, a horrifying story of a retired daimyo there who was said to cut down commoners for sword practice.[12]

While Masana had the freedom to sightsee because his purpose in Edo in 1828 was for personal study and not to perform a job designated by the domain, those retainers who were an official part of the retinue had some occasion to do so as well. According to a number of diaries, it is clear that some retainers were free to leave the procession and travel on their own on days they were off duty.[13] Also, retainers given leave in Edo to depart for home on their own (*okuni katte*) — which could happen any time of the year — had exactly the same opportunities as Masana. Through their travels to and from Edo, retainers like Mori Masana were able to observe conditions in, and talk to people from, other domains, helping to break down the cultural barriers inherent in the early modern political system.[14]

While the discussion here has focused on retainers, it is important to note that much of their experience was also shared by the daimyo himself. From his palanquin, on foot, or riding his horse, he could observe his surroundings as he passed through others' domains. Like Mori Masana, the Matsura lord of Hirado could draw conclusions about the way a domain was governed based on what he saw. Passing through Odawara in 1800, for example, he found "the land abundant, the people prosperous." At every rest stop or overnight stay he would ask the proprietor and local persons if there was anything unusual about the area — not just local sights but customs, dialects, and curious tales.[15] As noted earlier, stopping in Osaka and sometimes Kyoto, daimyo were able to meet and to interact with many people, including religious and intellectual elites.

The Transmission of Material Culture: Domainal Retainers as Consumers

Through their participation in alternate attendance, retainers were drawn into the commercial economy in a number of ways. The journey, particularly the return leg to the domain, provided ample opportunity to acquire souvenirs and other commodities, which were an important part of what made the trip to Edo a memorable experience.[16]

From the diaries kept by Tosa samurai we can get a detailed picture of the type of material culture they were transporting from the country's political center and from areas along the route to and from the domain castle town. On the way to Edo in 1828, Mori Masana purchased a few items, including a sword guard, scroll, dictionary, and an official document written by a daimyo,[17] but on the return to the domain a year later he shopped at no fewer than seven places, buying six scrolls (including ones by Confucian scholar Itō Tōgai and Nativist scholar Motoori Norinaga), calligraphy, a parasol, a diagram of Hachiman shrine, and a written explanation of the temple exhibition of treasures at Shinnyō-dō in Kyoto. He loaded up on souvenirs and other gifts in Osaka before boarding the ship for Kōchi, purchasing fifteen items, including a desk, an animal-skin blanket, pottery, sake cup, and a hanging scroll from an imported

TABLE 7.1. Miyaji Umanosuke's Purchases En Route, Edo to Kōchi, 1833

Date	Location	Item(s) Purchased	Price
4/20	Yumoto	Japanese sweets	1 *shu*
4/29	Kusatsu	11 candles	200 *mon*
	Tsuchiyama	Bag of tea	100 *mon*
	Fushimi	Folding fan	2 *shu*
5/1	Osaka	2 *tan* of silk material (*Nara shima*)	46 *monme*, 3 *bu*
		1 *tan* of silk material (*Beniita-jime kinu*)	30 *monme*, 2 *bu* 5 *rin*
		Black Hachijōji silk material	21 *monme*, 8 *bu*
		Kuroten sōzoku (black velvet material)	8 *monme*, 7 *bu*
		Sarasa wrapper (*furoshiki*)	6 *monme* 5 *bu*
		Silk gauze	2 *monme*, 8 *bu* 5 *rin*
		Pipe	1 *shu*
		18 kg. cotton thread (*shinomaki*)	76 *monme*, 5 *bu*
		1 piece of luggage (*ryōkake*)	25 *monme*
		2 raincoats	2 *monme*, 2 *bu*
		9 liters of sake	2 *shu*, 130 *mon*
		25 writing brushes	600 *mon*
		Fishing line	2 *monme* 26 *mon*
		Sea kelp	50 *mon*

goods store (*karamonoya*). Here we see alternate attendance as a mechanism through which both domestic and foreign goods were circulated across the country.

Masana's friend and teacher, the Confucian scholar Miyaji Umanosuke, likewise made a number of purchases — eighteen different types of goods — on the way home from his second period of service in Edo during 1832–1833 (see Table 7.1).[18] He picked up a few of these items (e.g., sweets, candles, tea, a folding fan) at post stations on Tokugawa Japan's main thoroughfare, the Tōkaidō, but the bulk of his purchases were made, again, in Osaka. There, he purchased a pipe, a piece of luggage, sake, writing brushes, kelp, raincoats, fishing line, a large amount of cotton thread, a cloth wrap of *sarasa* (tie-dyed) material, and four different types of silk cloth.[19]

The shopping list of gifts purchased by Tosa retainer Ogura Sadasuke in 1862 likewise reveals a number of items that were not made in Edo and provides more evidence of the function of alternate attendance as a mechanism by which material culture was circulated from local area to local area, or sometimes abroad, via the center (Edo). Those items consisted of nine pairs of *geta* with thongs made of *sanadao*, a kind of cord from Sanada in central Japan (Shinshū area) and undisclosed amount of Thai cloth. His shopping list also included[20] thirty-eight round fans, a wallet, child's hairpin, picture book, silk thread, a narrow belt used to hold a tucked-up kimono in place, thirty spools of thread, fourteen wooden tea ladles, six teacup saucers, medicine, six bundles of moxa, three pairs of pocket chopsticks, five fans, and a tobacco pouch. The diverse origins of Miyaji Umanosuke's purchases are also identifiable: for example, vermillion ink from Ryukyu, lacquer bowls from Aizu, and a sake cup from Karatsu. The turnip and daikon seeds Miyaji Umanosuke gave an acquaintance to take back to Tosa were likewise probably from someplace other than Edo.[21] Another Tosa retainer, Gotō Masahisa, was able to take make a side trip to Arima hot springs on the route back to Kōchi, where he purchased a broadsheet detailing a major fire in Edo in 1730, a couple of paper game boards with religious themes, a pictorial guide to Tennōji, and several single-sheet poems written by Arima bath girls.[22]

Purchasing commodities did not take place only when traveling. Just a day after reaching Edo in 1846, an anonymous rural samurai from Tosa purchased sixty woodblock prints, and three days later he added ten more. While he does not state what he did with them, he might have sent them home to various friends and acquaintances as an acknowledgment — much like postcards today — that he had arrived safely in the big city.[23] Items like woodblock prints, also known as *Edo-e*, *doro-e*,[24] as seen in chapter five, and Yamamoto-yama tea were popular gifts because of their association with the city of Edo. They served as "markers," giving concrete proof that the retainer had actually been there.[25] This was particularly evident with *doro-e* of daimyo compounds, which often highlight some famous spot in Edo and focus on place rather than on human activities (see Figure 7.1).[26] When Mori Masana went out to buy souvenirs a few days before leaving for Kōchi at the end of his first stay in Edo, he must have been distressed: Finding nothing at Asakusa, Shitaya, or Hongō that could be described as "Edo-like" (*Edo mae ni naki*), he felt compelled to go on to Koishi-kawa and Otansu-chō to look some more. Of course he could have consulted a shopping guide such as *Edo kaimono hitori annai* (1824) for a list of merchants in the city.

During that first period of residence in Edo, Mori Masana shopped frequently. He purchased the first sword guard of his trip at Akasaka post station on the Tōkaidō road, but during his time in Edo added at least twenty more to his collection. Shopping for books, scrolls, and documents written by famous persons, in addition to sword guards, seems to have preoccupied Masana during this trip, as he amassed 101 of these items in ten months (see Table 7.2).

Masana clearly had considerable economic means, making purchases beyond what most retainers could afford, but he does not disclose the source of his funds. He did not seem to lose any opportunity to spend money on his first

FIGURE 7.1. Souvenir *doro-e* of Hiroshima and Fukuoka domain residences at Kasumigaseki (top) and Arima residence at Akabane-bashi (bottom). Courtesy of Watanabe Shin'ichiro Collection.

TABLE 7.2. Mori Masana's Purchases in Edo, 1828/3–1829/3*

Date	Item Purchased	Notes
1828/5/12	Ornamental tassle	Placed on top of flag put on back of horse during ceremonies; cost: 1 *shu* gold
5/14	Sword guard	Bought in Atago area
5/15	Leaf-shaped inkstone	Cost: 2 *monme*
5/17	Brush and ink	
5/22	*Shisho* (The Four Books)	Annotated edition by his teacher Satō Issai; 20 *monme*
5/27	Calligraphy primer	Cost: 3 *monme*
6/4	Sun umbrella (*higasa*)	Cost: 200 *mon*
6/7	Scroll	By Kaga lord Toshitsune; cost: 2 *monme*; location: Yanagiwara
6/8	Potted plant	
6/10	2 or 3 books	Purchases from Shiba Shinmei area book dealer
6/18	Scroll	At Yanagiwara purchases scroll with calligraphy by Confucian scholar Koga Seiri (1750–1817) of Saga domain; cost: 2 *monme*
6/19	Pictorial scroll	By Kuki Fumitora; cost: 1 *bu* 1 *shu*
	Chinese drawing	*Kara-e*
7/4	Scroll	4 *monme*; later realizes it is a fake
7/8	*Sentetsu sōdan*	1 *bu* gold
7/10	*Shōgaku*	(*Lesser Learning*); cost: 2 *monme* 2 *bu*
	Konjaku monogatari	17 vols.; cost: 5 *monme* 9 *bu*
7/17	Scroll	120 *mon*
7/18	Scarlet coat	*Jin baori*; cost: 2 *ryō* 2 *bu* 2 *shu*
7/28	2 pairs of glasses	One for his mother, the other for person named Genzō
8/2	Inlaid sword guard	10 *monme* gold
	Framed calligraphy	By a daimyo
8/20	Calligraphy	
	Long narrow poem hanging	
9/2	2 sword guards	200 *mon*
9/3	Scroll by Itō Tōsai	1 *shu*
	Framed calligraphy	
	Writing sample	Of Kii daimyo
9/5	Sword accoutrement	160 *mon*
9/9	Sword guard	Purchased at Yamashita area
9/22	Sword guard	Purchased at Kiridōshi (Yushima)
10/18	Sword guard	Purchased at Kiridōshi
	6 scrolls	One by Confucian scholar Itō Tōgai (1670–1736); he later returns 3 of them.
10/17	Sword guard	

TABLE 7.2. (Continued)

Date	Item Purchased	Notes
11/9	Copy book	220 *mon*
11/?	Portrait	Of Kusunoki Masashige; cost: 2 monme 5 *bu*
	Small dagger	200 *mon*
12/20	Calligraphy	Returns 2 pieces previously purchased and buys 2 others
	Calligraphy	By Ōishi [Kuranosuke] for 2 *shu*; pays to have its authenticity checked
12/22	Letter	By Date Masamune; has it checked for authenticity; cost: 3 *monme 7 bu 5 rin*
12/23	2 sword guards	3 *monme*
	Sword handle	
12/24	3 pieces of calligraphy	Shitaya area; 2 *shu*
	Sword guard	At Kiridōshi area; 4 *monme 5 bu*
12/28	Sword	1 *ryō 2 shu*
	3 sword guards	
12/29	Sword	At Minami Ōdōri
	Old sword	1 *ryō 1 bu*; describes it as "a fine sword that he can wear with pride"
1829/1/20	2 pieces of calligraphy	6 *monme 5 bu*
1/21	Sword knot (*sageo*)	
	Book stand	
2/12	2 pieces of calligraphy	At scroll shop near Miyuki
	Painting	
2/13	Calligraphy, sword guards	Several of each; 5 *monme*
2/20	Sword guard	
	Collection of calligraphy	By a daimyo
2/21	*Shikan yōhō*	
	5 pieces of calligraphy	By Inoue Kinga, Hayashi Dōshun
2/28	3 pieces of calligraphy	
	Sword guard	Chrysanthemum patterned
3/8	Painting	By Yanagisawa Gondayu
	Calligraphy	By Kamei Dōsai
3/11	Calligraphy	
3/13	Sword guard	Purchased at Shiba area; 2 *monme*
3/18	Scroll	By Matsudaira Etchū no kami
	Short sword	
3/25	2 scrolls	By Eisen; 1 *bu* gold
	2 poem cards	3 *monme*
	ukiyoe	1 *shu*
	paper	1 *shu*
	3 scrolls	By Eisen; 1 *bu* gold

* Mori Masana 1828–1856, vols. 1–2.

trip to Edo, and when not purchasing he frequently browsed stores in different areas across town that specialized in armor or scrolls and other types of written works. With the large sum of money (seven *ryō* gold) that Masana earned as a reward for accompanying the Tosa lord in his escape from a fire at the main residence at Kajibashi, he went on a shopping binge, purchasing two scrolls (by a famous artist named Eisen), two long poem cards, woodblock prints, writing paper, and a few other items.[27]

Retainers acquired many goods toward the end of their stay in Edo, either through personal purchases or as gifts from friends and colleagues. Numerous friends stopped by Masana's residence in the weeks prior to his departure to give him going-away presents, some of them pooling their resources to do so. For example, five friends gave him an unspecified number of woodblock prints, ten friends got together to purchase him five round fans, and three others bought him seven prints and three tobacco pouches. Still others purchased gifts singly, as did one friend who brought him seven paintings; one of his teachers of Neo-Confucianism, Yamaguchi Sadaichirō, also presented him with a single-line piece of calligraphy, two stone rubbings, and three sheets of colored paper with poems.[28] Miyaji Umanosuke, who made many purchases in the weeks prior to his departure, likewise received gifts, including soap (*arakona*), folding fans, and woodblock prints, the latter two of which were popular going-away gifts because of their low cost and easy portability.

While Masana's diary is silent on the matter, Miyaji records from time to time that he sent some purchases home on the domain boat, which plied regularly between Kōchi and Edo. The porcelain, paper, Yamamoto-yama tea, futon, and other items given to Miyaji by his students as customary, end-of-year gifts were loaded in a trunk and shipped on the domain boat. Since there was room left over in his trunk, Miyaji allowed three others to send a few items in it (e.g., a six-paneled screen, box for Noh chanting, books, flower vase box).[29] Three times in his stay he sent home vases with the domainal messenger, and another time he sent home a rice pot and several other household goods on the domain boat. In still other cases, Miyaji, in turn, asked retainers heading for Tosa to carry some purchases back for him. Umanosuke and Masana were not unique; most samurai purchased souvenirs in Edo as well as when traveling, and domainal authorities sometimes tried to restrict their purchases.[30]

While Masana had unusual economic means, it is still instructive to compare the two men's purchases for an idea of what domainal samurai bought in Edo. In doing so one finds that Masana's purchases were primarily of scholarly and artistic interest — e.g., sword guards, books, scrolls, and pieces of calligraphy. Miyaji, on the other hand, while he did acquire a number of books, mostly purchased items related to clothing (e.g., thread and cloth) or various items for the kitchen or general household.

Masana exhibited great interest in collecting two types of art, sword guards and calligraphy. As in China, "[e]steemed calligraphy was rarely anonymous . . . owning it provided the most intense degree of identification with a famous owner."[31] This identification may have been a driving force behind Masana's collecting, as he accumulated scrolls or calligraphy from such cultural and political figures as Koga Seiri, Kusunoki Masashige, Ōta Kinjō, Itō Tōgai, Ōishi Kuranosuke, Motoori Norinaga, as well as a number of noted daimyo. The numerous purchases of calligraphy also relates the high place accorded that art form in the Japanese cultural system.

Masana was unusual in that he was able to purchase many expensive items, but Miyaji was perhaps more representative of the majority of retainers who did not have that luxury. With a fief of one hundred *koku*, Miyaji, who held an appointment as Confucian scholar as well as professor at the domain school, was able to amass — through purchases or gifts — eighty-three items during a year's residence in Edo. (Those purchased or received during the final three months of his stay are listed in Table 7.3.) His purchases made during the entire year were largely for household use: ceramics, vases, cloth, clothing, footwear, cooking pots, lacquerware, candles, and soap. While it may seem incongruous that the Confucian scholar only bought books on four occasions, in his position as a professor of the domain school, the Kōjūkan, and as Confucian scholar in-residence at Edo, he had easy access to books, which probably made it unnecessary to purchase many, particularly when volumes could be borrowed and copied as needed from the domain's libraries (in Edo and Kōchi) or from scholar friends. Masana spent money freely and was apparently not concerned about finances, but Miyaji rarely ventured out on the town to spend money, preferring instead, it seems, to save for the purchases he would make before leaving Edo. He was thrifty with his funds — sometimes shopping at second-hand stores, even for gifts — and always looking for the best price available. For example, Miyaji noted that a store in Kita Hatchōbori was "much cheaper than other second-hand stores." He also searched about town for the least expensive, most effective medicine. At Kinokuni-ya Denpei's pharmacy, Miyaji noted that "no place sells it [a Chinese-style medicine made from oysters] cheaper."[32] The Yanagiwara area in particular was popular with retainers like Umanosuke and Masana for its vast array of second-hand clothing, artwork, and other goods. A retainer from Nagoya named Enkōan (1756–1831), a prolific writer and artist, further popularized the area in a woodblock print (Figure 7.2) from his published illustrated account of life in the capital, "Edo juranki," based on his experiences while on a tour of duty.[33]

Masana's purchases in Edo and while traveling to and from it reveal the degree to which art had become commercialized in the early nineteenth century. He appears to have made some purchases on approval, for in a couple of in-

TABLE 7.3. List of Major Purchases and Gifts Received in Edo by Miyaji Umanosuke (1832–1833)*

Date	Item	Note
1832/5/4	*Shisho taizen*	*The Complete Version of the Four Books*; given to him by Shinagawa tea master Nishikawa Ryōhei
	Reiki shūchū	20 vols.; given by same
	Reiki shūchū, tama hen	12 vols.; given by same
	2 brass vases	Sends them home to Kōchi with domainal messenger
5/8	*Shokukanshi*	4 vols.; purchases them at cost
5/12	2 vases	Both with small mouths; sends them to Kōchi with the domainal messenger
5/26	Pair of footwear	*Sekida*, a high-quality *zōri*
	Tea tray	
	Karatsu ware sake cup	
5/29	Vermillion ink	From Ryūkyū—purchased from the domain supply chief (*nando*) for 272 *mon*
6/5	2 brass vases	Sends to family in domain
6/14	Obi material	Same as above
7/6	Turnip and daikon seeds†	Sends them to Kōchi with an homeward-bound retainer
Int. 11/8	Rice pot	Items sent to Kōchi on domain boat
	Bamboo for wrapping goods	
	Straw container	
12/1	10 lacquer soup bowls	Aizu-ware; paid 1 *bu* 200 *mon*
	Pot (*kama*)	Purchased in Kosai-chō for 8 *monme* 8 *bu*
	Pot (*kannabe*)	Purchased in Higashi Naka-dōri for 700 *mon*
	30 fans	Assorted sizes; purchased in Hori-chō for 55 *mon*
12/2	3 pair of *geta*	*Hikisuri* (*hiyori geta*)—i.e., "good weather" or low *geta*; gift purchase
	5 thongs for *geta*	*Geta* of *bokkuri* type (*geta* with replaceable platform); purchased in Kita Hatchōbori for 67 *mon*; gift purchase
	Box	*Uchimawashi no hako*; purchases at bric-a-brac store for 200 *mon*; notes that it is cheaper than other second-hand stores.

TABLE 7.3. *(Continued)*

Date	Item	Note
12/4	Pair of *geta*	Kyoto-style; cost, 200 *mon*; all items for this day are noted as "gift purchases" (*kudari miyage*)
	Pair of low *geta*	*Hiyori geta*; 334 *mon*
	Dried salmon	250 *mon*
	Dried salmon trout	*masu*; 188 *mon*
	Bundle of sea kelp	180 *mon*
	2 bags of sea kelp	328 *mon*
	8 women's *nemaki*	Sleeping robes; 72 *mon*
	Piece of bamboo	40 *mon*
	Hemp thread	820 *mon* for 375 *monme*
12/13	Umbrella	650 *mon*
12/25	2 padded under-kimono for cold-weather use	
1833/1/20	Pearl tongs	For use with charcoal brazier
	Small saw	2 *monme* 5 *bu*
	Small sake jar	Bizen ware; 2 *monme*, 8 *bu*
	2 square-tipped awls	28 *mon*
	Iron hammer	116 *mon*
	Saw file	40 *mon*
2/7	183 candles	For special use (*tokuyō*); 1 *bu* 2 *shu*
	5 bags of soap	*Abura nuki arai kona*; purchased in Kōjimachi at specialty store
	Box for small sake cups	24 *mon*
	2 pieces of sharkskin	19 *monme*, 5 *bu*; purchased at shark merchants, used to decorate sword sheath
	Gift envelope of colored paper	*chiyogami no noshi*: 100 *mon*
2/11	1 bundle of wicks	140 *mon*
	Rope	64 *mon*
	Black edges for six-panel screen	184 *mon*
	Sake container	88 *mon*
	Bamboo pincher for hot sake bottle	64 *mon*

TABLE 7.3. *(Continued)*

Date	Item	Note
2/14	10 soup bowls	Borrowed an old chest to send in; given as year-end gifts
	Ceramic sake cup	
	Large sake bottle	
	Pot	
	Small sake bottle	
	Tea bowl with lid	
	3 bundles of paper	
	Wajishi (3 vols.)	
	Kanjishi (3 vols.)	
	Nihon saijiki (3 vols.)	
	5 plates	
	1 box of tea	Yamamoto-yama brand
	1 large bowl	
	5 bundles of thread	
	1 soup bowl	
	3 small boxes	
	8 folding fans	
	1 big bundle of thread	
	5 bags of soap	
	1 futon	
3/1	New sword handle, new handle covers	Replaces handles on and has rust removed from second sword; sharkskin covers applied to both. Cost, 81 *monme, 5 bu*
4/12	2 tobacco containers	2 *monme*
	Futon bag	4 *monme, 4 bu*
	3 pipes	350 *monme*
4/13	*Kami nuno*	Cotton cloth? All items here are gifts given to Miyaji
	3 folding fans	
	2 books of woodblock prints	
	Prints	
	1 bag of soap	*Arakona*

* Miyaji Umanosuke 1832, vols. 1, 3, 4.

† In regard to the daikon seeds, Miyaji's diary notes that they were "*ninen bun daikon,*" which probably refers to a type of daikon rather than being "two years' worth of daikon" seeds.

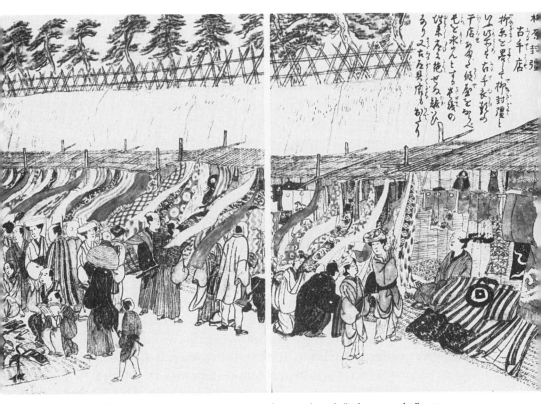

FIGURE 7.2. Shopping area at Yanagiwara-chō, from Enkōan's "Edo junranki," 1788. Courtesy of Tōyō bunko.

stances he returned the items soon after they were bought. To avoid purchasing fakes (which he had one known experience with), Masana paid an art evaluator to check the authenticity of two pieces of calligraphy, by the famous daimyo Date Masamune and the famous retainer Ōishi Kuranosuke. While it would be wonderful to know whether Masana traded or resold some of the sword guards he purchased, he does record on one occasion that he traded fifteen pieces of calligraphy, plus an additional sum of money, for an expensive scroll (two *ryō*) by the noted Confucian scholar Itō Jinsai. On one occasion he purchased a framed piece of calligraphy he had seen in an advertisement, giving further evidence of the commercialization of art.

Some retainers were clearly able to purchase beyond their own economic means. As in the case of a retainer from Hachinohe named Toyama Tamuro, friends and relatives often gave a departing retainer "send-off" money, to be used to buy souvenirs and other items in Edo.[34] Gifts would naturally be purchased for those who made such donations, thus spreading the cultural artifacts more widely, beyond the scope of those personally drawn into the system of alternate attendance.

Many retainers acted more directly as conduits by which people back in the domain acquired goods from Edo (including those shipped from other localities to Edo). Toyama Tamuro departed from Hachinohe in 1828 with a shopping list of twenty items his father had given him. While on his tour of duty he purchased at least eighty goods for various other members of his family, including his sister, who was getting married later in that year, his cousin, and at least nine other people.[35]

Edo as Cultural Nexus

Every year about half the ruling daimyo made their way from the castle towns in their domains to Edo, and along their designated routes, as well as in Kyoto, they were able to meet an educated elite.[36] Once in the Tokugawa capital, the basic requirements of their service to the shogun — attending audiences and, in the case of Tosa, fire watch duty — did not occupy much of their time. Ancillary activities such as visits to high-ranking shogunal officials and pilgrimages to Tokugawa temples likewise were not demanding. As a result, daimyo had ample free time, during which they transformed their principal residence compounds into cultural centers. Alternate attendance, which placed the daimyo in "long periods of splendid captivity" in Conrad Totman's words, resulted in a process of aristocratization — a civilizing, culturally edifying force. By the middle of the seventeenth century the daimyo had become the new cultural elite, patrons as well as practitioners of the arts.[37]

In Edo, the daimyo interacted with their peers, often inviting one another to their compounds for theatrical performances or the tea ceremony.[38] In the main compounds, and often in the middle ones, they constructed theatrical stages, where the Noh and Kyōgen masters in their employ performed. Performances were for the enjoyment of the lord's family and his retainers, but also for other daimyo, special merchants, and town officials. In 1681, for example, the Yamauchi lord sponsored large-scale performances of Noh at the main residence, inviting sixteen Tokugawa officials, including three senior advisors and twenty-eight daimyo. In addition, more than two hundred townsmen, including town officials and merchants with business relationships with Tosa, were in attendance.[39]

Noh actors under domainal employ performed an alternate attendance of their own. Many of the househeads of the various schools resided in Kyoto, but traveled periodically to the seat of the daimyo sponsor (Kanazawa in the case of the Takeda family) and Edo to perform.[40] Similarly, the Horiike family head was usually by the Yamauchi lord's side and rotated his residence between Tosa, Kyoto, and Edo during the first half of the eighteenth century.[41]

Theater was not restricted to the Noh and Kyōgen. Kabuki, puppet theater, dance, *jōruri*, and acrobatic performances were also held in Edo at the compounds.[42] Noted tea masters and other artists such as Morita Kyūemon and Shiba Kōkan were also invited to perform before various daimyo.[43] Morita, a potter in the Tosa lord's employ, put on thirty demonstrations—pottery making as performance—in Edo for Toyomasa, other Yamauchi family members, other daimyo, *dōboshū* (cultural advisors to the shogunate), and Tokugawa government administrators.[44] The daimyo of Yamato Kōriyama, a well-known figure in the cultural world of late eighteenth-century Edo, used commoner servants employed by the domain as amateur actors to put on kabuki performances at his main residence, even commissioning woodblock prints of the event.[45]

The daimyo in Edo took the Tokugawa's lead in hiring the best painters in the realm. The early shoguns summoned the Kano painters, Japan's "de facto painting academy," from Kyoto to Edo,[46] a movement that "mirrored a larger 'brain drain' of human resources that accompanied the expanding shift of power, resources, and culture from the Kinai region to the Kantō region around Edo."[47] By the middle of the seventeenth century, all Kano painters except those who remained in Kyoto were working for the Tokugawa or their vassals, the daimyo. Those in the domain's employ frequently painted the screens and walls in the various Edo residences of the lord, as we saw in the Kurume scroll in chapter six.

Painters and Noh actors were part of a broad spectrum of educated *bushi* attracted to service in Edo. Others included Confucian scholars, tea masters, poets, potters, doctors, those interested in the serious study of Kangaku (Chinese studies), martial arts or military studies, and a variety of artisans. Daimyo competed for the services of the best tea masters, landscape architects, poets, and actors. While this cultured elite often traveled with the lord's retinue, sometimes they also journeyed separately to Edo.[48]

Confucian scholars, in fact, seemed to be a part of every daimyo retinue from Tosa from the mid-eighteenth century on. At least one period of residence and study in Edo was routine for them. Members of Tosa's four main Confucian scholar families made frequent trips east, as shown in Table 7.4. These scholars often stayed for a one year, but in some cases it is known that they remained there on long-term assignment. Tani Manroku, for example, was there from 1789 to 1795, during which time he became a close friend of the loyalist Takayama Hikokurō.[49] While in Edo, Confucian scholars like Tosa's Miyaji Umanosuke lectured to the lord and to the heir on a regular basis, usually three times a month.[50] They also taught in the schools established in the domains' Edo compounds, some of which were started before those back in the provinces.[51]

Edo was important to the professional advancement of scholar-teachers. For Tsuda Izuru (1832–1905, Wakayama) and Unuma Kuniyasu (1755–1824, Kameda),

TABLE 7.4. Trips to Edo by Tosa's Confucian Scholar Families*

Miyaji Family	
Haruki	1759, 1765
Nakae[†]	1788, 1795, 1804
Umanosuke	1828, 1832
Tani Family	
Kakimori	1714, 1752
Tannai	1741, 1746, 1754, 1761, 1763, 1765, 1767, 1772, 1775, 1788
Manroku	1784, 1789
Masashige	1820, 1837
Miura Family	
Keirin	1804, 1813
Naotsune	1764, 1769, 1784, 1787
Sadayoshi	1787, 1802, 1808
Kōu	1816, 1829
Shōseki	1811, 1839, 1843
Tobe Family	
Haruyuki	1791, 1797, 1800, 1822

*The dates are compiled mainly from "Osamuraichū senzogaki keizu chō" n.d., but Kōchi-ken jinmei jiten henshū iinkai 1971 was also consulted. The various scholars did not necessarily always serve as lecturers-tutors to the lord or heir: e.g., Tobe Haruyuki acted as a scribe during the first three of seven stays in Edo. Even when appointed as professor, Confucian scholars, like Noh actors and every other type of retainer, sometimes also had to perform guard duty or some other service on a periodic basis.

According to the Kōchi-ken jinmei jiten henshū iinkai 1971, 210, Tani Kakimori (?–1752) also traveled to Edo "frequently," but I have been able to uncover only two dates, 1742 and 1752. In Edo he studied under noted Nativist scholar Kamo Mabuchi (1697–1769). For a short biography of Kakimori, see Matsuyama 1971, 1–18.

[†]Nakae traveled to Edo in 1788 to become a student of Hanawa Hokiichi, with whom he later edited the *Gunsho ruijū*. Miyaji Saiichirō 1970, 203–209. Many Tosa scholars likewise studied with Hanawa. Matsuyama Hidemi 1956, 4.

appointments as teachers in their respective domain schools followed periods of study in the shogunal city.[52] In Tosa, on the other hand, it appears that an appointment to the position of domain school professor was often followed by a tour of duty in Edo.[53]

Confucian scholars were not the only educated elite to make the trip to Edo. For example, the Tosa potter Morita Kyūemon, mentioned above, was sent there in 1678 by the Yamauchi lord to improve the quality of Tosa's ceramic ware, known as Odo-yaki, and stopped along the way at pottery centers such as Kyoto, Uji, Shigaraki, and Seto. In Edo, Morita, as noted, was kept busy by the lord putting on pottery-making demonstrations.[54] Similarly, the fifth generation head of the Rihei workshop, an official potter of Takamatsu domain, was ordered by the lord to spend a year in Edo, where he would have "a chance to see various fine wares from Kyoto and other centers."[55]

Numerous *bushi* artists from various domains traveled to Edo on regular assignments and while there studied with local artists. A number from Tosa studied in Edo, mainly with teachers of the Kanō school, but also occasionally with those of the Nanga school. For example, four different Tosa retainers studied in Edo with fourth-generation Surugadai Kanō artist Tōshun (Yoshinobu, 1747–1797) in the late eighteenth century,[56] and three other Tosa retainers studied Nanga painting under Tsuyama domain samurai Hirose Daisan at approximately the same time.[57] The number of examples from other domains are plentiful, but two will suffice: While in Edo, Watanabe Kazan studied with the famous Tani Bunchō, frequently met other painters, borrowed copies from them, and visited shows of their works. He also read voraciously and painted even while on guard duty at night.[58] Matsumae domain's Kakizaki Hakyō, who later became a senior advisor, began traveling to Edo at an early age in 1773, just when Odano Naotake was in town studying Western painting on his lord's orders. Hakyō lived in one of the domain's compounds for ten years, during which time he studied painting in the Nagasaki style under its best master in Edo, Sō Shiseki. He gained fame for his series of colorful, realistic portraits of Ainu leaders who fought on the Japanese side, paintings of which many daimyo are said to have borrowed a copy.[59]

A period of residence in Edo could have a transformational effect on retainers with varied interests. According to one biographer of Saigō Takamori, the trip to Edo "was a major turning point in his life." This was for several reasons, most basically because it "took him out of the narrow provincial world of Kagoshima and plunged him into the wide-open society of Edo."[60] In Edo he entered a "turbulent intellectual environment . . . and [a]lthough Saigō read and studied almost everything available in Kagoshima, Edo was another world entirely. Within months Saigō was swept away by what was for him a new ideology: Mito learning. Saigō's exposure to Mito learning in 1854 and 1855 would change his worldview forever."[61] He interacted with a group of samurai from at least four other domains, further demonstrating how Edo acted as an entrepot for ideas developed elsewhere.

For Confucian scholar Kaibara Ekiken (1630–1714), it was not only the period of residence in Edo, but the trip to and from there that was critical. For him, "travel, insofar as it enabled the direct and unmediated inspection of the world, was critical to . . . [his] intellectual enterprise."[62] Ekiken had of course traveled widely during his youth with his father, an attending doctor in the employ of the Kuroda lord, on official business to Edo, as many sons of samurai did.

While there his father introduced him to important Edo-based retainers as well as to members of the Hayashi family, the Tokugawa's hereditary Confucian scholars.[63] After a period of rōnin status (1650–1657), he was rehired and sent to Kyoto for an extended period of study. After this he accompanied the lord to Edo no fewer than twelve times, and on some of these occasions he received permission to stay for various amounts of time in Kyoto, where he renewed old acquaintances and shopped at the city's bookstores.[64] His periods of residence in Edo were not for a full year, but tended to vary from one to six months.

Nevertheless Ekiken's experiences were meaningful to his personal development as a Confucian scholar; his extensive book purchasing while on alternate attendance further reveals how the institution acted to circulate material goods. It also suggests that the three metropolises, Edo, Kyoto, and Osaka, and the castle towns had strong connections as early as the late seventeenth or early eighteenth century. The books Ekiken brought back to Fukuoka were purchased primarily in Kyoto and Edo. There were 861 titles listed in a family book catalogue, but it is believed that he acquired several thousand. Acting like a regional library, he lent them in Fukuoka, most often to a close circle of almost sixty people — to high-ranking samurai, other Confucian scholars, doctors, and to his students (sixteen of whom were from other domains) — and less frequently to a larger circle of acquaintances. When Ekiken was not in Edo himself, particularly after he retired, he could rely on his students traveling to Edo on alternate attendance to keep him informed of the latest developments in the book world, to buy volumes for him in Kyoto and Edo, and then either to ship the books or deliver them in person after their tour of duty. In this way Ekiken was "able to acquire information about books in close to real time."[65] Others perhaps without students or friends in Edo could obtain the same through official domain merchants in Edo or Kyoto.

Ekiken's experience as a conduit for books was not uncommon. Wakayama domain's Confucian scholar Ishibashi Shōan purchased texts from one of ten bookstores in the castle town there, as well as in Kyoto, Osaka, and Edo, when he traveled on alternate attendance, and he too lent them frequently to other retainers. Similarly, Tosa Confucian scholar Tani Tanzan formed the nucleus of a book-lending confraternity and mediated the purchase of books for its members.[66] In Hachinohe, Toyama Heima and his son Tamuro, both of whom served repeatedly in Edo, were part of a similar group with thirty-eight other samurai families, which pooled resources to amass more than 2,500 volumes.[67]

For those retainers pursuing cultural activities, the Edo experience exposed them to new sources of knowledge, new technologies, and cultural experiences not available in the domain. While serving in Edo, Shōnai retainer Katō Daini (1675–1741) became a serious student of Confucianism under Satō Naokata (1650–1715). Back in Shōnai, Katō became known as the founder of

Confucian studies in the domain.[68] Okunomiya Zōsai (1811–1877), like many of his colleagues from Tosa, studied in Edo with Satō Issai, becoming one of the Iwamura domain scholar's best students. After three years at Issai's private academy, Okunomiya returned home to establish his own institution, the Hasuike shoin, and to take up a post as instructor of the domain school.[69] Gion Nankai (1676–1751), one of the three earliest, outstanding figures of the Nanga school, followed a common pattern, accompanying his father, who was serving as an official physician of Kii domain, to Edo. While in Edo, Gion studied Confucianism and Chinese literature and pursued his artistic interests. Of significance to the development of "Southern School" or literati painting in Japan was that in Edo he was able to go to the original sources for artistic inspiration and see a few actual Chinese works rather than Japanese woodblock editions of them (some entirely in black and white).[70]

Odano Naotake (1749–1780) of Akita and Aōdō Denzen (1748–1822) of Shirakawa both returned to their respective domains after a period of residence in Edo with new skills, Odano in Western-style painting and Aōdō in copper-plate technology. Odano actually had been sent to Edo by the Akita lord to study metallurgy, but spent most of his time studying Western-style painting under Hiraga Gennai. Odano used his newly acquired skills to illustrate Sugita Genpaku's famous translation of *Tafel Anatomia* (New Anatomical Atlas) and remained in Edo for most of the last years of his brief life. Aōdō, painter-in-residence of the domain, became the student of the foremost copper-plate artist of the time, Shiba Kōkan. After the retirement of his lord, Matsudaira Sadanobu, Aōdō brought the new technology back to Shirakawa, where he produced landscapes of Edo, among other works.[71]

Odano (1749–1780) and his lord, Satake Yoshiatsu (1748–1785), became the center of a Western-style art movement in Akita, known as *Akita ranga*. It also included Naotake's brother, Naorin, and Satake Yoshima, the castellan of Kakunodate, a type of branch domain of Akita's of fifteen thousand *koku*.[72] Influenced by Odano, Yoshiatsu became one of a small group of daimyo who proudly saw themselves as infatuated with "things Dutch" (*ranpeki daimyō*). He became a practitioner himself under the name Shozan and wrote several books on Western art theory, the first of their kind in Japan. This was the starting point for late Edo period Western-style painting, which was to have a wide impact, influencing for example the perspective techniques used by noted woodblock print artists Hokusai and Hiroshige. Teaming up as many Western-style artists did, Yoshimi and Akita retainer Tashiro Chūgoku combined efforts to produce a painting that nicely illustrates some of the mechanisms of cultural flow made possible by alternate attendance. The painting (Figure 7.3) depicts a glass bowl housing Japanese fruit and Dutch flowers. The bowl was itself a foreign import, a gift from Akita domain's Edo liaison to Yoshimi. The

FIGURE 7.3. Painting by Satake Yoshimi and Tashiro Chūgoku. Source: Miwa Hideo
1993, 62.

bowl thus traveled on its own alternate attendance route from Europe to Edo
to Akita, to become part of a Western-style painting of foreign and Japanese
subject matter.[73]

A period in Edo had similar importance for medical practitioners. Kurume
domain doctor Furukawa Hōei's (?–1841) study in Edo at the shogunal medical
school under Katsuragawa Hoken (1797–1844), a practitioner of Dutch (European) surgery, gave him the polished skills and high reputation that enabled
him to draw patients from afar once he returned home.[74] Inamura Sanpaku
(1758–1811), a townsman doctor who was adopted by a retainer from Tottori,
pursued medical studies in Fukuyama, Nagasaki, and Kyoto before obtaining
an assignment in Edo at the domain's compound. While there he became a
student of Ōtsuki Gentaku and later wrote the first Dutch-Japanese dictionary,
which had obvious importance to the development of Dutch Studies (*Rangaku*)
in Japan.[75] Kure Kōseki (1811–1879) of Hiroshima domain accompanied his father, a domain doctor, to Edo at the age of fourteen to engage in Dutch Studies
with Itō Genboku (1800–1871) and Takeuchi Gendō (1805–1880) and earned a
high reputation as a doctor in that city.[76]

Some doctors in official service of daimyo in Edo on alternate attendance
formed their own cultural networks. One of them was Sugita Genpaku, mentioned above, who, like his father, was a physician in the employ of the daimyo
of Obama domain (Wakasa province). His group, which collaborated with him

on the famous translation of *Tafel Anatomia* in 1774, included Maeno Ryōtaku (Nakatsu domain), Nakagawa Jun'an (like Genpaku, from Obama), and Katsuragawa Hoshū (soon thereafter in shogunal employ).[77]

For those who sought to become instructors in the martial arts or simply to improve their skills under noted teachers, a period of residence in Edo could be crucial. For example, after five years of instruction in the shogunal capital under Numata domain samurai Naganuma Chōhei, Kurume retainer Imai Tansai (1769–1840) returned home with a license to teach his master's school of sword-fighting and became a domain instructor. In the closing decades of the Tokugawa period, numerous retainers traveled to Edo to acquire skills in Western-style military arts. Nakamura Shūhō (1832–1918) of Matsuyama domain, accompanying his father in Edo on a long-term posting, studied gunnery under Tokugawa retainer Shimosone Kinzaburō (1806–1874). Returning to Matsuyama, Shūhō became the first in his domain to teach Western-style military arts.[78] Okayama retainer Kagawa Shin'ichi (1835–1920) also traveled to Edo in 1853 with eight other colleagues to study with Shimosone, where he learned the importance of Western technology. "The gun is a divine weapon (*shinki*) that will strengthen our country. We must not waste a single day [adopting this technology]," he asserted. Returning home, he joined a faction of retainers advocating greater openness to Western culture.[79] Sakamoto Ryōma received permission from the domain on two occasions to study swordsmanship in Edo, and this "opened up tremendous vistas of activity for the young samurai from Tosa."[80]

The "Edo experience" also had a pyramid effect, affecting many people beyond those who actually traveled to and lived in the city. Some Tosa artists returned from Edo with not only the art work of their teachers but new creative skills, which they put to use in part by taking on students of their own.[81] Sendai domain lancer Saijō Unnoshin (1775–1834) acquired more than a thousand students in Edo, and upon his father's death in 1804 returned home with the title of professor to teach in the domain school.[82] In the few decades after returning to Kurume, Imai Tansai, mentioned above, counted more than one thousand students as his own; more than fifty of these earned their own licenses to teach.[83] One Kurume domain school professor, Honjō Ichirō (1786–1858), took some of his students with him on his third (of five) trips to Edo. During his first stay there he studied with noted Confucian scholar Koga Seiri (1750–1811) of Saga domain.[84] Aizu retainer Kagayama Tasuku (1811–1871), like most doctor's children who wanted to follow in their father's footsteps, went to Edo to study both Dutch-style and Chinese medicine. Not only was his proposal to establish a Dutch Studies school in the domain's Edo compound approved, but he also succeeded in establishing a similar school back in Aizu.[85] Nativist scholar Aoyama Kagemichi (1819–1891), from Mino Naegi domain, traveled to Edo on long-term status and became a follower of the Hirata school. Through his influence it is said that as many as fifty-six other retainers did likewise.[86] Edo thus played an important role as a cultural entrepot. It was a place where artists and scholars could gain exposure to new forms of knowledge and acquire excellent training, and perhaps professional certification, from teachers whose geographic origins were probably as diverse as their own. They then took this knowledge and passed it on to others in the domains.

The vast majority of retainers who traveled to Edo did not fall into the category of domain scholar, artist, or teacher of some martial art, but they nonetheless actively participated in and contributed to the cultural life of the city. Domainal samurai did more than shop while in Edo. Interested people could practice the so-called "polite accomplishments" (e.g., Noh chanting, tea ceremony, poetry writing, the playing of musical instruments) and took these developed skills home. They were also able to join any of the multitude of schools to pursue martial or intellectual interests. In their spare time there were books to read from a variety of sources, including lending libraries that catered to samurai; kabuki performances to see; and, for those who could afford it, the pleasure quarters to frequent. Even the most boorish of "country samurai" could not help but be affected by the urban culture of Edo.

Despite initial linguistic difficulties and unfamiliarity with a new urban landscape, retainers in Edo on alternate attendance could become involved in the cultural and intellectual life of the city and participate in the various cultural networks created there.[87] Many of these networks formed during the second half of the eighteenth century and, like the salons of contemporary France, were for the enjoyment of scholarship and the arts. Unlike the salons of France, though, they lacked the influence of a strong patron of higher social status than the other members. A few notable examples are Hiraga Gennai's botanical group, which stimulated the study of medicinal herbs; Ōkubo Jinshirō's picture-calendar exchange group; and Ōta Nanpo's literary and Watanabe Kazan's Dutch Studies circles. Kazan, for example, "participated in a group of some twenty-five Edo samurai and scholars who were interested in rangaku and met periodically to discuss current events and exchange information on Europe."[88] Tosa Confucian scholar Miyaji Umanosuke, whose main task in Edo was lecturing to the lord and his heir, was the center of a small network of individuals within Tosa's various Edo compounds. His group of seventeen regular and eight less regular students came to his residence for instruction in reading Confucian texts.[89] However, as Confucian scholar for one of the country's many domains, Miyaji also became part of an informal network of similarly employed scholars, all of whom exchanged visits with one another, during which time they could discuss intellectual problems or simply reinforce friendships.[90] Through their network they also had access to books not otherwise available.[91] In addition, Miyaji became part of a more formal network that met every month on the twentieth day for a "question-and-answer study meeting" (*gimon kai*). According to Miyaji, this was "popular amongst Confucian scholars in Edo," but he still found this type of unfettered intellectual climate "unusual" (*kōzu naru koto nari*).[92]

During his first period of residence in Edo (1828–1829), Mori Masana was fully engaged in the martial and scholastic studies for which he asked leave from his duties in Tosa. In the realm of the martial arts, he went almost daily to either of the two horse-riding ranges at the domain's Kajibashi compound and rode whenever he was not experiencing chronic pain in his legs. He also became the occasional student of military scholar and swordfighting teacher Nakayama Emonshichirō.[93] Given his interest in martial matters, it is not surprising that Masana also became the student of another noted military scholar and swordfighting teacher, Hirayama Shiryū.[94] Masana's purpose in becoming his student was to discuss military affairs, to borrow books (which were quickly copied), and to see his fine collection of armor.

The focus of Masana's activities, however, was in the scholarly world. Within the domainal residence at Kajibashi he attended the study sessions held by his friend and teacher Miyaji Umanosuke, where the students read and discussed biographies of famous people.[95] This perhaps inspired him to write his own book of biographies of notable Tosa people, which he did during a period of residence in Edo in 1834.[96] His interests also frequently took him outside the domain compound, and consequently he requested and received special permission to come and go as needed.

Masana often attended the lectures and study sessions given by Iwamura domain Confucian scholar Satō Issai at his domain's main compound.[97] Masana was able to become a student through the recommendation of Tosa Confucian scholar Oka Mansuke, who was on his fifth tour of duty in Edo.[98] The identities of the members of this class of "about twenty or thirty students" are not known, but at least one of them was a Tokugawa bannerman. Toward the end of his first stay in Edo, Masana also became the student of Obama domain's Confucian scholar Yamaguchi Sadaichirō (1772–1854). While Masana was one of a small number of retainers from other domains to be admitted as a student, there was some mixing of samurai across political boundaries in Edo.[99] His father Yoshiki, as noted earlier, participated in an informal reading group at the domainal residence and was an avid student of Noh chanting and dance as well as the art of *bonseki* (miniature landscape of sand and stone in a tray), which was the rage in Edo at the time. He also found time to join a study group focusing on the ancient text *Nihon shoki* (Chronicles of Japan), in which, he noted, one retainer from Echigo and two Tokugawa bannermen also participated.[100]

It was even possible for some commoners, such as Iwasaki Yatarō (1835–1885) of Mitsubishi fame, a farmer who later (in 1859) purchased rural samurai status, to travel to Edo for studies by working as the attendant of a retainer who had received a posting there. In obtaining employment with Okunomiya Chūjirō, Iwasaki noted that this was the only way the domain would give him permission to leave Tosa. Iwasaki's main objective in going to Edo was to become a student of Confucian scholar Asaka Gonsai (1791–1860), which he was for two years.[101] Okunomiya was apparently given a long-term assignment, since he was taking his family along. With his family and Iwasaki in tow, Okunomiya's party took a leisurely sixty days to reach Edo (on 11/23, just months after Commodore Perry reached Japan), stopping to sightsee in Kyoto and other places on the way, and were able to enjoy an experience that was perhaps in many ways similar to Masana's first trip to Edo.

Kuwagata Keisai (also known as Kitao Masayoshi), from Tsuyama, and Yamamoto Baiitsu, from Owari, are two notable examples of artists of commoner origin who were also drawn into the alternate attendance system. Kuwagata, born the son of an Edo tatami maker, was appointed as an official painter-in-attendance to the Tsuyama lord, and in 1810 accompanied the daimyo to Tsuyama, where he painted a bird's-eye panorama of Edo on *fusuma* (sliding-door panels) in the castle, which was frequently reproduced in numerous versions.[102] A less well-known example is that of the *bakumatsu*–early Meiji townsman painter Ekin, or Hirose Kinzō (1812–1872). The son of a hairdresser, Ekin studied with a local townsman painter and then with Ikezoe Yoshimasa, a painter in the employ of the Tosa lord. Able to secure employment as a page with a long-term assignment in Edo, Ekin traveled there in 1829 in the procession of Lord Yamauchi's daughter Tokuhime. Alternate attendance thus provided him with a means to travel to Edo, where he was able to improve the artistic skill he had developed in Kōchi and become part of the art world in that city. While in Edo he studied painting with the sixth-generation (Surugadai) Kanō artist Tōhaku and Tosa official artist Maemura Tōwa (Yōsai). After only three years, Tōhaku gave Ekin the name Tōi, and with this artistic name (and license) in hand Ekin returned home. Though Ekin studied in the Kanō school, the kabuki paintings he completed, not to mention his highly sexualized pictures, are said to betray the Edo influences of the renowned woodblock print artist Katsushika Hokusai and the Utagawa school.[103] In fact, one of the treasures Ekin brought back from Edo with him was a copy of Hokusai's cartoon drawings, *Hokusai manga*.[104]

Upon his return to Tosa in 1832, Ekin became artist-in-attendance under the employ of domain senior advisor Kirima. Later, after losing his official position sometime during the Tenpō era (1830–1844), he went on to complete a series of large paintings, drawing his subjects mainly from kabuki plays he might have seen while in Edo or Osaka. These paintings, as well as those of some of his more than one hundred disciples in the Kōchi area, are still displayed at numerous local temples during summer festivals.[105] The examples of Ekin and

Kuwagata demonstrate that alternate attendance was open to some commoners involved in the arts and offered them the same opportunities as *bushi*. They also demonstrate that Edo was the crucial nexus, for it was there they learned the skills that enhanced their reputations and careers.

Local Culture and Edo

Alternate attendance has been seen largely as a one-way process, spreading culture from Edo to the localities, where it was absorbed in the castle towns, and from there perhaps into the surrounding areas. The reverse flow of culture, from the domains to Edo, is in many ways difficult to document. However, if alternate attendance as a historical subject begs for our attention, it is largely because of its role as an agent of elite circulation or migration from the domainal castle towns to Edo. As noted earlier, probably 25 to 30 percent of Edo's population lived in the compounds constructed by the domains in that city, and their numbers were continuously replenished by others from the castle towns. The system brought retainers from local urban centers (ranging in population from several thousand to 100,000) to what was arguably the largest city anywhere in the eighteenth century. The vast majority of retainers in Edo did not fall into the category of domain scholar or artist, but they nonetheless created human links between the domains and Edo by becoming part of the various cultural networks formed for the enjoyment of scholarship and the arts, by participating in other forms of popular life in the city, or simply through their physical presence. All retainers who traveled on alternate attendance were in one sense products of their localities, bringing with them local customs, speech patterns, and values.

The flow of material culture from the localities to Edo was no doubt much smaller in volume, but it formed an important current nonetheless. As noted in chapter five, it is difficult on the domainal level to get as complete a picture of how much the Edo compounds were tied to their local economies as we would like, but on a more individual level, we discover, from the diaries of retainers, that there were also important economic ties between the domain and Edo. For example, Miyaji Umanosuke occasionally acquired goods in Edo that were shipped to him from Kōchi. In 1832/7/6 he received five sacks of charcoal and one roll of cotton cloth, material for *tabi* footwear, and five pairs of finished *tabi*.[106] The charcoal and socks were probably meant to help Miyaji, who was not in good health, through the Edo winter. An avid fisherman, Umanosuke was no doubt overjoyed to receive several hundred small, dried fish from his father. On another occasion he received a large box and a barrel, but unfortunately the contents of each are not noted. Mori Yoshiki periodically received from home what we might today call a CARE package. Friends and family sent him a large quantity of six different types of dried fish (small sea bream, mullet, Tosa's still-famous bonito, *mase*, *nirogi*, sweet sea bream), edible seaweed, pickled plums, and two salted ducks.[107] Similarly, Mori Masana was delivered salted mullet and twelve mandarin oranges by a retainer who had just made the trip from Kōchi.[108] With fine weather it was possible to ship goods to and from Edo in a week or two — fast enough for many food products to retain their freshness. Also, on numerous occasions Masana gave local Tosa specialty products such as dried bonito and Kosugihara paper as gifts to acquaintances and teachers. In this way local products were distributed in the shogunal capital. As the case of mandarins demonstrates, these local products were often recirculated back to the localities.

The practice of gift giving between daimyo and the Tokugawa was an important ritual that grew out of alternate attendance. All lords made periodic gifts to the shogun and his officials, as well as their peers, of local specialty products. Most of these consisted of local food products (e.g., various types of fish, abalone, tea, fruit), silken goods, or sometimes ceramics. One of the most famous examples of the latter was enameled Nabeshima ware, which was specially produced for the consumption of the lord's household and for presentation to the shogun and other daimyo.[109] Although less well known, the Takatori ware of Kuroda domain was often given as official gifts in Edo, frequently in conjunction with other items, such as domestically produced Hakata silk material for *obi* or various marine products.[110] Some of the largest domains, like Satsuma, gave these gifts to the shogunate every month of the year. Tosa's Odo ceramic ware was given to Tokugawa officials and other lords, but was never deemed of high enough quality to present to the shogun.[111] Since the shogunate could not consume all of these, many were recycled through merchant agents.[112] Alternate attendance, then, became a mechanism by which these official gifts were centralized in Edo and spread through the populace. Some of them no doubt found their way back to the domains.

Material culture was also circulated from local area (or abroad) to local area via Edo. As Edo was the entrepot for daimyo, shogun Yoshimune, for example, was able to encourage his policy of import substitution among them more easily. In doing so he demonstrated the shogunate's concerns about protecting and building the national wealth of Japan. To stop the outflow of previous specie, Yoshimune distributed sugar cane and ginseng seedlings to daimyo, instructing them to try them out in their fiefs. The imported Korean ginseng was grown experimentally in Nikko before the seedlings were distributed to a number of domains in the 1730s. Owari, Mito, and Kii experienced good success with the program and even presented some of the results as part of the periodic gift giving to the shogun. In Mito, ginseng seedlings were distributed to farmers, who were encouraged to try the crop. To encourage the discovery of medicinal herbs to fight epidemic disease, the shogun also instructed the daimyo to investigate the plant life along the nation's main highways and encouraged them to establish medicinal gardens, which his government itself did at Komaba and Koishikawa. These became the center of a national medicinal garden network.[113]

Individual retainers were involved, too, in the dissemination of plants across Japan. While it is not clear whether the two varieties of azaleas, *satsuki* and *kirishima* (*Rhododendrum indicum* and *Rhododendron obtusum*, respectively), that Tosa retainer Shimamura Muemon brought back from Edo in 1704 were a foreign or domestic variety, he gave or sold some plantings to a rural samurai named Fukushima Yasaku, who cultivated them for profit in Tosayama, not far from Kōchi castle town.[114] While on a tour of duty in Edo, Shimamura had learned about azaleas from a book Kirishima-ya Ihei published a decade before titled *Chōsei karin shō* [A Short Volume on Long-living Flowers and Trees]. He then sought out Kirishima, from whom he obtained the plantings.[115]

Material culture was also diffused from local area to local area without going through the center; this occurred on the trip to or from Edo. One notable example involves a type of fermented tea from Tosa known as *goishi-cha*, so named because of its square shape and black color. This high-class tea spread along the Tosa lord's travel route across Shikoku during the early eighteenth century. As a result of alternate attendance, merchants from Nio (Iyo province) in northern Shikoku discovered the product and paid for special rights to market it in the Inland Sea area, where they sold it as Nio tea. In the mid-Tokugawa period, eighteen Nio merchants handled it, and by late in the period almost all large-scale sake and soy sauce merchants were also trading it.[116] On the return from Edo, the Tosa senior advisor Nonaka Kenzan observed the production of honey in Kii province and transported honeybees with him back to Kōchi, where he encouraged the industry as part of a policy of import substitution.[117] Also on the return trip, a retainer who later served as Tosa city magistrate observed the construction of a particular type of well in Ōmi province and invited four local artisans to Kōchi to employ their craft, which improved the quality of drinking water in the castle town.[118] In general, then, the trip to and from Edo provided domainal retainers many opportunities to observe and learn about local lifestyles, commercial goods, and modes of production, information that was personally meaningful and which might be of some utility back in the domain.

The impact of local culture on Edo is also evident in the practice of establishing branches of provincial shrines or temples in that city's domainal compounds, as discussed in chapter five. Nishiyama Matsunosuke, one of Japan's leading cultural historians, asserts that "most Edo temples and shrines were branches of temples and shrines located in a daimyo's home province."[119] About half of the fifty-three shrines and temples found in daimyo compounds in Edo were actually transplants from the domains, including the daimyo household deity. The more famous of these transferred deities (*utsushi gami*) were Toyokawa Inari (Nishi Ōhira domain, Mikawa province), Dazaifu Tenmangū (Fukuoka domain, Chikuzen province), Okayama Yuga-san gongen (Okayama shinden domain, Bitchū province), Suitengu (Kurume domain, Chikuzen province) and Marugame Konpira shrine (Sanuki province). They were popular with both commoners and samurai and a number of diarists from Tosa paid visits. Likewise, the family temple of Katō Kiyomasa (1562–1611), lord of Higo, was moved from Kumamoto to the domain's lower compound in the Togoshi Ginza area; it too was opened up to the public and became a bustling pilgrimage site for Edoites.[120] It has also been observed that the Inari faith spread with the movement of daimyo, "who often took their protective *kami* with them when they relocated."[121] The shrines and temples established by daimyo in Edo, many of which became fashionable places to visit in the early nineteenth century, were part of a complicated system of popular belief in Edo and formed an important link between the daimyo residences and commoners in the city. The religious statuary and other objects displayed during periodic exhibitions and festivals were physical manifestations of local culture to those visiting or living in Edo, including the domainal retainers on duty in Edo, part of the circulation of culture engendered by alternate attendance.[122]

The reverse flow occurred as well, although probably much less often. For example, the tutelary deity from Shiba Shinmei-gū (Shrine) in Edo, which had become the guardian deity for the third and fourth Tosa lords, was transmitted to Hijima village near Kōchi castle.[123]

Of great importance as well was the circulation of ideas, surely a topic deserving a focused study: While early in the Tokugawa period ideas and policies flowed largely from the shogunate (which consisted in part of a small number of domain lords) to the domains, later the domains interchanged ideas. For example, the senior advisor from Aizu domain who led the Kansei reform in the 1790s received many ideas while in Edo from his Kumamoto counterpart. Policies devised by local leaders in turn affected the Tokugawa's efforts.[124] In this way, culture in its various forms, intellectual, material, and religious, among others, circulated from the localities to the center, where it was transformed and often disseminated across the country, adding to the common body of knowledge and experience that defined the Japanese of early modern times.

Conclusion

THE TOKUGAWA STATE mobilized its elite in an unprecedented fashion, calling on the daimyo to attend the shogun in his capital of Edo every other year, a practice that continued for more than two centuries. They squandered great wealth getting to and from Edo, yet this both helped to keep the peace and to generate economic growth across the country. Year after year, the daimyo and their entourages plied the highways between their castle towns and Edo, making visible for all to see the social and political hierarchy of the land. Daimyo paraded through the political landscape, performing their status but at the same time also demonstrating their fealty to the Tokugawa. The shogun's centrality was routinely exhibited as well through the attendance of the daimyo at receptions and ceremonies in Edo Castle and through other rituals of gift giving. While some lords might have occasionally delayed their attendance in Edo or, conversely, tried to extend their stays in the capital, the fact that there were no serious challenges to this system that so occupied their minds and bodies, not to mention consumed their local economies, demonstrates the hold of the state. Alternate attendance was a central pillar of the early modern polity. Once altered in 1862, there was no going back. The hybrid state was no longer adequate to meet the challenges of the modern, industrialized world.

The impact of alternate attendance was widespread. It created economies of service that affected the nature of domainal governance, the lifestyle of daimyo retainer bands, their support staffs, and more broadly the vast numbers of people who tilled the soil and whose labor supported the samurai. The requirements of service also transformed the shape of the former regional castle town of Edo and remade it into a national capital, the vestiges of which can still be seen across Tokyo today, primarily in its parks and public gardens.

Conceived as a military system, alternate attendance remained, in effect, a peacetime draft throughout the early modern era. Retainers (and subretainers) from the domains were drawn into service, in attendance upon their lord in the fulfillment of his responsibilities to the shogun, but little was required of the men in terms of military tasks other than the march to and from Edo, to protect the Tokugawa family's temples from fire, and in some cases to stand guard at gates around the shogun's castle. Even the requirements of service to their own lord, through the performance of assigned jobs at one of the domain's compounds in Edo, were not terribly demanding, leaving retainers with ample free time while on their tours of duty. Life in Edo was less restrictive than in the castle towns and offered far more opportunities for recreation, cultural activities, academic study, or military training.

While not a modern system of conscription imposed on all adult males, as would be imposed by the Meiji government in 1873, alternate attendance might be thought of as a type of "disciplinary institution" imposed on the samurai body, requiring the daimyo and large numbers of their retainers to remove themselves from their domains, to travel to Edo, to take up residence in the capital, and to experience a bachelor's life (if only temporarily) in barracks in service to their lord.[1] The "Edo experience" was shared by a significant portion of samurai and allowed retainers from domains across the country to interact face to face. This was an important part of the process by which a consciousness of national identity was forged.

While alternate attendance was an individual, lived experience, collectively those experiences had a tremendous impact on the cultural landscape of early modern Japan. The rich historical record has revealed that the process of cultural production, dissemination, and integration was not unidirectional, but rather the result of a number of currents. It occurred all along the metaphorical road of alternate attendance. The flow from Edo to the domain capitals was dominant; retainers returning to the castle towns enriched the cultural life there and in the surrounding areas, thus raising the cultural level of the country as a whole. However, these domainal samurai and other retainers were not simply empty vessels that absorbed the culture of the center while in Edo. They were vehicles that carried local culture from the various domains to Edo and, to a lesser extent, to the cities of Kyoto, Fushimi, and Osaka, where the domains maintained permanently staffed residences. These other cities must be included in our conceptualization of the cultural flows created by alternate attendance. It is crucial therefore to recognize that "Edo culture" was nothing less than an amalgam of continually changing influences from early modern Japan's large number of domains. In addition to these important currents from the domains to Edo, there were also flows from domain to domain, through the center. The city of Edo, in this sense, not only exported culture, but acted as an entrepot where the various cultural currents from the more than two hundred domains interacted and, at times, took on new configurations. As a result, Edo was transformed into a cultural nexus, a place to which scholars, artists, and artisans from the domains were drawn. Moreover, the effects of the system went far beyond those with direct experience of work and study in Edo. Those trained in that city brought those skills back to the castle towns and transferred them to innumerable others.

While Japan during the early modern period may in some respects be referred to as a "closed country," within the country's borders the regular flow of human traffic across political boundaries created by alternate attendance was instrumental in helping counteract local tendencies toward isolationism and cultural fragmentation. This political institution, which perhaps more than any other defined the early modern era, was instrumental in producing a population with a high level of shared culture and experience.

Notes

Introduction

1. Cortazzi 1985, 215–216. Mitford found the necessary paraphernalia hard to locate and the stage management of the affair difficult because few men still remembered such a procession. Twenty years earlier the re-enactment would have been unthinkable, as early Meiji Japanese endeavored to forget the recent Tokugawa past. The staging of this re-enactment thus might be seen as further evidence of the return of Japanese pride in their own past. The Meiji leaders were thus demonstrating, with the safety that the passage of almost forty years since the Meiji Restoration allowed, that there was a continuity of strong central government in Japan.

2. Cortazzi 1985, 15.

3. Kenneth Pyle is representative, calling it "by far the most important method devised for controlling the daimyo." Pyle 1978, 14.

4. For example, while there were almost 100 attainders during the first fifty years of the seventeenth century, over the next two hundred years there were only 118 more. Bolitho 1991, 208.

5. Louis XIV's preference for Versailles as his permanent residence necessitated construction of a whole city of administrative buildings clustered around his palace. His lavish court society forced the nobility's personal attendance; its members often became hard-pressed and sometimes ruined by Louis' demands that his courtiers be "well turned out." Mitford 1994, 97–98. On *hoffahrt*, see Kasaya 1993, 138.

6. Roberts 1998, 20–21.

7. Ping-ti Ho refers to this as "blood circulation, so to speak, of a large and complex society." Ho 1982, xii. Benjamin Elman refers to the circulation of elites as "more limited" in explaining that "[i]n much of the recent scholarship about the late imperial civil service exam system, scholars still emphasize the social mobility, rather than the more limited circulation of elites, which civil and military examinations permitted in a premodern society." Elman 2000, xxvi.

8. Recently, Mizuhara Mitsuhiro has written, "While the system is recognized as one of the hallmarks of Tokugawa rule, its profound impact on Japan's premodern cultural and economic development is often overlooked." Mizutani 2003, 1. In English, a single dissertation, written in 1951 and published unrevised in 1966 (Tsukahira 1966), briefly treats the institutional history of alternate attendance. In Japanese, two books have been written which focus squarely on the subject. One, largely political in nature, is concerned most with diplomatic relations between the shogunate and the domains (Yamamoto 1998); the second is concerned almost solely with the mechanics of the institution (Chūda 1993). While there is a larger body of work on the subject in aca-

demic journals, the scholarship here too has been largely institutional in nature. See, for example, Maruyama 1976. Judging by the number of museum exhibitions organized on the topic and coverage in some popular periodic literature, there has been a surge of popular interest in alternate attendance, though, as noted, this has not translated into much greater scholarly output. See, for example, Tōkyō-to Edo-Tōkyō hakubutsukan 1997; Ishikawa kenritsu toshokan 1991; Toyohashi shi Futagawa-juku honjin shiryōkan 1997; many others are cited in chapter two.

9. See Edo iseki kenkyūkai 1991, 1992, 2000. The Edo hantei kenkyūkai (Edo Compound Study Group), run out of the University of Tokyo and headed by Miyazaki Katsumi of the Shiryō hensanjo, has produced, among other works, Miyazaki and Yoshida 1994.

10. Tsukahira 1966, 4. Luke Roberts' study of mercantilism in Tosa domain is from one perspective a study of the economic impact of alternate attendance on Tosa domain and its fiscal policy. Roberts 1998.

11. Nishiyama 1992, 10. Exactly what Nishiyama meant by "full-scale" is unclear, as is the question of whether or not the two Japanese volumes cited above would cause him to change his view.

12. The cultural impact of alternate attendance has received some attention in Japan recently, but the focus has been largely on culture at the high level, specifically the lord. Two essays that examine the daimyo's cultural role in alternate attendance are Nishiyama Matsunosuke, "Sankin kōtai kara umareru bunka," in Nishiyama 1992 and Kasaya 1993.

13. McClain, Merriman, and Kaoru 1994.

14. Yokota 2003, 389–408.

15. Siebold 1973, 62.

16. For example, Matsudaira Tadanao (1628) and Bessho Yoshiharu (1623) were punished with attainder of their fiefs, Nambu Ienao with house arrest (1638), and Hotta Masanobu with attainder (1660). Fujino 1975, 39–45, 260–264, 271–273. Later, tardiness, when penalized, was more likely to result in censure, as in the case of Nabeshima Naoyuki (1744) of Hasunoike domain. *HDJ*, vol. 7, 122.

17. Kumazawa wanted the daimyo (and samurai) to return to the land. For his most notable work, see Galen Fisher's translation of *Daigaku wakumon*: Fisher 1938.

18. Tsukahira 1966, 103–125, presents an excellent summary of a number of important critics of the system.

19. Dōmon 1998, 114–117.

20. Nakai Chikuzan is quoted in Najita 1987, 172.

21. Kiyokawa 1969, 177. For Hayashi Shihei, see Ōshima 1959, 201, and Keene 1959, esp. 39–45.

22. James White includes alternate attendance as part of the controls on daimyo in White 1988, 15–17. While his argument about the nature of Tokugawa authority is sound, I would simply like to assert that a much stronger case should be made for the importance of alternate attendance in defining the nature of that absolute authority.

23. White 1988, 17.

24. Kodama 1969–1974, vol. 8, Doc. #427, 315–316.

Chapter 1: Beginnings

1. Mass 1990, 80, 206–208. On Hideyoshi's requirement of attendance, see Berry 1989, 168.

2. Hatanobu 1977, 50.

3. Maruyama 1992, 211–212.

4. Fujino 1964, 92.

5. Kodama 1986a, 103.

6. Robert Sakai, "The Consolidation of Power in Satsuma-han," in Hall and Jansen 1968, 132.

7. Tsukahira 1966, 50.

8. On the *sekisho* system, see Vaporis 1994a. Shiba Keiko discusses a number of travel diaries written by daimyo wives in Shiba 1997, 79–100. There are several other diaries from early in the seventeenth century of daimyo wives making the trip from the domain to Edo, where they would serve as hostages. The wife of Tokugawa Yoshinao, lord of Nagoya, in her poetic diary "Michi no ki" expressed unease at leaving home in 1633 and uncertainty over what lay ahead. Shiba 1997, 80–84.

9. Chūda 1993, 18–19.

10. Tōkyō-to Edo-Tōkyō hakubutsukan 1997, 30. The names of those retainers and their family members who served in Edo as hostages can be found in the first two volumes of the *Yamauchi-ke shiryō*. Tosa domain senior advisors all sent hostages to Edo in 1606; the hostages rotated duty, but at least one remained in Edo more than sixteen years (*TYK*, vol. 2, pp. 370–371). There apparently was no direct correlation between the size of the domain and the number of hostages, as Kaga (1.19 million *koku*) maintained three, Takada domain (255,000 *koku*) four, and Owari (619,000 *koku*) five; many smaller domains, however, maintained only one.

11. Miyaji Nakae 1845, vol. 1, fol. 53; *YKS*, vol. 2, 412–414.

12. On the issue of the Tokugawa's monopoly of the legitimate use of physical force, see White 1998; on Japan's foreign policy, especially vis-à-vis Asia, see Toby 1991; on the Tokugawa centralized road system, see Vaporis 1994a.

13. Bolitho 1991, 200.

14. Kodama 1986b, 103.

15. On Yoshimune's Kyōhō-period reform, see Yamamoto Hirofumi 1998, 52–73. Muro argued that a relaxation in the requirement that the *shugo daimyō* attend the Ashikaga shogun led to a decline in his authority.

16. Notehelfer 1992, 452–453.

17. Geertz 1983, 138. The case of Elizabethan England will also be explored in chapter three.

18. Tōkyō-to Edo-Tokyo hakubutsukan 1997, 31. Twenty-one others had mixed schedules; thirty were permanently stationed in Edo. The data are from 1818.

19. According to a chart on display at the Edo-Tōkyō hakubutsukan in Tokyo, in 1808 there were 160 daimyo in Edo (120 on alternate attendance, 25 permanently stationed in Edo, and 15 there due to job assignments in the shogunate), leaving a minority (104) in the domains.

20. Tōkyō-to Edo-Tōkyō hakubutsukan 1997, 32. All bannermen held fiefs, whether

real or fictive, less than ten thousand *koku*. One group of them were treated as daimyo and hence performed the requirement every other year, just like daimyo. The other group was treated as *hatamoto* and therefore required to reside in Edo only for short periods of time and to retain their families in the fief. Hirayama 1994, 489–502.

21. Tōkyō-to Edo Tōkyō hakubutsukan 1997, 31. The timing was based on status, more specifically the chamber room in which the lord sat at Edo Castle, rather than on the location of the domain. Hence a daimyo's schedule could change given a sufficient rise in status.

22. As per Article 4 of the Laws for the Military Houses of 1635. Ishii 1981a, 63.

23. The Nakamura Yamauchi line and domain came to an end in 1689, and the thirty thousand *koku* territory reverted to the main domain.

The daimyo of a single domain, collectively, made a total of roughly two hundred trips to and from Edo during the years 1635–1862: e.g., the Maeda of Kaga 188; the Shimazu of Satsuma 196; and the Yamauchi of Tosa 211 (104 times to Edo, 107 times back to the domain). There were far fewer trips than if the domain had maintained a regular schedule, because of delays in the confirmation of a new lord after the previous one's death or, as will be explained below, due to exemptions that were granted under certain circumstances.

24. Matsudaira 1964, 334–354. Nevertheless, the Mito lord could request permission to return to the domain for a few months, though this was not referred to as *kōtai*. Few actually did. The first three lords, for example, made the trip once every three to six years, and the sixth lord only once in forty years. Matsudo shiritsu hakubutsukan 1998, 10–11, 63.

25. *HDJ*, vol. 7, 136.

26. This early, more Kyoto-centered pattern of movement is discussed in Asao 1975, 20–21. The second Tosa lord, Tadayoshi, along with many other daimyo, attended the shogun Hidetada in Kyoto in 1619. *TYK*, vol. 2, 472.

27. For example, the lord traveled there in 1606 to supervise Tosa's imposed contribution of corvee labor for the construction of Edo castle, and also in 1613, 1616, 1618, 1620, 1624, 1626, and 1632. *TYK*, vol. 2, p. 4 (1606), pp. 26–27 (1613), p. 458 (1618), p. 545 (1620), pp. 674–675 (1624); *TYK*, vol. 3, pp. 91–92 (1626), pp. 447–451 (1632). In 1626 the third Tosa lord, Tadayoshi, spent five months in Kyoto before traveling to Edo, where he remained for another five months. (*TYK*, vol. 3, 91–92.) The Shimazu lord traveled to either Kyoto or Edo to wait upon the shogun almost every year from 1604 to 1618, with a break during 1615 to 1616 due to the Battle of Osaka. Hatano 1977, 95–96.

28. Jansen 2000, 57. Unfortunately, this idea has been often repeated and thereby has come to be accepted as fact — e.g., as in Kassel 1996, 17, and Ikegami 1995, 295–296.

29. The experience of Tosa suggests that the notion of daimyo as Edo born and bred needs some qualification. The Yamauchi made frequent use of adoption from collateral families to maintain the family line, particularly during the nineteenth century with the last five lords.

30. Tsukahira 1966, 118. Tsukahira asserts that the heir apparent could visit the domain while the lord was in Edo, but he must report to Edo sixty days after the lord returned to the domain. He also states that those not of age were proscribed from leaving Edo. It is not certain whether there were special circumstances surrounding Yamauchi Toyooki's two trips as a youngster or whether this occurred in other domains as well.

TKK Kansei 5 [1793], gogatsu-jūnigatsu, "Nijūshichi nichi ushigorō. Toyooki kimi Edo hatsuga," fols. 1–10. Toyooki died in 1809, in Edo, just three months after making his first trip there as lord.

31. *TYK*, vol. 3, 296, 321, 372, 388, 424, 427. The same pattern continued for Tadatoyo and his son Toyomasa (fourth lord).

32. *TYK*, vol. 3, 85–86.

33. Mutō 1990–97, vol. 6, 396–397. The document is dated Genroku 9 (1696/5/18). This is only a portion of a much longer address. The remainder of it focuses on the negative effects that Toyofusa's inaction had been having on his retainers. It is discussed at length in chapter four.

Despite Asahina's supplications and his thinly veiled warnings, Toyofusa did not step foot in Kōchi until 1700/8/3, another four years. Just one month later Toyomasa died in Edo, passing on the title of lord to Toyofusa, who was then required to return quickly to Edo. Thereafter, Toyofusa performed the alternate attendance regularly until his untimely death in 1706. His retainer Asahina Genba had criticized his laying in bed all day, even taking his meals there, telling the heir he should resolve to get better in a day, but Toyofusa's ills apparently were quite real.

34. Lord Asano was ordered to commit ritual suicide that same day. His domain was confiscated and all his retainers made masterless samurai. This story, including the revenge enacted by a group of his retainers, is generally known as the Tale of the 47 Rōnin. For the puppet play based on these events, see Keene 1971.

35. This material on Satsuma domain is based on Hatano 1977, 95–96, 112–113.

36. Myōjin 1983, 27–30. The various occasions were in 1605, 1669, 1720, 1791, 1843, and 1857.

37. Mori Yoshiki 1793–1807, fols. 49–64. The order was *goyō aisumi sōrō yue, katte shidai okuni e kaere sōrō yō* (since your duties have been completed, you are free to return to the domain). He also recorded that at Fujisawa he met a retainer from Tsuyama domain and they took a rest break together.

38. See for example Konishi, Jugaku, and Muragishi 1974, 2–3. Another proof is in the numerous petitions for relief from corvee labor submitted by assisting villages along alternate attendance routes. See Vaporis 1986, 377–414.

39. The following account of preparations for the trip is based on a number of different sources for different domains, e.g., Miura 1994, 18–19; Ichimura and Ōishi 1995, 6–7; Ōta Kōtarō 1966, 13–14; and Chūda 1993.

40. For Mori, see Mori Hirosada, "Hirosada kō dōchū yorozu nikki," fol. 1; for Toyama, see Miura Tadashi 1992, vol. 1, 3. Of course retainers might receive informal notice earlier.

41. Takakura 1987, 22–23.

42. Toyohashi shi Futagawa honjin shiryōkan, 1996, 49–50.

43. Kirima Hyōgo [Yoshitaka] 1802.

44. *TMK*, vol. 15, Kanbun 11 [1671] ichigatsu tsuitachi-jūichigatsu itsuka, "Shigatsu jūni nichi Edo rusui . . . dōchū hattosho o mōshiwatasu," fols. 30–31. The source for the instructions is the official record of the senior advisor on duty, "Karō tsukiban kiroku."

45. The concern about conflict with men from other domains is made clearer in a slightly later version of the travel rules, from 1677, which elaborates on the second ar-

ticle in instructing "do not approach places where people from other domains can be heard to be arguing." *TMK* dai nijū kan, Enpō 5 [1677] ichigatsu-gogatsu, fols. 50–53.

46. Regulations and exhortations issued to Okayama domain indicate a similar concern with order on the road and in the post stations: "Fights among retainers are expressly forbidden. Walking in the post station at night is prohibited, unless on official duty. Do not act improperly with shopkeepers, when purchasing items, or with innkeepers. Private drinking parties are forbidden. There is to be no singing or chanting in a loud voice while at the post stations." Miyamoto 1987, 87.

47. Fujisawa Hiroshi 1977, 338.

48. For example, high-ranking retainer Soeda Gizaemon was given ten days' rest after returning to Tsugaru in 1682. Namikawa 2004, 236.

49. Mori Yoshiki 1793–1807, vol. 6, fol. 5. However, having "just" returned from Edo the previous fifth month, Yoshiki did not feel the need to make the formal rounds again when he departed for Edo on 1802/4/18, on what would be his third and final trip to Edo (vol. 7, fol. 38.)

50. Miyaji Umanosuke 1832, vol. 4, fol. 31.

51. *TMK*, vol. 51, Jōkyō san nen [1686] sangatsu tsuitachi-rokugatsu misoka, "Sangatsu mikka Kōchi yamashiro hatsuga," fols. 48–49.

52. Kasumi kaikan n.d., *Sankin kōtai gyōretsu ezu*.

53. Miyamoto 1987, 11–12.

54. Fujisawa 1977, 341.

55. Miyamoto 1987, 63–65.

56. Miyamoto 1987, 66.

57. Kagoshima ken ishin shiryō hensanjo 1981, Docs. #689–690, 319–320.

58. Miura 1994, 54.

59. Miura 1992, vol. 1, 152. Tamuro returned to Hachinohe on 1829/4/13.

60. His experience is recounted in Gotō Seikō 1790, fol. 18.

61. Yamamoto 1998, 164–175; Date 1935, 1936; Tsukahira 1966, 96–102; Tōkyō-to Edo hakubutsukan 1997, 100–101.

62. Kaihō Seiryō, "Keizaidan," quoted in Nishiyama 1989, 146.

63. Roberts 1998.

64. Maruyama 1992, 601–606.

65. Given fifty-three stages, this meant an average of more than three inns per station. On the other Gokaidō roads, there were 102 on the Nakasendō, 29 on the Nikkō dōchū, 11 on the Oshu dōchū and 44 on the Kōshū dōchū. Toyohashi-shi Futagawa honjin shiryōkan 1994, 4.

66. Toyohashi shi 1996, 53. For a detailed study of these official inns, see Ōshima 1955; see also Vaporis 1994a, 22, 79, 167, 273–274.

67. During Kaga's procession in 1866, 128 men had to be lodged in three neighboring villages and 93 others in six different area shrines and temples because not all could be accommodated at Itoigawa station on the Hokkoku kaidō, a relatively undeveloped highway. There were a total of 2,600 men in Kaga's large-scale procession that year. Chūda 1993, 185–186.

68. Maruyama Yasunari appears to be the only Japanese scholar who has written on the subject of provisioning processions, and he devotes all of three pages to the subject.

Clearly it is a problem of sources. Maruyama 1992, 600–602. The following discussion of food is based on this source, unless otherwise indicated.

69. Chūda 1993, 111–112.

70. Hirao Michio n.d. On the next trip to Edo two years later there were twenty-one cooks, all again in the main body of the procession. *TMK*, vol. 65, Genroku 3 [1690] ichigatsu-sangatsu, "Sangatsu muika Kōchi yamajiro hatsuga," fols. 59–68.

71. Inagaki 1988, 95. The Nabeshima example is from Ōshima 1959, 177–181. The story of the tea caddy is told in Paul Varley, "*Chanoyu* from Genroku to Modern Times," in Varley and Kumakura 1994, 181.

72. Maruyama 1992, 600–602. The cost for this was one *ryō* gold, or about fifty-five *mon* per person.

73. Takakura 1987, 23–25.

74. Rutherford Alcock and many other foreigners made note of them. Alcock 1863, vol. 2, 129. The sand piles and other forms of courtesy offered the daimyo will be discussed at some length in chapter three.

75. These comments of the Dutch representative van Polsbroek, from 1858, are quoted in Jansen 2000, 132.

76. Miyamoto 1987; Vaporis 1994a, chaps. 1–2. The daimyo were supposed to pay some compensation to the inns when they had to cancel reservations. When reservations for the Kaga procession were cancelled at Nou post station in Niigata, the inn officials there complained that the twenty-five *ryō* cancellation fee was too little and petitioned for more. When they were refused, these officials followed after the procession. Their tenacity paid off, but not until they had traveled all the way to Edo. This was an exceptional case but the officials netted an additional thirty *ryō*. Chūda 1993, 222–224.

77. Vaporis 1994a, chap. 2.

78. "*Okuni wa Yamato no Kōriyama/Otaka was jū to go man koku / Chadai ga tatta nihyaku mon*." Konno 1986, 228–229. Apparently this form of lyric could apply to any number of daimyo. This one was found in the rural samurai Kiyokawa Hachirō's diary: "*Rokudaka wa jū to goman koku/ Matsudaira Kai no kamisama ochadai nihyaku mon/ Arigataku zonjitatematsuru*" (His domain, 150,000 *koku* / Lord Matsudaira of Kai / A tip of only 200 *mon* for tea). Kiyokawa 1969, 192.

79. Chūda 1993, 198. Another similar expression was "*O Edo Nihonbashi o nanatsu*" (wake up at 4 a.m. [every day] in order for the procession to make it to Edo on time). Miura 1994, 25. Late in the period there were seven groups of lantern bearers in one of Kaga's processions, which allowed the procession to travel at night. In no case, however, was passage permitted through checkpoints after dark. "Nariyasu kō Edo yori okikoku gyōretsu zutsuki" 1872.

80. Sasakawa 1986, 179–181. The Tosa officials used the occasion of confirming their reservation, two to three months prior to departure, to bargain for a lower price.

81. Apparently this was a problem, as the Tokugawa enjoined the daimyo not to demand lower prices after arrival at post stations. Officials from Aizu domain were able to negotiate at one post station a four *mon* per person reduction in 1842 and free lodging for the ten of them. Chūda 1993, 212.

82. Kodama Kōta 1986b, 106. For a full-length treatment of daimyo inns, see Ōshima 1955.

83. Kodama 1969–1974, vol. 9, pt. 2, 226–227. This particular petition from a group of *honjin* and *waki-honjin* operators from stations on the Tōkaidō, from Shinagawa to Hakone, was addressed to the Tokugawa's magistrate of roads and dates from 1830/12th month.

84. Toyohashi shi 1994, 54.

85. Tosa retainer Mori Yoshiki reported this in his diary, Mori Yoshiki 1793–1807, vol. 7, fol. 47.

86. Chūda 1993, 215. He also details an extremely long list of purchases made by the domain at Kashiwabara post station on the Hokkoku kaidō on the return trip to Kanazawa—such as twenty-nine tobacco trays, thirty-two candlesticks, three water buckets, a chopping board, mortar, kitchen knife, tongs, five charcoal braziers, twelve portable candlesticks, ten small trays, fifty teacups, twenty plates, lantern, a single-leaf screen, two iron kettles, charcoal, and warming stones (for bedding)—but does not offer any reasons for this extraordinary amount of shopping on the road. These goods, obviously, would have to have been carried to Kanazawa.

87. These numbers were for daimyo with holdings of more than twenty thousand *koku*; lesser lords could use half the number. Kodama 1969–1974, vol. 9, 219–220. On the three-tiered system of rates charged on Tokugawa highways, see Vaporis 1994a, 26–27, 76–77.

88. *HDJ*, vol. 1, 79.

89. Hirao 1979, 45–46.

90. On the nature of and problems with transport corvee labor on the Gokaidō, see Vaporis 1994a, 57–97. On Tosa's problems, see Roberts 1998, 87. Exactly how frequent is not clear, but Roberts cites eight examples of petitions (out of a total of 149 surviving examples from 1759–1771) that demanded that the domain government lighten the corvee burden. He concludes that "domain officials reformed the unpopular transport corvee system after receiving many complaints." Roberts 1998, 128, 105. The quote is from page 105.

Boat corvee also caused problems. See Roberts 1998, 45–46. Tsuzuki Takeyasu briefly discusses an example of peasant contention in Tosa in 1797 leading to the arrest of thirteen people when villagers refused to transport the lord's baggage. Tsuzuki 1988, 40–45. Elsewhere, Okayama domain officials requisitioned 1,189 villagers for corvee duty on boats transporting the lord and his entourage from the castle town to Osaka in 1692. This figure represented about 90 percent of the labor force used on the boats. On the return trip the following year, 1,339 men were called up. Okayama kenshi hensan iinkai 1985, 595.

91. Of the 181 persons in Kuwana's procession, 103 were hired laborers who worked the entire route from Kuwana to Edo. Yoneya maintained offices in Edo, Kuwana, Numazu, and the castle towns of the other lords he serviced. Tōkyō-to Edo-Tōkyō hakubutsukan 1997, 70–72.

92. Chūda 1993, 76. The *senryū* is *gohyaku ryō/ijikarimashita ni/arukaseru*. In other words, carrying five hundred *ryō* in gold would make the porters' legs bow.

93. This section on daimyo encounters on the road is based on Wada 2000, 157–164, unless otherwise indicated.

94. *TKK*, Kansei 11 [1799] ichigatsu-nigatsu no kan, "Nigatsu mikka byō ni yori," fols. 1–3.

95. Tōkyō-to Edo-Tōkyō hakubutsukan 1997, 65. The request was made the same day due to a disruption in the schedule.

96. "Odōchū ikkan chō" 1808, fol. 7.

97. Hirao 1979, 65.

98. Wada 2000, 159.

99. See, for example, the comments of Overmeer 1978, 215.

100. Retainers traveling on their own or in groups might have run into problems more often. Taniguchi Shinko discusses several cases in which retainers became involved in fights with commoners, often pack-horse drivers or other types of laborers, that ended in bloodshed. Taniguchi 2000, 225–229.

101. This incident, recounted in the *Fujioka nikki*, is discussed in Taniguchi 2001, 54–70.

102. Satow 1983, p. 52.

103. Notehelfer 1992, 447–448.

104. *Journal van Jonkheer Dirk de Graeff van Polsbrowk* (Assen: Van Gorcum, 1987), quoted in Jansen 2000, 813 n. 3.

105. Satow 1983, 52. After the incident, a British doctor, William Willis, bravely rode by the same procession, "whose swords were reeking with the blood of the Englishmen," on his way to treat the wounded, and passed unharmed.

106. This account in based on Miyazawa 1987, 84–92, and Tokutomi 1994, 408–410.

107. Notehelfer 1992, 448.

Chapter 2: The Road to Edo (and Back)

1. With no major delays, the 225-*ri* (883 km) trip to Edo could be made in thirty days. For comparison, this was approximately the same number of days as for Fukuoka (Kyushu) and Hagi (western Honshu) domains. For more distant Satsuma, about forty days were required. For Kaga (fifteen), Fukushima (twenty), and Tsugaru (nineteen), it was a far shorter trip.

2. Einosuke was the second son of the Tosa senior advisor Gotō Geki. Gotō Einosuke 1791, #939. This was the second of his four trips to Edo.

3. Mori Hirosada 1732, fols. 1–2.

4. Gotō Seikō 1790, fols. 18–19.

5. On the discomfort of palanquins, see Vaporis 1994a, 221.

6. Ōta Kōtarō 1965, 12.

7. This segment on Toyotsune is from Mutō 1990–1997, vol. 7, 122–123.

8. Hirao 1979, 64. The Maeda lord rode his horse to the outskirts of the castle town, where the procession was fully organized, then climbed into his palanquin. Chūda 1993, 44–45.

9. Toyotsune exhibited similar compassion for his men when the retinue stopped for a rest in the Hakone mountains at a place called Honzaka. After relaxing for some time, a high-ranking retainer named Mutō Mataemon informed him that everyone had rested and suggested that they prepare for departure. When another retainer advised that that was not the case, Mutō looked around and determined that what he had said was true, so again he suggested that the retinue depart. This time the lord replied that indeed not *everyone* had rested. "What about the man who had been holding a sun

umbrella over my head all during the rest break? Why had no one been sent to replace him?" Toyotsune queried. Getting the hint, Mutō ordered that a substitute be sent immediately. The original umbrella holder, a man named Hachiemon, was forever grateful for his lord's kindness and reportedly was moved to tears every time he recounted this story. There may be the inclination perhaps to dismiss this contemporary account as hagiography, but there is no similar laudatory account of Toyotsune's father, Toyotaka, in the *Nanroshi*. Mutō 1990–1997, vol. 7, 123–124.

10. This was true of Satsuma as well. See Hatano 1977, 46–56.

11. This is the conclusion of Fujisawa 1977, 338. The first Ikeda lord, Mitsumasa exclusively used boat transport to Osaka. Fujii, Mizuno, and Taniguchi 1967. His successor, Tsunamasa, used the overland route in 1705 for the first time and thereafter he and his successors rarely went by boat. Fujisawa 1977, 338–341.

12. Maruyama 1992, 213–214. He maintains that the same was true of daimyo from other parts of Japan as well.

13. While the domains were ordered by the Tokugawa in 1605 to turn over large vessels of five hundred *koku* and above, they still maintained large numbers of smaller ones, as evidenced by the 731 vessels that nine western lords provided at shogunal behest to meet the challenge posed by two Portuguese vessels in Nagasaki harbor in 1647. These smaller vessels are mostly known as *sekibune*. Fujisawa 1977, 334–337.

14. Kodama 1969–1974, vol. 9, pt. 2, 95.

15. On these de facto prohibitions, see Vaporis 1994a, 38–55. On the route taken by the Korean embassies, see Toby 1986, 419. Of course, the prohibition on large oceangoing vessels would have discouraged such travel, even were it legal.

16. In contrast, the first two lords (Kazutoyo, 1545–1605, and Tadayoshi, 1592–1664) usually traveled by boat from Urado to Osaka before going overland on the Tōkaidō. This was the most direct route available and could be accomplished under ideal conditions in as little as seventeen days. Tadayoshi apparently enjoyed travel by boat, opting for an overland route only on one occasion (1646) during his long reign, and that was during his later years after his health deteriorated.

17. "Motone nikki," quoted in *TCK*, Tenmei hachinen [1788] shichigatsu no kan, "Nijūni nichi Kōchi yamashiro hatsuga," fol. 68.

18. Miyaji Umanosuke 1832, vol. 1, fol. 4. It was precisely because of delays such as this that individuals most often wished to travel by land.

19. *TMK*, vol. 58, Genroku 1 [1688] ichigatsu futsuka-rokugatsu, "Tōka Kōchi yamashiro hatsuga," fol. 30.

20. *TMK*, vol. 35, Tenna ninen [1682] ichigatsu-shigatsu, "Tōka Kōchi yamashiro o hatsuga," fols. 53–70; Miyaji Sukeyoshi 1781–1817, n.p. In 1692, the figures were 1,507 sailors and fifty-one boats.

21. *TMK*, vol. 70, Genroku 5 [1692] ichigatsu futsuka-nenmatsu, fols. 12–29. For example, the landed senior advisor Gotō saw the lord off from the center of his fief, in Aki. Similarly, local shrine and temple officials came to pay their respects to the lord at the official resting place (*goten*) at Nahari.

22. Yamazaki 1971. It was one to two meters in width, typical for a provincial road. For comparison, most stretches on the Tōkaidō were 5.5 to 7.3 meters wide. Vaporis 1994a, 36.

23. Ishikawa Yasurō 1997, 48–53. The Kitayama road was surveyed by Kōchi pre-

fecture and a section of it designated a prefectural nature walking route. Kōchi ken 1995.

24. *TtaK*, vol. 10, Shōtoku 5 [1715], "Shigatsu jūgonichi kikoku no itoma o tamawari," fol. 10.

25. See Vaporis 1986.

26. Luke Roberts writes, "Village records suggest the scale of the burden on peasants. In the nineteenth century, one village of fifteen hundred people situated along a domain highway — which gave it a particular burden — reported a year's total of 15,104 man-days plus 708 horse-days of labor." This and the quote in the main text come from Roberts 1998, 87. In 1800, Mori Yoshiki noted that several villages on the Kitayama route had petitioned the domain authorities for relief due to their claims of "excessive" labor requisitioning. As a result, he said, it took the villagers four days to do what should have been one day's service. Mori Yoshiki 1793–1807, vol. 6, fol. 31.

27. A number of sections of varying lengths were paved, though according to signposts on the road these probably date only back to the early nineteenth century.

28. He stated this in a letter to the shogun requesting permission to take the Chūgokuji. *TCK*, Tenmei gannen [1781] ichigatsu-sangatsu, "Jūsan nichi kikoku no oitoma o tamawari," fols. 16–25.

29. This is according to a signboard at Hara Bōchō Pass, which I visited in 1995.

30. It was also his job to meet the procession on its return at the designated port on Honshu. Yoshida Tōyō 1929, 321–329; Hirao 1959, 44–45. For comparison, late in the Edo period Satsuma maintained fifty boats; Kumamoto sixty-seven; Hagi seventy-four; and Tokushima about thirty. Maruyama 1976, 85–86.

31. This account is based on Mori Yoshiki 1793–1807, vol. 7, fols. 37–56.

32. Mori Yoshiki 1793–1807, vol. 7, fol. 49.

33. As a result, two top domain officials, including a senior advisor, were dismissed. Kimura, Fujino, and Murakami 1988–1990, vol. 1, 428. Heirs and lords were often sickly, perhaps due to the relatively small social circles from which they selected mates. Toyoteru's doctor, Imajiri Yōjun, left a daily record of the lord's (poor) health as well as the drugs he prescribed for the lord on his alternate attendance trip in 1847. "Dōchū haishin nikki" [Diary of Medical Exams while Traveling], quoted in Matsumoto 1997, 16.

34. *TCK*, Tenmei gannen [1781] ichigatsu-sangatsu no kan, "Jūsannichi kikoku no oitoma o tamawari," fols. 16–25. The standard reply from the senior councilor on duty to the formal request submitted by the Edo liaison was, "You may do as you wish" (*Katte shidai*).

35. This paragraph is based on Mori Hirosada 1732, fols. 1–4.

36. *TNK*, vol. 26, Kyōhō 17 [1732], ichigatsu tsuitachi-gogatsu tsuitachi, fols. 20–21.

37. *TNK*, vol. 26, Kyōhō 17 [1732], ichigatsu tsuitachi-gogatsu tsuitachi, fol. 25.

38. Mori Hirosada 1732, fol. 49.

39. *TMK*, vol. 5, Kanbun 11 [1671], fols. 45–46. Maruyama 1992, 215, says that many western daimyo also went sightseeing at the Imperial Palace, but the Tosa lord apparently did not. He notes that early in the Tokugawa period the shogunate admonished the lords not to contact the court aristocracy but with time relaxed its attitude.

40. *TMK* 23, Enpō 7 (1679) ichigatsu nanoka-shichigatsu misoka no kan, "Nijūichi nichi shūhō no oitima o tamawari, nijū nichi Edo hatsuga," fols. 24–26; for 1680, *TMK*, Enpō 8 [1680], fols. 51–52.

41. According to Ishifumi Reii, ordinarily daimyo were not allowed to stop in Kyoto, but Tosa was given permission when it requested it because of its strong connection with the imperial court. The Yamauchi lords Tadatoyo, Toyokazu, Toyoteru, and Yōdō all married aristocratic women from the Sanjō family. Ishifumi 1933, 25–26. But according to Katsuhisa Moriya, more than one hundred daimyo were allowed to maintain residences in that city. Surely they were allowed to stop in Kyoto, or the permission given them by the Tokugawa to maintain the mansions would have been meaningless. Moriya 1990, 99.

42. *TYB*, vol. 26, Kyōhō 17 [1732], ichigatsu tsuitachi–gogatsu tsuitachi, fols. 24–26.

43. Daimyo usage, by road, was as follows: Tōkaidō, 119; Nakasendō, 31; Ōshū dōchū, 52; Kōshū dōchū, 4. Figures are from 1821 and are based on Kodama Kōta 1969–1974, vol. 10, pt. 3, Doc. #58, 106–116.

44. *Koban furu / haru sankin no / Shimada kana* (Dropping a gold coin / Alternate attendance in springtime / Shimada). A river-crossing office was located at Shimada. Takeuchi 1967, 343.

45. Mori Hirosada 1732, fol. 19.

46. Miyaji Umanosuke 1832, vol. 1, fols. 12–14.

47. River crossings were a concern for most domains, not just for those who used the Tōkaidō. Kaga domain had to cross seventy-three rivers wider than five meters, only forty-three of these (about 60 percent) of which were bridged. The others had to be crossed in boats, by wading across on foot, or over temporary boat-bridges. Chūda 1993, 158.

48. Mori Hirosada 1732, fols. 6–7.

49. For more on river stoppages and their consequences, see Vaporis 1994a, 48–55.

50. Harris 1983, 59.

51. Mori Hirosada 1732, fol. 18. According to Chūda 1993, 86, the vanguard in Kaga domain's procession was divided into on-duty and off-duty groupings, which rotated days of service while traveling. The off-duty group traveled at some distance, about four kilometers, in front of the main group.

52. Mori Hirosada 1732, fols. 23–24, 38.

53. This appears to have been standard practice. Lord Maeda changed out of his travel clothes at Kaga's auxiliary compound at Itabashi before proceeding to the main residence at Hongō. Chūda 1993, 44–45. Kodera Kiyoaki, a retainer of Nagoya domain, writes that in 1841 the procession stopped for lunch in Shinagawa, then its members shaved their heads, fixed their hair, and changed clothes before proceeding to the main residence at Ichigaya. Kodera Kiyoaki 1916, 263.

54. Mori Hirosada 1732, fol. 12; *TKK*, Kansei san nen [1791] ichigatsu–jūnigatsu no kan, "Sangatsu itsuka Kōchi yamashiro hatsuga," fols. 50–51.

55. *TMK*, vol. 15, Enpō 3 [1675], "Urū shigatsu itsuka itoma o tamawari," fols. 33–37; *TMK*, Enpō 8 [1680], "Muika Kōichi yamashirō o hatsuga," fol. 51.

56. Kasumi kaikan n.d.

57. Nishiyama Matsunosuke 1983, 12–13.

58. Lord Yamauchi Toyotsune, leaving Edo for the first and only time as lord in 1725, took special care of the sword he received from the shogun. Shortly after departing from Edo in 1725 (3/23), it began to rain hard. A vassal close to Toyotsune gave him covers for his two swords, but the lord used only the long one to cover the sword the shogun had given him, tossing the other one back to the retainer.

59. This is described briefly in Mori Hirosada 1732, fol. 17. The shogunate much reduced gift giving as part of the Kyōhō reforms in the early eighteenth century; the amount of silver given to the largest domains, like Kaga, was reduced from one thousand pieces to one hundred. Due to economizing measures in the closing decades of the Edo period, gift giving would fall to even lower levels. Chūda 1993, 45–50.

60. *TTK*, vol. 2, pp. 396–398; *TKK*, vol. 9, Kansei 3 [1791] ichigatsu-jūnigatsu, fols. 24–59.

61. Dutch travelers remarked on this as well. See Thunberg 1795, 218.

62. *TMK*, vol. 31, Tenna gannen [1681] shigatsu futsuka-gogatsu misoka, "Shigatsu jūyokka shūhō no oitoma o tamawari," fols. 16–18.

63. Quoted in Tsukahira 1966, 109–110.

64. Bolitho 1991, 203–205.

65. *TNK*, Meiwa ninen [1765], jūgatsu-jūnigatsu no kan, "Meiwa ninen jūgatsu jūichinichi kikoku no oitoma o tamawari," fols. 1–11. Similar delays were granted in 1814 and 1824. The delays allowed the daimyo some time to recoup before having to make the expensive trip back to the domain.

66. Tsukahira 1966, 55.

67. Chūda 1993, 40–47.

68. Tsukahira 1966, 54.

69. *TCK*, An'ei kyūnen [1780] ichigatsu-jūnigatsu no kan, "Jūgatsu jūyokka jōtei shukka," fols. 8–12. Likewise Tosa was instructed to reduce its numbers in Edo during Lord Toyokazu's prolonged stay in Edo from 1800 to 1803. *TKK*, Kyōwa gannen [1801] no kan, "Jūsan nichi byō ni yori," fol. 16.

70. The earliest example found thus far of such an instruction from the shogunate to the lords dates from 1738. *TNK*, Genbun sannen [1738] kugatsu-nenmatsu, "Bakufu yūshi yori kikoku no toshi ni atari shodaimyō to taifu," fols. 1–2.

71. *HDJ* 1988–1990, vol. 7, 122. There were different types of branch domains. Hasuike, Ogi, and Kashima were classified as *naibun bunchi*, rather than simply *bunchi* (as were Kaga domain's branches of Toyama and Daishōji), which meant that they were not as independent in political terms and therefore could not petition the shogunate directly.

72. *TshK*, vol. 5, Ka'ei gonen [1852] no kan, "Kokonoka Kōchi-jō hatsuga," fols. 1–7.

73. *TKK*, Kansei jūichi nen [1799], ichigatsu-nigatsu no kan, "Nigatsu mikka byō no yue ni yori," fols. 1–2. The request cited a recent precedent in which the lord of nearby Tokushima had been allowed to remain in the home domain to recuperate.

74. *TKK*, Kansei jūnin nen [1800], ichigatsu-sangatsu no kan, fols. 20–44.

75. *TKK*, Kyōwa gannen [1801] ichigatsu-sangatsu no kan, "Jūsan nichi byō ni yori," fols. 1–25.

76. *TKK*, Kyōwa gannen [1801] ichigatsu-sangatsu no kan, "Jūsan nichi byō ni yori," fol. 16.

77. *TKK*, Bunka san nen [1806] ichigatsu-gogatsu no kan, "Shōgatsu tsuitachi byō ni yori tsukai o motte," fols. 1–8.

78. According to Konno Nobuo, "[t]here is no end to these stories of daimyo impoverishment." Konno 1986, 53.

79. The Japanese reads: *Kyōto e shinobi nite nobori kudari*. *TCK*, Tenmei gannen [1781], ichigatsu-sangatsu no kan, "Jūsannichi kikoku no oitoma o tamawari," fols. 1–15.

It has been suggested to me that perhaps the lord purchased a prostitute in Gion but the language is not clear (*Gion atari no hana kenbutsu seshime, kure mutsu doki Fushimi e kaeru*).

80. *TYK*, An'ei kyūnen [1780], ichigatsu-jūichigatsu no kan, "Jūgatsu yokka Kajibashi jōtei shukka," fols. 1–12. The retired lord Toyosuke made a similar request to remain in Kōchi to take the waters after retiring in 1843, and asked for extensions in 1846, 1847, and 1855. *TteK* table of contents.

81. *TCK*, Tenmei hachinen [1788] shichigatsu no kan, "Nijū nichi Kōchi yamashiro hatsuga," fols. 1–69. Departure was delayed until 7/22.

82. *TCK*, Tenmei hachi nen [1788] shichigatsu no kan, "Nijūni nichi Kōchi yamashiro hatsuga," fols. 1–69.

83. *TKK*, Bunka sannen [1806] ichigatsu-gogatsu no kan, "Nijūgo nichi kore yori saki byō yori kikoku no oitoma o tamawari [1806/4/26]," fols. 1–5.

84. Gotō Seijun 1801b, fol. 25.

Chapter 3: The Daimyo Procession

1. Toby 1986, 415–456; and Toby 1991. In Japanese, see Kuroda and Toby 1994; and Watanabe Hiroshi 1985.

2. Geertz 1983, 134–142. The quote is on page 138. The K'ang-hsi [Kangxi] emperor in Qing China was famous for his travel around the empire. His journeys served multiple purposes: to familiarize himself with the land he ruled; to collect plants, birds, and other animals encountered; for hunting and exercise; and to train his troops. Spence 1988.

3. Geertz 1983, 138. The Moroccan saying went, "The king's throne is his saddle, the sky his canopy."

4. Cole 1999. She actually made twenty-three progresses during her forty-four year reign. On Elizabeth, see also Strong 1977.

5. After the large-scale processions to Kyoto by the first three shoguns, no Tokugawa ruler made the trip until 1862. The shoguns also periodically made trips, accompanied by a large number of daimyo, to Nikkō to pay their respects to the founding members of the dynasty enshrined there, and for the occasional hunting trip, but otherwise they rarely left Edo. See Watanabe Hiroshi 1985, 25–27, for a brief account of these trips.

6. The quote is from Cole 1999, 10. The notion of the interplay between structure and antistructure is from Turner 1969.

7. This notion of "august authority" being supported and maintained through ritual is developed in Watanabe Hiroshi 1985.

8. Kurushima 1986, 60–62, 85, 91. The sand also had a practical use: if rain muddied the road the sand piles could be spread over the road surface. These and other practices were not restricted to the daimyo on alternate attendance, but applied to Tokugawa officials as well.

9. The following discussion is based on Kurushima 1986, 60–92. There were of course other forms of *gochisō* — e.g., all official travelers, including daimyo on alternate attendance, were allowed a prescribed number of no-cost and subsidized numbers of porters and post horses. See Vaporis 1994a, 26–27.

10. For Englebert Kaempfer's comments on hospitality, see Kaempfer 1999, 370.

11. Kurushima 1986, 18. The example of Odawara is from Miyamoto 1987, 79. The example of Nagoya is from Enkōan 1986, 374.

12. Alcock 1863, 124–125.

13. Alcock 1863, 409. See also Kaempfer, 1999, 350–351; Siebold, 1973, 68; Fortune 1863, 45.

14. Notehelfer 1992, 132.

15. Notehelfer 1992, 133.

16. This account is based on Notehelfer 1992, 135.

17. Notehelfer 1992, 135.

18. Notehelfer 1992, 141–42.

19. The anonymous man began his account responding to a question about the mark on his face. The story he told had taken place fifty years earlier, around 1853. Shinoda 1971, 93–94. The other account of being pushed is from Ikeda Sadatsune, "Omoide kusa," in Mori Senzō 1980, vol. 7, 275–276. Harry Heusken also reported that in Edo, "when one happens to get in the middle of the procession of a Daimyo, then they shove aside the intruder who broke the train." Heusken 1964, 181–182.

20. Kuga machi kyōiku iinkai 1990, 129–131.

21. The scroll is housed at the Sakai-shi Hakubutsukan (Sakai City Museum), and segments of it have been reproduced in various exhibition catalogues on alternate attendance. I would like to express my gratitude to the head cultural arts supervisor, Yoshida Yutaka, for sharing with me his insight on this rich document.

22. Jilly Traganou posits that daimyo scrolls present the procession facing left, as if "leaving Edo," and are an implicit political statement on the part of their patrons, whereas procession scrolls of foreigners commissioned by the Tokugawa depict the people facing right, as if on the way to Edo, emphasizing their submission to the Tokugawa government. Traganou 2004, 156–157. In most daimyo scrolls the procession does indeed face left—not only those in western Japan but also those from northern parts of the country such as Aizu and Sendai, where "going left" might be said to be toward Edo. Daimyo procession scrolls facing right are rare, Morioka being the most famous example. Occasionally people in other, nondaimyo procession scrolls face right, as in Utsunomiya's procession scroll for the Nikkō pilgrimage. That the vast majority of daimyo scrolls depict the procession facing left has more to do, it seems, with artistic convention than ideology. By unfurling the scroll one segment at a time, with the people facing left, the procession appears to move. Reproductions of all of the scrolls mentioned here can be found in Fukushima kenritsu hakubutsukan, 2001.

23. Toby 1986, 418.

24. Fukushima kenritsu hakubutsukan 2001, 6, 7, 45.

25. Lindau 1986, 162.

26. Toby 1986, 454.

27. See, for example, the reproductions in Narasaki 1964, vol. 2.

28. Toyohashi shi Futagawa honjin shiryōkan 1998, 72–73.

29. On Nihonbashi, see Yonemoto 1999, 49–70.

30. Shinoda 1971, 351. Kaempfer, too, was awed: "Watching the procession of a territorial lord, one cannot help but be impressed and praise high enough, firstly, how with

the exception of the norimono bearers everybody is dressed in black silk, and secondly, how so many people travel in close and well-ordered formation with only the sound of their clothes, feet, and the horses being heard." Kaempfer 1999, 273.

31. Shinoda 1969, 93–94.

32. Mutō Hiroki 1842, scroll 11.

33. Craig 1961, 78.

34. Mori Yoshiki 1793–1807, vol. 6, fol. 17.

35. Quoted in Watanabe Hiroshi 1985, 138.

36. McClellan 1985, 11.

37. This discussion of the definition of a procession is based on Toby, "Gaikō no gyōretsu — ikoku goikō kenbutsunin," in Kuroda and Toby 1994, 37–38.

38. Sean Wilentz, in "Introduction," in Wilentz 1985, 3, refers to them as "theaters of power."

39. Davis 1986, 5.

40. These three functions are suggested by points made by Maurice Asulhon, "Political Images and Symbols in Post-Revolutionary France," in Wilentz 1985, 177.

41. Kaempfer 1999, 331.

42. Kaempfer 1999, 418.

43. Caron and Schouten 1935, 30.

44. Shuri-man 1998, 125.

45. Siebold 1973, 66. He contrasted this with his retinue of only two hundred, which he wrote "does not very extravagantly exalt the mercantile foreigner."

46. Chūda 1993, 60–62, 74–76. The Kaga lord brought to Edo as many as twenty horses for his personal use, and each horse required a person to lead it. Not all of these were in the main part of the procession.

47. Furukawa Koshōken 1964, 7.

48. The scroll "Rakusan-kō ogyōrestu zukan," which depicts the Sendai lord's procession of 1842, is housed in the Sendai shi hakubutsukan. Painted by retainer Mutō Hiroki, it was presented to the lord as a gift. A small portion of it is reproduced in Toyohashi shi Futagawa honjin shiryōkan 1997, 10.

49. Kobayashi Issa, quoted in Kameda and others 1995, 22.

50. On the rising burden of the corvee labor tax for transport on the Tokugawa's official highways, see Vaporis 1986, 377–414.

51. Kodama 1969–1974, vol. 8, pt. 1: Doc. #169, 106; Doc. #222, 148; Doc. #397, 291–292 (1701); Doc. #450, 346–347 (1712); Doc. #494, 391–392 (1721).

52. TMK, 23 kan, Enpō 7 (1679)/1st–7th Month, "Onnikki," fol. 24.

53. Yamamoto Takeshi and others 1982–1986, vol. 6, Doc. #2, 4–6. The men were also known variously as watari chūgen.

54. Limits, as set in 1721, were as follows: for daimyo over two hundred thousand koku, 15 to 20 mounted samurai, 120 to 130 footsoldiers, 250 to 300 petty attendants; for daimyo over one hundred thousand, the numbers are reduced to 10, 80, and 140 to 150; for daimyo over fifty thousand, 7, 60, and 100; and for those below fifty thousand, 3 to 4, 20, and 30. Kodama 1969–1974, vol. 8, pt. 1, Doc. #494, 391–392.

55. TMK, vol. 86, fols. 55–57.

56. Reductions were made in 1674 as a result of a flood in Kōchi. TMK, vol. 14, Enpō 2 (1674), fols. 33–34.

57. Quoted in Ishifumi 1933, 39.

58. Maruyama 1987, 25.

59. *HDJ*, vol. 1, 120. The numbers were reduced again by one-half in 1815. Unfortunately no numbers are given in either case.

60. Mutō Hiroki 1842, scroll 11. There was, to be sure, some bravado here. Certainly at least Kaga maintained its high numbers.

61. Kasei jikki kanpon hensan iinkai 1977, vol. 3, 483–484.

62. Regulations are quoted in Ōshima 1959, 174–175. According to the one issued in 1712, the practice was "completely useless."

63. Mutō Hiroki 1842, scrolls 10–11.

64. For example, in 1764 there were 2,184 persons; in 1816, 2,144 persons. George Tsukahira notes that "Maeda's retinue was reduced in 1747 to about 1500 persons" (Tsukahira 1966, 80), but this was only a temporary deviation. Louis G. Perez, quoting Susan Hanley, repeats a statement that exaggerates the numbers: "Most daimyo brought at least 500 samurai. Many brought more than 1,000, and one, the Maeda, commonly brought more than 4,000." Note that the numbers he gives are only for samurai, who made up only a modest portion of the retinues. Perez 2002, 144. Harold Bolitho, on the other hand, underestimates the size of the largest processions: "The daimyo gyōretsu, or procession, numbering as many as a thousand men with spears and pennants, was one of the most splendid sights Tokugawa Japan had to offer." Bolitho 1991, 220. Part of the confusion may lie with the acceptance of Kaempfer's figures as representative for the entire period. He reported that "the processions of the greatest daimyo consisted of about two thousand people, those of the *shōmyō* have half that number." Kaempfer 1999, 271. In footnote 1 (p. 488) the translator/annotator notes, "The original states twenty thousand, but this seems to be a slip of the pen in view of the figures stated elsewhere in this chapter."

65. Chūda 1993, 58–61, 67.

66. As was the case with the tenth lord of Kumamoto, Hosokawa Narimori. Tōkyō-to Edo-Tōkyō hakubutsukan 1997, 38.

67. For Yonezawa, see *HDJ*, vol. 1, 511. For other domains please refer to the note with Table 2.1.

68. Maruyama 1987, 25. Totman notes, "Daimyo retinues commonly numbered in the hundreds." Totman 1993, 100. Shimabara, a domain of forty-three thousand *koku*, had 148 people in its Bunka-era (1804–1817) processions. *HDJ*, vol. 7, 233. Some were considerably less: Hisai domain (53,103 *koku*, Ise province) usually had 78 in its procession in the 1830s but that number was reduced to 69 in 1843. *HDJ*, vol. 4, 490.

69. Tōkyō-to Edo hakubutsukan 1993, 40–43.

70. Available statistics for Komatsu domain (ten thousand *koku*, Iyo province) range from forty-seven to fifty-eight people, about a third of whom were full samurai. *HDJ*, vol. 6, 488.

71. Chūda 1993, 68–70.

72. Chūda 1993, 79. If this percentage held for the entire procession of two thousand, this would translate to eighty people just to carry raincoats!

73. Chūda 1993, 83.

74. Chūda 1993, 98.

75. The comment was made by Kanzawa Tokō during the Kyōhō period (1716–1736). Quoted in Chūda, 1993, 121.

76. Davis 1986, 159–160.

77. Chūda 1993, 100–101.

78. Takagi 1985, 54–55. A retainer was instructed to have his subretainers dress uniformly so they would "look smart." They were not to talk in line and not to look around, nor should they use a fan while marching. In discussing warriors decorating their military equipment, Takagi concludes that those of the Sengoku and early modern period were "the same" (p. 55).

79. Kaempfer 1999, 369.

80. Enkōan 1986, 332.

81. Kaempfer 1999, 369.

82. Kaga's procession did this at forty-six of the sixty-seven post stations through which it passed. Chūda 1993, 94–95.

83. Shuri-man 1998, 148.

84. The crowd in Elizabethan England made "an enormous amount of noise," according to R. Malcolm. He explains, "If an entry was simply an assertion of power and status, we should expect the crowd to have assumed a passive deferential posture. Instead it aggressively asserted its presence, treating the monarch less as an awesome symbol of authority than as a popular hero." Smuts 1989, 74. The quiet in Tokugawa Japan was maintained in part through explicit prohibitions on loud voices, the playing of instruments and noise due to construction. Chūda 1993, 203–204.

85. Ryan 1989, 147.

86. Mori Hirosada reported that the children of Tosa samurai based in Edo whose service was completed traveled separately, departing the day before the main body of the procession. Mori Hirosada 1732, fol. 10. Of course it was unheard of for high-ranking women to appear in public in any circumstance.

87. Kaempfer 1999, 273.

88. Fukumochi 2002, 9–14. The late seventeenth century dating of the screen would make it roughly contemporaneous with Kaempfer. While difficult to prove, it seems there was likely a direct connection between kabuki and the yakko.

89. Dazai is quoted in Konno 1986, 52.

90. Darnton 1984, 113.

91. "Daimyō gyōretsu zu," Kanazawa shiritsu Tamagawa toshokan, Doc. #2676.

92. Mutō Hiroki 1842.

93. The procession was that of Hosokawa Narimori (1804–1860), who was making his first entry into the domain as lord. The total of three thousand includes an unidentified number of men who met the lord at the domain's border for the final leg of the journey to the castle town. Kanagawa kenritsu rekishi hakubutsukan 2001, 53, 109. The intended audience for the surimono is an important but unknown issue. Was it made for the local Kumamoto audience, for Edoites, for people who would watch along the roadways between these two cities, or for all of the above? As this was the lord's first trip to the domain as ruler the procession was no doubt larger than normal. Another example of this type of surimono is from Sendai. Matsudo shiritsu hakubutsukan 1998, 22.

94. There were roughly two hundred commercial editions by 1700 and twelve hundred by 1860. Berry 2006, 45, 108.

95. Kumon kodomo kenkyūjo 2003, Doc. #32, 57. This volume also contains a num-

ber of *mitate-e* of children's daimyo processions, e.g., Doc. #42, 61. On *mitate-e*, see Clark 1997.

96. For Iwataki, see Fukumochi 2002. For Hagi, Kuga machi kyōiku iinkai 1990. The processions in Ōi, like the one in Niimi, have been declared an intangible folk cultural property. It took place yearly, beginning in 1816, until recent times. Since 1963 it has been held every three years. Ōi-machi kyōiku iinkai 2000, 1–3. For Yuzawa, see Ashkenazi 1993, 54–64.

97. Hasegawa Akira 1969, 293–297; Niimi daimyo gyōretsu hozonkai, 1997.

98. Niimi daimyo gyōretsu hozonkai 1997.

99. For more on the procession in Niimi today, see Vaporis 2005.

100. The quotation is from Milton Singer, *Traditional India: Structure and Change*, quoted in MacAloon 1984, xiii.

101. Notehelfer 1992, 198–199.

102. Toby 1986, 421. The quote refers of course only to the foreign embassies.

103. Fukushima kenritsu hakubutsukan 2001, 32.

104. See for example, Walthall 1986 and Taniguchi 2001, 54–70.

105. Taniguchi 2001, 63. Jippensha Ikku's fiction also indicated that a certain lack of respect was not unknown, as Yaji, one of his two main characters in *Hizakurige*, fails to bow to the procession and jokes about its members. Ikku 1960, 25.

106. Kawata 1990, 46. The same is true in the scene at Bakuro-chō.

107. This and the following description are from Kaempfer 1999, 272–273.

108. Fukushima kenritsu hakubutsukan 2001, 32–34.

109. *HDJ*, vol. 6, 194.

110. Kuwata 1988.

111. Kasaya 2001, 28–32. This unit acted as the central headquarters for command of the battle but didn't participate directly in combat unless needed. Its primary task was defending the lord. "*Sonae*" refers to military unit; "*hatamoto*" indicates that the head is a bannerman or high-ranking retainer of the lord, usually a senior advisor.

112. See Ogawa 1992, vol. 2, 195–202, for a discussion and diagrams of the various types of palanquins. Those of higher quality had hinged roofs to allow the rider great ease in entering and exiting the vehicle.

113. Kaempfer 1999, 271.

114. Notehelfer 1992, 133, 135. Hall was clearly overwhelmed by the numbers. Beyond his "seven hundred" he asserted that "it is impossible to reckon the number" of attendants behind the main bodyguard around the lord. "I think it not all improbable that several thousand persons passed preceding and following this immediate body guard," he wrote (135).

115. Miyamoto 1987, 85. The statistics are from 1697.

116. The procession dispatched on Tokugawa orders from Kanazawa to take possession of Takayama castle began in a similar fashion, namely with thirty gunners, twenty bowmen, and twenty spearmen. The takeover occurred in 1693. Doc. #2680, Kanazawa shiritsu Tamagawa toshokan, Kanazawa city.

117. Jansen 2000, 131.

118. The Shimabara screen is beautifully illustrated and discussed at length in Kuwata 1988.

119. Takagi 1985, 50–51.

120. *HDJ*, vol. 1, 150. For Chōshū, *HDJ*, vol. 6, 194. For Kaga, see Chūda 1993, 68–70.

121. In Hitoyoshi domain (Kumamoto), *shi* made up 46.6 percent of the total in 1781 (90 of the 193 men were of *shi* status). Maruyama 1987, 24.

122. There were variations from trip to trip — e.g., in 1797 samurai made up 23 percent, pages 23 percent, and hired workers 10 percent — but the variations were not substantial. Miura 1994, 23; and *HDJ*, vol. 1, 97.

123. The comment on American parades is from Davis 1986, 159–160.

124. A detailed study of the regulations informing the use of implements in the daimyo processions can be found in Ogawa 1992, 3 vols. The following discussion of implements is, unless otherwise indicated, based on vol. 1, 185–205 of this work.

125. Kornicki 2001, 69. For a complete set of *bukan*, see Fukai and Fujizane 1996–2003, 36 vols.

126. Tsukahira 1966, 73. Perhaps the progress of the sultan in late nineteenth century Morocco was equally "decadent." Its vanguard "was formed of a cavalry escort, headed by standard bearers, carrying flags of every hue and colour, the poles topped with glittering balls." Harris 1983, 57.

127. The Japanese is "Daimyō no yari wa damatte na o nanori." Chūda 1993, 106.

128. Chūda 1993, 106.

129. Chūda 1993, 106.

130. Kondo Eiichi 1984, 244–245.

131. A reproduction of the Morioka domain procession is most conveniently available in Tōkyō-to Edo-Tōkyō hakubutsukan 1997, 40–43. Photographs of some of the paraphernalia discussed here can be found on pages 47, 51; for Sendai, see Mutō Hiroki 1842.

132. Tōkyō-to Edo-Tōkyō hakubutsukan 1997, 52.

133. "Odōchū ikkan chō" 1808, fol. 6.

134. Kasei jikki 1977, vol. 3, 458–468.

135. Brown 1993, 233.

136. Brown 1993, 233.

137. The quote is from Kornicki 2001, page 69. He is referring only to office-holding daimyo.

Chapter 4: Assignment: Edo

1. Zhang 2003, 11. There were approximately twenty thousand officials in the civil service during the Qing period (1644–1911), though not all of them circulated since they also had to staff the imperial city in Beijing. Smith 1983, 50.

2. Zhang 2003, 8.

3. In Kaga a rotation system was implemented in 1734 whereby two of the eight senior elders alternated tours of duty. Prior to this, service was restricted to just two of the families. Chūda 1993, 134.

4. Naitō Meisetsu 1982, 141–142. This is a written compilation of an oral account given in the early Meiji period by a retainer whose father was on a long-term posting there.

5. "Yontō shizoku jōseki nenpu" n.d., vol. 12, pt. 1. The five generations of Befu never served in Edo.

6. The schedule was irregular in 1670, with both a *kōtai* (departing Edo 4/30) and a *sankin* (departing Kōchi 10/3) that year. The following number of names were listed: for 1670, fifty-four names; for 1671, seventy-three names; for 1675, sixty-two names; and, for 1676, eighty-five names. *TMK*, vol. 2, Kanbun 10 [1670], "Shigatsu nijūichinichi tsuihō no itoma o tamawari," fols. 11–23; *TMK*, vol. 15, Enpō 3 [1675], "Urū shigatsu itsuka itoma o tamawari," fols. 33–45; *TMK*, vol. 18, Enpō 4 [1676] ichigatsu-shigatsu, "karō tsukiban kiroku," fols. 19–24 *TMK*, vol. 35, Tenna 2 [1682] ichigatsu-shigatsu, "Tōka Kōchi yamashiro hatsuga," fols. 53–62.

7. *TMK* 65, Genroku sannen [1690] ichigatsu-sangatsu, "Sangatsu muika Kōchi yamashiro hatsuga," fols. 61–63.

8. "Jō otomo ashigaru nezue" 1866, 4 vols. This source consists of genealogies of ninety such footsoldiers' families, not all of which were in existence at the same time.

9. This incident is recounted in "Mori Yoshishige nikki" 1828, vol. 7, Bunsei 11 [1828]/3/2 entry. In one of his plays Chikamatsu tells of a samurai who avoided service in Edo by claiming to be ill. Chikamatsu 1961a, 65.

10. "Osamurai chū senzogaki keizu chō" n.d., vol. 24, entry for Mori Masakatsu.

11. *TMK*, vol. 21, Enpō 5 (1677), "Jūnigatsu tsuitachi kachū shoshi ni meijite senyaku o reikō seshimu," fols. 9–11.

12. Zhang writes, "References about sons accompanying fathers to official posts are abundant." Zhang 2003, 11.

13. The only other time Kusumose Ōe left the domain was on domain orders to Nagasaki. Ōta Motoko 1994, 4.

14. Miyaji Sukeyoshi 1781–1817, fol. 10.

15. "Yontō shizoku jōseki nenpu" n.d., vol. 21, pt. 1. Entry for Okuda Shin'eimon family. Sons replaced their fathers in their fathers' old age, but did not usually succeed formally as household until the father's death.

16. "Yontō shizoku jōseki nenpu" n.d., vol. 12, pt. 1, entry for family of Odate Gōhachi. Gōhachi began with a stipend of seven *koku* and a two-man rice allowance.

17. "Yontō shizoku jōseki nenpu" n.d., vol. 12, pt. 1, entry for family of Heiuchi Gon. He had a stipend of 5.71 *koku* and a two-man rice allowance.

18. The genealogies of service reported changes in status or job, or unusual events in the life of a retainer. For example, while it records that he was appointed to regular position in the force accompanying the lord in 1835, it is impossible to know with certainty that he continued traveling to Edo every other year. The next entries in the record tell us that he held the position of police supervisor for the procession in 1842, but that does not clarify the issue of whether he continued the biennial trips from 1835 to 1846; in 1846 he was appointed to a position in Tosa, so we know his Edo service ended.

19. Moriguchi 1986, 23–41.

20. Mori Masana 1828–1856, vol. 1, fol. 6.

21. Masana's relation, Mori Oki'emon, was himself in Edo for the third time in 1828, having made previous trips there in 1821 and 1825, during which time he was given important assignments. In 1827 he was called back to duty in Edo, where he remained for twenty-three years. In 1829 his position was officially made long term and consequently

he brought his family to Edo. Oki'emon returned to Kōchi sometime after 1850 and spent his last days there before passing away in 1854. "Osamurai chū senzogaki keizu chō" n.d., vol. 24, pt. 1.

22. This argues against the view put forth in Nihon fūzoku shi gakkai 1994, 188: "Domainal retainers sent to Edo were given a small allowance and suffered from poverty." On the next page the author of the text also claims that "young people like going to Edo" even though it impoverished their household for "several years."

23. Shimamura Taeko 1972, 65–67. Sakai's Edo subsidy seems high, at least in comparison with those granted by Tosa.

24. This discussion of Tannai is based on Tani Tannai 1791. In 1752 he received an Edo allowance of ten *koku* rice and a service allowance (*gohōkōryō*) of ten *koku*. According to the merchant Saitaniya, Tannai's father, Kakimori, who was already in Edo, should be able to bring back (i.e., save) seven *ryō* gold in an average year. I discuss the economic impact of Edo service on Tani Tannai more fully in Vaporis 2000, 205–222.

25. "Osamurai chū senzogaki keizu chō" n.d., vol. 24, entry for Tani Tannai.

26. "Ohōkōryō osadamegaki nuki chō" 1781, fol. 3. This document presents evidence of a subsidy program for different dates from the beginning of the seventeenth century until the 1720s. Retainers on long-term postings were able to receive their moving subsidies in either rice or silver. Similar information from the mid-eighteenth century is available in "Edo tsutome ōfuku kōgi yori watarimono kitei" 1750.

27. Miyaji relates a communication relayed to all Edo-based personnel that stated that "they have been adequately provided for, but that in case of emergencies the domain would assist with a loan, if requested and approved, to be repaid within five years. Miyaji Umanosuke 1832, fols. 37–38. The notice explained the domain's role in providing this service as being due to the difficulty of retainers securing loans in Edo (i.e., away from their native place where they likely had personal contacts and guarantors).

28. Miyagi ken 1966, 441–443. In Wakayama the allowances were referred to as *watarimono*. Two domain senior advisors serving in Edo in the early nineteenth century received 1,670 *ryō* each at departure, 310 *ryō* every other month while in Edo, and 650 *ryō* upon departure. They also received a 90-*ryō* supplement. Presumably these substantial funds were for dispersal to their retainers as well as for their own personal use. Wakayama kenshi hensan iinkai 1991, 561–562.

29. For a study of financial assistance program in Nanbu domain, see Morita 1952. Similar systems, some dating to the mid-seventeenth century, existed in Ogaki, Hachinohe, Tsugaru, Tsushima, and Kaga.

30. Isoda 2003, 31. The following quote is from the same page.

31. Isoda 2003, 41–47.

32. Almost 12 percent of the budget went toward entertainment of relatives and acquaintances. Isoda 2003, 77. Debt was also exacerbated of course by high rates of interest (18 percent) on loans. Isoda 2003.

33. Some retainers in fact may have lived better in Edo. Mori Yoshiki was able to purchase two horses while in service there, though he was not able to afford one back in Kōchi. He paid the considerable sum of six *ryō* for one of them. Mori Yoshiki 1793–1807, vol. 7, fol. 65.

34. For more on Tani and Saitaniya, see Vaporis 2000.

35. It is unclear here whether Tannai is referring to the three-man rice allotment he

was granted in 1748 after returning home from Edo or the raise his father received more recently, in 1750/1/9, or both. His father rose in status and income by a two-man rice allotment and four *koku* to the level of a seven-man allotment and twenty-four *koku*.

36. Tani Tannai 1791, fol. 12.

37. It was common practice to make two annual payments for staple items. Other major expenses for the household included brushes, dyeing costs, medicine, and salary for household help. Tani Tannai 1748–1754, fols. 3–4. Tannai was also required to pay a land tax on his residence in Kita Hōkōnin-chō of less than one-half (0.4519) *koku*, payable in low-quality rice, but he expected that this would be covered by a special subsidy granted retainers, such as his father, who accompanied the lord to Edo on alternate attendance. Specifically, the subsidy entailed the return of a portion of the payback to the lord.

38. Tani Tannai 1791, fols. 2–3.

39. Tani Tannai 1791, fols. 2–3.

40. Tani Tannai 1791, fol. 3–5. These payments (in *mon*) included 2,438 to Kon'ya (for dyeing? or for cloth and dyeing?); 2,331 for sake; 1,844 for medical expenses; 800 salary for maid; 757 for paper; 270 for fish; 240 for brushes; 538 for miscellaneous; and 837 unclear, for a total of 9,963 (144.93 *monme*).

41. Tani Tannai 1791, fols. 6–7.

42. Tani Tannai 1791, fol. 5.

43. Tani Tannai 1791, fol. 24

44. Tani Tannai 1791, fol. 5.

45. Tani Tannai 1791, fol. 6.

46. Tani Tannai 1791, fol. 6.

47. Tani Tannai 1791, fol. 17.

48. Tani Tannai 1791, fol. 6.

49. Craig 1961, 76–77.

50. Tani Tannai 1791, fols. 8–9.

51. Tannai's calculations were missing the land tax (0.4591 *koku*) and another, extraordinary impost (*nijū bu ichi*, 0.9 *koku*), a 5 percent tax on his actual intake of eighteen *koku*. These reduced Tannai's summer stipend payment to 4.6481 *koku*. Together with his year-end payment, Tannai's income stood at 16.6481 *koku*, which Saitaniya noted must cover additional rice purchases as well as the salaries of the household help and other expenses. The rice returned to retainers serving in Edo, according to Saitaniya's comments, appears to have been affected by the size of the domain's annual rice crop. Since the harvest was not good that year, he noted the payment would probably be less — 0.3 or 0.4 instead of 0.87 *koku* (fol. 10); in fact it ended up being more than Saitaniya thought: 0.57 *koku* (fol. 13).

52. Tani Tannai 1791, fol, 11.

53. Tani Tannai 1791, fols. 15–19.

54. Kōchi chihōshi kenkyūkai 1975. Another fire in 1751 destroyed more than three hundred households.

55. Hirao Michio 1965, 101–103.

56. Yamamura 1974, 129–131.

57. Shinji 1984, 123.

58. Shinji 1984, 123.

59. Yamakawa 2001, 154–155.

60. Tani Tannai 1791, fols. 9–10.

61. *TNK*, vol. 27, Kyōhō 17 [1732] 5th–9th month, "Jūhachi nichi kachū shoshi ni kari-age mai o ka suru" and Kōchi kenshi kensan iinkai 1968, 514. For example a 25 percent cut for the general retainer corps would mean a reduction of 12.5 percent for those on long-term Edo postings. Only the base stipend or fief, not office salary, was affected.

62. A contemporary record of subsidies offered by Tosa is "Ohōkōryō sadamegaki nuki chō" 1781. Even a low-ranking footsoldier like Tosa's Ogura Sadasuke, who had a salary of 9.2 *koku*, was able to send money home. On 1861/5/8 he sent a money envelope with three *ryō* to his family via the domain's messenger service. Sadasuke, like other Edo-based retainers, received supplements for service in the Tokugawa capital, includ-ing for his performance of guard duty. On other domains, see Morita 1952.

63. There was some cause for confusion perhaps, since the figure apparently changed from year to year. Kakimori received a subsidy (*Edo gohōkōryō* and *ongorikimai*) of 23.312 *koku* for his service in Edo in 1749–1750. (fols. 16–17)

64. Dates compiled from entry for Tani Tannai in "Osamurai chū senzogaki keizu chō" n.d., vol. 10; Kōchi ken jinmei jiten henshū iinkai 1971, 213–214; and Matsuyama 1971, 22–23. According to Shimamura Kaname, Tannai's father Kakimori went eight times but does not disclose his sources. Shimamura Kaname 1988, 32–35. "Osamurai chū senzogaki keizu chō" n.d., vol. 10 — hardly a complete source — only lists one occa-sion, in 1736, but we know from the "Record" that he was in Edo in 1750 as well. Father and son made the trip together a single time, in 1741.

65. Tani Tannai 1791, fols. 20–22.

66. Tani Tannai 1791, fol. 22.

67. Tani Tannai 1791, fol. 20.

68. Tani Tannai 1791, fols. 22–23.

69. Tani Tannai 1791, fols. 24–25.

70. Tani Tannai 1791, fol. 25.

71. Matsuyama 1971, 23–24.

72. Although the two arms routinely communicated with each other through high-speed messengers, this did not prevent tension from occurring between them. The per-manent Edo staff in particular was naturally more focused on the lord's responsibilities in terms of service to the shogunate and tended to prioritize this over problems and concerns in the domain. Roberts 1998, especially chapters 4 and 5. These differences between the two branches could lead to real political turmoil, including conflict over succession in the lord's house. Ravina 2004, 51.

73. Merchants were known to bribe domain officials to acquire these lucrative con-tracts. The compounds also provided an important source of by-employments for com-moners; Totsuka village, for example, had a contract with Owari domain to clean the garden at its Ichigaya compound. Shinjuku rekishi hakubutsukan 1994, 30.

74. In 1672, 262 Tosa men were assigned such duty, including 11 full samurai, 120 footsoldiers, and 131 pages. Mutō Yoshikazu 1990–1997, vol. 6, 242. *TMK*, vol. 23, Enpō shichinen [1679] ichigatsu nanoka-shichigatsu getsumatsu, fols. 32–42.

75. *TDK*, vol. 4, 33–38.

76. Iwasaki 1984, 81–84 and 132 n. 6.

77. The actual origins of the position are unclear, but Tosa may well have been the

first domain with a *rusui* (1609). Harafuji 1984, 41–42. That different domains established the position at different times lends credence to the assertion that the system was not a result of shogunal directive. This description of the Edo liaison, unless otherwise stated, is based on Harafuji's lengthy tome.

78. *TNK, Hōreki rokunen* [1756], jūgatsu-jūnigatsu no kan, "Nijūsan nichi jōtei ruishō su," fols. 11–12.

79. Roberts 1998, 168.

80. Kasaya 2000a, 77–85. The meetings were known as *yoriai* or *konkai* (lit. "hospitality gathering").

81. Kasaya 2000a, 88–102, 168–170.

82. Harafuji 1984, 271–276. Typically they came from the middle portion or bottom rungs of upper samurai rank in the retainer corps. Kasaya 2000a, 7–8.

83. "Nijūnichi oboegaki," quoting the "Miyaji nikki," in *TNK*, vol. 23, Kyōhō jūroku nen [1731], ichigatsu-shigatsu no kan, fol. 13.

84. Mori Yoshiki 1793–1807, vol. 6, fols. 49–51.

85. Mori Masana 1828–1856, vol. 1, fol. 59.

86. See, for example, the prohibition order from 1789, quoted in Harafuji 1984, 218 n. 4.

87. On Matsushiro's petition for target practice (accepted), see Kasaya 2000a, 17–21, for Chōshū's request to print paper bills, see pages 142–144. It was best to find a precedent involving one's own house, but if that did not exist then one involving houses of about the same status was next best.

88. The Edo liaison for Morioka carried a handbook containing a song, *otōjō no uta* (Song for Attending at Edo Castle), that made it easier to remember audience days, which were irregular. Yamamoto Hirofumi 1991, 25–27.

89. Henry Smith 1986a, 351.

90. See, for example, the directive issued to retainers in Kanazawa in 1746. Ishii 1981b, Doc. #172, 102–103.

91. Notehelfer 1992, 592.

92. Hata 2001, 11–12, 86. Shibue Io, whose story is beautifully recounted in McClellan 1985, was employed in a daimyo compound. Unusual for a merchant daughter, she was given instruction not only in reading, writing, various ladylike accomplishments (singing, dancing, and calligraphy), and Confucian studies, but also training in the martial arts. The substantial costs of service in a daimyo compound indicated that there were real social benefits for the young women. As she had to hire and pay for two maids as well as feed herself and them, this amounted to subsidizing the operation of the compound.

93. Walthall 1990, 473. It no doubt facilitated Shibue Io's marriage across status boundaries to Shibue Chūsai, a doctor in the employ of the Tsugaru lord. McClellan 1985. Sekiguchi Tōemon, the head of a family of landlords, moneylenders, night soil merchants, and village officials in Namamugi, near Edo, sent all three of his daughters to serve in the households of high-ranking daimyo. Walthall 1990, 465–469. The village headman of Shimoshioka, near Ōme, sent his only daughter, Michi, fifty kilometers to Edo to serve in the Tayasu house; later she married a doctor in the Tokugawa's employ. Masuda 1992, 109–111.

94. While there were differences from domain to domain, many had the following

hierarchy of ranks within the inner quarters: *rōjo, ochūrō, osoba, otsugi, okoshō, onakai,* and *osue.* Ego 1999, 11–12, 37–38. For Inoue's literary diary she kept in Edo, see Inoue Tsūjo 2001, 299–344.

95. Toyokazu's visits to his father at the main compound often did not go well. On one occasion, Toyooki repeatedly reprimanded Toyokazu, telling him to return to his residence at Shinagawa if he could not behave properly. Toyokazu, for his part, was often quite recalcitrant, once refusing a gift of some cloth from the lord, telling him that he did not need it. Interestingly, the lord instructed him, "Even if you receive something like an Edo picture of sumo wrestlers [i.e, a base gift], you should just accept it." Instead the lord gave the cloth to a number of the heir's attendants. Subsequently he criticized the heir for collecting silver pipes, grilling him, "What do you plan to do with them?" This exchange is related in Mori Yoshiki 1793–1807, vol. 7, fols. 94–95.

Chapter 5: The Daimyo Compounds: Place and Space

1. As quoted in Bodart-Bailey 2003, 100.

2. Oliphant 1860, 130–131.

3. E.g., Frenchman Marquis de Moges, who held that "the capital of Japan . . . contains two millions and a half of inhabitants." De Moges 2002, 315.

4. As in *Edo meisho hanagoyomi* (Famous Sites of Edo: An Almanac of Flowers, 1827), *Ehon Edo miyage* (Souvenir of Edo, published sometime between 1850 and 1868), *Tōtō saijiki* (Chronicle of Annual Events in the Eastern Capital, 1838). Tosa retainer Mori Masana referred to it as "Etō," "E" being the first character in "Edo" and "tō" meaning "capital." Mori Masana 1828–1856, vol. 1, fol. 37.

5. An exception is Coaldrake 1981, 1996, 2003, who discusses various architectural features of the compounds.

6. Coaldrake 1981, 246.

7. The story of how Edo castle and the surrounding areas were constructed is well known. See, for example, Yazaki 1968; McClain and Merriman, "Edo and Paris: Cities of Power," in McClain, Merriman, and Ugawa 1994, and a number of other essays in this volume are relevant. In Japanese, Naitō Akira 1972 is the standard work.

8. Coaldrake has a number of convenient maps and a reproduction of the spiral design as found originally in Naitō Akira 1972. Coaldrake 1981, 244–245, 247.

9. Bendix 1978, 333.

10. According to the survey, dating from 1869, *buke-chi* made up 68.6 percent, townsman districts (*machi-chi*) 15.8 percent, and shrine and temple land 15.6 percent. However, about 20 percent of the land classified as *machi-chi* was actually controlled by warrior households. At the same time, some warriors built tenement housing on their property and rented it out to commoners. The daimyo compounds, according to a Tokugawa census from 1856, comprised 7.48 million *tsubo,* or 57 percent of all warrior land in the city. Miyazaki 1992, 130–133.

11. Fujioka 1977, 248–249, 260–261. The figure of six hundred *daimyō yashiki* appears in Nishiyama Matsunosuke and others 1989, 143, but the documentary basis for that figure is unclear. Fujino Tamotsu writes that according to the *Edo zusetsu* of 1799, there were 265 upper compounds and 734 middle and lower ones, a total of 999. Fujino 1964, 95. Still, Fujino's figure does not take into consideration the many other auxiliary

compounds that domains had. In the English-language literature, Timon Screech, for example, states that there were "near one thousand official compounds and their associated stores." Screech 1996, 21–22. In part the numbers depend on when and what one is counting. According to a shogunal census from 1856 there were 874 pieces of land granted to the daimyo and 163 other pieces used by daimyo that were under the administration of the city magistrate or an intendant (*daikan*). Miyazaki 1992, 132–133.

12. This paragraph is based on Jinnai 1995, 22–24. The quote below is on page 23.

13. This and the following quote are from the Englishman George Smith 1861, 303.

14. Hirai 2004, especially page 25 (residences of the Asano and Kuroda houses). Of course, many of Tokyo's parks have their origins in the gardens of the daimyo lords, Kōrakuen (Mito) and Rikugien (Kōriyama) parks and Meiji shrine perhaps being the most famous examples.

15. Jinnai 1992, 27.

16. "Daimyō yashiki no kadan," in Shinjuku rekishi hakubutsukan 1994, 76–80. The standard work on daimyo gardens is Shirahata 1997.

17. Alcock 1863, vol. 2, 230–231, 131.

18. Ujiie 1991, 78–81, 101.

19. Kodera 1989, especially 2–34, 94–125.

20. Pitelka 2005, 142. He also notes that the Owari lord had another kiln in his garden (Rakurakuen) at his main residence. In the early nineteenth century Raku wares were also produced there.

21. Tōkyō-to Edo-Tōkyō hakubutsukan 1997, 4.

22. Eighteen others had property between 50,000 and 100,000 *tsubo*, and three had estates covering from 100,000 to 300,000 *tsubo*. Tsukahira 1966, 92.

23. McClatchie 1890, 167.

24. Suzuki 1992, 180. E.g., Tatsuno domain purchased a *kakae yashiki* of 867 *tsubo* contiguous with its middle compound of 17,115 *tsubo*. Tōkyō-to kyōiku bunka zaidan 1997, vol. 1, 333.

25. The remaining 77.6 percent was land granted by the shogunate (*hairyō yashiki*). Miyazaki 1992, 132–133. This survey contained information on 260 of the 266 daimyo. According to a shogunal survey in 1856 there were 888 plots of land identified as *kakae yashiki*. Of these, 668 (75 percent) were controlled by daimyo and the Tokugawa's direct retainers. Iwabuchi 2004, 131–168.

26. McClatchie 1890, 157.

27. There are a number of these screens, most notably those at the National Museum of History (Rekihaku), the Idemitsu Museum, and the Tsuyama Museum (Tsuyama kyōdo hakubutsukan). Only the Rekihaku's focuses on the *bushi* part of town. Unfortunately, Tosa's main residence is obscured by clouds in this work. For a study of the screens, see Ozawa Hiromu and Maruyama Nobuhiko 1993.

28. "Ochiboshū," 89, as quoted in Coaldrake 1981, 255.

29. Coaldrake 1996, 197. He notes that none remain today. The only example of an *onarimon*, a gate built for a shogunal visit, is now located at Nishi Honganji in Kyoto.

30. A contemporary record describes the most famous *onari* gate, that of the daimyo of Fukui: "Carvings of dragons are wrapped around the pillars. The pillars and all the beam ends, together with the end of the main architrave above the entrance, and the fittings above, have sculptures of *shishi*. The tiebeams, cornice and architrave, all have

relief carvings depicting scenes of the 'Eight Sages of the Bamboo Grove' on the door panels and above the waist ties at the sides of the gate. It is entirely covered with gold leaf." "Kōnen oboegaki," quoted in Coaldrake 1981, 267.

31. Coaldrake 1981, 198. Still, some of the roof tiles dating from the eighteenth and nineteenth centuries excavated from Kaga's main compound were found to have been covered in gold leaf. Oikawa 2004, 20.

32. *TKK*, Bunka 3 [1806], ichigatsu-gogatsu no kan, "Shigatsu futsuka Bakufu Ōmetsuke yori kasaku ni kanshitaru kaijō ni settsu."

33. Coaldrake 1996, 199. *Aobyōshi*, a compendium of regulations and etiquette published in 1840–1841, devotes an entire section to them.

34. Coaldrake 1996, 199. After the Meireki fire, roof tiles were allowed only for the daimyo compounds, which must have made them stand out that much more to observers. Coaldrake 1981, 255.

35. Nishigori Gohei, "Tobu nikki," in Harada Tomoko 1975, 687–688.

36. Kaempfer 1999, 353.

37. Coaldrake 1981, 280, describes the gate. Other compound gates exist from Hikone domain at Gōtokuji temple, from Tokushima domain at Saichōji, both in Setagaya ward, and from Okayama shinden domain at Renkōin in Ōta ward. Edo Tōkyō tatemono no en 2001, 13–14.

38. Naitō Akira 1972, 10–11. On post–Meireki fire reconstruction, see Kikuchi 1987, 69–108.

39. There was a chronic shortage of warrior land, creating a waiting list of Tokugawa retainers and daimyo who had been approved land grants but for whom there was no land available at the time (e.g., in 1815, there were 35 such parties; from 1815 to 1828 there were 240). To even apply for land to the magistrate of construction (*fushin bugyō*) one had to first find available land and then beat other competition for it. Miyazaki 1992, 137–138.

40. The *akamon* are visible in many woodblock prints and *doro-e*. See, for example, Hiroshige's prints of Kasumigaseki and Hibiya. Henry D. Smith 1986a, prints #2–#3.

41. "Jōkyō gannenbun jōge ninzu aratamegaki" 1684. The location of the middle compound was a puzzle to local historians. In fact, until 1698 the middle compound was contiguous with the main residence. As a result, in Tosa documents they are treated as one, the middle compound subsumed into the main one. The same was true in some shogunal maps, as in the magistrate of construction's image of the Kajibashi area before 1698 (Bakufu fushin bugyō 1985–1988, 133), but not in the earlier (Kan'ei 1624–1633) period map of Edo.

42. "Kōdai hyakuninjūgo, Shotoku monjo, gan ni, san yon" 1711–1714. This census was compiled in 1712. Other followed in 1712, 1725, 1768, and 1842.

43. See Miyazaki 1992, 132, for a discussion of the dual nature of this type of land.

44. "Shiba oyashiki no mōyō zu" n.d.; Gotō Seijun 1800b, fols. 15–16.

45. "Kōdai hyakuninjūgo, Shotoku monjo, gan ni, san yon" 1711–1714.

46. These requests to live in townsman lodging appear to have been common early in the period. Yamamoto cites evidence from Satsuma, Kumamoto, and Choshu domains. Yamamoto Hirofumi 1991, 96; Miyazaki Katsumi, "Daimyō Edo yashiki no kyōkai sochi," in Miyazaki and Yoshida 1994, 17.

47. *TCK*, vol. 1, Meiwa 5 [1768] first month, fols. 98–100.

48. Approximately the same figures were reported to the shogunate in 1802, although the domain in giving up some land (1,524 *tsubo*) at Shiba was also granted a second middle compound, at Hibiya (1,126 *tsubo*).

49. Tsukahira 1966, 91–93, for example, makes no mention of change in his account of the compounds.

50. Miyaji Nakae 1845, vol. 1, fols. 10, 22.

51. Years later it would do so again, confiscating a Tosa residence at Hatchōbori in 1721 for reasons that are unclear. The domain had apparently displeased the shogunate because a request for an extension on the evacuation order to have sufficient time to clean the premises was declined. *TtsK*, vol. 3, Kyōhō rokunen [1721], ichigatsu-shichigatsu, "Gogatsu kokonoka meini yori Hatchōbori tei," fols. 1–5.

52. "Tadayoshi sama otomodachi narabini Edo jōzume hitodaka chō," Shōhō 2 [1645], *KNS*, Doc. #17–10; Mutō Yoshikazu 1990–1997, vol. 6, 33–34. The Levee Residence was granted in 1658. It is not known precisely when Tosa was granted land for the middle compound, but in the general literature on Tosa it has heretofore been held, incorrectly, that the middle compound was always at Shiba.

53. Miyaji Nakae 1845, vol. 2.

54. Maps of this area before and after 1698 are available in Bakufu fushin bugyō 1985–1988, vol. 1, 133–134. See also Vaporis 1994b, 4–5. On how to read these and other maps of Edo, see Soda 1999). A small portion of Tosa's Kajibashi residence was subject to a rescue excavation in 1992 before the building Kokusai foramu was constructed on the site. Except for some ceramics and the stone wall and moat dividing Tosa's and Awa's compounds, a relatively small quantity of artifacts were recovered. See Tōkyō-to kyōiku bunka zaidan, Tōkyō-to maizō bunkazai senta- 1994.

55. Miyaji Nakae 1845, vol. 3, fol. 22.

56. Miyaji Nakae 1845, vol. 2, fol. 23; *TNK*, vol. 37, Kyōhō 20 [1735]/sixth month–twelfth month.

57. Miyaji Nakae 1845, vol. 2, fol. 32.

58. *TKK*, vol. 5, Kansei 2 [1790]/first month–fourth month, fol. 50.

59. Tōkyō-to Chiyoda ku 1998, 424. This six-way exchange was carried out to acquire a much larger residence for Sadanobu's retirement. Miyazaki 1992, 144–145. All "fixtures" — tatami matting, translucent paper doors, opaque sliding doors, *fusuma*, rain shutters, garden trees, and rocks — were considered private property and therefore to be taken to the next compound when an "exchange" occurred. Suzuki Masao 1992, 182–183. Tosa's compound at Tsukiji was obtained in 1826 in the same fashion described above; that is, a portion of Tosa's Shinagawa compound was, pro forma, offered in exchange. Its borders were then expanded through a series of three purchases of adjoining land, and finally the entire area was enclosed before the teenaged heir Toyoteru made it his residence in 1832. Miyaji Nakae 1845, vol. 3, fols. 16–17; *TSK*, vol. 64, Tenpō 1 [1830] and vol. 66, Tenpō 3 [1832].

60. Kelly 1994, 313. The expression in Japanese is "*hanabi to kenka wa Edo no hana.*"

61. For a chart detailing the extent of damage in Edo due to fire, by decade, see Nishiyama 1983, 18–19.

62. The lower compound at Shinagawa, near Edo Bay, burned only once. Warehouses at Hatchōbori, Shindenjima, and Kon'ya-chō each burned several times. Information

on fires at Tosa's compounds is drawn from a number of sources, including Miyaji Umanosuke 1832; Miyaji Nakae 1845; Mutō Yoshikazu 1990–1997; ms. "Edo Fushimi oshakan enjōki" n.d.; and, *YKS*. For a complete list of fires affecting Tosa's Edo residences, see Vaporis 1994a, 9. Earthquakes caused damage in and of themselves, of course, as in 1649 when Tosa's three major compounds were damaged, but also due to the fires that sometimes followed them.

63. "Nijūichi nichi Edo Kanda Sakuma-machi shukka taika to naru," *TSK*, vol. 62, Bunsei 11 [1828], fols. 15–16.

64. Gotō Seijun 1800c, vol. 1, fol. 32.

65. Mori Yoshiki 1793–1807, vol. 7, fols. 117–118. These events took place during the winter of 1802.

66. *TMK* 37, Tenna ni nen [1682] shichigatsu tsuitachi-jūnigatsu getsumatsu no kan, "Nijūhachi nichi Shibatei ruishō," fols. 66–73; *TCK*, An'ei kyūnen [1780] ichigatsu-jūnigatsu no kan, "Tōka jū yokka Kajibashi jōtei shukka," fols. 1–6. Kururi domain designated evacuation areas in the four cardinal directions. Chiba ken 1990, 446–447.

67. *TCK*, Tenmei 7 [1787], rokugatsu-kugatsu no kan, "Nijūshichi nichi kore yori saki jūman koku no kakaku ni jun shite," fols. 1–18.

68. On the fire of 1756, see *TNK dai 126 kan*, Hōreki 10 [1760], fourth–twelfth months; on the 1780 and 1784 cases, see Miyaji Nakae 1845, vol. 2, fols. 49, 55.

69. *TCK*, An'ei 9 [1780], jūnigatsu no kan, "Jūgatsu jūyokka Kajibashi jōtei shukka," fols. 13–16. Tosa was blamed for causing a fire at its Shiba compound that affected its neighbor (Awa) and was ordered under restraint in 1756. Tosa records claim, however, that the fire had spread there from elsewhere. (Mutō Yoshikazu 1990–1997, vol. 5, 422.) Again in 1866 Tosa was ordered under restraint for twenty-one days even though just a small area of the neighboring compound had been affected. *BMI*, vol. 5, 465–469.

70. The document that related this information is from a later date, 1769/7/12. *TCK* Meiwa rokunen [1769], rokugatsu-jūnigatsu no kan, "Jūichinichi Kyōto Edo kami ya-shiki ruishō," fols. 1–2.

71. Miyaji Nakae 1845, vol. 2, fols. 44–45. Participating in this annual event could be costly, as there was great social pressure to appear in fine clothes with the proper equipment and adequate number of subretainers and menials.

72. Mutō Yoshikazu 1990–1997, vol. 6, 2. The account comes from the "Haramiishi-ke ki" (1657).

73. After the Meireki fire in 1657, fourteen daimyo, including Tosa's, were given leave, twenty-two were ordered to postpone their trips to Edo, and seventeen were excused from attendance altogether. Similar concessions were granted after major fires in 1721, 1772, and 1855. Tsukahira 1966, 54. Yamauchi Toyochika was already en route to Edo when he received word of a major fire in Edo from a Tokugawa messenger, who relayed instructions that the Tosa lord had the option to delay his departure for Edo for several months. Having already crossed the Inland Sea and proceeded as far as Harima province, Toyochika continued on to Edo. Mutō Yoshikazu 1990–1997, vol. 5, 420–421.

74. Roberts 1998, 20.

75. McClain, "Space, Power, Wealth and Status in Seventeenth-Century Osaka," in McClain and Wakita 1999, 64; Hayashi Reiko, "Provisioning Edo," in McClain, Merriman, and Ugawa 1994.

76. Mori Yasuhiro 1991, 123–138.

77. Mori Yasuhiro 1991, 47–55, 52–53. The number of warehouse compounds was as follows: 25 (1657), 95 (1690), 125 (1830–1844). Almost without exception these belonged to western domains, a few of which had more than one compound. A map of Osaka indicating the location of the warehouses has been reproduced in McClain and Osamu 1999, 66.

78. *TYK*, vol. 1, 569.

79. A crude, hand-drawn map of Tosa's Osaka compound can be found in Gotō Seijun 1800a, fol. 5. Four images from Kurume domain's Osaka compound have been reproduced in Ōsaka shiritsu hakubutsukan 1996, 12–13, 23.

80. Morishita Tōru, "Hagi han kura yashiki to Ōsaka shichū," in Tsukada and Yoshida 2001, 69–96. Saga had twenty rental units along the western moat of its compound. In Tosa's case there were rental properties in both parts of the compound amounting to about 267 *tsubo* (764 sq. m). The space enclosed by a fence containing the tenements and gardens in both parts amounted to about 20 percent of the area. Tosa's rental properties ran all along the southern part of its land, though they were placed outside the domain's compound. Luke Roberts and I "discovered" this map (GM Doc. #4442), the only extant map of the domain's Osaka compound, in the Gotō family collection in Aki city, an event that made the local Kōchi newspaper.

81. Mori Yasuhiro 1994b, 18–20. Tosa had thirty-five retainers permanently stationed there. Mori Yasuhiro 1990, 34–35.

82. *TNK*, vol. 7, Kyōhō 12 (1727), fols. 1–84. While recuperating from an illness in Osaka in 1727 on his first trip home as lord, Yamauchi Toyonobu (r. 1725–1767) hosted Noh performances on five separate occasions, with actors brought in from Kyoto.

83. Kaempfer, quoting the Kyoto investigator of population, recorded that there were 137 daimyo compounds in the city. Kaempfer 1999, 323. Tosa sold its residence at Kawaramachi in 1646 and purchased one in Buzenjima machi, 1,522 *tsubo* in area, where it remained for the duration of the period. Uematsu, Nakajima, and Tani 2000, 33–34. For a map of the Kyoto residence dating from 1795, see GM Doc. #4434 (misclassified as a map of Edo: "Edo kami yashiki heimen zu").

84. A Tosa census from 1697 lists 186 people from the domain living in Kyoto: 110 males and 76 females. Most of the males and probably all the females were support staff. Some of the males could be domain scholars studying in the city. For Osaka, the number of women was substantially fewer: 32 females (and 111 males). *TMK* 86, Genroku jūnen [1697] "Jūichigatsu kokonoka kirishitan shūmon aratamesho o bakufu ni dasu," fols. 55–57.

85. The residence was also lent to Tokugawa officials on occasion. For one example, see *TKK* Kyōwa gannen [1801] ichigatsu–jūnigatsu no kan, "Nanoka ukeoi ni yori Kyōto shitei o rōjū," fols. 72–77. The domain also had another residence at Kuwahara-chō, where the first Tosa lord's wife had lived, but it was sold in 1647. *TYK*, vol. 3, 501–503.

86. The Kyoto liaison helped to coordinate Tosa potter Morita Kyūemon's tours of kilns in places such as Kyoto, Zeze, Kuwana, Seto, and Shigaraki. Cort 2004, 107–108.

87. Sugimori 1999, 25–27. Some of these purveyors worked for more than one domain and about seventy daimyo without residences in Kyoto employed them as well.

88. Alcock 1863, vol. 2, 116.

89. Kaga's residence at Hongō was exceptional in that it was not enclosed by perimeter barracks to the same extent as most main compounds.

90. These comments are based on the study of a number of compound maps for domains such as Tosa, Awa, Kaga. Kururi: Tōkyō-to kyōiku bunka zaidan, Tōkyō-to maizō bunka senta- 1994, 712–714; Chiba ken 1990, 416–418.

91. McClatchie 1890, 167.

92. McClatchie 1890, 173.

93. Tosa's riding ground was located next to the archery range at its main residence. Gotō Seijun 1800c, fol. 31. There was a second riding area as well outside the compound. Because of this, he notes, townsmen were prohibited from using carts in the area. Gotō Seijun 1800c, fols. 9–10.

94. Chiba ken 1990, 416–418. This description is largely based on a rough map sketched by a retainer (p. 418).

95. Naruse Kōji, "Edo hantei no chika kūkan: Tōkyō daigaku Hongō kōnai no iseki o rei ni," 95–96, in Miyazaki and Yoshida 1994. These underground spaces generally did not exist in the lowland commoner sections of the city, where the soft soil was not suited to such use.

96. Hosokawa Tadashi, "Bunken shiryō kara mita Rigakubu Nanagōkan chite," 495–498, in Tōkyō daigaku iseki chōsashitsu 1989.

97. Ozawa Emiko 1998, 17. Not all underground spaces were related to concerns with fires. In at least one domain residence (Arima), an underground passage was dug from near the front gate to the stage area near the inner quarters. This was apparently a direct underground route used by actors invited by the lord. Ozawa Emiko 1998, 28–29.

98. See Naruse Kōji, "Edo hantei no chika kūkan — Tōkyō daigaku Hongō kōnai no iseki o rei ni," in Miyazaki and Yoshida 1994, 94–99, for an analysis of the various types of underground spaces. The Tokugawa used cellars near the Fujimi tower in Edo Castle to store gold. Temples also used them to safeguard their treasures. Ozawa Emiko 1998, 18–27.

99. Koizumi 1990a, 193–194; and Koizumi 1990b, 152.

100. Terashima Kōichi, "Kaga han Edo hantei ato no hakkutsu," 52–53, in Edo iseki kenkyūkai 1991.

101. Edward Kidder, "Summary," in Toritsu gakkō iseki chōsakai 1990, 256–257.

102. Edward Kidder, "Summary," in Toritsu gakkō iseki chōsakai 1990, 256; Terashima, "Kaga han Edo hantei ato," 33–34. I observed this bracing system at the Shiodome site during several visits there in 1994. For photos, see Tōkyō-to kyōiku bunka zaidan, Tōkyō-to maizō bunka senta- 1997, vol. 1, 339–340, 371.

103. See Itō 1982.

104. A large amount of material, including thirty-five refined sea-salt containers, was disposed of in the garden pond at Kaga domain's main compound after a shogunal visit in 1629. Ogawa Nozomu, "Daimyō yashiki shutsudo no yakishio," in Edo iseki kenkyūkai 1992, 151.

105. Tōkyō-to kyōiku bunka zaidan Tōkyō-to maizō bunkazai senta- 1994, vol. 1, 20–26, 724.

106. Hagio Masae, "Edo jidai shoki no enkai no shokki rui," in Edo iseki kenkyūkai 1992, 205–206; Nishida Yasutani, "Shutsudo tōjiki ni saguru shoku bunka," in Edo iseki kenkyūkai 1992, 56–62. It has been suggested that disposable chopsticks, which have been found at a number of sites other than the Kaga residence, may have been used

when eating meat. The use of disposable chopsticks has been recorded as far back as the Nara period.

107. Population density for the samurai population in Edo (650,000 in 1721) is estimated to have been 16,816 people per square kilometer, roughly one-fourth the figure for the townsmen population of 600,000 (67,317 people per sq. km). There was also an estimated townsman population of 50,000 living on shrine and temple land (with a population density of 5,682 people per sq. km). Based on figures in Sekiyama 1958, 227–230.

108. This regulation for Hagi dates from 1686. Yamamoto Hirofumi 1991, 153.

109. Ishii 1981b, vol. 10, 1291, 1313, 1319. The notice is from 1820/2/23.

110. Vaporis 1996, 296.

111. Alcock 1863, vol. 2, 116.

112. Ishii 1981b, vol. 10, 1319–1320. This caused great discomfort to the men on hot days, and because of negative reaction these regulations were later relaxed.

113. Yamamoto Hirofumi 1991, 155.

114. Yamamoto Hirofumi 1991, 56–57.

115. Yamamoto Hirofumi 1991, 100–102.

116. Yamamoto Hirofumi 1991, 156–157.

117. Suzuki Eizō 1993, 263–266. The lord of Hirado lists all the compounds Nezumi stole from as well as the amounts taken in Matsura Seizan 1978–1982, vol. 7, 26–37, 111.

118. Miyaji Umanosuke 1832, vol. 1, fols. 25–27. According to Miyaji, the daimyo were ordered to submit to the shogunate a list of goods stolen. The thief was a particular headache for a handful of daimyo, including that of Hitotsubashi domain, whose residences he broke into repeatedly. Nezumi kozō became the source of legend, including that he stole to give to the poor, like Robin Hood. In fact, he never stole anything other than money nor hurt a single person. He is also said to have left a note on the Noh stage in one daimyo compound to the effect that he had viewed the performance put on for the lord. Suzuki Eizō 1993, 201.

119. As a rule, commoners were prohibited from extending their buildings out into the road in Edo, although they were permitted an angled overhanging or awning of three *shaku* (about 91 centimeters). In key business areas such as Nihonbashi dōri and Honchō dōri it was permissible to extend into the road one *ken* (1.82 meters) as long as traffic was not being obstructed. Tamai 1986, 85–95.

120. Tōkyō-to Chiyoda-ku 1998, 451.

121. Tōkyō-to Chiyoda-ku 1998, 459–460.

122. The same occurred in Osaka and other Tokugawa-administered cities as well. Tōkyō-to Chiyoda-ku 1998, 459.

123. Similarly, daimyo were ordered to dispatch men outside the compound in case of fire within several hundred meters of the compound. *TtaK* jūgo kan, Kyōhō san nen [1718], "Jūgatsu nijūichi nichi rojū yori teigai ni san chō," fol. 37.

124. The guard posts, first established in 1629/3, were assigned to either one daimyo (220 such posts in the early eighteenth century) or more commonly to a group of several lesser daimyo and/or bannermen (680 posts). Some daimyo, though, turned to contracting labor to fulfill this obligation, particularly from the middle of the period. The number of guard posts was related to the size of the daimyo compound, with larger

compounds having more posts. Itō 1987, 167–169, 179–186. On the *tsujiban* system, see also Iwabuchi 2004, 189–273.

125. Quoted in Itō 1987, 169–170.

126. Gotō Seikō 1790, fols. 44–45.

127. "Zai Edo tsukaiban, koshō, wakatō, monban nado shohatto" 1622–1629.

128. Tōkyō-to Chiyoda-ku 1998, 460–461.

129. Ikegami 1995, especially chapters 5–7.

130. Kasaya 1980, 211–212.

131. Kasaya 1980, 215–217.

132. Kasaya 1980, 213. Kawai was avenged by the murdered man's older brother.

133. Kasaya 1980, 226–228.

134. "Bushi kokoroegaki," quoted in Kasaya 1980, 237.

135. Hatano Jun, "Edo's Water Supply," in McClain, Merriman, and Ugawa 1994, 234–246.

136. *TYK*, vol. 4, 477–478.

137. E.g., Toritsu gakkō iseki chōsakai 1991, 7.

138. Few toilets have been positively identified as such in Edo samurai sites, perhaps because whenever a cavity is excavated, it is usually described simply as a "hole" (*dokō*), without its function or use being fully examined. One reason for the difficulty in identifying toilets is probably that human waste from the daimyo compounds was removed from the premises and transported to the countryside, where it was used by farmers as fertilizer. On toilets and waste disposal, see Itō 1987, 268–279; Hanley 1997, 110–124; and Walthall 1998, 279–303.

139. "Shinpojiumu Edo o horu: happyaku yachō no kōkogaku," in Ōtsuka and Koizumi 1994, 182–183. On the cleanliness of Edo water relative to contemporaneous Europe, see Hanley 1997, 104–128.

140. A table listing thirty-seven of them and a map indicating their locations can be found in Tōkyō-to Edo Tōkyō hakubutsukan 1997, 147. Iwabuchi Reiji has identified fifty-three. Iwabuchi 2003, 139–140. This discussion of daimyo compound shrines and temples is based on Iwabuchi 2003, unless otherwise noted. At least twelve residences of Tokugawa bannermen or housemen also had religious institutions on their premises that were sometimes opened to commoners. On the topic of religious sites in daimyo residences, see also Yoshida Masataka 2000, 64–82.

141. Pilgrims to Kururi domain's Fudō temple gained access through a rear gate and traversed a path that took them between the official-administrative part of the compound and the space where retainers lived. Chiba ken 1990, 418.

142. This amount represented the equivalent of 4.6 percent of the income collected by the shrine's main branch in Marugame domain from the 1780s on. Thal 2005, 337 n. 10. Income was also forwarded from the domain's Konpira shrine in Osaka as well.

143. Nakagawa Sugane, "Inari Worship in Early Modern Osaka," in McClain and Wakita 1999, 23–24. Townsmen in Osaka in the early nineteenth century visited the Inari shrine within the precincts of Matsue's compound in the belief that it would help children to overcome smallpox.

144. Hauser 1974, 23, 59–64. For a list of commodities shipped by Osaka wholesalers in 1714, see Hayashi Reiko, "Provisioning Edo," in McClain, Merriman, and Ugawa

1994, 219. In 1724 103,500 bales of cotton, 112,196 casks of soy sauce, and 265,395 casks of sake were shipped from Osaka to Edo.

145. The classic study of the Kantō economy is Itō 1966.

146. Hayashi Reiko, "Provisioning Edo," in McClain, Merriman, and Ugawa 1994, 218.

147. Najita 1987, 173.

148. Hitotsubashi officials in Edo sold the rights to night soil from the domain residence to one Hanbei from Tanashi village (Tama district) for the price of 1,500 large daikon, 2,000 middle-sized daikon, or two *ryō* in cash. Hanley 1987, 1–26.

149. Hachinohe shishi hensaniinkai 1977–1982. The domain also regularly shipped indigo and horses to Edo, presumably for sale. Miura 1990, 29. Of course a variety of commercial goods were also being shipped both ways (pp. 37–40). This trend, Miura notes, became discernible during the late seventeenth and early eighteenth centuries.

150. Some available figures for the volume of rice in *koku* shipped from Kaga to Osaka for the following years (in parentheses) are: 107,790 (1705), 132,000 (1746), 80,000 (1788), 73,000 (1848). Rice shipped to Edo varied as well: 33,075 (1705), 21,570 (1746), 18,375 (1788), 18,360 (1804), 18,260 (1848). Mori Yasuhiro 1994a, 46–48.

151. Neville 1958, 60.

152. E.g., Tosa relied on Kōchi lumber to an undetermined degree to rebuild its Edo residences after periodic fires, and on at least one occasion local carpenters were brought to Edo to do the work. Ironically, this produced cost overruns rather than savings. *TYK*, vol. 1, 409–414. For Okayama, see Okayama kenshi hensan iinkai 1985, 588–591; for Kanazawa, see McClain 1982, 52.

153. See, for example, Miyaji Umanosuke 1832, vol. 1, fol. 41; vol. 3, fols. 6, 10–11, 13; vol. 4, fol. 30.

154. The trip of 250 *ri* (1,061 km) went from Urado Bay to Tosa's warehouses, located in the early eighteenth century at Minami Kon'ya-chō or Minami Hatchōbori. "Tosa no kuni kenchichō" n.d..

155. Deetz 1966, 4.

156. Tōkyō-to kyōiku iinkai, ed. 1991, 48–49; Iidamachi iseki chōsakai 1995, 590–591; Edward Kidder, "Summary," in Toritsu gakkō iseki chōsakai 1991, 269–270. Table salt was sold in *yakishio* jars, in which the salt had been baked to remove bitterness. Ogawa Nozomu, "Daimyō yashiki shutsudo no yakishio tsubo," in Edo iseki kenkyūkai 1992, 128–162; Watanabe Makoto, "Yakishio tsubo," in Edo iseki kenkyūkai 1992, 107–127.

157. Tōkyō-to Chiyoda-ku 1998, 468–469.

158. Hasegawa Kōtoku, "Hongoku no miso, shōyu chinchō" (part of series "Kaga-han Edo yashiki seikatsu kō), *Hokkoku shinbun*, 1987/8/19, 8.

159. Harada Nobuo 2004, 98–99.

160. Tōkyō-to kyōiku iinkai, ed. 1991, 60–61. According to the text, most roof tiles for the daimyo compounds were made in Imado, a manufacturing center located northeast of the city (present-day Taitō ward); however, no support is offered for this statement. Imado ware (*Imado yaki*) and Imado dolls (*Imado ningyō*) were famous products in the Edo period. I have been unable to find any systematic study of roof tiles. Stamped impressions that give the place of production inform us that certain tiles were made in the domains. Further study of roof tiles and other commodities promises to enlarge

our understanding of the development of the regional Edo economy and the economic relationship between the domains and Edo.

161. Nagoya shi hakubutsukan 2002, 49.

162. Miyazaki 1999, n.p. The lumber was sized and pieced together in Hagi, then disassembled, shipped, and reassembled in Edo; 11,000 pieces of lumber and 265,562 copper and ceramic roof tiles were also acquired from Osaka.

163. For example, after the devastating Meireki fire, Tosa restocked its Edo compounds with local Odo-yaki ceramic ware. *TTK*, vol. 1, 135. The document dates from 1657/3/13. In 1681, after another fire in the lord's residence destroyed all the plates and other ceramic eatery, the senior advisor Hiramiishi had replacements sent from Kōchi. Mutō Yoshikazu 1990–1997, vol. 6, 282.

164. Richard Wilson, "Kyoto Ware and Rihei Ware," in Iidamachi iseki chōsakai 1995, 563–568.

165. Richard Wilson, "Kyoto Ware and Rihei Ware," in Iidamachi iseki chōsakai 1995, 564–565.

166. Richard Wilson, "Kyoto Ware and Rihei Ware," in Iidamachi iseki chōsakai 1995, 563. Rihei wares, however, were not perfect Kyoto copies. They suggest the requirements of the military elite, "where official display and the need to impress are more important than personal enjoyment and intimacy" (p. 577). I.e., samurai aesthetics and values were still important, despite the strength of Kyoto influences on Rihei ware.

167. Morimoto Ichirō, "Edo shichū no busshi ryūtsū to seikatsu yōgu," in Edo iseki kenkyūkai 1991, 145–148. At the Naitō domain compound (Shinjuku), wares from thirty-seven different kilns were unearthed. Tōkyō-to Shinjuku-ku 1992, vol. 3, 20. It might be tempting to interpret the large number of ceramics found in pits as evidence that Tokugawa Japanese treated them as a disposable commodity, but the many examples of repaired pieces that have been excavated testify to a concern for economizing. Kobiki Harunobu, "Dewa Matsuyama tei no hakkutsu: Hakuō iseki no hakkutsu," in Edo iseki kenkyūkai 1991, 68.

168. For example, according to "Shinpojiumu Edo o horu," in Ōtsuka and Koizumi 1994, 219, the five hundred *tokkuri* found at a Tosa site confirms what big drinkers Tosa men were (and by reputation still are). About three-quarters of all ceramic artifacts at the Hakuō site, Matsuyama domain's main compound, were *tokkuri,* some of them with merchant trademarks stamped on them. Kobiki Harunobu, "Dewa Matsuyama tei no hakkutsu: Hakuō iseki no hakkutsu," in Edo iseki kenkyūkai 1991, 68. In theory the sake bottles were to be returned when empty, but in late Edo this system stopped for some reason. Kobiki posits that perhaps the cost of production declined, that it became too much trouble to recycle them, or that there was a drop in consumers' sense of social responsibility.

169. Store names have been found not only on sake bottles but also on dishes, indicating that food and drink were sometimes delivered to domain compounds. Tōkyō-to kyōiku iinkai 1991, 48. In Edo the most common type of *tokkuri* by far was the ash-glazed Seto-Mino variety, whereas in the Kinai region Bizen and Tanba wares predominated. Nagasako Shin'ya, "Kinsei 'tokkuri' no sho yōsō," in Edo iseki kenkyūkai 1992, 76–79.

170. Nagoya shi hakubutsukan 2002, 52–53, 150.

171. Tōkyō-to Shinjuku-ku 1992, 10–13.

172. Cort 2004, 112.

173. For example, Owari domain imported clay from Seto for use in the garden (Rakurakuen) kiln at the main compound at Ichigaya. Shinjuku rekishi hakubutsukan 1994, 30–39.

174. Kobiki 1991, 65–67, and Toritsu gakkō iseki chōsakai 1990, vol. 2, 93–95, 270–271.

Chapter 6: Life in the Capital

1. McEwan 1962, 36.

2. Vaporis 1996, 296.

3. Smith 1986b, 346. Tokyo did not recover its Edo-period population levels until 1890.

4. McClain, Merriman, and Ugawa 1994, 13.

5. Sekiyama 1958, 228.

6. While the figures for the Tokugawa retainers are based on hard evidence, the remainder of his estimates are very rough. For example, as we have seen, the percentage of a domain's retainer corps serving in Edo varied. Sakura domain (110,000 *koku*), for example, maintained almost a third (31.7 percent) of its retainer corps, 777 out of 2,448 men, in its compounds (although we do not know the overall size of its support staff).

7. Izushi-chō yakuba sōmuka chōshi henshūshitsu 1982, 358–359.

8. Kenneth Pyle asserts that the largest daimyo had a permanent staff of ten thousand in the mid-eighteenth century, but the documentary basis for this statement is unclear. Pyle 1978, 24.

9. The quotation is from Alcock 1863, vol. 1, 116.

10. In 1697, slightly more than 1 percent of Tosa's population lived outside the borders of the domain, in Edo (4,201), Kyoto (186), Fushimi (21), and Osaka (143). *TMK* 86, Genroku jūnen [1697], "Jūichigatsu kokonoka kirishitan shūmon aratamesho o bakufu ni dasu," fols. 55–57.

11. *TMK* 86, Genroku jūnen [1697] "Jūichigatsu kokonoka kirishitan shūmon aratamesho o bakufu ni dasu," fols. 55–57.

12. The figures for Okayama in 1698 are 992 males (71 percent) and 400 females (29 percent). *HDJ*, vol. 6, 194; for Uwajima, in 1771, 654 males (67 percent) and 320 females (33 percent). Yasuzawa 2002, 24–25.

13. Quoted in Screech 1996, 22.

14. Mori Masana 1828–1856, vol. 1, fols. 49–50.

15. The figures here do not add up. Excluding cleaning ladies from the calculation, there were 2,971 Tosa people residing in Edo. If this category of women is included the figure is 3,117. In either case, the figures do not match the total of 3,046 given. Although mathematical errors are common in the early modern documentation, assuming there is no error in calculation, one can deduce that there were 76 Tosa people living in auxiliary residences.

16. Figures from 1644 are from *TDK*, vol. 3, 295–297; for 1708, from Hirao and Yamamoto 1976, 328–330; and for 1731, "Nijūichi nichi oboegaki o tōban yakunin ni," *TNK*, vol. 23, Kyōhō 16 [1731] ichigatsu-shigatsu no kan, fols. 13–14.

17. Naitō Meisetsu 1982, 145.

18. Sakai Banshirō 1983, 531–559.

19. Mori Yoshiki 1793–1807, vol. 9, fols. 19–22.

20. Miura 1992, vol. 1, 71–85. During a four-month period in 1828, Tamuro worked forty-eight out of sixty-eight days. The day was divided into three shifts: early shift (*hayaban*), second shift (*atoban*), and an overnight shift (*hayadomari*).

21. The same schedule was true for retainers in the domain. Tosa's Mori Hirosada, for example, was assigned guard duty an average of thirty days a year and actually served only twenty of them. He was sick, or feigned sickness, one-third of the time. Moriguchi 1986, 23–26.

22. Miura 1992, vol. 1, 73.

23. The only full transcription of the text, in Japanese or English, can be found in Vaporis 1996, 296–307. The account of the scroll contained herein is taken from this article (pp. 279–307). The quote is on page 300.

24. *TSK*, vol. 63, Bunsei jūni nen [1829], fols. 18–20. In another case Kurume was relieved of duty at Zōjōji because of pestilence at home, and Tosa was assigned to take over. Mori Hirosada 1732, fols. 14–15.

25. Shinohara 1981, 468. Shōha's father, Mitani Eishū, like many domain retainers, accompanied his father to Edo in 1778 to further pursue his art studies although he had no official duties. Kashin jinmei jiten hensan iinkai 1987–1989, vol. 7, 120–121.

26. Kashin jinmei jiten hensan iinkai 1987–1989, vol. 7, 105. Toda was a lover of Japanese and Chinese poetry and authored some twenty books.

27. The scroll appears to be the only visual source extant depicting the living quarters of domanial samurai in Edo. It does so from the inside looking out rather than from the outside in, as do woodblock prints, *doro-e,* and even the *Edo-zu byōbu.* It is also unusual in that four of the paintings (3, 4, 7, and 8) have partial double layerings — pieces of paper appended to the surface of the paintings. In two cases (3 and 4), lifting the paper, which shows an interior wall of a retainer's room, allows a full view of the garden outside. This device, sometimes used in erotic prints for a "peek-a-boo" effect, gives a three-dimensional sense to the paintings. In two other instances (7 and 8), the second layers are in the form of *shoji,* and, when lifted, reveal scenery outside the barracks. The entire thirteen paintings were published, in color, in *Tōkyōjin* 1995, 26–33.

28. *Tōkyōjin* 1995, 297.

29. Tōkyō-to 1960, 698–701. For comparison, the main residence of Tosa (two hundred thousand *koku*), at Kajibashi was 7,052 *tsubo* in 1725.

30. Harada (no first name) 1938, 411.

31. Beato's photograph shows the first floor of the outer barracks to be in the *sasarako shitami itabari* style: wooden board siding with battens, and the second floor done in white plaster. But *doro-e* and Hirosohige's woodblock prints of the same compound depict it as being decorated with *namako kabe* (wall covered with square tiles jointed with raised plaster). See Hara 1993, front pages. The various works are roughly contemporaneous in time. Given the photographic evidence, we must conclude that the *doro-e* and woodblock prints represented idealized depictions. For one of Hiroshige's prints of the Kurume compound, see Henry Smith 1986a, print 53.

32. Vaporis 1996, 300.

33. Vaporis 1996, 301.

34. Vaporis 1996, 301.

35. McClatchie 1890, 166–167.

36. Vaporis 1996, 305.

37. Mori Masana 1828–1856, vol. 6, fol. 15.

38. Gotō Seijun 1801b, fol. 19. Gotō was a senior advisor of Tosa domain. When Tosa Confucian scholar Miyaji Umanosuke was reassigned from the main residence of the domain at Kajibashi to the lower compound at Tsukiji, he found the tatami matting in his new room spotted with oil stains and one of the window lattices damaged. This was duly reported to the official in charge of maintenance. Another official responsible for the tatami was sent to inspect the mats, and he replaced four of them; the damaged window was also repaired. Miyaji Umanosuke 1832, vol. 1, fols. 26–29. At the end of his tour of duty, Miyaji noted that he was given a receipt for the furnishings he had used during the year. Miyaji Umanosuke 1832, vol. 4, fol. 35.

39. *Yu ni deru* or *machiyu ni deru* were the expressions used when they went into town to use public facilities. Mori Masana 1828–1856, vol. 2, fol. 5; Mori Yoshiki 1793–1807, vol. 6, fols. 20–21. Sakai also writes occasionally of taking a sitz bath. Sakai Banshirō 1983, 550.

40. Harada (no first name) 1938, 427. There one could relax, drink tea, have a sweet, smoke a pipe, or play a game of *go*. Harada noted that there were separate areas for men and women and that only the men's had two stories.

41. Mori Yoshiki 1793–1807, vol. 7, fols. 103, 106, 107.

42. The hierarchy of military ranks in the daimyo's household usually took the following order for upper (mounted) samurai: *daimyō — ichimon/karō — kumigashira — monogashira — hirashi*. Lower ranking samurai (infantry) ranks went: *kachi — ashigaru — chūgen — komono*. Kasaya 2000b, 45–47.

43. Undated regulations for Wakayama are quoted in the introduction to Sakai Banshirō 1983, 530.

44. A rough, hand-drawn map of the compound can be found in Gotō Seijun 1800b, fol. 11.

45. Introduction to Sakai Banshirō 1983, 530.

46. Miyazaki Katsumi, "Daimyō Edo yashiki no kyōkai sochi," in Miyazaki and Yoshida 1994, 19–21. Tosa's Mori Yoshie, for example, was assigned a single room, but two other men, his brother Masana, who was in Edo for studies, and another man, Sakai Genjirō, were "attached" (*fuzoku*) to him and residing unofficially in the same room. Mori Masana 1828–1856, vol. 1, fols. 19–20, 28. The three men lived in a ten-mat room in the northern barracks at Kajibashi. Masana found the room too crowded for him to study in and removed his desk to that of his relative, Mori Oki'emon.

47. Gotō Seijun 1800b, fol. 30.

48. Naitō Meisetsu 1982, 146. Retainers usually received their rice allowance and regular Edo allowance, the latter in cash, in two-month installments. See, for example, Miyaji Umanosuke 1832, vol. 1, fols. 16, 43.

49. Shimamura Taeko 1972, 57–59. Sardines cost only five *mon* each, whereas salmon, bonito, and tuna cost sixteen. Banshirō usually bought one or two at a time. In all he ate thirty different types of fish. For seasonal vegetables, he ate, for example, bamboo shoots during the third and fourth months and eggplant during the sixth through ninth months.

50. "Edo iseki kenkyūkai dai-ikkai taikai zentai tōgi kiroku," in Edo iseki kenkyūkai

1992, 284–285. According to *Ryōri monogatari*, a record of the Date daimyo family published in 1643, seven types of four-legged game (deer, badger, boar, rabbit, otter, bear, and dog) were prepared in a variety of ways: dried, incorporated into soups, cooked in a pot or shell, or coated in miso bean paste and grilled. *"Ryōri monogatari" shōkai* 1975, 44–46; Ebara 1986, 36–40; Harada Nobuo 1989, 18–23. Perhaps to assuage guilt or to deflect social approval, game meat was often known by different code names: for example *yama kujira* ("mountain whale") for boar, and *momiji* ("maple leaves") for deer. The place name Kōjimachi, location of the meat store Yamaoku-ya in Hirakawa-chō, also became a password for meat; similarly, rabbits were counted with the term used for birds (*wa*). *"Ryōri monogatari" shōkai* 1975.

51. Harada Nobuo 2003, 38–40.

52. Iidamachi iseki chōsakai 1995, 433–437; Bunkyō furusato rekishikan 1993, 26–27. Kobiki 1991, 64, likewise states that it "seems that dog was eaten quite a bit."

53. "Shinpojiumu Edo o horu," 171–172; Sakurai Jin'ya, "Iseki shutsudo no dōbutsu itai kara mita daimyō yashiki no shoku seikatsu," in Edo iseki kenkyūkai 1992, 272–273.

54. On dogs and hawking, see Bodart-Bailey 2006, 46–49. Tosa's fighting dogs are still a popular tourist attraction today.

55. Occasionally incidents were reported of bear and wild boar running loose through the city, but whether these were animals that had wandered into the city or simply broken out of their cages in the compounds is unknown. Kaneko Hiromasa, "Edo shichō no dōbutsu (gyokai rui to tori, kedamono rui): Shoku bunka to no kakawari kara," in Edo iseki kenkyūkai 1991, 202–203.

56. Kaneko Hiromasa, "Edo shichū no dōbutsu (gyōkairui to tori kedamono rui) — shoku bunka to no kakawari kara," in Edo iseki kenkyūkai 1992. At the San'ei-chō site, boar and deer were the most numerous of the wild animals unearthed, followed by *kamoshika* (seven), bear (three), and several wolves, badgers, foxes, and otters.

57. Tosa samurai Mori Masana bought a large boar's head in Yamashita and took it to the domain compound at Tsukiji, where he and a few friends tried out their new blades on it. After they were finished — and one of his friend's blades had chipped — they boiled the head and ate the meat. Mori Masana 1828–1856, vol. 2, fols. 34–35.

58. Hanley 1997, 67.

59. Duck was eaten more than domesticated fowl. Swans and cranes were for banquets and other formal occasions. Canaries, golden pheasants, and peacocks, not native species, found their way to Edo via the foreign-trade port of Nagasaki. Kaneko Hiromasa, "Edo shichū no dōbutsu (gyōkairui to tori kedamono rui) — shoku bunka to no kakawari kara," in Edo iseki kenkyūkai 1992, 157–159.

60. Koizumi 1990b, 184.

61. Sakurai 1992, 266.

62. Kaneko Hiromasa, "Edo shichū no dōbutsu (gyōkairui to tori kedamono rui) — shoku bunka to no kakawari kara," in Edo iseki kenkyūkai 1992, 236. Perhaps the fish were cleaned at specialty shops, with the result that the bones do not appear in the consumers' garbage.

63. Akimoto Chiyako, "Kaga han kami yashiki 'okashikoya' ni okeru shoku seikatsu no ittan," in Edo iseki kenkyūkai 1992, 252–254.

64. Akimoto Chiyako, "Kaga han kami yashiki 'okashikoya' ni okeru shoku seikatsu no ittan," in Edo iseki kenkyūkai 1992, 252–253.

65. Kaneko Hiromasa, "Edo shichū no dōbutsu (gyōkairui to tori kedamono rui) —shoku bunka to no kakawari kara," in Edo iseki kenkyūkai 1992. Short-necked and freshwater clams were also consumed by upper samurai.

66. Kaneko Hiromasa, "Edo shichū no dōbutsu (gyōkairui to tori kedamono rui) —shoku bunka to no kakawari kara," in Edo iseki kenkyūkai 1992, 183–85.

67. It appears that some retainers from Kaga domain routinely were required to stay in Edo for longer than a year. In 1780 the period of service was set at two and a half years, but this was reduced the following year to eighteen months. This requirement did not cover those serving the immediate needs of the lord (*kinshū*). This meant there was substantial movement of personnel to and from Kaga in the fall in addition to the usual spring season when the lord Maeda alternated residences. Ishikawa kenritsu toshokan 1991, 58.

68. Najita 1987, 172.

69. Ōta Makoto 1994, 196. The sickly Suzu had great difficulty coping on her own.

70. Miyaji Umanosuke 1832, vol. 3, fol. 12.

71. Gotō Seijun 1800c, fols. 60–61. Retainers routinely died due to natural causes during their tours of military service in Edo, though the disposition of their corpses is not clear from the documentary record for Tosa. See, for example, Takeichi Saichirō 1967, 49.

72. Yoshiki's separation in Edo serving the lord meant that his son's audience with the lord had to be held in absentia. While this may seem odd, it was done to ensure that the Mori line would continue even if Yoshiki died. Mori Yoshiki 1793–1807, vol. 7, fol. 69 and vol. 8, fol. 29.

73. Mori Yoshiki 1793–1807, vol. 6, fol. 23.

74. Mori Masana 1828–1856, vol. 1, fol. 23. He paid eighty-four *mon* for the service. Mori Yoshiki 1793–1807, vol. 7, fol. 55.

75. The arrival of letters from home was frequently followed by a notation expressing "relief" (*anshin*). No news could be unsettling, as when Umanosuke noted, "I didn't receive any letters from home and this troubles me." Miyaji Umanosuke 1832, vol. 1, fol. 19.

76. Suzuki Yuriko, "Jūke jōsei no seikatsu — Rai Baishi no shigoto to shussan, ikuji," in Hayashi 1993, 129–166. During his husband's first absence she returned to her family home in Osaka, but on the six subsequent occasions she remained in Hiroshima with her children.

77. Mutō Yoshikazu 1990–1997, vol. 6, 396–398, 404–407.

78. Keene 1961, 270–312. On "wife-revenge," see Ikegami 1995, 244, 245–257.

79. Keene 1961, 57–90.

80. Ravina 2004, 59.

81. The lessons in Noh chanting were given by Horiike Shōbei, an actor who was attached to the Yamauchi lord. Mori Yoshiki 1793–1807, vol. 7, fol. 57.

82. Mori Yoshiki 1793–1807, vol. 7, fols. 57, 70, 111.

83. Ravina 2004, 61. This was during 1854–1855.

84. Shinohara 1981, 235, 468.

85. Ravina 2004, 59.

86. Yamakawa 2001, 79.

87. Anonymous 1846, 412–428.

88. Matsuyama domain may have been stricter. According to Naitō Meisetsu, retainers were given leave to go outside the compound only four days a month. If Naitō's memory was correct, then Matsuyama's policies were rather severe. Permission usually took the form of a wooden tag, obtained from one's immediate superior. Naitō Meisetsu 1982, 141. I viewed one such wooden tag unearthed at the excavation site at Shiodome, of Sendai domain's main residence, and wish to thank the archaeologist Chiba Motoji for two guided tours of the site. Thomas McClatchie notes the existence of the tag system in McClatchie 1890, 173–174.

89. Ego 1999, 12; "Edo oyashiki gomonsei okakitsuke," in Maeda Akinari n.d., vol. 4. A later return required written permission. Of course in "unavoidable circumstances" no punishment was imposed if a retainer's ex post facto written explanation was approved. Either Nakatsu domain's policy was unusually late or Yukichi Fukuzawa's memory was incorrect, for in his memoir he wrote that the gate at his compound closed at midnight. Yukichi Fukuzawa 1966, 97–98. Other evidence from Tosa also suggests that its retainers had a later curfew than Matsuyama's. According to the undated document, the curfew was the fourth hour in the evening (about 10 p.m.). "Edo oyashiki gomonsei okakitsuke," twelfth month, year unknown, in Yamauchi Akinari, "Yōsha zuihitsu," vol. 4.

90. This account of beating the curfew is based on Naitō Meisetsu 1982, 143–144. The method of announcing the time is described in Gotō Seijun 1800c, fol. 22.

91. Mori Yoshiki 1828–1856, vol. 9, fol. 23.

92. Miura 1992, vol. 1, 71–85. The period was 1828/5/18–7/8.

93. Sakai Banshirō 1983, 531–559. The ledger covers one year of his stay in Edo, which lasted about two years. Unfortunately he kept the diary for only seven months. Sakai's normal stipend was twenty-five *koku*. Background information on him is discussed in Shimamura Taeko 1972, 45–68.

94. Sakai Banshirō 1983, 535.

95. According to Sakai's diary, soba cost sixteen *mon* per plate and sushi eight *mon* per piece.

96. He visited thirty-six different shrines and temples during a nine-month period, some of them multiple times (e.g., Asakusa Kannon five times; Atago-san, Sakanoshita Fudō, and Hirakawa tenjin three times); went to the bath forty-three times; went to see plays six times; and went to listen to storytellers eight times.

97. Sakai Banshirō 1983, 540.

98. The first month he had twelve lessons. During the eighth and ninth months there was a break, but then he resumed the lessons thereafter with similar frequency.

99. Upper samurai would have their manservant do their hair, but lower samurai usually paid directly for the service. Banshirō paid him twenty *mon* per time.

100. He purchased candles only during the twelfth and first months, suggesting that probably he had received a fixed number by the domain and had exhausted the supply toward the end of the year.

101. A bath and cut of tea with sweets cost eighteen to twenty-four *mon*. At other times, Banshirō took a sitz bath or tub bath at the barracks. In his ledger, 9.9 percent of his budget is unaccounted for.

102. Mori Masana 1828–1856, vol. 1, fols. 35–36; Miura 1994, vol. 1, 71–106; Kodera Kiyoaki 1916, 257–287.

103. Mori Masana 1828–1856, vol. 1, fols. 34–35.

104. When leaving the compound, Seijun, as befitting his status, was supposed to be accompanied by a messenger, two retainers, one steward (*wakatō*), one sandal bearer, and one umbrella holder. By "stealthily" he probably only meant that he and Tamba went out singly, without entourages. They might also have dressed inconspicuously so as not to draw attention to themselves. Gotō Seijun 1800c, fols. 18–19, 59.

105. Sakai Banshirō 1983, 533.

106. Mori Masana 1828–1856, vol. 1.

107. This paragraph is based on Kodera Kiyoaki 1916, vol. 2, 257–287, and Suzuki Shōsei 2001, 144–158.

108. Miyaji Umanosuke 1832, vol. 1, fols. 28–29.

109. *TKK*, vol. 57, Kyōwa gannen [1801] nenmatsu, "Shobatsu," fols. 103–104. In this case it was for eleven days.

110. "Zai Edo tsukaiban, koshō, wakatō, monban nado shohatto" 1622–1629, fols. 1–11.

111. "Jō otomo ashigaru nezue" 1866, vol. 1. See, for example the entries for Takechi Masuhei, Okano Hannojō, or Nomoto Ikuzō.

112. "Jō otomo ashigaru nezue" 1866, vol. 1. Entry for Okuda Otoji. He had a stipend of 8.7 *koku* with a two-person rice allowance.

113. Miyaji Umanosuke 1832, vol. 4, fols. 25–26.

114. Tōkyō-to Chiyoda-ku, ed. 1998, 457–459.

115. Akizawa Shigeru and others 2003, vol. 6, 159.

Chapter 7: Carriers of Culture

1. Its cultural effects have received some attention in Japan recently, but the focus has been largely on culture at level of the daimyo. Two essays which examine the daimyo's cultural role in alternate attendance are Nishiyama 1992 and Kasaya 1993.

2. Tsukahira 1966, 3; Ōishi Shinsaburō 1991, 124–125; Tōkyō-to Edo-Tōkyō hakubutsukan 1997, 6. The on-line dictionary of the Japanese publisher Gakken, under the term "*sankin kōtai*," notes, "Due to the influence of alternate attendance (Japan's) road system developed and the culture of Edo spread to the localities." Gakken's on-line dictionary is available at http://dbgakken.co.jp/jiten/sa/204030.htm. John Hall has noted that "the castle cities took on a remarkable uniform guise as the necessities of alternate attendance . . . circulated the ideas and practices of the center to the periphery." John Hall, "The Castle Town and Japan's Modern Urbanization," in Hall and Jansen 1968, 184. According to a Japanese prefectural history, "[a]s a result of the institutionalization of alternate attendance and the growing prosperity of Edo, from the second half of the seventeenth century, and particularly during the eighteenth century, the castle town [of Matsushiro] absorbed Edo culture; the effect on the neighboring districts was also great" and "Edo culture passed through the castle town of Matsushiro to every part of the Shinano area." Nagano kenshi kankōkai 1988, 355.

3. Masana's elder brother Yoshie served as a chamberlain (*osoba monogashira*) to the daimyo heir and was a part of his procession, which left Kōchi on 3/27. The lord had departed earlier in the month, on 3/5. This account of Masana's 1828 trip is based on Mori Masana 1828–1856, vol. 1, fols. 1–20. Textual citations which follow are from this volume.

4. Masana in 1828 passed through or by Marugame, Okayama, Himeji, Amaga-

saki, Akō, Osaka, Yodo, Zeze, Minakuchi, Kuwana, Yoshida, Hamamatsu, Kakegawa, Fuchū, Numazu, and Odawara. Mori Masana 1828–1856, vol. 1.

5. Similarly, a doctor named Harada on duty in Edo compares the Kamigata culture of his native Wakayama with Edo culture in terms of food, custom, and language, among other areas, in his "Edo jiman" (1860), in Harada 1938, 411–438.

6. The British Bishop of Victoria (Hong Kong) noted in 1861 that Mt. Atago "commands an extensive view of the city and surrounding country, commonly called by foreign visitors the 'Grand Vue' of Yeddo [Edo]." To him, "There is no spot in Yeddo from which a better view is gained of the vast expanse of inhabited space lying in the city and suburbs below." George Smith 1861, 309–310.

7. Sakai Banshirō 1983, 535–536.

8. Clarke 1989, 70. The contemporary writer Ōta Nanpo relates that samurai in Edo who wanted to succeed in life imitated the Mikawa dialect, which was the strongest strain in Edo language. Mizuhara 1994, 22–24.

9. Mori Masani 1828, vol. 1, fols. 30–31.

10. Teruko Craig 1999, 80.

11. Leutner 1985, 187.

12. Mori Masana 1828–1856, vol. 2, fols. 55–59.

13. Mori Yoshiki 1801–1802, vol. 7, fols. 47–49.

14. Mori Masana 1828–1856, vol. 2, fols. 39–60. Of course, retainers were also able to better get to know their own domain. On their way back home in 1829, Masana, his elder brother Yoshie, and a few other men traveled a different course than the Kitayama route they had taken to Edo a year earlier, riding a boat from Osaka to Kan-no-ura, in eastern Tosa, from which they went overland on the Noneyama route. This gave them the opportunity to pass through and observe conditions in that sparsely populated part of the domain.

15. Quoted in Kasaya 1993, 148–151.

16. The author discusses the purchasing habits of two Tosa domain retainers while on alternate attendance in Vaporis 1994c, 52–67.

17. Mori Masana 1828–1856, vol. 1, fols. 9–15.

18. Miyaji Umanosuke 1832.

19. Miyaji Umanosuke 1832. The fishing line was probably in anticipation of some days of relaxation fishing back in Kōchi, but he died just a couple of months after returning home. The four types of silk cloth were *Nara shima*; *beni itajime*; black Hachijō silk, which was used most often for the neck of under-kimono; and silk gauze. During the Tokugawa period *sarasa*, dyed cloth with patterns of people, birds, or flowers, was imported from India, Indonesia, Vietnam, and Siam before domestic production started. Japanese-made material was sometimes referred to as *Wa-sarashina* to distinguish it from imported items, but just as often no distinction in terminology was made. Late in the period almost all *sarasa* was domestically produced. Personal communication with Tanaka Yuko, October 6, 1994.

20. Ogura 1862. He also brought six pairs of low geta (*hiyori geta*) for members of the main family, from whom he probably received going-away gifts of money.

21. Miyaji Umanosuke 1832, vol. 1, fol. 41.

22. "Arima nyūtō miyage-e nado" 1730.

23. The sixty prints (*nishiki-e*) cost 2 *shu*, 50 *mon*; the other ten cost 144 *mon*. "Edo otomo no ki," in Kami-gun Tosa Yamada chō kyōiku iinkai 1979, vol. 2, 412–416.

24. *Doro-e* were paintings done in the European style, using opaque pigments. Usually small in size, they were produced mainly for visitors to Edo, Kyoto, or Nagasaki. Hirai Kiyoshi 2004; and the classic study by Ōkuma 1939.

25. Hachinohe retainer Toyama Tamuro gave Yamamoto-yama tea as gifts to several people from the domain, in addition to *furoshiki*, a tobacco pouch, bath towel, paper, face power, and other unspecified gifts. Miura 1992, vol. 1, 284–285. Late in the Edo period, those retainers not familiar with Edo might consult the shopping guide *Edo kaimono hitori annai* (1824) for a list of merchants in the city. Many retainer diaries either fail to note any purchases made or simply state that the person in question went "shopping." In their attention to this type of detail, Miyaji Umanosuke's, Mori Masana's, and Toyama Tamuro's diaries are exceptional.

26. Satō Morihiro 2000.

27. Mori Masana 1828–1856, fols. 34–35.

28. Mori Masana 1828–1856, fol. 36.

29. Miyaji Umanosuke 1832, fols. 15–16.

30. E.g., a weight restriction on baggage (5 *kan* or 34.7 kg) established by Kaga domain was probably aimed at limiting the amount retainers brought with them. Chūda 1993, 47. However, Chūda does not state when this regulation was issued and whether or not it was effective. One Yonezawa lower samurai surnamed Saitō bought back from Edo a heavy, green-and-white glazed brazier, filling it with sugar, a precious commodity, for the trip home. Ōishi Shinzaburō 1991, 125. At various times Kaga tried to restrict the purchase of gifts in Edo by its retainers, instructing them when returning home not to buy them for anyone except their parents. In particular the notice singles out items such as containers (*utsuwamono*) for a total prohibition, probably because they were bulky. The regulation was part of a policy of economic retrenchment. For instructions from 1689, see Kanazawa shishi hensan iinkai 2001, 740. Kaga also discouraged going-away gifts, particularly since it was customary for the recipient of such gifts, in this case Edo-bound retainers, to respond with a gift in turn. Ishii 1981b, 87, 89. Of course the frequency of such exhortations indicates that the custom prevailed nonetheless.

31. Clunas 1991, 125.

32. Miyaji Umanosuke 1832, vol. 3, fols. 23, 36.

33. Enkōan 1828. See also Nagoya shi hakubutsukan 1986.

34. Miura 1992, vol. 1, 372. The same practice of giving money to someone about to embark on a trip was followed among commoners, who frequently made pilgrimages during the Edo period. See Vaporis 1994a, 322–328.

35. Miura 1992, vols. 1–2.

36. Kasaya 1993, 141–147, lists the travel schedule of the fourth and eighth lords of Hirado domain, with brief comments on whom they met along the way.

37. The quote about "splendid captivity" is from Totman 1967, 36. The notion of the aristocratization of the daimyo is from Nishiyama 1992, 64. The classic study of daimyo sponsorship of the arts is Fukui 1937.

38. The visits of Lord Yamauchi to the residences of other lords are assiduously noted in Gotō Seijun 1800c.

39. Moriguchi 1982, 213–260. There was the same level of commoner attendance as well at a puppet performance in honor of the lord's daughter's wedding in 1679. Mori Yoshiki 1793–1807, vol. 7, fol. 70. During the Genroku period, when the domain employed as many as forty-seven actors, performances were put on five times a month at the two principal residences. Yamauchi jinja hōmotsu shiryōkan 1990, 50–51.

40. Lord Maeda Tsunanori (r. 1645–1723) also took the Hōshō family head with him to Edo. McClain 1982, 139–140.

41. Moriguchi 1982, 215–217.

42. It was customary to put on Noh performances to mark auspicious events, such as to celebrate the lord's arrival in Edo or the completion of his service to the shogun, his promotion in rank, a birthday, marriage, or on any number of festive days. During the Genroku period, however, it became popular to perform jōruri in the daimyo compounds on these occasions. Torii 1998, 1–12.

43. Shiba performed for the lord of Sendai in his main residence. French 1974, 10.

44. Cort 2004, 103–112.

45. Tatsurō Akai, "The Common People and Painting," in Nakane and Ōishi 1990, 189–190. Yanagisawa's diary, "Enyū nikki," can be found in Yanagisawa 1988. Likewise, the diary of the lord of Shibata, Matsudaira Yamato no kami, also records many accounts of the cultural life of the lord, who often invited kabuki actors to his residence to perform. See "Matsudaira Yamato no kami," in Yanagisawa 1988.

46. Brendan G. Jordan and Victoria Weston, "Introduction," in Jordan and Weston 2003, 3–4. On the Kano school, see also Tōkyō-to Edo-Tōkyō hakubutsukan 1997.

47. Brendan C. Jordan, "Copying from Beginning to End?" in Jordan and Weston 2003, 18, 30. The quote is from page 18.

48. As discussed in chapter five, invariably these were men. Some women, however, such as Inoue Tsūjo (1660–1738), the daughter of a Marugame samurai, were sent to Edo on special assignment. Inoue, who was once referred to as the Murasaki Shikibu of her day, spent the years 1681 through 1689 in Edo as a lady-in-waiting for the mother of the lord.

49. "Nijūni nichi jūsha Tani Manroku (Yoshii) bossu," TKK, vol. 70, Bunka 2 (1805)/ eighth–twelfth months, fols. 93–97.

50. Miyaji Umanosuke 1832.

51. Dore 1965, 73.

52. Kashin jinmei jiten hensan iinkai 1987–1989, vol. 1, 285–286; vol. 5, 57–58.

53. Miyaji Umanosuke, for example, was appointed in 1827 and traveled to Edo in 1828; Miura Sadayoshi was appointed in 1784 and went to Edo in 1787. Tosa's domain school was established in Kōchi in 1760. Kōchi kenshi hensan iinkai 1968, 505–506. Elsewhere, Kurume domain retainer Inoue Kakuma (1829–1885) became an assistant at the domain school in 1842, at the age of sixteen, and two years later became an instructor. After a tour in Edo from 1849 to 1853, he became assistant lecturer. Another Kurume retainer, Ikejiri Monzaemon, became lecturer at the domain school after spending eight years in Edo, 1830 to 1838, where he became a student of Matsuzaki Kōdō (1771–1844). In the late 1840s he opened his own school. Kashin jinmei jiten hensan iinkai 1987–1989, vol. 7, 74–75, 79, 113.

54. Maruyama Kazuo, ed., Morita Kyūemon nikki. I would like to thank Louise Al-

lison Cort for sharing with me a copy of her draft translation of the diary (provisionally entitled *Morita Kyūemon Diary*). The diary is also discussed in Cort 2004.

55. Richard Wilson, "Kyoto Ware and Rihei Ware," in Iidamachi iseki chōsakai 1995, 567–568, 577.

56. Those samurai were Matsuzaki Keishin (1720–1813), Hashimoto Unzan (d. 1822), Ikezoe Yōsai (1755–1822), and Itō Koshigawa (d. 1836). Kattō 1994, 46–48, 53–55, 61–64, 70–72.

57. The Tosa retainers were Tokuhiro Sekimon (1777–1825), who changed from the Kanō to the Nanga school during his time of service in Edo, Furuya Chikugen (1788–1861), and Mibu Suiseki (1790–1871). Kattō 1994, 190–196, 214–249.

58. Keene 2006, 46–48.

59. Hakyō studied for a period in Kyoto as well. In his forties and fifties he made a number of additional trips to Edo accompanying the lord. Hakyō ronshū kankōkai 1991, 16–17, 151–166. See also Nagata 1988. In English, see Screech 2000, 79, 223–225.

60. Yates 1995, 26.

61. Ravina 2004, 59. Earlier, Yates came to the same conclusion, that Saigō "would never be able to return to the simple naivete of his earlier life." Yates 1995, 31.

62. Yonemoto 2003, 51.

63. Inoue Tadashi 1963, 22–23.

64. The following material on Kaibara is based on Yokota 2003, 389–408. On Kaibara, see also Tucker 1989, 32–39, 347–354.

65. Yokota 2003, 392.

66. Yokota 2003, 399–400. According to Yokota, the fact that books were circulating across the country through a variety of mechanisms, making it possible for people in the regional castle towns to acquire copies of Ekiken or Saikaku, for example, at the same time, revises our view of Genroku culture as a phenomenon in which only Kyoto-Osaka merchants took part. Yokota 2003, 406.

67. Kobayashi Fumio 2000, 68–78.

68. Kashin jinmei jiten hensan iinkai 1987–1989, vol. 5, 234.

69. Kashin jinmei jiten hensan iinkai 1987–1989, vol. 5, 235.

70. Cahill 1976, 9, 15–17. Another offspring of a domainal retainer who followed his father to service in Edo, Yanagisawa Kien (1704–1758), was the second of the three earliest important figures in Nanga. Cahill 1976, 17–22. Cahill writes that Nanga, which began largely as a Kyoto phenomenon, took root in Edo in the late eighteenth century, by which time it had also spread to other artistic centers (p. 107). Cahill considers Edo to have been the location of a "branch school" (pp. 108, 112), but to Calvin it was the "center of *bunjin* [i.e., literati] activity." French 1974, 78.

71. On Odano, see French 1974, 79, 182 n. 3; and Keene 1969, 62. On Aōdō, see Kashin jinmei jiten hensan iinkai 1987–1989, vol. 2, 117.

72. This paragraph is based on Miwa 1993, 17, 55–64, 95. Yoshiatsu and Odano are also discussed in Screech 2000, 59, 170. Other *ranpeki daimyō* included Matsudaira Yoritaka (Takamatsu domain) and Hosokawa Shigekata (Kumamoto domain).

73. The history of the painting after its execution is not elaborated upon. It is found in Miwa 1993, 62, image 28.

74. Kashin jinmei jiten hensan iinkai 1987–1989, vol. 5, 111.

75. Kashin jinmei jiten hensan iinkai 1987–1989, vol. 5, 314–315. In examining the careers of the cultured elite of *bushi* status, one cannot help but be impressed by their mobility. Not just Edo, but Kyoto, Nagasaki, Osaka, and a number of other cities were important centers that attracted students.

76. Kashin jinmei jiten hensan iinkai 1987–1989, vol. 6, 159–160. Kōseki was known as one of the Yamanote's three best doctors.

77. On Hiraga Gennai, see Screech 2000, 58.

78. Kashin jinmei jiten hensan iinkai 1987–1989, vol. 6, 85–86.

79. Kashin jinmei jiten hensan iinkai 1987–1989, vol. 6, 39. Shimosone's students had wide geographic origins. Gunnery specialist Oku Kunimasa (1813–1866) also studied under Shimosone and back in Hiroshima taught both Western-style gunnery and the traditional school his family had long taught. As part of a domain reform movement, only the Western-style was taught after 1862. Kashin jinmei jiten hensan iinkai 1987–1989, vol. 6, 150–151.

80. Hirao Michio 1979, 267–268. The quote is from Jansen 1961, 87.

81. For example, Tosa *bushi* and artist Maeno Kyūemon went to Edo in his father's place and stayed there five years, studying under Kanō Tenshin. Matsuzaki Keishin served in Edo during the An'ei period (1772–1781) and returned home with twenty-four works of his teacher, Kanō Yoshinobu. He mounted them in Kōchi, preserving them for his descendants. Kattō 1994, 45–46.

82. Kashin jinmei jiten hensan iinkai 1987–1989, vol. 1, 113.

83. Kashin jinmei jiten hensan iinkai 1987–1989, vol. 7, 81–82.

84. Kashin jinmei jiten hensan iinkai 1987–1989, 112–113.

85. Kashin jinmei jiten hensan iinkai 1987–1989, vol. 2, 27.

86. Asakura 1997, 7.

87. For a study of Edo's cultural networks in general, see Tanaka 1993.

88. Tōkyō-to Edo-Tōkyō hakubutsukan 1993, 80. Quote is from Totman 1993, 526–527. Kazan, like Nishima Jo, was the son of a daimyo retainer on a long-term posting in Edo.

89. Miyaji Umanosuke 1832, vol. 4, fol. 35.

90. Miyaji Umanosuke 1832, vol. 1, fol. 21. On 1832/5/1, for example, Umanosuke visited eight colleagues from eight different domains.

91. For example, Umanosuke was able to borrow books from his friend and scholar Yamasaki Kusaku (retainer of the Yanagiwa lord) "not available in Tosa." Miyaji Umanosuke 1832, vol. 4, fols. 17, 23.

92. Miyaji Umanosuke 1832, vol. 4, fols. 14–15.

93. Mori Masana 1828–1856, vol. 1, fols. 71–77.

94. Hirayama (1759–1828) authored the book *Kaibō mondō* (Questions and Answers on Coastal Defense).

95. Masana attended Umanosuke's biography study meetings (*idenkai*) ten times during a three-month period in 1828. Mori Masana 1828–1856, vol. 1.

96. The manuscript book "Tosa jinbutsu den" (A History of Tosa Personages) can be found in the Kōchi shimin toshokan.

97. E.g., he entered the school on 5/26 and went again fourteen times during the fifth through eighth months. Mori Masana 1828–1856, vol. 1, fols. 30–59.

98. Oka Mansuke replaced Miyaji Umanosuke as Confucian scholar in 1833. "Osamurai chū senzogaki keizu chō" n.d., vol. 6, entry for Oka Mansuke.

99. There were about forty students present at the study meetings, four or five of whom were from other domains. Mori Masana 1828–1856, vol. 2, fol. 11. Many other Tosa retainers were also students of Yamaguchi's, e.g., Yasunami Kage, who later became a professor at the domain school, Sagara Chūgo, and Nakayama Matasuke. Matsuyama 1971, 230–232.

100. Mori Yoshiki 1801–1802, vol. 7, fols. 57, 70, 111.

101. Shinba Eiji 1990, 19–25. Okunomiya Chūjirō came from the lowest rank of the upper portion of the vassal band in Tosa. Iwasaki had to return home in 1855, earlier than expected, because of his father's illness. Gonsai began as the famed Satō Issai's assistant, but opened up his own school at Kanda Surugadai in 1814. Meiji leader Itō Hirobumi also made the trip to Edo as an attendant of yet another oligarch-to-be, Kido Takayoshi. Kashin jinmei jiten hensan iinkai, ed. 1987–1989, vol. 6, 258–259.

102. On Kuwagata, see Atsumi 1996 and Henry D. Smith 1988.

103. Kōchōsha henshū bu 1978, 101; see also Chikamatsu Toshio 1990.

104. He also brought back with him Kanō-school copy books, *ukiyoe*, and puppet-theater texts. Kagioka 1999, 42–43.

105. Kagioka 1999, 4–24.

106. Miyaji Umanosuke 1832, vol. 1, fol. 46.

107. Mori Yoshiki 1801–1802, vol. 9, fols. 3–4.

108. Mori Masana 1828–1856, vol. 2, fol. 3. Toyama Heima sent his son in Edo local foodstuffs such as dried fish, miso, wheat gluten, and tangerines. Miura 1992, vol. 1.

109. Imaizumi 1981. One of the more unusual gifts given to the shogun, by Kaga domain, was ice. This was transported from Kaga by high-speed messenger, obviously well packed, in four days. Oikawa 2004, 16. Usuki domain (fifty thousand *koku*) in Kyushu gave more than two thousand freshwater trout and almost five thousand tangerines as winter seasonal gifts. Ego 1999, 24.

110. Maske 1994, vol. 1, 250–255. Records for 1855–1856 indicate that each year more than one hundred pieces of Takatori ware were taken to Edo. These included incense burners, flower vases, paperweights, tea bowls, water jars, sake flask warmers, and incense boxes.

111. *TFK*, vol. 3, Genroku 13 (1700), nenmatsu, nenmatsu zassai, "Zatsu," fols. 9–10, for a record of the bestowal of tea bowls and a flower vase of Odo ware to Tokugawa officials.

112. The merchants (known as *kenzan-ya*) also handled gifts exchanged between members of the samurai group in general. Nishiyama and others 1989, 220.

113. Ōishi Manabu, 1995, 176–183.

114. Shimamura had purchased these from the merchant Kirishimaya Ihei. Hirotani 1997b, 20–21. According to Hirotani, by the middle of the period azaleas were grown across the country. Today, azaleas are the official flower of Kōchi city. Hirotani 2003, 160–161.

115. Kamakura 1977, 7.

116. Hirotani 1978, 17–28; Nio-machi shi hensan iinkai 1984, 180, 186–195. There was also considerable stirring of the cultural melting pot when daimyo were transferred from one domain to another.

117. Hirotani 1997b, 18–19. This was part of Kenzan's policy to increase domestic

production of foodstuffs, other examples of which included koi, trout, catfish, and shiitake.

118. Hirotani 1997b, 20.

119. Nishiyama 1997, 78.

120. Nishiyama 1987, 99.

121. Smyers 1999, 20.

122. A senior advisor from Kururi ordered that a statue of Fudō Myōō be brought from the domain to the main residence in Edo and had a hall built for it, purportedly without the lord's permission. It was widely publicized, and large crowds made the pilgrimage, which drew the Tokugawa's attention and led to punishment for the senior advisor and other officials involved. Iwabuchi 2003, 134–135.

123. *TMK*, vol. 78, Genroku 8 (1695)/first–fifth months, fols. 75–83. The original shrine was located near Tosa's compound at Shiba; apparently prayers were said there for the safe births of the two Yamauchi lords, and thereafter they continued to support the shrine.

124. Totman 1967, 86.

Conclusion: Notes

1. Foucault 1995.

Works and Documents Cited

1. Abbreviations

BMI   *Yamauchi-ke shiryō: Bakumatsu ishin hen*. See published sources.

GM   Gotō-ke monjo collection. Aki shimin toshokan (Aki City Library).

HB   Hirao bunko collection. Kōchi shimin toshokan (Kōchi City Library).

HDJ   Kimura Motoi, Fujino Tamotsu, and Murakami Tadashi, ed. *Hanshi daijiten*. 9 vols. See published sources.

KNS   Kaganoi-ke shiryō, Kōchi shimin toshokan.

KTK   *Yamauchi-ke shiryō: Katsutoyo-kō ki*. See published sources.

TCK   Yamauchi-ke shiryō: Toyochika-kō ki. Yamauchi Shrine Treasury and Archives, Kōchi.

TFK   Yamauchi-ke shiryō: Toyofusa-kō ki. Yamauchi Shrine Treasury and Archives, Kōchi.

TKK   *Yamauchi-ke shiryō: Toyokazu-kō ki*. Yamauchi Shrine Treasury and Archives, Kōchi.

TMK   Yamauchi-ke shiryō: Toyomasa-kō ki. Yamauchi Shrine Treasury and Archives, Kōchi.

TNK   Yamauchi-ke shiryō: Toyonobu-kō ki. Yamauchi Shrine Treasury and Archives, Kōchi.

TOK   Yamauchi-ke shiryō: Toyooki-kō ki. Yamauchi Shrine Treasury and Archives, Kōchi.

TSK   Yamauchi-ke shiryō: Toyosuke-kō ki. Yamauchi Shrine Treasury and Archives, Kōchi.

TshK   Yamauchi-ke shiryō: Toyoshige-kō ki. Yamauchi Shrine Treasury and Archives, Kōchi.

TtaK   Yamauchi-ke shiryō: Toyotaka-kō ki. Yamauchi Shrine Treasury and Archives, Kōchi.

TteK   Yamauchi-ke shiryō: Toyoteru-kō ki. Yamauchi Shrine Treasury and Archives, Kōchi.

TtsK   Yamauchi-ke shiryō: Toyotsune-kō ki. Yamauchi Shrine Treasury and Archives, Kōchi.

TTK   Yamauchi-ke shiryō: Tadatoyo-kō ki. See published sources.

TMK   Yamauchi-ke shiryō: Toyomasa kō ki. Yamauchi Shrine Treasury and Archives, Kōchi.

TYK   *Yamauchi-ke shiryō*: Tadayoshi-kō ki. See published sources.

YKS   Yamauchi-ke shiryō. Kōchi Prefectural Library, Kōchi.

2. Manuscript and Pictorial Sources

Note: Most volumes in the Yamauchi-ke shiryō are unnumbered, unbound, and unfoliated. Each volume is titled with the name of the daimyo who was ruling at the time. This information together with the date of the volume and the document title will be given.

"Arima nyūto miyage-e nado." 1730. *GM*.

"Daimyō gyōretsu emaki." Edo period. 32 cm × 346 cm. Document [Doc.] #2673. Kanazawa shiritsu Tamagawa toshokan, Kanazawa city.

"Daimyō gyōretsu emaki." Edo period. 28 cm × 329 cm. Doc. #2674. Kanazawa shiritsu Tamagawa toshokan, Kanazawa city.

"Daimyō gyōretsu zu." Edo period. 24 × 34 cm. Doc. #2676. Kanazawa shiritsu Tamagawa toshokan, Kanazawa city.

"Edo Fushimi oshakan enjōki." N.d. Kōchi: Yamauchi Shrine Archives.

"Edo oyashiki gomonsei okakitsuke." N.d. In Yamauchi Akinari, "Yōsha zuihitsu," vol. 4.

"Edo okami yashiki sō oezu." Ca. 1840–1845. Kanazawa shiritsu toshokan Doc. #1777.

"Edo tsutome ōfuku kōgi yori watarimono kitei." 1750 [Enkyō 3]. *KNS* Doc. #20-24. Kōchi City Library.

"Edo zukan kōmoku." 1689. 2 vols. *YKS*. Kōchi Prefectural Library.

Enkōan [Kōriki Tanenobu]. 1828. "Edo junranki." Tōyō bunko, Tokyo.

Gotō Einosuke. 1790. "Dōchū no ki (utsushi)." *GM* Doc. #938. Aki City Library.

———. 1791. "Dōchū no ki (utsushi)." *GM* Doc. #939.

Gotō Geki. 1684–1685. "Nichō." *GM* Doc. #925.

"Gotō-ke keifu Seizen yori Seihō made." Undated. *GM* Doc. #32.

Gotō Seikō. 1790. "Seikō-sama ondōchū nikki." *GM* Doc. #937.

Gotō Seijun. 1800a. "Nikki. Ōsaka chaku igo shigatsu muika made." *GM* Doc. #947.

———. 1800b. "Nikki. Kansei jūninen shigatsu tsuitachi yori dō nijū kyū nichi made." *GM* Doc. #948.

———. 1800c. "Nikki. Kansei jūninen shigatsu muika yori dō sanjūnichi made." *GM* Doc. #949.

———. 1801a. "Nikki. Kansei jūsan/Kyōwa nen shōgatsu tsuitachi yori dō jūgonichi made." *GM* Doc. #960.

———. 1801b. "Nikki. Edo Ōsaka dōchūki shigatsu nijūyokka made." *GM* Doc. #964.

———. 1801c. "Nikki. Ōsaka-Kōchi dōchūki." *GM* Doc. #966.

"Gozai Edo oninzū shodōgu yōichō." N.d. Kōchi: Yamauchi Shrine Archives.

Ikoma Moku. 1683. "Senzo obogaki." *KNS* Doc. #1-06.

Imamura Yagosaku. 1700. "Edo yuki iriyō kinsu oboegaki." *KNS* Doc. #8-7.

"Jōkyō gannenbun jōge ninzū aratamegaki." 1684. Jōkyō documents. Kōchi: Kōchi Prefectural Library.

"Jō otomo ashigaru nezue." 1866. 4 vols. Kōchi: Kōchi Prefectural Library.

"Kirima Hyōgo (Yoshitaka)." 1802. "Wakadono hajimete shuppu otomo osetsukeraru ni tsuki kōjō." *KNS* Doc. #21-26.

"Kirima Ikoma ryōke senzogaki." 1688. *KNS* Doc. #01-08.

"Kishū han sankin kōtai gyōretsu zukan." Late Tokugawa. 8 rolls. Sakai: Sakai-shi hakubutsukan.

"Kurume han Edo kinban nagaya emaki." Early Meiji. Tōkyō-to Edo-Tōkyō hakubutsukan.

"Kyōhō ninen Edo kasaizu." 1717. *YKS* Doc. #211/238.

"Kōdai hyakuninjūgo. Shotoku monjo, gan ni, san yon." 1711–1714. Kōchi: Kōchi Prefectural Library.

Miyaji Haruki. N.d. (ca. 1785). "Ikō." Miyaji bunko. Kōchi: Kōchi Prefectural Library.

Miyaji Nakae. 1845. "Gotōke nendai ryakki." 3 vols. Kōchi: Kōchi Prefectural Library.

Miyaji Sukeyoshi. 1781–1817. "Bunken bibō." Miyaji bunko. Kōchi: Kōchi Prefectural Library.

Miyaji Umanosuke. 1832. "Edo nikki." 4 vols. (no. 2 missing). Miyaji-ke monjo. Kōchi: Kōchi Prefectural Library.

Mori Masana. 1828–1856. "Mori Masana Edo nikki." 10 vols. (no. 5 missing). Kōchi: Kōchi Prefectural Library (copy).

Mori Hirosada. 1732. "Hirosada-kō dōchū yorozu nikki." Kōchi: Kōchi Prefectural Library.

Mori Yoshiki. 1793–1807. "Nichi roku." 12 vols. Kōchi: Kōchi Prefectural Library.

———. 1801–1802. "Mori Yoshiki kō nikki." Hand-copied version of 1801–1802 original diary. Kōchi: Kōchi Prefectural Library.

"Mori Yoshishige nikki." 1828. vol. 7. Kōchi: Kōchi Prefectural Library.

Mutō Hiroki. 1842. "Rakuzan-kō ogyōretsu zukan." 11 scrolls. Sendai: Sendai shiritsu hakubutsukan.

"Nariyasu-kō Edo yori okikoku ogyōretsu zutsuki." 1872 [reprint of Edo-period images and text]. 8 scrolls. Doc. #2675. Kanazawa: Kanazawa shiritsu Tamagawa toshokan.

"Odōchū ikkan chō." 1808 [Bunsei 5]. Ogasawara-ke bunko. Hachinohe: Hachinohe shiritsu toshokan.

Ogura Uji (Sadasuke). 1858. "Ansei gonen umadoshi shichigatsu yori nikki shohikae." Kōchi: Kōchi Prefectural Library.

———. 1861. "Man'nen ni nen toradoshi nikki shohikae, shōgatsu chūjun yori." Kōchi: Kōchi Prefectural Library.

———. 1862. "Bunkyū gannen toradoshi nikki shokakae." Kōchi: Kōchi Prefectural Library.

"Ohōkōryō osadamegaki nuki chō." 1781 (copy of 1748 original). *YKS.*

"Osamurai chū senzogaki keizu chō." N.d. Kōchi: Kōchi Prefectural Library.

"Oumamawari Edo kinban shidai." 1799–1805. *GM* Doc. #5524.

"Rakusan kō ogyōretsu zukan." N.d. Sendai: Sendai shi hakubutsukan.

"Shiba oyashiki no mōyō zu." N.d. *GM* Kōchi: #4,439.

"Shōhō ninen, Tadayoshi sama ontomodachi narabini Edo jōzume hitodaka chō" 1645. *KNS* Doc. #17-10.

"Tadayoshi sama ontomodachi narabini Edo jōzume hitodakachō." 1645 [Shōhō 2]. *KNS* Doc. #17-10.

"Takayama-jō uketoru yakunin gyōretsu no zu." N.d. Doc. #2680, 27 × 615 cm. Kanazawa: Kanazawa shiritsu Tamagawa toshokan.

Tani Tannai (Mashio). 1748–1754. "Nichiyō beien roku." Kōchi: Yamauchi bunko, Kōchi Prefectural Library.

"Tōbun oboegaki" 1788 [*GM* Doc. #5500-5501], 1801 [*GM* Doc. #5735], 1839 [*GM* Doc. #5668], 1845 [*GM* Doc. #5583]. Aki shimin toshokan.

"Tosa han gyōretsu emaki." N.d. Nangoku city (Kōchi prefecture): Kōchi kenritsu rekishi minzoku shiryōkan.

"Tosa no kuni kenchichō." N.d. *YKS*.

"Toyoteru kō oniji." N.d. Yamauchi bunko. Kōchi: Kōchi Prefectural Library.

Yamauchi jidai shikō. N.d. [Manuscript copy written in 1927 from various Tokugawa period sources]. 11 vols. Kōchi: Kōchi Prefectural Library.

Yamauchi Akinari. N.d. "Yōsha zuihitsu." 6 vols. Private collection of Kattō Isamu, Kōchi.

"Yontō shizoku jōseki nenpu." N.d. Kōchi: Kōchi Prefectural Library.

"Zai Edo tsukaiban, koshō, wakatō, monban nado shohatto." 1622–1629. *KNS* Doc. #16-13.

3. Published Sources

Note: All Japanese works cited are published in Tokyo unless stated otherwise.

Abe Ayako. 2004. "Hirosaki han Edo hantei o meguru chōnin soshō no jittai." In Namikawa Kenji, *Kinsei bushi no seikatsu to ishiki. "Soeda Gizaemon nikki"— Tenna ki no Edo to Hirosaki*. Iwada shoin.

Akizawa Shigeru and others, ed. 2003. *Tosa (no) kuni gunsho ruiju*, vols. 5–6. Kōchi: Kōchi kenritsu toshokan.

Alcock, Sir Rutherford. 1863. *The Capital of the Tycoon: A Narrative of a Three Years' Residence in Japan*. 2 vols. London: Longman, Green, Longman, Roberts & Green.

Anonymous. 1846. "Edo otomo no ki." In *Tosa Yamada-chō shiryō*, vol. 2, ed. Kōchiken Yamada-machi kyōiku iinkai, 412–428. Kōchi: Kōchi-ken Yamada-machi kyōiku iinkai.

Aoki Michio, ed. 2001–2003. *Tōkaidō Kanagawa-juku honjin Ishii Junkō nikki*. 3 vols. Yumani shobō.

Asakura Haruhiko, ed. 1997. *Edo bunjin jiten*. Tōkyō-do shuppan.

Asano, Shugo, and Timothy Clark. 1995a. *The Passionate Art of Kitagawa Utamaro. Plates*. London: British Museum Press.

———. 1995b. *The Passionate Art of Kitagawa Utamaro. Text*. London: British Museum Press.

Asao Naohiro and Marius B. Jansen. 1981. "Shogun and Tennō." In *Japan Before Tokugawa. Political Consolidation and Economic Growth, 1500 to 1650*, ed. John Whitney Hall, Nagahara Keiji, and Kozo Yamamura. Princeton, N.J.: Princeton University Press.

Ashkenazi, Michael. 1993. *Matsuri. Festivals of a Japanese Town*. Honolulu: University of Hawai'i Press.

Atsumi Kuniyasu. 1996. *Edo no kufūsha. Kuwagata Keisai*. Geijutsu shimbunsha.

Bakufu fushin bugyō, compiler. 1985–1988. *Edo jōka hensen ezu*, 20 vols. Hara shobō.

Bendix, Reinhard. 1978. *Kings or People: Power and the Mandate to Rule*. Berkeley: University of California Press.

Berry, Mary Elizabeth. 1989. *Hideyoshi*. Cambridge, Mass.: Harvard University Press.

———. 2006. *Japan in Print. Information and Nation in the Early Modern Period.* Berkeley: University of California Press.

Black, John R. 1968. *Young Japan. Yokohama and Yedo, 1858–79.* New York: Oxford University Press.

Blomhoff, Jan Cock. 2000. *The Court Journey to the Shogun of Japan. From a Private Account by Jan Cock Blomhoff.* Edited by F. R. Effert. Introduced and annotated by Matthi Forrer. Leiden: Hotei Publishing.

Bodart-Bailey, Beatrice. 2003. "Urbanisation and the Nature of the Tokugawa Hegemony." In *Japanese Capitals in Historical Perspective, Place, Power and Memory in Kyoto, Edo and Tokyo,* ed. Nicholas Fieve and Paul Waley. London and New York: Routledge Curzon.

———. 2006. *The Dog Shogun: The Personality and Policies of Tokugawa Tsunayoshi.* Honolulu: University of Hawai'i Press.

Bolitho, Harold. 1991. "The Han." In *The Cambridge History of Japan,* vol. 4: *Early Modern,* ed. John Hall. Cambridge: Cambridge University Press.

Brown, Philip C. 1993. *Central Authority and Local Autonomy in the Formation of Early Modern Japan. The Case of Kaga Domain.* Stanford, Calif.: Stanford University Press.

Bunkyō furusato rekishikan, ed. 1993. *Hakkutsu sareta buke yashiki — hito to mono to dōbutsu no sekai.* Bunkyō-ku kyōiku iinkai.

Cahill, James. 1976. *Scholar Painters of Japan: The Nanga School.* New York: Arno Press.

Caron, Francois, and Joost Schouten. 1935. *A True Description of the Mighty Kingdoms of Japan & Siam.* Reprinted from the English edition of 1663, with introduction, notes, and appendixes by C. R. Boxer. London: The Argonaut Press.

Chiba ken, ed. 1990. *Kururi hansei ichihan.* Chiba ken.

Chikamatsu Monzaemon. 1961a. "The Drum of the Waves of Horikawa." In *Major Plays of Chikamatsu,* trans. Donald Keene. New York: Columbia University Press.

Chikamatsu Monzaemon. 1961b. "Gonza the Lancer." In *Major Plays of Chikamatsu,* trans. Donald Keene. New York: Columbia University Press.

Chikamatsu Toshio. 1990. *Ekin tokuhon.* Kōchi: Akaoka-chō kyōiku iinkai.

Chōno Enkei, ed. 1980. *Tosa han seiroku.* Rekishi tosho sha.

Chūda Toshio. 1993. *Sankin kōtai dōchūki — Kaga han shiryō o yomu.* Heibonsha.

Clark, Timothy T. 1997. "Mitate-e: Some Thoughts and a Summary of Recent Writing." *Impressions* 19, 6–27.

Clarke, H. B. D. 1989. "The Development of Edo Language." In *Eighteenth Century Japan,* ed. C. Andrew Gerstle, 63–72. Sydney: Allen & Unwin.

Clunas, Craig. 1991. *Superfluous Things. Material Culture and Social Status in Early Modern China.* Urbana and Chicago: University of Illinois Press.

Coaldrake, William H. 1981. "Edo Architecture and Tokugawa Law." *Monumenta Nipponica* 36, 3: 235–284.

———. 1996. *Architecture and Authority in Japan.* London and New York: Routledge.

———. 2003. "Metaphors of the Metropolis. Architectural and Artistic Representations of the Identity of Edo." In *Japanese Capitals in Historical Perspective, Place, Power and Memory in Kyoto, Edo and Tokyo,* ed. Nicolas Fieve and Paul Waley. London and New York: Routledge Curzon.

Cole, Mary Hill. 1999. *The Portable Queen: Elizabeth I and the Politics of Ceremony*. Amherst: University of Massachusetts Press.

Cort, Louise Allison. 2004. "A Tosa Potter in Edo." In *The Artist as Professional in Japan*, ed. Melina Takeuchi, 103–112. Stanford, Calif.: Stanford University Press.

Cortazzi, Hugh, ed. 1985. *Mitford's Japan. The Memoirs and Recollections, 1866–1906, of Algernon Bertram Mitford, the First Lord Redesdale*. London and Dover, N.H.: Athlone Press.

Craig, Albert M. 1961. *Choshu in the Meiji Restoration*. Cambridge, Mass.: Harvard University Press.

Craig, Teruko, trans. 1999. *Remembering Aizu: The Testament of Shiba Goro*. Honolulu: University of Hawai'i Press.

Darnton, Robert. 1984. "A Bourgeois Puts His World in Order: The City as a Text." In Robert Darnton, *The Great Cat Massacre and Other Episodes in French Cultural History*. London: Penguin Books.

Date Kenji. 1935. "Edo ni okeru shokō no shōhiteki seikatsu ni tsuite," pt. 1. *Rekishigaku kenkyū* 4, 1: 389–395.

———. 1936. "Edo ni okeru shokō no shōhiteki seikatsu ni tsuite," pt. 2. *Rekishigaku kenkyū* 6, 5: 555–565.

Davis, Susan G. 1986. *Parades and Power. Street Theatre in Nineteenth-Century Philadelphia*. Berkeley: University of California Press.

Deetz, James. 1966. *In Small Things Forgotten: An Archaeology of Early American Life*. New York: Anchor Books.

De Moges, Marquis. 2002. *Recollections of Baron Gros's Embassy to China and Japan in 1857–58*. London: Ganesha Publishing Ltd.

Dōmon Furuji. 1998. "Edo keizai o sasaete ita sankin kōtai to iu karakuri." *Kaizai kai* 33: 114–117.

Dore, Ronald P. 1965. *Education in Tokugawa Japan*. Berkeley: University of California Press.

Ebara Megumi. 1986. *Edo ryōri shikō*. Kawade shobō.

Edo iseki kenkyūkai, ed. 1991. *Yomigaeru Edo*. Shinjinbutsu ōraisha.

———. 1992. *Edo no shoku bunka*. Yoshikawa kōbunkan.

———. 2000. *Edo bunka no kōkogaku*. Yoshikawa kōbunkan.

Edo jidai o hakkutsu suru. Special edition of *Gekkan bunkazai* no. 338 (November 1991).

"Edo sanbyakunen yūmei tonosama to meibutsu kashin." Special edition of *Rekishi tokuhon* 17 (July 1992).

Edo Tōkyō tatemono no en, ed. 2001. *Uwajima han Date ke—shūzō kenzōbutsu 'Date-ke no mon' no haikei*. Edo Tōkyō tatemono no en.

Ego Michiko. 1999. *Inkyo daimyō no Edo kurashi*. Kōdansha.

Elman, Benjamin. 2000. *A Cultural History of Civil Examinations in Late Imperial China*. Berkeley: University of California Press.

Enkōan [Kōriki Tanenobu]. 1986. *Kinmei roku. Enkōan nikki*. Edited by Nagoya shi hōsa bunko. Nagoya sōsho, 3rd series, vol. 14. Nagoya shi kyōiku iinkai.

Fieve, Nicholas, and Paul Waley, eds. 2003. *Japanese Capitals in Historical Perspective, Place, Power and Memory in Kyoto, Edo and Tokyo*. London and New York: Routledge Curzon.

Fisher, Galen M., trans. 1938. "*Daigaku Wakumon*: A Discussion of Public Questions in the Light of the Great Learning." *Transactions, Asiatic Society of Japan*, 2nd series, 16: 259– 356.

Foucault, Michel. 1995. *Discipline and Punishment: The Birth of the Prison*. Translated by Alan Sheridan. New York: Vintage.

Fortune, Robert. 1863. *Yedo and Peking*. London: John Murray.

French, Calvin L. 1974. *Shiba Kōkan. Artist, Innovator, and Pioneer in the Westernization of Japan*. New York and Tokyo: Weatherhill.

Fuess, Harald. 1997. "A Golden Age of Fatherhood? Parent-Child Relations in Japanese Historiography." *Monumenta Nipponica* 52, 3: 381–397.

Fujii Shun, Mizuno Kyōichirō, and Taniguchi Sumio, ed. 1967. *Ikeda Mitsumasa nikki*. Okayama: Sanyō tosho shuppan.

Fujikawa Masaki. 2002. *Kinsei buke shūdan to toshi, kenchiku*. Chūō kōron.

Fujimoto Tsuyoshi. 1990. *Uzumoreta Edo. Tōdai no chika no daimyō yashiki*. Heibonsha.

Fujino Tamotsu. 1964. *Daimyō: sono ryōgoku keiei*. Jinbutsu ōraisha.

———. 1975. *Shintei bakuhan taiseishi no kenkyū*. Yoshikawa kōbunkan.

Fujioka Kenjirō, ed. 1977. *Nihon rekishi chiri sōsetsu: kinsei hen*. Yoshikawa kōbunkan.

Fujisawa Hiroshi. 1977. *Kinsei hōken kōtsūshi no kōzōteki kenkyū*. Fukubu shoten.

Fukai Masaumi and Fujizane Fumiko, eds. 1996–2003. *Edo bakufu daimyō bukan hennen shūsei*. 36 vols. Tōyō shorin.

Fukuda Kazuhiko. 2001. *Tōkaidō gojūsantsugi. Shōgun Iemochi-kō ojōraku zu*. Kawade shobō.

Fukui Kyūzō. 1937. *Shodaimyō no gakujutsu to bungei no kenkyū*. Kōsei kyoku.

Fukumochi Masayuki. 2002. *Iwataki no daisatsurei. Iwataki daimyo gyōretsu no rekishi to genkyo*. Iwataki: Iwataki shi.

Fukushima kenritsu hakubutsukan, ed. 2001. *Mushatachi ga tōru — gyōretsu ezu no sekai — tenji kaisetsu zuroku*. Fukushima: Fukushima kenritsu hakubutsukan.

Fukuzawa, Yukichi. 1966. *The Autobiography of Fukuzawa Yukichi*. Translated by Eiichi Kiyooka. New York: Columbia University Press.

Furukawa Kiyoyuki. 1995. *Daimyō gyōretsu o shiraberu*. Shōmine shoten.

Furukawa Koshōken. 1964. *Tōyū zakki*. Heibonsha.

Geertz, Clifford. 1983. "Centers, Kings and Charisma: Reflections of the Symbolics of Power." In Clifford Geertz, *Local Knowledge. Further Essays in Interpretive Anthropology*, 121–146. New York: Basic Books.

Gerstle, C. Andrew, ed. 1989. *Eighteenth-Century Japan*. Sydney: Allen & Unwin.

Hachinohe-shi shi hensan iinkai, ed. 1976. *Hachinohe-shi shi. Tsūshi hen*. Hachinohe: Hachinohe-shi.

———. 1977–1982. *Hachinohe shishi, shiryōhen. Kinsei*. 12 vols. Hachinohe: Hachinohe shi.

Hagio Masae. 1992. "Edo jidai shoki no enkai no shokki rui." In *Edo no shoku bunka*, ed. Edo iseki kenkyūkai. Yoshikawa kōbunkan.

Hakyō ronshū kankōkai, ed. 1991. *Hakyō ronshū*. Hakyō ronshū kankōkai.

Hall, John W., and Marius B. Jansen. 1968. *Studies in the Institutional History of Early Modern Japan*. Princeton, N.J.: Princeton University Press.

Hanley, Susan B. 1987. "Urban Sanitation in Preindustrial Japan." *Journal of Interdisciplinary History* 18, 1: 1–26.

———. 1997. *Everyday Things in Premodern Japan. The Hidden Legacy of Material Culture.* Berkeley: University of California Press.

Hanley, Susan B., and Kozo Yamamura. 1977. *Economic and Demographic Change in Preindustrial Japan, 1600–1868.* Princeton, N.J.: Princeton University Press.

Hara Kiyoshi. 1993. *Edo jijō*, vol. 5: *kenchiku hen*. Yūzankaku.

Harada (no first name given). 1938. "Edo jiman." In *Mikan zuihitsu hyakushu*, vol. 14, ed. Yamada Seisaku. Beisandō.

Harada Nobuo. 1989. *Edo no ryōri shi*. Chūō kōron.

———. 2003. *Edo no shoku seikatsu*. Iwanami shoten.

———. 2004. *Edo no ryōri to shoku seikatsu*. Shōgakkan.

Harada Tomoko, ed. 1975. *Nihon toshi seikatsu shiryōshū*, vol. 3: *jōkamachi hen*, pt. 1. Gakken.

Harafuji Hiroshi. 1984. *Daimyō rusui no kenkyū*. Sōbunsha.

Harris, Townsend. 1930. *The Complete Journal of Townsend Harris.* Introduction and Notes by Mario Emilio Cosenza. New York: Doubleday, Doran and Company.

Harris, Walter. 1983. *Morocco That Was.* London: Eland Books, 1983.

Hasegawa Akira. 1969. "Niimi no dogeza matsuri." *Okayama minzoku* 85: 293–297.

Hasegawa Kōtoku. 1987/8/19. "Hongoku no miso, shōyu chinchō" (part of series Kaga-han Edo yashiki seikatsu kō), *Hokkoku shinbun*, 8.

Hata Hisako. 2001. *Edo oku jōchū monogatari*. Kōdansha.

Hatano Tominobu. 1977. "Satsuma han no shoki sankin to sankin kōtaiji." *Komazawa daigaku shigaku ronshū* 7: 46–56.

Hauser, William B. 1974. *Economic Institutional Change in Tokugawa Japan: Osaka and the Kinai Cotton Trade.* London: Cambridge University Press.

Hayashi Reiko, ed. 1993. *Nihon no kinsei 15: josei no kinsei*. Chūō kōron.

———. 1994. "Provisioning Edo in the Early Eighteenth Century. The Pricing Policies of the Shogunate and the Crisis of 1733." In *Edo and Paris*, ed. James L. McClain, John M. Merriman, and Ugawa Kaoru. Ithaca, N.Y.: Cornell University Press.

Heusken, Henry C. J. 1964. *Japan Journal, 1855–1861.* Translated and edited by Jeannette C. van der Corput and Robert A. Wilson. New Brunswick, N.J.: Rutgers University Press.

Hirai Kiyoshi, ed. 1993. *Edo jijō 5: Kenchiku hen*. Yūzankaku.

———. 2004. *Doro-e de miru daimyō yashiki*. Gakken.

Hirao Michio. 1953. *Tosa nōmin ikki shikō*. Kōchi City Library.

———. 1959. *Yoshida Tōyō*. Yoshikawa kōbunkan.

———. 1965. *Zōho shinpan Kōchi han zaisei shi*. Kōchi: Kōchi shi shimin toshokan.

———. 1979. *Tosa shimin shiwa*. Kōchi: Kōchi shinbunsha.

———. N.d. "Kōchihan keizai shiryō" vol. 12: rokusei hen." Unpublished ms., Hirao bunko, Kōchi City Library.

Hirao Michio and Yamamoto Takeshi, ed. 1976. *Kaizanshū*, vol. 3, *rekishi* 2. Kōchi kenritsu toshokan.

Hirayama Toshijirō. 1994. "Sankin kōtai suru hatamoto." In *Ronshū bakuhan tai-*

sei shi, series one, vol. 5, *Hatamoto to chigyōsei*, ed. Fujino Tamotsu, 489–502. Yūzankaku.

Hirotani Kijūrō. 1978. "Maboroshi no Tosa no meicha, goishicha ni tsuite." *Ōtoyo shidan* 20: 17–28.

———. 1990. "Goishi-cha sunkō." *Ōtoyo shidan* 21: 55–60.

———. 1997a. "Sankin kōtai Kitayama-dō to Kōchi shi." *Tosa shidan* 206: 29–32.

———. 1997b. "Tosa no sankin kōtai to jōhō denpan no dōkō." *Tosa shidan* 206: 17–21.

———. 2003. "Engyōji no satsuki." In his *Kōchi shi rekishi sanpo*, 160–161. Kōchi: Kōchi shi bunka shinkō jigyōdan.

Ho, Ping-ti. 1982. *The Ladder of Success in Imperial China. Aspects of Social Mobility, 1368–1911*. New York: Columbia University Press.

Hohenberg, Paul M., and Lynn Hollen Lees. 1985. *The Making of Urban Europe 1000–1950*. Cambridge, Mass., and London: Harvard University Press.

Hōseishi gakkai, ed. 1958–1961. *Tokugawa kinreikō*. 11 vols. Sōbunsha.

Huber, Thomas. 1981. *The Revolutionary Origins of Modern Japan*. Stanford, Calif.: Stanford University Press.

Humbert, Aime. 1967–1970. *Anberu bakumatsu Nihon ezu*, 2 vols. Translated by Takahashi Hōtarō. Yūhōdo.

Ichimura Yōichi and Ōishi Shinzaburō. 1995. *Sakoku = yuruyakana jōhō kakumei*. Kōdansha.

Iidamachi iseki chōsakai, ed. 1995. *Iidamachi iseki*. Iidamachi iseki chōsakai.

Ikegami, Eiko. 1995. *Taming of the Samurai. Honorific Individualism and the Making of Modern Japan*. Cambridge, Mass.: Harvard University Press.

Ikku, Jippensha. 1960. *Shank's Mare: Being a Translation of the Tokaido Volumes of Hizakurige, Japan's Great Comic Novel of Travel & Ribaldry*. Translated by Thomas Satchell. Tokyo: C. E. Tuttle Books.

Imaizumi, Motosuke. 1981. *Nabeshima*. Tokyo and New York: Kodansha International.

Inagaki Shisei. 1988. *Omoeba Edo wa*. Yamato shobō.

Inoue Tadashi. 1963. *Kaibara Ekiken*. Yoshikawa kōbunkan.

Inoue Tsūjo. 2001. "Edo nikki." In *Edo jidai joryū bungaku zenshū*, vol. 1, ed. Furuya Akiyoshi. Nihon tosho senta.

Inuzuka Minoru. 1984. *Bunsei Edo machi saiken*. Yūzankaku.

Ishifumi Reii. 1933. "Daimyō sankin kōtai." *Tosa shidan* 42: 21–39.

Ishii Ryōsuke, ed. 1981a. *Tokugawa kinreikō*, vol. 1. Sōbunsha.

———. 1981b. *Hanpōshū*, vol. 4: *Kanazawa han*. Sōbunsha.

Ishikawa Eisuke. 1990. *Edo enerugi- jijō*. Kōdansha.

Ishikawa kenritsu toshokan, ed. 1989. *Santo to Kanazawa*. Kanazawa: Ishikawa kenritsu toshokan.

———. 1991. *Sankin kōtai*. Kanazawa: Ishikawa kenritsu toshokan.

Ishikawa Mitsuru. 1997. "Sankin kōtai Kitayama-dō to Shinomiya mura." *Tosa shidan* 206: 53–59.

———. N.d. "Tosa han sankin kōtai michi." Unpublished research paper.

Ishikawa Yasurō. 1997. "Sankin kōtai Kitayama-dō to Ōtoyo." *Tosa shidan* 206: 48–53.

Isoda Michifumi. 2003. *Bushi no kakei bo: 'Kaga han gosanyō mono' no bakumatsu*. Shinchōsha.

Itō Yoshiichi. 1966. *Edo no jimawari keizai no tenkai*. Kashiwa shobō.

———. 1982. *Edo no yume no shima*. Yoshikawa kōbunkan.

———. 1987. *Edo no machi kado*. Heibonsha.

Iwabuchi Reiji. 2003. "Buke yashiki no shinbutsu kōkai to toshi shakai." *Kokuritsu rekishi minzoku hakubutsukan kenkyū hōkoku* 103: 133–199.

———. 2004. *Edo bukechi no kenkyū*. Haniwa shobō.

Iwasaki, Haruko. 1984. "The World of *Gesaku*: Playful Writers of Late Eighteenth Century Japan." Ph.D. dissertation, Harvard University.

Izushi chōshi henshū iinkai, ed. and pub. 1987. *Izushi machi shi*, vol. 3: *shiryō hen* 1. Izushi machi (Hyōgo).

Izushi-chō yakuba sōmuka chōshi henshūshitsu, ed. and pub. 1982. *Izushi-chō shi bessatsu: "Goyō heya nikki."* Izushi machi (Hyōgo).

Jansen, Marius B. 1961. *Sakamoto Ryōma and the Meiji Restoration*. Princeton, N.J.: Princeton University Press.

———. 2000. *The Making of Modern Japan*. Cambridge, Mass., and London: Belknap Press of Harvard University Press.

Jinnai, Hidenobu. 1995. *Tokyo. A Spatial Anthropology*. Translated by Kimiko Nishimura. Berkeley: University of California Press.

Jordan, Brenda G., and Victoria Weston. 2003. *Copying the Master and Stealing His Secrets. Talent and Training in Japanese Painting*. Honolulu: University of Hawai'i Press.

Kaempfer, Englebert. 1999. *Kaempfer's Japan. Tokugawa Culture Observed*. Edited, translated, and annotated by Beatrice M. Bodart-Bailey. Honolulu: University of Hawai'i Press.

Kagioka Masanori. 1999. *Ekin to bakumatsu Tosa rekishi sanpo*. Shinchō sha.

Kagoshima ken ishin shiryō hensanjo, ed. 1981. *Kagoshima ken shiryō. Kyūki zatsuroku tsuiroku*, vol. 1. Kagoshima-ken.

———. 1984. *Kagoshima-ken shiryō. Nariakira-kō shiryō*, vol. 4. Kagoshima-ken.

Kagoshima ken shiryō kankō kai, ed. 1967. *Onobori odōchū nichō ogekō*. Kagoshima ken shiryō 7. Kagoshima ken shiryō kankōkai.

Kamakura Kōji. 1977. *Satsuki to haiku*. Kōchi: Published privately by author. (Copy in Kōchi Prefectural Library.)

Kameda Yasunori and others. 1995. "Sankin kōtai." *Daruma* 7 (vol. 2, no. 3): 12–15.

Kami-gun Tosa Yamada chō kyōiku iinkai, ed. 1979. *Tosa Yamada-chō shiryō*, vol. 2. Tosa Yamada: Kami gun Tosa Yamada chō kyōiku iinkai.

Kanagawa kenritsu kindai bijutsukan, ed. 1976. *Watanabe Shin'ichirō shi korekushon Edo no doroe ten*. Nihon bijutsukan kiga kyōgi kai.

Kanagawa kenritsu rekishi hakubutsukan, ed. 2001. *Tokubetsu ten "Edo jidai no Tōkaidō—egakareta kaidō no sugata to nigiwai."* Kanagawa kenritsu rekishi hakubutsukan.

Kanazawa shishi hensan iinkai, ed. 2001. *Kanazawa shishi, shiryōhen* 4, *kinsei* 2: *hansei*. Kanazawa: Kanazawa shi.

Kanzawa Tokō. 1978. "Okinagusa." In *Nihon zuihitsu taisei*, vols. 19–24, ed. Nihon zuihitsu taisei henshūbu. Yoshikawa kōbunkan.

Kasaya Kazuhiko. 1980. "Kinsei buke yashiki kakekomi kankō." *Shiryōkan kenkyū kiyō* 12: 211–237.

———. 1993. "Sankin kōtai no bunkashiteki igi." In *Bunmei to shite no Tokugawa Nihon*, ed. Haga Tōru. Chūō kōron.

———. 2000a. *Edo orusuiyaku. Kinsei no gaikōkan.* Yoshikawa kōbunkan.

———. 2000b. *The Origin and Development of Japanese-Style Organization.* Kyoto: International Research Center for Japanese Studies (Nichibunken).

———. 2001. *Shi (samurai) no shisō.* Iwanami shoten.

Kasei jikki kanpon hensan iinkai, ed. 1977. *Aizu han kasei jikki*, vol. 3. Rekishi shunjūsha.

Kashin jinmei jiten hensan iinkai, ed. 1987–1989. *Sanbyaku han kashin jinmei jiten.* 6 vols. Shinjinbutsu ōraisha.

Kassel, Marleen. 1996. *Tokugawa Confucian Education: The Kangien Academy of Hirose Tansō (1782–1856).* Albany: State University of New York.

Kasumi kaikan, ed. N.d. *Sankin kōtai gyōretsu zu.* Kasumi kaikan.

Kasuya Hiroki. 1997. *Tōkaidō meisho zue o yomu.* Tōkyō-dō.

Kattō Isamu. 1994. *Tosa gajin den.* Kōchi: Kōchi shimin toshokan.

Kawata Hisashi. 1990. *Edo meisho zue o yomu.* Tōkyōdō.

———. 1995. *Zoku Edo meisho zue o yomu.* Tōkyōdō.

Keene, Donald. 1959. *The Japanese Discovery of Europe, 1720–1830.* Stanford, Calif.: Stanford University Press.

———. 1961. *Major Plays of Chikamatsu.* New York: Columbia University Press.

———. 1971. *Chūshingura (The Treasury of Loyal Retainers).* New York: Columbia University Press.

———. 2006. *Frog in the Well. Portraits of Japan by Watanabe Kazan, 1793–1841.* New York: Columbia University Press.

Kelly, William W. 1994. "Incendiary Actions. Fires and Firefighting in the Shogun's Capital and the People's City." In *Edo and Paris,* ed. James L. McClain, John M. Merriman, and Ugawa Kaoru. Ithaca, N.Y.: Cornell University Press.

Kikuchi Kazuo. 1987. *Kinsei toshi no shakai shi.* Meicho shuppan.

Kikuchi Kazuo and Sugimoto Toshio, eds. 1963. *Fudai hansei no tenkai to Meiji ishin — Shimōsa Sakura han.* Bungadō ginkō kenkyūsha.

Kimura Motoi and Sugimoto Toshio, eds. 1969. *Fudai hansei no tenkai to Meiji ishin — Shimōsa Sakura han.* Bungeidō ginkō kenkyūsha.

Kitahara Itoko. 1991. "Edo no buke yashiki ni tsuite." In *Edo-Tōkyō o yomu*, ed. Ogi Shinzō. Chikuma shobō.

Kitahara Susumu. 1991. *Hyakuman toshi. Edo no seikatsu.* Kadokawa shoten, 1991.

Kiyokawa Hachirō. 1969. *Saiyūsō.* Heibonsha.

Kobayashi Fumio. 2000. "Buke no zōsho to shusho katsudō — Hachinohe han shomotsu nakama no shokai." *Rekishi hyōron* 605: 68–80.

Kobayashi Katsu. 1991. "Oranda kara kita kurei paipu." In *Yomigaeru Edo*, ed. Edo iseki kenkyūkai.

Kobayashi Tadashi. 2002. *Edo ukiyoe o yomu.* Chikuma shobō.

Kobiki Harunobu. 1991. "Dewa Matsuyama tei no hakkutsu — Hakuō iseki no hakkutsu." In Edo iseki kenkyūkai, *Yomigaeru Edo.*

Kōchi chihōshi kenkyūkai, ed. 1975. *Kōchi-ken rekishi nenpyō*, revised edition. Kōchi City Library.

Kōchi ken, ed. 1995. *Sankin kōtai Kitayamadō. Kōchi ken rekishi no michi chōsa hōkoku.* Kōchi ken.

Kōchi ken bunkyō kyōkai, ed. 1965. *Nonaka Kenzan kankei monjō.* Kōchi: Kōchi ken bunkyō kyōkai.

Kōchi ken jinmei jiten henshū iinkai, ed. 1971. *Kōchi ken jinmei jiten.* Kōchi: Kōchi shimin toshokan.

Kōchi kenshi hensan iinkai, ed. 1968. *Kōchi ken shi: Kinsei hen.* Kōchi: Kōchi ken.

Kōchōsha henshūbu, ed. 1978. *Ekin.* Kōchi: Kōchōsha.

Kodama Kōta. 1969–1974. *Kinsei kōtsū shiryōshū.* 10 vols. Yoshikawa kōbunkan.

———. 1986a. *Shukueki.* Shibundō.

———. 1986b. *Shukuba to kaidō: Gokaidō nyūmon.* Tōkyō bijutsu.

Kodate Chūzō. 1973. *Tsugaru hansei jidai ni okeru seikatsu to shūkyō.* Hirosaki: Tsugaru shobō.

Kodera Kiyoaki. 1916. "Edo migusa." In *Sohaku jisshu*, vol. 2, ed. Mitamura Enkyō. Kokusho kankōkai.

Kodera Takehisa. 1989. *Owari han Edo shimo yashiki no nazo.* Chūō kōron.

Koizumi Hiroshi. 1987. *Edo no kōkogaku.* Nyū saensu.

———. 1990a. *Edo o horu — kinsei toshi kōkogaku e no shōtai.* Kashiwa shobō.

———. 1990b. *Edo no ana.* Kashiwa shobō.

Kondo Eiichi. 1984. *Shukuba to kaidō.* NHK.

Kondō Toshio. 1988. *Ekin gafū.* Heibonsha.

Konishi Shirō, Jugaku Akiko, and Muragishi Yoshio. 1974. *Sugoroku.* Tokuma shoten.

Konno Nobuo. 1986. *Edo no tabi.* Iwanami shoten.

Kornicki, Peter. 2001. *The Book in Japan. A Cultural History from the Beginnings to the Nineteenth Century.* Honolulu: University of Hawai'i Press.

Kuga machi kyōiku iinkai, ed. 1990. *Daimyō gyōretsu to Kuga.* Kuga machi (Yamaguchi): Kuga machi kyōiku iinkai.

Kumamoto ken, ed. 1965. *Kumamoto ken shiryō, kinsei 3.* Kumamoto.

Kumon kodomo kenkyūjo, ed. 2003. *Asobeya asobe! Kodomo ukiyoe ten.* NHK.

Kuroda Hideo and Ronald Toby, eds. 1994. *Gyōretsu to misemono.* Special edition (vol. 17) of *Asahi hyakka: Rekishi o yominaosu.* Asahi shimbun.

Kuroita Katsumi. 1964–1966. *Tokugawa jikki.* Vols. 38–47 of *Kokushi taikei.* Kokushi taikei henshukai, ed. Yoshikawa kōbunkan.

Kurushima Hiroshi. 1986. "Morizuna, makizuna, kazari teoke, hōki. Kinsei ni okeru 'chisō' no hitotsu to shite." *Shigaku zasshi* 95, 8: 60–92.

Kuwata Tadachika. 1988. *Shimabara no ranzu, Sengoku gassenzu.* Chūō kōron.

Leutner, Robert W. 1985. *Shikitei Sanba and the Comic Tradition in Edo Fiction.* Cambridge, Mass.: Council on East Asian Studies, Harvard University.

Lindau, Rudolph. 1986. *Suisu ryōji no mita bakumatsu Nihon.* Translated by Morimoto Eifu. Shinjinbutsu ōraisha.

Lo, Winston W. 1987. *An Introduction to the Civil Service of Sung China.* Honolulu: University of Hawai'i Press.

MacAloon, John J., ed. 1984. *Rite, Drama, Festival, Spectacle: Rehearsals Toward a Theory of Cultural Performance.* Philadelphia: Institute for the Study of Human Issues.

Maeda Ikutoku kai. 1929–1958. *Kaga han shiryō.* 18 vols. Ishiguro Bun'kichi.

Martin, Ann Smart. 1993. "Makers, Buyers, and Users. Consumerism as a Material Culture Framework." *Winterthur Portfolio* 28, 2/3: 141–157.

Maruyama Yasunari, 1976. "Sankin kōtai sei no kenkyū (1) — sono josetsu hen." *Kyūshū bunkashi kenkyūjo kiyō* 20: 61–105.

———. 1987. "Sankin kōtaisei no kōzō to kōtsū (1) — sono sobyō." *Kōtsū shi kenkyū* 18: 1–25.

———, ed. 1992. *Nihon no kinsei 6: jōhō to kōtsū.* Chūō kōron.

Maske, Andrew Lawrence. 1994. "The Historical Development of Takatori Ware — Official Ceramic of the Kuroda Han of Chikuzen Province." 2 vols. Ph.D. thesis, St. Anthony's College (Oxford).

Mass, Jeffrey P. 1990. "The Kamakura Bakufu." In *The Cambridge History of Japan,* vol. 3: *Medieval,* ed. Kozo Yamamura. Cambridge: Cambridge University Press.

Masuda Toshimi. 1992. "Yoshino Michi no shōgai — sono tegami o tsūjite." In *Edo jidai no joseitachi,* ed. Kinsei joseishi kenkyūkai. Yōshikawa kōbunkan.

Matsui, Masato. 1975. "Shimazu Shigehide, 1745–1833. A Case Study of Daimyo Leadership." Ph.D. dissertation, University of Hawai'i.

Matsudaira Tarō. 1964. *Kōtei Edo jidai seido no kenkyū.* Kashiwa shobō.

Matsudo shiritsu hakubutsukan, ed. 1998. *Mito dōchū. Shukuba to tabibito.* Matsudo shiritsu hakubutsukan.

Matsumoto Eiko. 1997. "Tosa han no sankin kōtai." *Tosa shidan* 206: 4–17.

Matsunoo Shōkō, comp. 1973–1978. Hirao Michio and others, eds. *Kaizanshū,* 10 vols. Kōchi: Kōchi kenritsu toshokan.

Matsura Seizan. 1978–1982. *Kasshi yawa.* Edited by Nakamura Yukihiko and Nakano Mitsutoshi. 6 vols. Heibonsha.

———. 1981a. "Enpō kikō. In Matsura Seizan, *Kasshi yawa zokuhen* 7, ed. Nakamura Yukihiko and Nakano Mitsutoshi. Heibonsha.

———. 1981b. "Kansei kikō." In Matsura Seizan, *Kasshi yawa zokuhen* 7, ed. Nakamura Yukihiko and Nakano Mitsutoshi. Heibonsha.

Matsuyama Hidemi. 1971. *Kajin gunzō.* Kōchi: Kōchi shimin toshokan.

Matsuyoshi Sadao. 1930. *Tosa han keizai shi kenkyū.* Nihon hyōronsha.

McClain, James L. 1982. *Kanazawa.* New Haven, Conn.: Yale University Press.

McClain, James L., John M. Merriman, and Ugawa Kaoru, eds. 1994. *Edo and Paris. Urban Life & the State in the Early Modern Era.* Ithaca, N.Y.: Cornell University Press.

McClain, James L., and Wakita Osamu. 1999. *Osaka. The Merchants' Capital of Early Modern Japan.* Ithaca, N.Y.: Cornell University Press.

McClatchie, Thomas R. H. 1890. "The Feudal Mansions of Yedo." *Transactions of the Asiatic Society of Japan* 7: 157–188.

McEwan, J. R. 1962. *The Political Writings of Ogyū Sorai.* Cambridge: Cambridge University Press.

McClellan, Edwin. 1985. *Woman in the Crested Kimono. The Life of Shibue Io and Her Family Drawn from Mori Ōgai's 'Shibue Chūsai'.* New Haven, Conn., and London: Yale University Press.

Mitford, Nancy. 1994. *The Sun King.* New York: Penguin Books.

Miura Tadashi. 1990. "Hachinohe han no Edo yashiki to hanshū no kōyū." *Rekishi techō* 18, 3: 4–13.

————, ed. 1992. *Hachinohe han Tōyama ke nikki*. 2 vols. Aomori: Aomori ken bunka-zai hogo kyōkai.

————. 1994. *Hachinohe han no rikujō kōtsū*. Hachinohe: Hachinohe tsu'un sha.

Miwa Hideo. 1993. *Odano Naotake to Akita Ranga*. Nihon no bijutsu 327. Shibundō.

Miyagi ken, ed. 1966. *Miyagi kenshi 2: Kinseishi*. Miyagi kenshi kankōkai.

Miyaji Saichirō. 1970. *Miyaji-ke sandai nikki*. Kōfūsha shoten.

Miyamoto Tsuneichi. 1987. *Daimyō no tabi. Honjin o tazunete*. Yasaka shobō.

Miyazaki Katsumi. 1992. "Edo no toshi — daimyō, bakushin no tochi mondai." In *Nihon no kinsei*, vol. 9: *Toshi no jidai*, ed. Yoshida Nobuyuki. Chūō kōron.

————. 1995. "Buke yashiki." In *Iwanami kōza Nihon rekishi* 14, *Kinsei* 4. Iwanami shoten.

————. 1999. "Daimyō yashiki no sakuji — fushin to Edo iseki." Unpublished report from 13th Annual Meeting of Edo iseki kenkyūkai.

Miyazaki Katsumi and Yoshida Nobuyuki, eds. 1994. *Buke yashiki — kūkan to shakai*. Yamakawa shuppan.

Miyazawa Shin'ichi. 1987. *Satsuma to Igirisu no deai*. Takajō shobō.

Mizuhara Akito. 1994. *Edo-go, Tōkyō-go, hyōjun-go*. Heibonsha.

Mizutani, Mitsuhiro. 2003. "The Shogun's Domestic and Foreign Visitors." *Japan Echo* 30, 2: 1–6, online edition: <www.japanecho.co.jp/sum/2003/300315.html>.

Mori Senzō, ed. 1980. *Zuihitsu hyakkaen*, vol. 7. Chūō kōron.

Mori Yasuhiro. 1990. "Shoki no Kōchi han Ōsaka kura yashiki." *Keizaigaku ronkyū* 44, 3: 29–47.

————. 1991. "Ōsaka kura yashiki no hensen." *Shōgaku ronkyū* 38, 4: 47–55.

————. 1994a. "Kanazawa han Ōsaka kura yashiki." *Shōgaku ronkyū* 42, 1: 39–52.

————. 1994b. "Fukuoka han Ōsaka kura yashiki." In Hidemura Senzō, ed. *Sainan chiikishi kenkyū*, vol. 8. Bunken shuppan.

Moriguchi Kōji. 1982. "Tosa han nōgaku zakkō." In *Kōchi no kenkyū*, vol. 4: *kinsei-kindai*, ed. Yamamoto Takeshi. Seibundō.

————. 1986. "Josetsu 'Mori Kanzaemon Hirosada nikki' kōkyū (1)." *Ōtoyo shidan* 15: 23–41.

————. 1987. "Josetsu 'Mori Kanzaemon Hirosada nikki' kōkyū (2)." *Ōtoyo shidan* 16: 7–25.

————. 1988. "Josetsu 'Mori Kanzaemon Hirosada nikki' kōkyū (3)." *Ōtoyo shidan* 17:13–25.

————. 1989, 1994. *Tosa han oyakuninchō*, vols. 1–2. Kōchi shimin toshokan.

————. 1991. "'Mori Kanzaemon Hirosada nikki' no sekai." *Bungaku* 2–3: 38–42.

Morita Minoru. 1952. *Nanbu han ni okeru moyai seido no kenkyū*. Aomori: Morita nōmin bunka kenkyūjo.

Motosuke Imaizumi. 1981. *Nabeshima*. New York: Kodansha.

Mutō Yoshikazu, comp. and auth. 1990–1997. *Nanroshi. Tosa kokushi shiryō shūsei*. Yorimitsu Kanji, Akizawa Shigeru, and others, eds. 10 vols. Kōchi: Kōchi Prefectural Library.

Myōjin Kentarō. 1983. "Shita ni — Shita ni — Tōkaidō neriaruki (jō). Kokurō Fukao kō no Edo sankin kōtai." *Sakawa shidan: Kiriuseki* 8: 26–32.

N. A. 1981. *Shikoku no michi*, pt. 1. Kōchi shinbunsha.

Nagano kenshi kankōkai, ed. 1988. *Nagano kenshi, tsūshi hen*, vol. 5: *kinsei* 2. Nagano: Nagano kenshi kankōkai.

Nagashima Atsuko. 1986. "Bakumatsu nōson josei no kōdō no jiyū to kaji rōdō." In *Ronshū kinsei josei shi*, ed. Kinsei josei shi kenkyūkai. Yoshikawa kōbunkan.

Nagata Tomisato. 1988. *Matsumae eshi Kakizaki Hakyō*. Hokkaidō shimbunsha.

Nagoya shi hakubutsukan, ed. 1986. *Enkōan to sono jidai. Owari hanshi no egaita Nagoya*. Nagoya: Nagoya shi hakubutsukan.

———. 2001. *Tōkai benranzu ryaku*, pt. 1. Nagoya: Nagoya shi hakubutsukan.

———. 2002. *Nagoya jōka no 'gomi' jijō*. Nagoya: Nagoya shi hakubutsukan.

Nagoya shi hōsa bunko, ed. 1976. *Kinmei roku. Enkōan nikki*. Nagoya: Nagoya shi kyōiku iinkai.

Naitō Akira. 1972. *Edo no toshi to kenchiku*, supplementary volume to Suwa Haruo and Naitō Akira, eds., *Edozu byōbu*. Mainichi shinbunsha.

Naitō Meisetsu. 1982. "Kinban mono." In *Bakumatsu no buke*, ed. Shibata Shōkyoku. Seiabō.

Najita, Tetsuo. 1987. *Visions of Virtue in Tokugawa Japan: The Kaitokudō Merchant Academy of Osaka*. Chicago: University of Chicago Press.

Nakagawa Sugane. 1990. "Kinsei Ōsaka no daimyō kashi shōnin." *Nihonshi kenkyū* 329: 3–35.

Nakano Mitsutoshi. 1992. *Edo bunka hyōbanki: gazoku yūwa no sekai*. Chūō kōron.

Nakane, Chie, and Ōishi Shinzaburō. 1990. *Tokugawa Japan: The Social and Economic Antecedents of Modern Japan*. Translated and edited by Conrad Totman. Tokyo: University of Tokyo Press.

Namikawa Kenji. 2004. *Kinsei bushi no seikatsu to ishiki. "Soeda Gizaemon nikki"— Tenna ki no Edo to Hirosaki*. Iwada shoin.

Narasaki Muneshige. 1964. *Tōkaidō gojūsantsugi. Hokusai to Hiroshige*, vol. 2. Kōdansha.

Neville, Edwin L. 1958. "The Development of Transportation in Japan: A Case Study of Okayama han, 1600–1868." Ph.D. dissertation, University of Michigan.

Nihon fūzoku shigakkai. 1994. *Edo no kurashi 122 hanashi*. Tsukubane sha.

Niimi daimyo gyōretsu hozonkai. 1997. *Oshinkō buki gyōretsu. Niimi daimyo gyōretsu*. Niimi-shi, Okayama: Niimi daimyō gyōretsu hozonkai.

Nio-machi shi hensan iinkai, ed. 1984. *Nio-machi shi*. Kagawa-ken, Nio-machi.

Nishigori Gohei. 1977. "Tōbu nikki." In *Nihon toshi seikatsu shiryō shūsei*, vol. 2: *Santo hen* pt. 2, ed. Harada Tomohiko. Gakken.

Nishiyama Matsunosuke. 1983. *Edo no seikatsu bunka*. Vol. 3 in his *Nishiyama Matsunosuke chosakushū*. Yoshikawa kōbunkan.

———. 1987. *Edo bunka shi*. Iwanami shoten.

———. 1991. "Zenkoku ni hirogaru Edo bunka." *Rekishi tanjō* 8: 124–136.

———. 1992. *Yomigaeru Edo bunka*. NHK.

———. 1997. *Edo Culture: Daily Life and Diversions in Edo Japan, 1600–1868*. Translated and edited by Gerald Groemer. Honolulu: University of Hawai'i Press.

Nishiyama Matsunosuke and others, ed. 1989. *Edo gaku jiten*. Kōbundō.

Noguchi Tomomichi. 2004. "Kinsei zenki Nabeshima-ke no honke-bunke kankei." *Chihōshi kenkyū* 307: 5–21.

Notehelfer, F. G., ed. and annot. 1992. *Japan through American Eyes. The Journal of Francis Hall. Kanagawa and Yokohama, 1859–1866*. Princeton, N.J.: Princeton University Press.

Ōba Hideaki. 1997. *Edo no shokubutsugaku*. Tōkyō daigaku shuppankai.

Ogawa Kyōichi. 1992. *Edo bakuhan daimyō ke jiten*. 3 vols. Hara shobō.

Ogi Shinzō. 1991. *Edo-Tōkyō o yomu*. Chikuma shobō.

Ōgiura Masayoshi. 1993. *Edo hakkutsu*. Meichō shuppan.

Ōi-machi kyōiku iinkai. 2000. *Yoshinaga Hachimangū no daimyō gyōretsu*. Ōi-machi, Shizuoka: Ōi-machi kyōiku iinkai.

Oikawa Yoshio. 2004. *Edo no mikuro kosumosu. Kaga han Edo yashiki*. Shin'eisha.

Ōishi Manabu. 1995. *Yoshimune to Kyōhō no kaikaku*. Tōkyōdō.

Ōishi Shinzaburō. 1991. "Zenkoku ni hirogaru Edo no bunka." *Rekishi tanjō* 8: 124–128.

Oliphant, Laurence. 1860. *Narrative of the Earl of Elgin's Mission to China and Japan in the Years 1857, 1858, 1859*. 2 vols. Edinburg: Blackwood and Sons.

Okayama kenshi hensan iinkai, ed. 1985. *Okayama kenshi 7, kinsei* pt. 2. Okayama: Okayama ken.

Ōkuma Yoshikuni. 1939. *Doro-e to daimyō yashiki*. Ōtsuka kōgei.

Ono Ken'ichirō. 1931. *Tōki zenshū*. Tōki zenshū kankōkai.

Ōsaka shiritsu hakubutsukan, ed. 1996. *Shōnin no butai — tenka no daidokoro: Ōsaka*. Osaka: Ōsaka shiritsu hakubutsukan.

Ōshima Nobujirō. 1955. *Honjin no kenkyū*. Yoshikawa kōbunkan.

———. 1959. *Tabi fūzoku*, vol. 1: *sōgō hen*. Yūzankaku.

Ōta Kōtarō. 1965. *Nanbu han sankin kōtai zukan*. Morioka: Okubane shidankai.

Ōta Motoko. 1994. *Edo no oyako: Chichioya ga kodomo o sodateta jidai*. Chūō kōron.

Ōtsuka Hatsushige and Koizumi Hiroshi. 1994. *Happyaku hatchō no kōkogaku*. Yamakawa shuppansha.

Overmeer, F. Van. 1978. *Nihon fūzoku bikō*, vol. 2. Translated by Jōji Mitsuo. Heibonsha.

Ozawa Emiko. 1998. *Higai toshi Edo to*. Yoshikawa kōbunkan.

Ozawa Hiromu, Uchida Kinzō, and others. 1993. *Kuwagata Keisai, Eto meisho zue no sekai*. Ōkūsha.

Ozawa Hiromu and Maruyama Nobuhiko. 1993. *Edozu byōbu*. Kawade shobō.

Perez, Louis G. 2002. *Daily Life in Early Modern Japan*. Westport, Conn., and London: Greenwood Press.

Pitelka, Morgan. 2005. *Handmade Culture: Raku Potters, Patrons, and Tea Practitioners in Japan*. Honolulu: University of Hawai'i Press.

Pyle, Kenneth B. 1978. *The Making of Modern Japan*. Lexington, Mass.: D. C. Heath.

Ravina, Mark. 2004. *The Last Samurai. The Life and Battles of Saigō Takamori*. Hoboken, N.J.: John Wiley & Sons, Inc.

Roberts, Luke S. 1991. "The Merchant Origins of National Prosperity Thought in Eighteenth Century Japan." Ph.D. dissertation, Princeton University.

———. 1998. *Mercantilism in a Japanese Domain: The Merchant Origins of Economic Nationalism in 18th-Century Tosa*. Cambridge: Cambridge University Press.

Rozman, Gilbert. 1974. "Edo's Importance in the Changing Tokugawa Society." *Journal of Japanese Studies* 1, 1: 91–112.

Ryan, Mary. 1989. "The American Parade: Representations of the Nineteenth-Century Social Order." In *The New Cultural History*, ed. Lynn Hunt. Berkeley: University of California Press.

"Ryōri monogatari" shōkai. 1975. Tada shokumi kenkyūjo.

Sakai Banshirō. 1983. "Edo e hassoku nikki chō." In *Chizu de miru Shinjuku-ku no utsurikawari — Yotsuya hen*. Tōkyō-to Shinjuku-ku kyōiku iinkai.

Sakai Gankō. 1996. *Hiroshige. Edo fūkei hanga taishūsei*. Shogakkan.

Sakurai Junya. 1992. "Iseki shutsudo no dōbutsu itai kara mita daimyō yashiki no shoku seikatsu." In *Edo no shoku bunka*, ed. Edo iseki kenkyūkai. Yoshikawa kōbunkan.

Sasakawa Ryūhei. 1986. *Tsubaki no gohonjin*. Osaka: Kōyō shobō.

Satō, Kanzan. 1983. *The Japanese Sword*. Translated and adapted by Joe Earl. Tokyo and London: Kodansha.

Satō Morihiro. 2000. "Doro-e and Edo Urban Composition." Unpublished paper presented at the AAS Annual Meeting, Washington, D.C., March 11.

Satow, Ernest. 1983. *A Diplomat in Japan*. Rutland, Vt., and Tokyo: C. E. Tuttle Books.

Screech, Timon. 1996. *The Western Scientific Gaze and Popular Imagery in Later Edo Japan. The Lens within the Heart*. Cambridge: Cambridge University Press.

———. 2000. *The Shogun's Painted Culture. Fear and Creativity in the Japanese States, 1760–1829*. London: Reaktion Books.

Sekiyama Naotarō. 1958. *Kinsei Nihon no jinkō kōzō*. Yoshikawa kōbunkan.

Setagaya kuritsu kyōdō shiryōkan, ed. 1998. *Edo no bunjin kōyū roku. Kameda Bōsai to sono nakamatachi — Atsumi korekushon of chūshin ni-*. Setagaya kuritsu kyōdō shiryōkan.

Shiba Keiko. 1997. *Kinsei onna tabi nikki*. Yoshikawa kōbunkan.

Shimamura Kaname. 1988. "Tosa Yamada hōmen no sankin kōtai." *Tosa shidan* 179: 32–36.

Shimamura Taeko. 1972. "Bakumatsu kakyū bushi no seikatsu no jittai." *Shien* 21, 2: 45–68.

Shinba Eiji. 1990. *Iwasaki Yatarō*. PHP kenkyūjo.

Shinji Yoshimoto. 1984. *Edo jidai bushi no seikatsu*. Yūzankaku.

Shinjuku rekishi hakubutsukan, ed. 1991. *Edo no kurashi. Kinsei kōkogaku no sekai*. Shinjuku-ku kyōiku iinkai.

———. 1994. *Daimyō yashiki — gishiki, bunka, seikatsu no sugata*. Shinjuku-ku kyōiku iinkai.

Shinoda Kōzō. 1969. *Bakumatsu hyakuwa*. Kadokawa shoten.

———. 1971. *Bakumatsu Meiji onna hyakuwa*. Kadokawa shoten.

Shinohara Sadaichi. 1981. *Kurume jinbutsu shi*. Kurume: Kikuchiku Kinbundō.

Shirahata Yōzaburō. 1997. *Daimyō teien*. Kōdansha.

Shuri-man, H. (Schliemann, Heinrich). 1998. *Shuri-man ryokōki Shinkoku, Nihon*. Translated by Ishii Kazuko. Kōdansha.

Siebold, Philipp Franz von. 1973. *Manners and Customs of the Japanese in the Nineteenth Century: From the Accounts of Dutch Residents in Japan and From the German Work of Philipp Franz von Siebold*. Introduction by Terence Barrow. Rutland, Vt., and Tokyo: C. E. Tuttle Books.

Smith, George. 1861. *Ten Weeks in Japan*. London: Longman, Green, Longman, and Roberts.

Smith, Henry D. 1986a. *Hiroshige: One Hundred Famous Views of Edo*. New York: Braziller.

———. 1986b. "The Edo-Tokyo Transition: In Search of Common Ground." In *Japan in Transition. From Tokugawa to Meiji*, ed. Marius B. Jansen and Gilbert Rozman. Princeton, N.J.: Princeton University Press.

———. 1988. "World Without Walls: Kuwagata Keisai's Panoramic Vision of Japan." In *Japan and the World: Essays on Japanese History and Politics in Honour of Ishida Takeshi*, ed. Gail Lee Bernstein and Haruhiro Fukui. New York: St. Martin's.

Smith, Richard J. 1983. *China's Cultural Heritage. The Ch'ing Dynasty, 1644–1912*. Boulder, Colo.: Westview Press.

Smuts, R. M. 1989. "Public Ceremony and Royal Charisma: The English Royal Gentry in London, 1485–1642." In *The First Modern Society: Essays in English History in Honour of Lawrence Stone*, ed. A. L. Beier, David Cannadine, and James M. Rosenheim. Cambridge: Cambridge University Press.

Smyers, Karen A. 1999. *The Fox and the Jewel. Shared and Private Meanings in Contemporary Japanese Inari Worship*. Honolulu: University of Hawai'i Press.

Soda Kōichi. 1999. *Edo kiriezu o yomu*. Tōkyō-dō shuppan.

Spence, Jonathan D. 1988. *Emperor of China: Self-portrait of K'ang-hsi*. New York: Vintage.

Strong, Roy. 1977. *The Cult of Elizabeth: Elizabethan Portraiture and Pageantry*. London: Thames and Hudson.

Sugimori Tetsuya. 1999. "Gofukusho to Kyōto — Akita han o jirei to shite." *Nenpō toshi shi kenkyū 7: shutosei*. Yamakawa shuppan.

Sugitanai Akira. 1992. *Nabeshima Kansō*. Chūō kōron.

Suzuki Eizō. 1993. *Edo kōdan Fujiokaya banashi*. Shineidō.

Suzuki Masao. 1992. *Ienushi san no daigosan*. Sanseidō.

Suzuki Shōsei. 2001. *Edo no meisho to toshi bunka*. Yoshikawa kōbunkan.

Suzuki Yuriko. 1993. "Jūke jōsei no seikatsu — Rai Baishi no shigoto to shussan, ikuji." In *Nihon no kinsei 15: josei no kinsei*, ed. Hayashi Reiko. Chūō kōron.

Takagi Shōsaku. 1985. "'Hideyoshi's Peace' and the Transformation of the Bushi Class." *Acta Asiatica* 49: 46–77.

Takakura Jun. 1987. "Sankin kōtai no shidō shiryō ni tsuite." *Miyagi shigaku* 12: 19–30.

Takeichi Saichirō. 1967. *Takeichi Saichirōshū*, vol. 4: *rekishi shiryō hen*. Kōchi shimin toshokan.

Takeuchi Mitsuaki. 1967. *Ōigawa monogatari*. Takeda shuppan.

Tamai Tetsuo. 1986. *Edo. Ushinawareta toshi kūkan o yomu*. Heibonsha.

Tanaka Yūko. 1993. *Edo wa nettowāku*. Heibosha.

Tanigawa Akio. 1991. "Chika ni uzumoreta minzoku shiryō." In *Gekkan Bunkazai* 11: 20–25.

———. 1992. "Excavating Edo's Cemeteries: Graves as Indicators of Status and Class." *Japanese Journal of Religious Studies* 19, 2–3: 271–297.

Taniguchi Shinko. 2000. "Burei-uchi ni miru bushi mibun to shakai." In *Han sekai no ishiki to kankei*, ed. Okayama han kenkyūkai. Iwada shoin.

———. 2001. "Kinsei ni okeru 'burei' no kannen." *Nihon rekishi* 636: 54–70.

Terakado Seiken. 1974–1976. *Edo hanjōki.* 3 vols. Heibonsha.

Thal, Sarah. 2005. *Rearranging the Landscape of the Gods. The Politics of a Pilgrimage Site in Japan, 1573–1912.* Chicago: University of Chicago Press.

Thunberg, Charles Peter. 1795. *Travels in Europe, Africa, and Asia.* London: F. and C. Rivington.

"Tobu nikki." 1977. In *Nihon toshi seikatsu shiryō shusei,* vol. 2: Santo, pt. 2, ed. Harada Tomohiko. San'ichi shobō.

Toby, Ronald P. 1986. "Carnival of the Aliens. Korean Embassies in Edo-Period Art and Popular Culture." *Monumenta Nipponica* 41, 4: 415–456.

———. 1991. *State and Diplomacy in Early Modern Japan: Asia in the Development of the Tokugawa Bakufu.* Stanford, Calif.: Stanford University Press.

Tokushima kenritsu hakubutsukan, ed. 1999. *Daimyō gyōretsu. Yomigaeru Edo jidai emaki.* Tokushima: Tokushima kenritsu hakubutsukan.

Tokutomi Sohō. 1994. *Ishin e no taidō (chū). Namamugi jiken.* Kōdansha gakujutsu bunkō.

Tōkyō daigaku iseki chōsashitsu, ed. 1989. *Rigakubu 7 gokan chiten — Tōkyō daigaku Hongō kōnai no iseki.* Tōkyō daigaku iseki chōsa shitsu.

Tōkyō daigaku maizō bunka zai chōsa shitsu, ed. 1990. *Sanjō kaikan, Gotenshita kinenkan chiten.* 3 vols. Tōkyō daigaku shomubu shomuka kōkokushitsu.

Tōkyōjin 88 (1995): 26–33.

Tōkyō-to. 1960. *Tōkyō-shi shikō, shigai hen, shigai hen.* Tōkyō-to.

Tōkyō-to Chiyoda-ku, ed. 1998. *Shinpen Chiyoda kushi tsūshi hen 3, kinsei 1.* Tōkyō-to Chiyoda-ku.

Tōkyō-to Edo-Tōkyō hakubutsukan, ed. 1993. *Edo-Tōkyō hakubutsukan. Sōgō annai.* Tōkyō-to Edo-Tōkyō habubutsukan.

———. 1997. *Sankin kōtai kyodai toshi. Edo no naritachi.* Tōkyō-to Edo hakubutsukan.

———. 1998. *Kanō-ha no sanbyakunen.* Tōkyō-to Edo-Tōkyō hakubutsukan.

Tōkyō-to kyōiku bunka zaidan, ed. 1997. *Shiodome iseki.* 5 vols. Tōkyō-to maizō bunkazai senta-.

Tōkyō-to kyōiku bunka zaidan, Tōkyō-to maizō bunka senta-, eds. 1994. *Marunouchi sanchōme iseki.* 2 vols. Tōkyō-to seikatsu bunka kyoku sōmubu kokusai fōramu.

Tōkyō-to kyōiku bunka zaidan Tōkyō-to maizō bunkazai senta-, 1994. *Marunouchi sanchōme iseki.* 2 vols. Tōkyō-to seikatsu bunka kyoku.

Tōkyō-to kyōiku iinkai, ed. 1991. *Ōedo happyaku hatchō chika tanken — Tōkyō no iseki ten.* Asahi shinbunsha.

Tōkyō-to rekishi bunka zaidan Edo-Tōkyō tatemono en, ed. 2001. *Uwajima han Date-ke — shūzō kenzōmono "Date-ke no mon" no haikei.* Tōkyō-to rekishi bunka zaidan Edo-Tōkyō tatemono en.

Tōkyō-to Shinjuku-ku, ed. 1992. *Naitō-chō iseki.* Tōkyō-to kensetsu-kyoku, Shinjuku-ku Naitō-chō iseki chōsakai.

Torii Fumiko. 1998. "Genroku ki Edo no Tosa jōruri. Daimyō yashiki ni okeru jōen o megutte." *Kokugo to kokubungaku* 11: 1–12.

Torigoe Bunzō, ed. 1998. *Chikamatsu Monzaemon shū,* vol. 2: *Shinpen Nihon koten bungaku zenshū 75.* Shogakkan.

Toritsu gakkō iseki chōsakai, ed. 1990. *Hakuō Site,* vol. 2. Toritsu gakkō iseki chōsakai.

———. 1991. *Hongō Motomachi. Toritsu kōgei kōkōnai maizō bunkazai hakkutsu chōsa gaihō.* Toritsu gakkō iseki chōsakai.

Totman, Conrad. 1967. *Politics in the Tokugawa Bakufu, 1600–1868.* Cambridge, Mass.: Harvard University Press.

———. 1974. "Tokugawa Japan." In *An Introduction to Japanese Civilization,* ed. Arthur E. Tiedmann. New York: Columbia University Press.

———. 1980. *The Collapse of the Tokugawa Bakufu, 1862–1868.* Honolulu: University of Hawai'i Press.

———. 1993. *Early Modern Japan.* Berkeley: University of California Press.

———. 2000. *A History of Japan.* Malden, Mass.: Blackwell Publishers.

Toyohashi shi Futagawa honjin shiryōkan, ed. 1994. *Daimyō no yado. Honjin ten.* Toyohashi: Toyohashi shi Futagawa honjin shiryōkan.

———. 1996. *Honjin ni tomatta daimyōtachi.* Toyohashi: Toyohashi shi Futagawa honjin shiryōkan.

———. 1997. *Daimyō gyōretsu. Egakareta daimyō gyōretsu.* Toyohashi: Toyohashi shi Futagawa honjin shiryōkan.

———. 1998. *Dōchū sugoroku.* Toyohashi: Toyohashi shi Futagawa honjin shiryōkan.

Tōyō tōji gakkai. 1991, 1995. Nos. 14, 26.

Traganou, Jilly. 2004. *The Tōkaidō Road. Traveling and Representation in Edo and Meiji Japan.* New York: Routledge Curzon.

Tsuji Tatsuya. 1958. *Tokugawa Yoshimune.* Yoshikawa kōbunkan.

Tsukada Takashi. 1996. *Kinsei no toshi shakaishi. Ōsaka o chūshin ni.* Aoki shoten.

Tsukada Takashi and Yoshida Nobuyuki. 2001. *Kinsei Ōsaka no toshi kūkan to shakai kōzō.* Yoshikawa kōbunkan.

Tsukahira, Toshio G. 1966. *Feudal Control in Tokugawa Japan: The Sankin Kōtai System.* Cambridge, Mass.: Harvard University Press.

Tsukamoto Manabu. 1984. "Edo no mikan." *Kokuritsu rekishi minzoku hakubutsukan kenkyū hōkoku* 4: 29–54.

Tsuzuki Takeyasu. 1988. "Kitayama koe no michi." *Tosa shidan* 179: 40–45.

Tucker, Mary Evelyn. 1989. *Moral and Spiritual Cultivation in Japanese Neo-Confucianism: The Life and Thought of Kaibara Ekken, 1630–1740.* Albany: State University of New York Press.

Turner, Victor. 1969. *The Ritual Process: Structure and Anti-Structure.* Chicago: Aldine Publishing Company.

Uchiyama Junzō. 1992. "San'ei-chō and Meat-eating in Buddhist Edo." *Japanese Journal of Religious Studies* 19, nos. 2–3: 299–303.

Uematsu Kiyoshi, Nakajima Setsuko, and Tani Naoki. 2000. "Kōchi han yashiki no kenchiku kōzō ni tsuite — Ōsaka, Kyōto, Fushimi yashiki o chūshin ni." In Uematsu Kiyoshi, Nakajima Setsuko, and Tani Naoki, *Kinsei Ōsaka ni okeru kura yashiki no jūkyoshiteki kenkyū.* Yamakawa shuppansha.

Ujiie Mikito. 1991. *Tonosama to nezumi kozō.* Chūō kōron.

Umihara Tōru. 2003. *Edo no tabibito Yoshida Shōin.* Mineruva.

Vaporis, Constantine Nomikos. 1986. "Post Station and Assisting Villages: Corvee Labor and Peasant Contention." *Monumenta Nipponica* 41, 4: 377–414.

———. 1994a. *Breaking Barriers. Travel and the State in Early Modern Japan.* Cambridge, Mass.: Council on East Asian Studies, Harvard University.

———. 1994b. "Edo to Tosa — Toshū Edo hantei no ikkōsatsu." *Tosa shidan* 195: 1–11.

———. 1994c. "Edo e no michi. Tosa hanshi Mori-ke nikki nado ni miru sankin kōtai no sugata." *Kōtsūshi kenkyū* 34: 52–67.

———. 1996. "A Tour of Duty. Kurume hanshi Edo kinban nagaya emaki." *Monumenta Nipponica* 51, 3: 279–307.

———. 1997. "To Edo and Back: Alternate Attendance and Japanese Culture in the Early Modern Period." *Journal of Japanese Studies* 23, 1: 25–67.

———. 1998. "Digging for Edo. Archaeology and Japan's Premodern Urban Past." *Monumenta Nipponica* 53, 1: 73–104.

———. 2000. "Samurai and Merchant in Mid-Tokugawa Japan: Tani Tannai's Record of Daily Necessities (1748–54)." *Harvard Journal of Asiatic Studies* 60, 1: 205–227.

———. 2005. "Daimyo Processions: Authority and Theater." *Japan Review* 17: 3–52.

Varley, Paul, and Isao Kumakura. 1994. *Tea in Japan: Essays on the History of Chanoyu*. Honolulu: University of Hawai'i Press.

Wada Minoru. 2000. "Sashiai ni miru sankin kōtai no girei." *Aichi daigaku sōgō kyōdo kenkyūjo kiyō* 45: 157–164.

Wakayama kenshi hensan iinkai, ed. 1991. *Wakayama kenshi. Kinsei*. Wakayama-ken.

Walthall, Anne. 1986. *Social Protest and Popular Culture in Eighteenth-Century Japan*. Tucson, Ariz.: Published for the Association of Asian Studies by the University of Arizona Press.

———. 1990. "The Family Ideology of the Rural Entrepreneur in Nineteenth Century Japan." *Journal of Social History* 23, 3: 463–483.

———. 1998. "Village Networks. Sodai and the Sale of Edo Nightsoil." *Monumenta Nipponica* 43, 3: 279–303.

Watanabe Hiroshi. 1985. "'Goikō' to shōchō. Tokugwa seiji taisei no ichi sokumen." *Shisō* 740: 132–154.

White, James. 1988. "State Growth and Popular Protest in Tokugawa Japan." *Journal of Japanese Studies* 14, 1: 1–27.

Wilentz, Sean, ed. 1985. *Rites of Power: Symbolism, Ritual and Politics Since the Middle Ages*. Philadelphia: University of Pennsylvania Press, 1985.

Wilson, Richard L. 1991. *The Art of Ogata Kenzan. Persona and Production in Japanese Ceramics*. New York: Weatherhill.

Xia Nai. 1990. "What Is Archaeology?" In *Anthropology in China. Defining the Discipline*, ed. Gregory Eliyu Guldin. Armonk, N.Y., and London: M. E. Sharpe, Inc.

Yamakawa Kikue. 2001. *Women of the Mito Domain. Recollections of Samurai Family Life*. Translated with an introduction by Kate Wildman Nakai. Stanford, Calif.: Stanford University Press.

Yamamoto Hirofumi. 1991. *Edo orusui yaku no nikki: Kan'eiki no Hagi hantei*. Yomiuri shinbunsha.

———. 1998. *Sankin kōtai*. Kōdansha.

Yamamoto Takeshi, ed. 1969. *Kōchi-ken no rekishi*. Yamakawa shuppansha.

———, ed. 1983. *Kōchi no kenkyū*, vol. 3. Osaka: Seibundō.

Yamamoto Takeshi and others, eds. 1982–1986. *Kenshōbo*. 7 vols. Kōchi: Kōchi kenritsu toshokan.

Yamamura, Kozo. 1974. *Samurai Income and Entrepreneurship*. Cambridge, Mass.: Harvard University Press.

Yamashita Shigeru and Tada Tetsunosuke, eds. 1975. *"Ryōri monogatari" shōkai*. Tada shokumi kenkyūjo.

Yamauchi jinja hōmotsu shiryōkan, ed. 1990. *Yamauchi ke no meihōten*. Kōchi: Yamauchi jinja hōmotsu shiryōkan.

Yamauchi-ke shiryō-bakumatsu ishin hen. 1983–present. Kōchi: Yamauchi jinja hōmotsu shiryōkan.

Yamauchi-ke shiryō — Katsutoyo-kō ki. 1980. Kōchi: Yamauchi jinja hōmotsu shiryōkan.

Yamauchi-ke shiryō — Tadatoyo-kō ki. 1980–1981. 3 vols. Kōchi: Yamauchi jinja hōmotsu shiryōkan.

Yamauchi-ke shiryō — Tadayoshi-kō ki. 1980. 4 vols. Kōchi: Yamauchi jinja hōmotsu shiryōkan.

Yamauchi Toyoaki. 1988. "Tosa han no shoki sankin nittei ni tsuite." *Tosa shidan* 179: 18–31.

Yamazaki Kiyonori. 1971. *Noneyama kaidō*. Aki city: Kōchi ken Aki-gun Kitagawa-mura kyōiku iinkai.

Yanagisawa Kien. 1988. "Enyū nikki." In *Nihon shomin bunka shiryō shūsei*, vol. 13: *Geinō kiroku*, pt. 2, ed. Geinō shi kenkyūkai. San'ichi shobō.

Yasuzawa Shōichi. 2002. "Edo yashiki ninzū, Edo yashiki hiyō oyobi sankin kōtai hiyō." *Gakusai* 6: 23–32.

Yates, Charles L. 1995. *Saigō Takamori: The Man Behind the Myth*. London and New York: Kegan Paul International.

Yazaki, Takeo. 1968. *Social Change and the City in Japan: From Earliest Times through the Industrial Revolution*. Tokyo: Japan Publications.

Yokogawa Suekichi. 1967. *Bakumatsu ishin no Tosa no shakai*. Kōchi: Kōchi City Library.

Yokohama shi rekishi hakutsukan, ed. 1996. *Tōkaidō to Kanagawa shuku*. Yokohama: Yokohama shi rekishi hakubutsukan.

Yokota Fuyuhiko. 2003. "Santo to chihō jōkamachi no bunkateki kankei." *Kokuritsu rekishi minzoku hakubutsukan kenkyū hōkoku* 103: 389–408.

Yonemoto, Marcia. 1999. "Nihonbashi: Edo's Contested Center." *East Asian History* 17/18: 49–70.

———. 2003. *Mapping Early Modern Japan: Space, Place, and Culture in the Tokugawa Period (1603–1868)*. Berkeley: University of California Press.

Yoshida Masataka. 2000. "Edo toshimin no daimyo yashiki nai chinju e no sankei kōdō." *Chihōshi kenkyū* 284: 64–82.

Yoshida Tōyō. 1929. "Nankai Sanyō zakki." In *Yoshida Tōyō ikō*, ed. Ōtsuka Takematsu. Nihon shiseki kyōkai.

Zhang, Cong Ellen. 2003. "The Culture of Travel in Song China (960–1279)." Ph.D. dissertation, University of Washington, Seattle.

Index

Page numbers in **boldface** type refer to illustrations.

Aizu, 57, 76–77, 99, 234
Alcock, Sir Rutherford, 65, 132, 149
alternate attendance: and authority, 7, 8, 9, 11, 14–16, 22, 56, 60, 63, 69, 80, 96–101, 129, 132, 158–163, 172, 241n8; and categories of service, 104–105; and changes in schedule, 21, 26–27, 33, 126, 179; and commoners, 42–43, 231–233, 289n101; comparisons with other countries, 2, 3, 15, 63, 103, 106, 231nn7, 8, 254n2, 255n84, 260n1; as control mechanism, 1, 5, 11, 242n22; and culture, 4, 6, 37, 54–55, 71, 98, 133, 149, 167–171, 191, 205–206, 210–233, 238–239, 242n12, 283nn1, 2, 284n5; delays in schedule of, 45, 57, 61, 147, 253n65, 270n73; and domain economic policy, 3, 27, 237, 242n10; as economic stimulant, 2, 17, 43, 103, 166, 231n8; exemptions from, 16–17, 56–57, 121, 147; expenses related to, 2, 3, 8, 11, 22, 27–32, 43, 51, 59, 139–140, 173, 247nn76, 78; as feudal service, 2, 102–103; historical precedents for, 11–12; legal requirements of, 7, 12, 40, 51, 131; military character of, 13, 25, 27–28, 62, 72–73, 76–77, 79–81, 83, 94–96, 102, 237; and modes of transport, 39–40; and nature of domain government, 3, 123; and Noh actors, 222; and Osaka economy, 3, 166–169; and peasants, 28, 102 (*see also* daimyo processions, and corvee labor for); preparation for journey on, 11, 51–52, 55, 63; and punishments of

daimyo, 7, 12, 19, 146, 242n16; reforms of, 14, 173, 253n59; retainer assignments on, 52–53; schedule for, 15–20, 36, 43, 49, 50–51, 243nn18, 19, 21; and travel time, 206. *See also* shogunate
Arima. *See* Kurume
Asahina Genba, 18, 195, 245n33
auxiliary daimyo inns (*waki honjin*). *See* daimyo inns

bakufu. *See* shogunate
baths, 23, 186–187, 201
Beato, Felice, 134, **136–137**, 181, 208, 278n31
bloodshed, incidents of, 35, 160–163, 176–177, 204
books, 6, 212, 214–218, 220, 226, 230–231, 235, 287n66, 288n91
books of heraldry (*bukan*), 63, 87, 96, 99, 140
bukan. See books of heraldry

calligraphy, 214–217, 221
Caron, Francois, 72
ceramics, 153, 155, 218–220, 224–225, 228, 234, 289nn110, 111. *See also* daimyo compounds, ceramic wares in
checking stations (*sekisho*), 12, 26, 55, 82, 247n79
cloth, 166, 193, 200, 211–212, 214, 219–220, 233–234, 284n19
clothing. *See* cloth
Chōshū, 12, 25–26, 65, 67, 70, 91, 95, 119, 121, 134, 157–159, 169
Confucian scholars, 111, 113, 125, 149, 223–234, 226, 229, 286n53. *See also* books; Kaibara Ekiken; Miyaji Umanosuke; Ogyū Sorai; Tani Tannai

daimyo: encounters on the road, 34–35; families of, 12–13, 172, 243n8; hereditary lords (*fudai daimyō*), 16; illness, 8, 33, 42, 45, 47, 56–61; official requests to shogunate, 21, 58, 60–61. *See also* Chōshū; Hiroshima; Kaga; Mito; Sendai; Tosa; Wakayama

daimyo, families of, 152, 167, 176, 232, 244n30

Daimyo Avenue (*daimyō kōji*), 129, **130**, 134, 137, 140, 158, 202

daimyo compounds, 4; animals in, 189–191; barracks in, 137, 149, 152, 155–156, 160, 278nn27, 31; bathing in, 186–187, 279n39; boundaries of, 149, **151**, 155, 157–159, 271n89; ceramic wares in, 169–172, **170**, **172**, 276nn163, 166, 168, 169, 289nn110, 111; and commoners, 25, 124, 126, 165, 265nn92, 93, 286n39; confiscation of, 143–144, 269n51; as cultural centers, 222–225, 286nn39, 42, 45; descriptions of, 132, 134–135, 149; and diplomatic immunity, 158–159, 162; disposal of refuse from, 153, 155, 163; establishment of, 129–134; excavations of, 4, 152–155, 168–171, 189–192; and garbage disposal, 191–192; gardens in, 132–133, 149, 152–153, 267n14; garden kilns in, 133, 171, 267n14, 277n173 (*see also* ceramics); gateways of, 136–137, 139, 149, 267nn29–30; images of, **136–137**, **138**, **140–141**, **156**; land transactions involving, 143–144; maps of, 5, **130**, **150**, **151**, 153, 269n54, 272n90; and merchants, 51, 264n73; numbers and size of, 7, 103, 131, 133–135, 142, 181, 266n11; *oku* (inner quarters), 25, 126–127, **150**, 152, 167–168, 265n94; organization of space in, 149–152, **150**; overcrowding in, 57, 60, 142, 144, 150, 188; populations of, 133, 277n6; and power, 136–137, 139, 155–160; provisioning of, 123–124, 153, 165–171, 275n150; relationship to domain economies, 165–171; relationship to Edo, 163, 165; and roof tiles, 136, 155,

169, 183, 268nn31, 34, 275n160; shrines and temples in, 163–165, 274nn140, 141, 290nn122, 123; space around, 160–161; toilets in, 185, 188, 274n138; use of underground space in, 152–155, **154**, 272n97; warehouse compounds (*kura yashiki*), 107, 134, 168; water supply in, 135, 142, 163, **164**, 185; women in, 25, 175–178, 183–184, 187, 200 (*see also* daimyo compounds, *oku*)

daimyo inns (*honjin*), 27, 30, 32, 65, 73, 248n83

daimyō kōji. See Daimyo Avenue

daimyo processions: animals in, 78, 82, 92–93, 98–100, 280n54; and attire, 78–80, 97, 252n53, 258n78; and clearing of the road, 95; and corvee labor for, 31–32, 245n38, 248n90, 250n26; as cultural performance, 54–55, 62, 70–91, 97–98; departure of, 24–25, 44–45; descriptions of, 37, 70–91, 91–101, 255n30; and gender, 83–85; images of, 37, **40**, **41**, 77–78, **80–81**, **84–85**, **88**, 90–91, 255n22; implements used in, 92–93, 94–100, 260n124; limits on, 73–74, 256n54; and local festivals, 87–90; and kabuki, 84–85; provisioning of, 22, 27–29, 37–38, 77, 98, 246nn68, 69; reception of, 20, 64–69, 83, 85, 87, 91; reenactments of, 1, 88–89, 90, **91**, 259n96; religious elements of, 81–82; of senior advisors, 20; size of, 44, 66–74, 75–77, 96, 257nn64, 68, 258n93, 259n114; and spectators, 67–69, 71, 87, **88**; and temporary laborers, 77, 248n91; transport charges for, 31–32. *See also* "hospitality"

daimyo yashiki. See daimyo compounds

domain boats, 216, 218

domains, Edo populations of, 172–174

doro-e ("mud pictures"), 132, 181, 212, 285n24. *See also* daimyo compounds, images of

Edo, 6–7, 23, 54–55, 61, 80, 91, 103, 205, 212, 221, 238; economic links to localities, 166–171; land usage in, 129, **130**, 131, 140, 142–143, 266n10, 267n25; population of, 5, 128, 172–174, 266n3, 273n107; shrines and temples in, 235–236. *See also* daimyo compounds, populations of

Edo allowance, 111–112, 117, 118–119, 262nn24, 26, 28, 29, 33, 264n62, 279n48

Edo castle, 13, 20, 54, 58, 73, 126, **130**, 132, 138, 167, 179, 201–202

"Edo culture," 6, 205, 238

Edo language, 208–209, 284n8

Edo liason (*Edo rusui*), 58, 124, 227, 264n77, 265nn87, 88

Edo service: extension of, 192, 195–196; financial incentives for, 111–123, 204, 262n22; selection process for, 103–108. *See also* Edo allowance

Edo subsidy. *See* Edo allowance

Edozu byōbu, 136, **138**, 278n27

Ekin, 112, 232–233

Enkōan. *See* Kōriki Takenobu

fires, 57, 132–133, 137, 145–147, 152, 169, 273n123. *See also* Meireki fire; Tosa, fires in Edo compounds

fire-watch duty, 13, 124, 144, 146, 177, 179, 278n24

food, 114–116, 123, 190, 211, 212, 219–220, 233, 235, 272n104, 279n49. *See also* daimyo procession, provisioning of; plants

Fukui, 65, 70

Fukuoka, 16, **213**, 226

Furukawa Koshōken, 72, 76

gift-giving, 24, 26, 31, 51, 54–55, 59, 125, 186, 190, 192, 199, 221, 234, 237, 285n34, 289n109

goishi-cha, 43

Gokaidō, 13, 31, 40, 43, 68, 246n67; cleaning of, 21

Gotō Seiko, 26, 37

Gotō Seijun, 145, 188, 193, 201, 279n38

guard houses, 137, 160, 273n124

Hachinohe, 15, 21, 26, 77, 99, 121, 167

Hall, Francis, 14, 66, 90, 94, 126

Hideyoshi. *See* Toyotomi Hideyoshi

Hiroshige. *See* Utagawa Hiroshige

Hiroshima, 77, 139, **140–141**, 155, 195, **213**, 228

Hokusai. *See* Katsushika Hokusai

honjin. See daimyo inns

"hospitality" (*gochisō*), 64–66, 83, 254n9. *See also* daimyo procession, reception of

hostages, 12, 13, 192, 243n10

Inari, 50, 148, 165, 236, 274n143. *See also* daimyo compounds, shrines and temples in

inns, 22–23, 30. *See also* daimyo inns

jōfu. See retainers, long-term postings in Edo

kabuki, 223, 232, 286n45

Kaempfer, Englebert, 71, 78, 82–83, 85, 92–93, 96, 128, 137

Kaga, 4, 17, 57, 77, **78–79**, 112–113, **151**, 168; compounds of, 131, 134, 188; Inoyama household of, 112–113; lord of, 12, 73; processions of, 23, **24**, 28, **29**, 32–33, 72, **88**

Kaibara Ekiken, 225–226

Kanō school, 223, 225, 232, 287n57, 288n81, 289n104

kariage (funds "borrowed" by the lord), 114–115, 118, 120, 122, 264n61

Kasumigaseki, 91, **140–141**, 155, 160, **213**

Katsushika Hokusai, 227, 232

Kii. *See* Wakayama

Kishū han sankin kōtai gyōretsu zu (Kii domain procession scroll), 68, 83, 90, 94–95. *See also* Wakayama

Kitayama route. *See* Northern route

Kōchi. *See* Tosa; Yamauchi

Kōriki Takenobu, 82, 217, **221**

Kumamoto, 70, 76, 87, 100–101, 124, 236

Kurume, **156**, 160, 172, 179–186, **180**, **183**, **184**, **186**, 213

Kyoto, 6, 17, 20, 33, 59, 104, 128, 207–208, 219, 222, 271n83. *See also* "three metropolises"

"Laws for the Military Houses" (*buke shohatto*), 2, 9, 17, 73, 161. *See also* shogunate; Tokugawa
leave of absence (*oitoma*), 9, 23, 37, 55, 58, 104
loans, 111, 113, 114–116, 118–120, 123, 262n27. See also *kariage*
local specialty products, 31, 54, 168, 233–235, 289nn108, 112, 114

Maeda. *See* Kaga, lord of
Marugame, 69, 107, 210
Matsumae, 16
Matsura Seizan, 133
Meireki fire, 26, 132, 136, 139, 141–143, 153, 270n73
messengers, 106, 109–110, 151, 178, 193–194, 264n72
Mitford, Lord Algernon, 1, 62, 241n1
Mito, 17, 131, **138**, 160, 165, 234, 244n24
Miyaji Umanosuke, 24, 41–42, 52, 145, 158, 211–212, 217, 223, 230, 233
Mori Hirosada, 21, 37, 47, 49, 52–54, 108–110
Mori Masana, 108–110, 125, 176–177, 187, 194, 202, 206–210, 212–217, 231, 233, 283nn3, 4
Mori Yoshiki, 20, 24, 45–46, 70, 108–109, 125, 127, 145, 179, 187, 194, 233
Morita Kyūemon, 223–224, 271n86
Mount Atago, 132, 134, **136–137**
Mutō Hiroki, 70, 76, 87, 256n48

Nabeshima, 16, 28, 125
Nabeshima ware, 170, 234
Naitō Meisetsu, 104, 179, 187–188
Nakai Chikuzan, 166, 192
Nakasendō, 31, 51. *See also* Gokaidō
Namamugi incident, 34–35, 249n105
Nanbu (Morioka), 25, 31, 37, 54, 77, 98, 100, 121
Nanga school, 225, 227, 287n702

networks, 205, 224–225, 227–231
Noh, 51, 99, 148, 152, 197, 216, 222–223, 231, 281n81, 286n42
Nonaka Kenzan, 49, 235
Northern (Kitayama) route. *See* Tosa, Northern route

Odano Naotake, 225, 227
Odawara, 37, 210
Odo-yaki. *See* Tosa, Odo ware
official inns. *See* daimyo inns
Ogura Sadasuke, 188, 192, 211
Ogyū Sorai, 15, 56, 172
Okayama, 25, 33, 167
Oliphant, Laurence, 128
Osaka, 6, 25, 40, 42–43, 47–48, 67, 69, 168, 207–208, 210–211, 271nn77, 80; Battle of, 13, 17. *See also* "three metropolises"
Owari, 66, 94–95, 132–133, **138**, 202

parades. *See* daimyo processions
pax Tokugawa (Great Peace), 3–4, 161
picture game boards (*esugoroku*), 20, 62, 69, 85
pilgrimages, 24–25, 42, 51, 55, 59, 207, 282n96
plants, 218, 220, 235
post stations, 20, 22, 29–30, 33, 51, 64–65, 77, 87, 133, 211
puppet theater, 179, 201, 286n39

"Record of Daily Necessities." *See* Tani Tannai
retainers: consumptive behavior of, 148, 188–189, 192–193, 198, 210–222, 282nn100, 101, 285n30 (*see also* cloth); curfews on, 198, 282nn89, 90; diets of, 188–192, 279nn50, 57, 59, 62, 282n95 (*see also* food); hardships of Edo service, 193–196, 281nn67, 72, 75, 76; independent travel of, 207–210, 249n100; indiscretions and crimes of, 23, 110, 159, 203–204 (*see also* bloodshed, incidents of); leisure activities of, 70, 81, **180**, 181, 183, 184, **186**, 196–202, 282nn96, 98; living quarters of, 180,

181–188, **184, 186,** 279n46; long-term postings in Edo, 17, 104, 110, 112, 126, 174–175, 188, 192, 260n4, 261n21 (*see also* jōfu); pilgrimages by, 181, 198–199, 201–202; regulating behavior of, 22–23, 156–157, 162, 198, 202, 244nn45, 46; selection for Edo service, 103–108, 260n3; stipends of, 111–118, 122–123; subsidy programs for, 111–114, 123; workload of, 110, 179, 278nn20, 21

retinue. *See* daimyo procession

Saga, 12, 16, 28, 70, **140–141**
Saigō Takamori, 197, 225
Saitaniya Naomasa (Hachirōbei), 111, 113–121
Sakai Banshirō, 111, 113, 179, 188, 197–202, 207–208
samurai. *See* retainers
sankin kōtai. See alternate attendance
Satō Issai, 209, 214, 227, 231
Satow, Sir Ernest, 34
Satsuma, 12, 20, 26, 34–35, 69, 72, 76, 97, 125, 155
Schliemann, Heinrich, 72, 82
Sendai, 21, 29, 33, 66, 70, 72, 76, 78, **80–81,** 87, 97–98, 134, 153, 157–159, **164,** 170
Shiba Kōkan, 176, 227
Shimabara, Battle of, 13, 94–95
shogun, 1, 7, 8, 14, 48, 126. *See also* shogunate; Tokugawa
shogunate, 2, 12, 34–35, 73–74, 80, 96, 124–125, 128, 37, 142–144, 147–148, 159–161, 162, 203; daimyo petitioning of, 31, 57, 97, 99, 124–125, 148; and land grants to daimyo, 129–133, 143–144, 158; senior councilors of, 21, 47, 50–51, 54–55, 58–61, 125, 159. *See* Tokugawa
sightseeing, 51, 53, 207–210, 232, 251n39, 253n79
status, 30, 33, 64, 70, 73, 78, 82, 94, 97–100, 108, 112, 143, 146, 163, 177–178, 188, 191, 198
Sugita Genpaku, 227–229
Suitengū, 165, 202, 236
sumo, 25, 47, 70

swords, 214–215, 220, 253n58. *See also* sword guards
sword guards, 212, 214–215, 221

Tani Kakimori, 115–117, 121, 193
Tani Tannai (Mashio), 106, 111–123
Tani Tanzan, 226
tea ceremony, 28, 99, 113, 182, 197, 222
theater, 124, 207, 222–223. *See also* puppet theater
"three metropolises," 6, 226. *See also* Edo; Kyoto; "Laws for the Military Houses"; Osaka
tobacco, 37, 193, 201, 220
Tōkaidō, 1, 20, 27, 29, 31, 33, 38, 51–52, 59, 65–66, 70, 148, 211. *See also* Gokaidō
Tokugawa, 2, 61; family mortuary temples of, 13, 73; magistrate of residence lands, 158; Three Related Houses (*gosanke*) of, 33, 97–98, 139, 162. *See also* shogunate; Tokugawa Hidetada; Tokugawa Iemitsu; Tokugawa Ieyasu; Tokugawa Tsunayoshi; Tokugawa Yoshimune
Tokugawa Hidetada, 98, 136
Tokugawa Iemitsu, 13, 136
Tokugawa Ieyasu, 11, 13, 44, 129
Tokugawa Tsunayoshi, 19, 98
Tokugawa Yoshimune, 14, 17, 56, 234
Tosa, 4, 5, 17, 30, 37, 39, 55, 73–74, 77, **98,** 102, 206, 236; alternate attendance routes, **39,** 41–48, 250n16; Confucian scholar families of, 223–224, 226–227, 230–231 (*see also* Miyaji Umanosuke; Tani Tannai); daimyo compound in Fushimi, 147–148; daimyo compound at Kajibashi, 54, 57, 60, 139–140, 143, 163, 216, 231; daimyo compound in Kyoto, 5, 107, 147–149, 252n41, 271nn84, 85; daimyo compound in Osaka, 49–51, 147–148, 271n79; daimyo compound at Shiba, 58, 124, 139, 144–146, 177, 268n4, 269n52; daimyo compound at Shinagawa, 54, 107, 139–140, 142–143, 177; domain boat service, 106, 167; economic reform programs in, 60,

124–125, 142, 146, 178; Edo liason, 58, 60, 124–127; fires in Edo compounds, 18, 145–147, 269nn61, 62, 270n69; Kan-no-ura route, 41–43; lower compound (*shimo yashiki*), 133–134; Northern route, 43–48, 74, 250nn22, 23; and Odo ware, 170–171, 224, 234; population of Edo compounds, 133, 174–178, 277nn10, 15; processions of, 28, **40–41**, 48; secondary compounds (*naka yashiki*), 132, 139; senior advisors (*karō*) of, 13, 20–22, 25, 44, 46; use of sea transport, **39**, 41–43, 45–48, **50**. *See also* daimyo processions; fire-watch duty; retainers
Toyama Tamuro, 21, 26, 179, 221–222, 226. *See also* Hachinohe
Toyotomi Hideyoshi, 11, 147
travel, 206–210, 249n1; delays in, 42–43, 250n18; instructions for, 22, 24; preparations for, 21–26. *See also* daimyo procession; Tosa, Kan-no-ura route; Tosa, Northern Route; Tosa, use of sea transport
Tsugaru, 70, 121
Tsushima, 16

Ukiyoe. See woodblock prints
Utagawa Hiroshige, 30, 69, 90, 165, 227

Wakayama, 67, **68**, 82–83, 87, 90, **138**, 188. *See also* Kishū han sankin kōtai gyōretsu zu; Sakai Banshirō
Watanabe Kazan, 225, 230
woodblock prints, 64, 69, 85, 90, 212, 215–216, 217, 220, 223, 227, 232

yakko (footmen), 62, **84–85**, **86**, 87. *See also* daimyo procession
Yamauchi. *See* Tosa
Yamauchi, daimyo heir of, 17–19, 22–23, 45–46, 51, 110, 195
Yamauchi Tadatoyo, 17, 41, 144
Yamauchi Toyofusa, 18, 19, 178, 195, 244n33
Yamauchi Toyokazu, 58–60, 266n95
Yamauchi Toyomasa, 18, 19, 24, 41, 178
Yamauchi Toyonobu, 55, 124
Yamauchi Toyooki, 18, 45
Yamauchi Toyosuke, 41, 145
Yamauchi Toyoteru, 18, 38
Yamauchi Yōdō, 38, 110
Yanagiwara, 217, 202, **221**
Yoshiwara, 124–125, 200

Zōjōji, 124, 177, 179–180, 183, 202

About the Author

Constantine Nomikos Vaporis received his doctorate in history from Princeton University. He has received major grants from the National Endowment for the Humanities, the Fulbright Program, and the Japan Foundation. In 1993–1994 he was a visiting research professor at the International Research Center for Japanese Studies (Nichibunken). Among his publications is *Breaking Barriers: Travel and the State in Early Modern Japan* (1994). He is currently associate professor and director of the graduate program in the Department of History, University of Maryland, Baltimore County (UMBC).

Production Notes for Vaporis | TOUR OF DUTY
Cover and interior design by April Leidig-Higgins
   in Minion, with display type in Mantinia.
Composition by Copperline Book Services, Inc.
Printing and binding by Edwards Brothers
Printed on 60# EB Opaque, 500 ppi